CW01192819

AN UNEASY HEGEMONY

Sri Lanka has been regarded as a model democracy among former British colonies. It is lauded for its impressive achievement in terms of human development indicators. However, Sri Lanka's modern history can also be read as a tragic story of inter-ethnic inequalities and tensions, resulting in years of violent conflicts. Two long spells of anti-state youth uprisings were followed by nearly three decades of civil war, and most recently a renewed upsurge of events are examples of the ongoing uneasy project of state-building. This book discusses that state-building in Sri Lanka is centred on the struggle for hegemony amidst a kind of politics that rejects individual and group equality, opposes the social integration of marginalised groups and appeals to narrow, fearful and xenophobic tendencies among the majority population and minorities alike. It answers the pressing questions of: How do the dynamics of intra-Sinhalese class relations and Sinhalese politics influence the trajectories of post-colonial state-building? What tensions emerge over time between Sinhalese hegemony-building and the wider state-building? How do these tensions manifest in majority and minority relationships?

Shyamika Jayasundara-Smits is an Assistant Professor in Conflict and Peace Studies at the International Institute of Social Studies of Erasmus University Rotterdam, The Netherlands. Her main areas of work include violent conflicts, security, development and peace. Geographically, her work focuses on South Asia, Europe and Sri Lanka.

SOUTH ASIA IN THE SOCIAL SCIENCES

South Asia has become a laboratory for devising new institutions and practices of modern social life. Forms of capitalist enterprise, providing welfare and social services, the public role of religion, the management of ethnic conflict, popular culture and mass democracy in the countries of the region have shown a marked divergence from known patterns in other parts of the world. South Asia is now being studied for its relevance to the general theoretical understanding of modernity itself.

South Asia in the Social Sciences will feature books that offer innovative research on contemporary South Asia. It will focus on the place of the region in the various global disciplines of the social sciences and highlight research that uses unconventional sources of information and novel research methods. While recognising that most current research is focused on the larger countries, the series will attempt to showcase research on the smaller countries of the region.

General Editor
Partha Chatterjee
Columbia University

Editorial Board
Pranab Bardhan
University of California at Berkeley

Stuart Corbridge
Durham University

Satish Deshpande
University of Delhi

Christophe Jaffrelot
Centre d'etudes et de recherches internationales, Paris

Nivedita Menon
Jawaharlal Nehru University

Other books in the series:

Government as Practice: Democratic Left in a Transforming India
Dwaipayan Bhattacharyya

Courting the People: Public Interest Litigation in Post-Emergency India
Anuj Bhuwania

Development after Statism: Industrial Firms and the Political Economy of South Asia
Adnan Naseemullah

Politics of the Poor: Negotiating Democracy in Contemporary India
Indrajit Roy

South Asian Governmentalities: Michel Foucault and the Question of Postcolonial Orderings
Stephen Legg and Deana Heath (eds.)

Nationalism, Development and Ethnic Conflict in Sri Lanka
Rajesh Venugopal

Adivasis and the State: Subalternity and Citizenship in India's Bhil Heartland
Alf Gunvald Nilsen

Maoist People's War and the Revolution of Everyday Life in Nepal
Ina Zharkevich

New Perspectives on Pakistan's Political Economy: State, Class and Social Change
Matthew McCartney and S. Akbar Zaidi (eds.)

Crafty Oligarchs, Savvy Voters: Democracy under Inequality in Rural Pakistan
Shandana Khan Mohmand

Dynamics of Caste and Law: Dalits, Oppression and Constitutional Democracy in India
Dag-Erik Berg

Simultaneous Identities: Language, Education and the Nepali Nation
Uma Pradhan

Deceptive Majority: Dalits, Hinduism, and Underground Religion
Joel Lee

Colossus: The Anatomy of Delhi
Sanjoy Chakravorty and Neelanjan Sircar (eds.)

When Ideas Matter: Democracy and Corruption in India
Bilal A. Baloch

In Search of Home: Citizenship, Law and the Politics of the Poor
Kaveri Haritas

Bureaucratic Archaeology: State, Science, and Past in Postcolonial India
Ashish Avikunthak

The Odds Revisited: Political Economy of the Development of Bangladesh
K. A. S. Murshid

AN UNEASY HEGEMONY

POLITICS OF STATE-BUILDING AND STRUGGLES FOR JUSTICE IN SRI LANKA

SHYAMIKA JAYASUNDARA-SMITS

CAMBRIDGE
UNIVERSITY PRESS

CAMBRIDGE
UNIVERSITY PRESS

University Printing House, Cambridge CB2 8BS, United Kingdom

One Liberty Plaza, 20th Floor, New York, NY 10006, USA

477 Williamstown Road, Port Melbourne, vic 3207, Australia

314 to 321, 3rd Floor, Plot No.3, Splendor Forum, Jasola District Centre, New Delhi 110025, India

103 Penang Road, #05–06/07, Visioncrest Commercial, Singapore 238467

Cambridge University Press is part of the University of Cambridge.

It furthers the University's mission by disseminating knowledge in the pursuit of education, learning and research at the highest international levels of excellence.

www.cambridge.org
Information on this title: www.cambridge.org/9781009199247

© Shyamika Jayasundara-Smits 2022

This publication is in copyright. Subject to statutory exception and to the provisions of relevant collective licensing agreements, no reproduction of any part may take place without the written permission of Cambridge University Press.

First published 2022

Printed in India by Avantika Printers Pvt. Ltd.

A catalogue record for this publication is available from the British Library

ISBN 978-1-009-19924-7 Hardback

Cambridge University Press has no responsibility for the persistence or accuracy of URLs for external or third-party internet websites referred to in this publication, and does not guarantee that any content on such websites is, or will remain, accurate or appropriate.

To Amma and Thaattha

CONTENTS

List of Tables and Figure — xi
Preface — xiii
Acknowledgements — xvii
List of Abbreviations — xxi

1 Introduction — 1
2 Politics of Judgement — 36
3 From Nationalism to Ethnic Supremacy — 57
4 Political Patronage: Underbelly of Everyday Politics — 113
5 State Institutions and Patronage Politics — 173
6 War and Peace as Politics by Other Means — 223
7 What Came after War? — 275

Afterword — 301
Appendix 1 Map of Sri Lanka — 304
Appendix 2 Indication of Background of Key Interviewees (from January to May 2009) — 305
Bibliography — 306
Index — 351

TABLES AND FIGURES

TABLES

4.1	Major occupational groups in Sri Lanka, 1921–1970 (% working population)	123
4.2	Party profiles of UNP and SLFP	124
4.3	Improvement in physical quality of life in Sri Lanka, 1946–1981	137
4.4	Change in external resources, 1945–1975	139
4.5	Population size and rate of growth in Sri Lanka, 1871–1981	140
4.6	Government expenditure on social welfare, 1955–1975	141
4.7	Differences between traditional and broker clientelism	150
4.8	Defence expenditure, 2007–2011 (in LKR million)	164
5.1	Europeans and Ceylonese, including others, in the Ceylon Civil Service	177
5.2	Growth of public service, number of employees, 1948–1980	190
5.3	Types of bureaucracies	193
5.4	Comparison between the First and the Second Republican Constitutions	198
5.5	Public and private sector employment: male and female distribution, 1998–2008 ('000)	201
5.6	Distribution of semi-government sector employees by sex, 2001–2007	201

5.7	Total employment in each sector from 2005 to 2009	203
5.8	Distribution of semi-government employees by major occupational group, 2007	203
5.9	Distribution of semi-government sector employees by institution, 2007	204
5.10	Public sector employment, 2007–2009	204
5.11	Unemployment, 2003–2008 (%)	204
5.12	Registered unemployed female graduates, 1994–2001	205
5.13	Ethnic composition of occupational categories of males 18–30 years of age	206
6.1	Votes (percentage) secured by UNP and SLFP in general elections, 1994–2004	241
6.2	Colombo Consumer Price Index and Greater Colombo Consumer Price Index	242

FIGURE

5.1	Structure of government (as of 2008)	195

PREFACE

Sri Lanka has always been a fascinating case study due to its gradual transformation from a model democracy to a case of perpetual political violence. The aim of this book is to present a nuanced account of Sri Lanka's trajectory of politics of state-building by situating it in the intersections of state-building and hegemony-building. The book delves into a number of social categories and relations, mainly class, caste and gender, beyond the usual analyses centred on ethnic and inter-religious identity conflicts. It discusses four key state-building processes that came to be converged with Sinhala right-wing hegemony-building processes that were invented and nurtured by the majority Sinhalese elites who occupied state power throughout the post-colonial period. Paying close attention helps analyse how these processes have come about and have been utilised and adapted according to the prevailing global and national ideological and material conditions at a given historical moment. The book aims to re-problematise Sri Lanka's trajectory of state-building by redrawing attention to class relations, specifically intra-ethnic class relations of the majority Sinhala-Buddhist community as a perpetual source of violence. The primacy given to a class-based analysis of the roots and manifestations of social and political violence is aimed at a deeper and multi-level analysis, weaving historical–contemporary, material–ideational and global–national–local elements into one coherent and complex whole.

The book is written from a critical, reflective and interpretivist perspective. It is situated within critical approaches to politics and the state, specifically influenced by the Gramscian concept of hegemony. This is central to the analysis, which shows how ideological hegemony was pursued by the ruling class through the use of various ways of combining coercion with consent.

These strategies for securing hegemony were often resisted and contested by countervailing social and political forces, ultimately manifested as a series of violent encounters, protests and forms of opposition. The book has its origins in the author's PhD thesis, defended in 2013. It benefits from in-depth field interviews conducted as part of doctoral work, and subsequently up to 2020, across Sri Lanka, with a wide range of actors, including high-profile political actors, civil servants, civil society actors, non-state armed groups and ordinary citizens from the north to the south. Many interviews were conducted under extraordinary conditions, at the height of civil war in the first quarter of 2009 and then in its immediate aftermath. This makes the interviews a rare form of public testimony as to how public servants, political elites, intellectuals, practitioners and citizens reflected on the roots of Sri Lanka's violent political conflicts and thought about prospects for a peaceful transition to democracy. However, this research is mindful of the fact that, given the circumstances the interviews were conducted in (here referring to the imminent victory of the government forces against the LTTE), apart from being manipulated, the fear of consequences for not subscribing to the prevailing political discourse at the time of interviews might have also played a major role in expressing such hard-line views. This book greatly benefitted from the author's continued scholarly and applied research and practice in Sri Lanka on the post-war political dynamics and social transformations, and from graduate-level teaching in conflict, peace and conflict transformation.

Competing elements of the Sinhalese political elite have dominated the trajectory of Sri Lankan state-building since independence. The Sinhala-Buddhist hegemonic right-wing political project has become more dominant over time and bears the heaviest political and moral responsibility for the political violence both past and present. This study places their political designs for overall hegemony within broader, past and ongoing regional and global geo-strategic and geo-economic contestations for domination and legitimacy in representing and controlling Sri Lanka's economy and politics. The main challenge in the book remains to show that the premise of inequality and social injustice, which underpins the right-wing political ideologies of elites, is not shared by all Sinhalese, let alone by all Sri Lankans. Although alternative progressive political projects are often co-opted, this is not always the case, even within the Sinhala-Buddhist communities. Making these distinctions between broad, fluid identities and the project of political hegemony of specific classes and elites is vital amidst the current rapid and global resurgence of populist and authoritarian politics. The struggles of Sri Lankan social justice movements undoubtedly have appeal and relevance beyond Sri Lanka, just as much as the strivings of elites for economic and political hegemony. Last but not least, this book cautiously explores inter-linked local, national and global roots of right-wing, exclusionary and fundamentalist politics in the neo-liberal and post-liberal era.

ACKNOWLEDGEMENTS

This book is an extension of my PhD thesis that was defended at the International Institute of Social Studies (ISS) at Erasmus University Rotterdam, the Netherlands. Therefore, I am immensely grateful to my PhD supervisors, Professor M. R. M. Salih and Dr David Dunham, for their wonderful support and guidance throughout my PhD journey.

I am also thankful to my academic peers at ISS for many years of inspiring discussions on politics and social justice, which I drew on to shape the new content. I am especially thankful to my senior colleagues Wil Hout, Des Gasper, Mansoob Murshed, Karin Arts, Dubravka Zarkov and Helen Hintjens who continue to support my intellectual journey at ISS, where this book was written. Thanks go to my colleagues in the Governance, Law and Social Justice (GLSJ) research group too. Special thanks to Helen for reading, editing and commenting on many parts of the draft chapters of this book. I want to also thank my fantastic scholar-activist colleagues in the ISS teaching programme, the Social Justice Perspective Major (SJP), whose work has been an inspiration to think through issues from the perspective of social justice. Thanks to Julien-Franciois and Farhard, with whom I often take the pleasure of hanging out for the much-needed academic detox. I also want to thank my current and past MA and PhD students for helping to push my horizons of thinking with your questions, comments and encouragements, inside and outside of the classroom.

A few of words of thanks are not enough to express my gratitude to Professor Jayadeva Uyangoda, Professor Amal Jayawardena and Professor Nira Wickramasinghe, who have always been my towers of support and inspiration in academia, for more than two decades. You always had time for me when I visited you in Sri Lanka and in the Netherlands, sometimes for a quick catch-up or for a long conversation to fill me in with what is going on in Sri Lanka. Professor Wickramasinghe's (Nira's) corky ultimatum is what really led me to embark on this 'always postponed' book project. I am also grateful to my mentors across the Atlantic, Professor Lisa Schirch and Professor Jayne Docherty at the Eastern Mennonite University, in Virginia, USA, for their continued support and inspiration to engage with topics of war, peace, violence and social justice, with my head and heart in the right places.

I very much appreciate my friends and colleagues in Sri Lanka who always made time to meet up, strike up long conversations and keep me up to date with the latest developments in Sri Lanka with all their seriousness, much-needed sense of humour and irony. Kassapa, Udan, Ayoma, Munas and Rajith, I am thinking of you. Many thanks to our new and old friends from many different corners of the world for your friendship, encouragement, support and interest shown in my work. Thank you, Bilisuma, Anteneh, Hugo, Cathelijne, Sussane, Harry, Loes, Kees, Georg, Suba, Fabio, Angelica-Maria and Rosanne.

I had a fantastic editorial team at Cambridge University Press. Immense thanks to Qudsiya Ahmed, Anwesha Rana and Anwesha Roy for setting up a smooth process to materialise this book. Aniruddha De's patient and careful final copy-editing of the manuscript made it a much better read. Thank you very much to the three anonymous reviewers who spent their valuable time to read through the draft manuscript and showed a great deal of intellectual generosity with very helpful comments and communicating them in an uplifting and positive note. Not forgetting to appreciate those who shared their views on Sri Lanka's political developments under undesirable political conditions and risking own safety, during my many visits to Sri Lanka in the last 15 years. Their views and life experiences living in Sri Lanka certainly enriched this book.

I want to thank my family, especially my father, Nandadasa, my late mother, Helen Jayasundara, my two sisters, Buddhika and Indika, my nieces, Sandali and Yuthara, and nephews, Heshan and Sonal, for their appreciation for my work. I very much wished that my mother was here with me to turn the pages of this book together – she tragically passed away due to COVID when I was finalising the last two chapters of the book. My memories of her heydays of trade union activism in a red saree kept me going. I want to thank my parent-in-laws and Mireille for their interest in my work and checking up on my well-being. I especially thank my paternal uncle, Dayananda Jayasundara, whose past political activism has been a source of inspiration for my work on Sri Lanka's politics, which I did not fully realise until much later in my adult life. Thank you very much for allowing me to use the image you crafted on a coconut shell capturing the aspirations of the Sri Lankan youth while you were locked up in a prison cell for taking part in the first anti-state youth uprising. To me, nothing comes closer than this image to capture the essence of this book.

Last but not least, I want to express my gratitude to my husband, Marcel, and daughter, Selah. Their unconditional love and patience helped me to get on with this book project, especially during the darkest days since losing my mother. I very much hope one day my daughter will be inspired to learn more about Sri Lanka's horse-trading high politics, which I bet she will not find as fun as riding real horses.

ABBREVIATIONS

ADB	Asian Development Bank
APRC	All Party Representative Committee
BBS	Bodu Bala Sena (Buddhist Power Force)
CIABOC	Commission to Investigate Allegations of Bribery and Corruption
CNC	Ceylon National Congress
COPE	Committee of Public Enterprises
CP	Communist Party
CPA	Centre for Policy Alternatives
CWC	Ceylon Workers Congress
DDC	District Development Councils
DUNF	Democratic United National Front
EPDP	Eelam People's Democratic Party
GOSL	Government of Sri Lanka
GST	goods and services tax
ICES	International Centre for Ethnic Studies
IDEA	Institute for Democracy and Electoral Assistance
IMF	International Monetary Fund
IPKF	Indian Peace Keeping Force
ISGA	Interim Self-Government Administration
JHU	Jathika Hela Urumaya

JVP	Janatha Vimukthi Peramuna
LLRC	Lessons Learnt and Reconciliation Commission
LMSL	Lanka Marine Services Limited
LSSP	Lanka Sama Samaja Party
LTTE	Liberation Tigers of Tamil Eelam
MEP	Mahajana Eksath Peramuna
MOU	Memorandum of Understanding
MP	member of parliament
NFF	National Freedom Front
NIPU	National Integration Project Unit
NPC	National Peace Council
NPM	New Public Management
NUA	National Unity Alliance
OECD	Organisation for Economic Co-operation and Development
PA	People's Alliance
PCs	Provincial Councils
PEs	Public Enterprises
PR	Proportional Representation
PSC	Public Service Commission
PSIP	Public Sector Investment Programme
PTA	Prevention of Terrorism Act
P-TOMS	Post-Tsunami Joint Operational Management Structure
R	Respondent
SLFP	Sri Lanka Freedom Party
SLIC	Sri Lanka Insurance Company
SLMC	Sri Lanka Muslim Congress
SLMM	Sri Lanka Monitoring Mission
SSA	Social Scientists' Association
TMVP	Tamil Makkal Viduthlai Pulikal
TNA	Tamil National Alliance
TULF	Tamil United Liberation Front

ABBREVIATIONS

UN	United Nations
UNDP	United Nations Development Programme
UNF	United National Front
UNHCR	United Nations High Commissioner for Refugees
UPFA	United People's Freedom Alliance
UNP	United National Party
VAT	value added tax
WB	World Bank

1

INTRODUCTION

Sri Lanka's trajectories of state-building and politics remain interesting topics in scholarly research and public discussion, sometimes but not always for the right reasons. For decades, Sri Lanka has attracted attention as a general topic of interest in a fairly narrow scholarly set of circles, mainly with a focus on Asian studies, area studies and Indian Ocean studies. The country has also been an interesting case study for academic research on subjects ranging from politics, state-building, democracy and post-conflict peacebuilding. The primary lens across the political science studies on the country, however, has come to be that of ethnic conflict. The popularity of the category of 'ethnic conflict' in the post–Cold War period was not unique to Sri Lanka[1] (Sadowski 1998), but a global phenomenon, much of it thanks to the popularity of the 'new wars' thesis[2] and the West's promotion of liberal peace[3] in pursuit of a new 'global interventionary order' by effectively promoting and instrumentally using the non-governmental organisations, at an industrial scale (Richmond 2020).

The country's most spectacular achievements seem firmly stuck in the rapidly retreating past. Once celebrated as a model democracy in the former British Empire, after independence Sri Lanka was lauded for its impressive achievement in terms of human development indicators. Compared to its neighbours, its social welfare policies were seen as a model of social democracy. Among such jubilatory observations, there were periodic incidents of communal violence, even before the idyll was shattered by the onset of civil war in 1983.

Since the island's civil war began officially in 1983, fighting between the Sri Lankan government and the Liberation Tigers of Tamil Eelam

(LTTE) has led to the country being recast as no longer 'Paradise' but as 'Paradise Lost'. In much of academic literature, the public media and private portrayals of the country, discourses have become negative, dramatising the grim overtones and persistence of inter-ethnic enmities. A powerful Sinhala-Buddhist nationalism, recurring cycles of inter-ethnic violence and corruption at the level of Sri Lanka's political and economic elites are all ingredients in the new mix. These are all dominant themes in recent accounts of the condition of Sri Lanka's state, society and politics. The intensity of the discussion, whether among serious scholars or in a public gathering or in a family discussion, can result in heated debates. Polarisation can be worsened, risking making enemies of colleagues, friends and even family members.

For any long-term observer of Sri Lanka's trajectories of state-building and politics, it is not difficult to notice that too often these fierce debates and discussions around identity politics and violence tend to confuse the trees for the woods and fail to see the forest. Heated scholarly debate is not unique to Sri Lanka, being a characteristic of much South Asian scholarship, where many scholars are either unable or unwilling to let go of their political background, and embrace identity politics as if it were part of their professional and civic responsibility as citizens, quite consciously becoming ethno-intellectuals (Ludden 2002: 4).

Regardless of whether the discursive communities are locally rooted, hybrid or international, what is often missing in their debates and discussions are the way complex linkages between politics, economy and societal transformation have influenced the story of state-building in the country (Venugopal 2018). These linkages often have their roots and dynamics beyond the immediate local and national economic and political environment, at the regional and the global level. Given how rapidly such dynamics unfold, their complex local manifestations for politics and society mean that researchers on Sri Lanka hardly have the luxury of taking time to reflect on events and connect the dots before completing their analysis.

With this monograph my intention is to fill in this gap of necessary reflection, to connect at least some of the dots, including some that extend well beyond Sri Lanka itself. My hope in this way is to prevent another exercise of chasing geese. Instead, I wish to understand 'the way things are' and 'how they got this way'. To frame and explain Sri Lanka's trajectory of state-building and nationalist politics, the civil war itself is treated as more marginal than is usually the case, since despite the attractions of warfare for many observers, civil war and ethnic conflict are in many ways quite marginal to the wider general story of post-colonial state-building in Sri Lanka. By not adopting ethnic conflict and violence as my primary frame of investigation, I make a consistent effort to paint a bigger picture and tell a longer and more complex story of how Sri Lanka came to be what it is today.

In this way my aim is to contribute to the fast-unfolding scholarly and policy discussions about the 'dramatic' post-war developments in Sri Lanka since 2009, reflecting on the background to contemporary dynastic politics, the militarised state, and authoritarian and populist trends, all of which are very much in the headlines. Departing from the majority of scholarly and policy-related works of the past 30 years, inter-ethnic relations and ethnic conflict are not the only or even primary prism through which the many decades of post-colonial state-building of Sri Lanka and politics (of state-building) are understood in this book. Here I echo recent work that invites one to look beyond the familiar tropes in Sri Lanka's political developments along the narratives of colonial divide and rule politics, the rise of ethno-nationalist lobbies, structural discriminations and majoritarian democracy (Pieris 2019). I assign greater importance than is usual to intra-ethnic conflictual, competitive and collaborative relations among Sinhalese elites. I find that vertical ethnic relationships across classes are key to painting a more nuanced picture of how Sri Lankan politics has come to be expressed overwhelmingly in 'ethno-religious' terms. My approach is guided by an understanding that identity and large-group identity formation are relational processes, equally influenced by vertical class and horizontal inter-group relations. My inquiry into state-building thus rests on a longer-term historical analysis of intra-group dynamics, class relations and the slow construction of an ethno-religious form of identity politics.

The main questions I ask in this book are as follows:

- What are the key hegemony-building processes identified in Sri Lanka's state-building project?
- How do the dynamics of Sinhalese politics and the broader political and economic context over time influence these processes of hegemony-building and reproduction of elite dominance?
- What have been the key tensions between hegemony-building and state-building in Sri Lanka since independence?
- How have these tensions affected prospects for specifically democratic state-building?

In this book I have had to cover a wide range of topics, from the politics of anti-colonial nationalism, to class relations within the Sinhalese majority and among elites, to capitalist transformation, intra-elite competition, subaltern politics, political party development, state reforms, administrative reforms, state bureaucracy, patronage politics, economic liberalisation, the civil war, peace processes, dynastic politics, post-war reconstruction, militarisation, human rights and relations with the global economy. The central claim will be that *the state-building process of Sri Lanka has been a struggle for establishing the hegemony of the right*. This type of politics rejects individual and social equality, opposes social integration of marginalised groups into the nation, both fosters and appeals to popular xenophobic tendencies, and engages in political projects to achieve hegemony. In this political project of the Sinhala-Buddhist right, Sinhalese political elites and the broader Sinhalese community have played a decisive role.

This book relied on several sources, mainly semi-structured interviews with experts, whom I considered rich sources of information. These interviews were conducted in Sri Lanka and in person, most during the first quarter of 2009, as the war was at its height and coming to an end. Therefore, these interviews stand as rare testimonies to what was happening during this very specific time period in Sri Lanka's recent history. They were also helpful to gain deeper and honest insights into sensitive topics, which were not possible to document due to the dangers they could bring upon some of my interviewees. However, given their everyday engagement with local realities, the personal-political narratives they shared with me became an invaluable set of resources. In some cases, interviewees even considered the interview(s) therapeutic.[4] Some interviewees had first-hand experience working within specific political regimes and had close relationships with some significant political leaders, even knowing them in a personal capacity. This meant they were often able to share 'insider accounts', including information mostly hitherto undocumented. In this way, interviews threw a different light on most written accounts of key political events. I treat these interviews as 'hidden transcripts', in the same way that James Scott suggests (Scott 1990).[5] Although a majority of the interviewees opted to have these interviews in English, frequently they switched to everyday vernacular in Sinhala and Tamil, using specific culturally rooted expressions and metaphors to express deeper feelings they felt unable to express in English.

I also relied on observations during my visit to Sri Lanka in early 2009, at a time when interviewees' emotions were running high given the highly contentious political environment at that time. The government forces were preparing for a 'final military assault' on the LTTE forces, and these military battleground events were complicated further by strategically planned provincial council elections, organised by the ruling regime in the hope of capitalising politically on the government's 'strong' military action in the Northern and Eastern Provinces.[6] These observations I made amidst these events were useful for reflecting on how emotions expressed by interviewees could relate to their unspoken fears and suspicions, to a sense of frustration and to hyper-vigilance within the local highly polarised environment. On certain topics, they appeared to look for a quick escape and their bodily expressions of power and powerlessness. The election campaigns of the time were dominated by themes of war and military victory on the battlefield. It was hardly possible to distinguish between war victories and election victories at that time. On closer observation, election campaigns, televised debates, and cultural and political rituals revolved around the notion of battlefield victories in war as part and parcel of elections victories, and vice versa. Both were viewed as equally imperative by the ruling regime. I also took two additional short field visits to Colombo in the aftermath of the war, first in 2010 and then in 2011. In the jubilatory environment that followed the end of the war in the south of Sri Lanka, collective celebrations of the recent military victories were a frequent sight. In addition to the aforementioned, this book also benefitted from many published literature on the social, economic and political history of Sri Lanka, written from a number of disciplinary areas, in social and economic history, sociology, cultural and social anthropology, political science, economics, administrative science, cultural and conflict studies and studies of colonialism, and also 'grey literature', and locally and internationally published official reports in English and Sinhala.

I analysed all these materials using a critical lens, aiming not only to evaluate but also to identify ideas about transforming social reality by explicitly recognising the possibilities and capacities people have to change their material and social circumstances (Orlikowski and Baroudi 1991). Further, the critical lens was helpful to read and make sense of the written work and to remain focused on issues of power and asymmetrical power relations among various forces in society. Unlike the relatively obvious dimensions of power, exploring the deeply grounded hegemonic relationship that constitutes the state-in-society relations of Sri Lanka requires taking a critical approach to digging deeper into the manipulated consciousness of society. My approach also helped develop a deeper level of understanding of the significance of various kinds of political engagement and be more attentive to possible alternative, less conventional explanations of such political engagements. By combining critical with narrative approach, I wanted to pay attention to each respondent's unique story, their own analysis, the sequencing of narrative episodes, the reference to linguistic and cultural symbols, and bring out the authenticity of each narrative (Reisman 1993: 2). The narrative approach also helped me uncover 'what was meant beyond what was said' and thus explore respondents' close personal experiences and perceptions on state-building and Sri Lankan politics. Most importantly, combined narrative and critical approaches helped to reveal how the respondents made sense of events and actions in their own lives, through metaphors, ambiguous emotions, body language, jokes and other elements in the interview. All these are part of how each person expressed their worldview. In this way I was able to identify four main narrative themes: (*a*) nationalism, (*b*) patronage politics, (*c*) state reforms and (*d*) war and peace. These themes are presented in this book as the four main chapters, with due attention to relevant sub-themes under each heading.

I then fed these four narratives into a larger framework, a heuristic device partially modelled on Gabriel Almond's political system model and his functional approach to politics (Almond and Coleman 1960; Almond and Powell 1966; Almond et al. 2004; Almond and Sidney 2007). In his framework, Almond distinguishes between input (in my inquiry: ideology, material struggles) and output functions (in this inquiry: consent and coercion) within a given political system. These in turn are distinguished from end goals (in my inquiry: state-building cum hegemony-building) that actors strive to achieve. Having first identified these disparate elements, I then sought to anchor them in a coherent framework. By identifying overlaps and connections between various components relevant to my inquiry, each chapter examines elements and relationships that help to gauge the broader picture of Sri Lankan elite state-building and hegemonic politics. Overall, hegemony-building was found to be the oil that runs the political machinery of the state. Using this framework, I was able to place both the internal and external structures, processes and the historical and contemporary specificities each in their appropriate place within the broader story of Sri Lankan state-building.[7]

I categorised each of the four processes, dividing them into consent- and coercion-oriented elements, which is more an analytical than empirical distinction. In practice, coercive and consensual elements are often presented simultaneously in all four processes of nationalism, political patronage, state reforms and war and peace. In each of the four hegemony-building processes, I have also identified key actors and alliances, those dominating, supporting and challenging such processes as they evolve, persist and are dynamically transformed. While in Almond's original framework, political processes are divided between the formal and informal (Almond and Powell 1966: 17), this particular distinction was not taken on in this study, since in Sri Lankan politics formal and informal processes are so completely enmeshed as to be almost indistinguishable.

THE BACKGROUND: POPULATION AND DEMOGRAPHY

At present, the total population of Sri Lanka is approximately 21 million. Ethnicity is one of the major categories of identity. Although these ethnic identities were present throughout history, with the introduction of official censuses by the British colonial rule in the late 18th century, as elsewhere in the British Empire, divisions that had been fluid became hardened and an awareness arose of identities as antagonistic and immutable among the various communities, redefined through the colonial administrative apparatus (De Silva 1981).

The majority ethnic group is Sinhalese, constituting 74.9 per cent of the total population, whereas the Sri Lankan Tamils constitute 11.2 per cent. In addition to these two main ethnic groups, Indian Tamils constitute 4.1 per cent, Sri Lankan Moor (Muslims) 9.3 per cent and others 0.5 per cent (Central Bank of Sri Lanka 2020).[8] The Sinhalese ethnic group is also divided along an upcountry and low-country distinction based on the regions of the country from which Sinhalese originate. Meanwhile, there is a significant cultural difference between Indian and Sri Lankan Tamil people. While Sri Lankan Tamils claim to have their origins within the island, the Indian Tamils were brought to the island as workers during the British colonial era for casual and agricultural labour, for instance, to work on road construction and in plantations. Given the main locations of the tea plantations, in the hilly areas in the central province, it is here that the Tamil community of Indian descent is mainly concentrated.

Among Sinhalese and Tamils, two separate caste systems are practised. Compared to the caste system in neighbouring India, the caste systems in Sri Lanka are practised in a considerably less rigid manner (Rogers

2004). The Sinhalese caste system consists of a few caste groups, in which Goyigama (cultivator caste) occupies the top tier of the caste hierarchy (Jiggins 1979: 36–37); Goyigama members constitute more than 50 per cent of the total Sinhalese population. However, the members of the Goyigama caste originating from up-country areas claim superiority over those from the lower-country regions. This is because up-country Goyigama believe themselves to be descendants of the pre-colonial Kandyan aristocracy. Although these differences appear subtle, in electoral politics and in everyday affairs – for instance, when seeking a marriage partner or seeking political nomination in elections – such caste differences still play a role (Jiggins 1978: 7, 15). In addition to the Goyigama caste, there are also sub-castes that trace their origins to specific regions and a set of traditional occupations. Among these sub-castes are Karava (fisherfolk), Salagama (cinnamon peelers) and Durawa (coconut cultivators and toddy tappers).[9] In the history of political party development, especially in the founding of the two main rival Sinhalese-led political parties – the United Nations Party and the Sri Lanka Freedom Party – such caste distinctions have played a major role in political mobilisation in later years, resulting in tensions and inter-family rivalries that influence Sri Lanka's national political life, as it were, behind the scenes (Roberts 1982). Both historically and in contemporary Sri Lanka, caste-based mobilisation and state-building have a complex set of interdependencies (see Chapter 3).

Among the Sri Lankan Tamils, there are caste differences between those living in northern Sri Lanka and those in the eastern parts of the country (Thiranagama 2018: 365). In both regions, the Vellala caste of farmers occupies the highest rank in the Tamil hierarchy (Thiranagama 2018: 371). Although during the civil war, there were forms of politically orchestrated unity that cut across caste in both northern and eastern Tamil areas (Thiranagama 2011), underlying caste tensions remain, as does domination of eastern Tamils by northern Tamils. This is an intra-ethnic source of tensions in political relations within minority parties and within the organisational structure of the LTTE.

The Muslim population in Sri Lanka is believed to have arrived on the island during medieval times; their origins are usually traced to trading in spices, ivory and gems (Ali 2001: 1). For most Sri Lankan Muslims, their mother tongue is Tamil, a language they share with the Tamil community 'proper'. Nevertheless, most Muslims are also fluent in Sinhalese. This community includes two sects also present elsewhere in the Muslim world – Shia and Sunni. Most Sri Lankan Muslims are Sunni and are concentrated in the Eastern Province. In addition, there is a concentration of Shia Muslims in the North and Eastern Provinces and in the Kandyan Hill areas. In 1990, an expulsion of around 72,000 Muslims from north-eastern Sri Lanka by the LTTE resulted in the mass displacement of a large part of this northern Muslim population, many of whom resettled in other parts of the country, and especially in the North Western Province (Imtiyaz and Iqbal 2011: 380). According to McGilvray, this incident further exacerbated the Muslim and Tamil divide, a development that was received favourably by Sinhala nationalists who wished no political alliance formation between Tamil nationalists and Muslims (2010: 53). Despite occasional outbursts of violent communal incidents, before the end of the civil war in 2009, Muslims had relatively cordial relationships with the majority Sinhalese. In the post-war period, however, this relationship has become strained under the governments of the two Rajapaksa brothers (DeVotta 2019b). Sadly, in the post-war period under both Rajapaksa regimes, the Sri Lankan Muslim community was being targeted as the new enemy of the Sinhalese hegemony-building project (Holt 2016: 5). Until 2009, no apparent major clashes took place among the Muslims; a violent encounter between a Sufi sheik and a reformist congregation sparked some fears among the majority Sinhalese of Islamic militancy and jihadism in Sri Lanka (McGilvray 2010: 57). Despite such incidents, Muslim political elites have played a visible role in both national and regional politics since at least the early 1990s and are especially active in the Eastern Province. As for Sinhalese and Tamil political representation, most of the Muslim community is organised and represented through a few political parties primarily founded on a common Islamic identity. However, there are also key Muslim political figures and a substantial proportion of their Muslim followers who are members and supporters of the main Sinhalese political parties.

In religious terms, 70.1 per cent of Sri Lankans are estimated to be Buddhist. Almost all Sri Lankan Buddhists are followers of the Theravada Buddhist tradition, an orthodox school of Buddhism ('doctrine of the elders') with its literary traditions in the Pali language (Pieris 2006: 336). Some of the key beliefs of the Theravada followers are spirituality, the enlightenment of the individual, self-discipline and pure thought and deed. The Sangha, the main Buddhist priestly order in Sri Lanka, plays a dominant and important role in the everyday life of its followers and in national politics as well. Next to the Buddhists,[10] about 12.6 per cent of Sri Lankans are estimated to be

Hindus, 9.7 per cent follow Islam and 7.6 per cent are Christian and Roman Catholic (Central Bank of Sri Lanka 2020). While the majority of Tamils are Hindu, there is also a relatively small Tamil Christian community.

As per the latest figures, the rural population constituted 77.4 per cent of the total population, whereas the urban and estate population represented 18.2 and 4.4 per cent, respectively (Central Bank of Sri Lanka 2020). The geographical distribution and concentration of communities along ethnic and religious lines have a significant impact on political and electoral dynamics in Sri Lanka. Around 90 per cent of all Sinhalese are concentrated in the southern, western, central and north central parts of the country (Pieris 2006: 342) (see Appendix 1 for the map of Sri Lanka). However, since the 1930s, state-sponsored peasant colonisation projects in the eastern part of the country have dramatically altered the ethnic composition of these areas. The result is that today there are almost equal numbers of Tamils, Muslims and Sinhalese in the Eastern Province (Department of Census and Statistics 2007: 16). From time to time, various politically motivated demographic changes to electoral boundaries have been introduced by the ruling Sinhalese political parties, and the eastern part of the country is especially susceptible to communal tensions, particularly around the time of elections. In the recent past there have been some violent clashes between Sinhalese and other communities in Trincomalee district, the capital of the Eastern Province.

The majority of Sri Lankan Tamils live in the northern and eastern parts of the country, although there are small pockets of Tamil people living in other parts of the country too, for example, in the capital, Colombo, where there is a significant percentage of Tamil inhabitants. As per the 2012 official census and statistics, about 31.5 per cent of the population in Colombo are Tamils (Department of Census and Statistics 2012). According to some reports, there has been a significant reduction in the proportion of Muslims in the Eastern Province, mainly due to war-induced mass displacement towards the southern parts of the island. Meanwhile, several waves of trade-related migration of Muslims to various parts of the country have taken place (Pieris 2006: 342). As far as provincial distribution of the overall population is concerned, the Western Province records the biggest share. The Southern Province is the next most populous, followed by the North Western Province. In these three provinces alone, the Sinhalese represent the highest percentage of the population (Department of Census and Statistics 2012).

There is hardly any data available on the class composition of the population along the notions of relations of production. One way of tracing this is to go by the key occupational categories. Since 1977, with the open economy system in place, there has been some degree of diversification of the occupations of the working-age population. Sector-wise, 36 per cent of the working-age population is engaged in agriculture, whereas 40 per cent is in the services and 23.6 per cent is in the industrial sector (www.statistics.gov.lk). In the service sector, there are new types of occupational categories compared to the traditional ones. Placing these new occupations in a traditional class system (that is, Marxist class schema or purely based on relations of production) is difficult. Nevertheless, any analysis of the socio-economic backgrounds and the various current occupational categories suggests that the majority of the working population belong to what is considered the lower-middle class or below. A detailed analysis of the latest official labour force data that is categorised according to different economic sectors can be useful to get a broader sense of the class belonging of the population.

Sri Lanka has also been experiencing an interesting trend in its population growth, which has had some significance for the island's politics, and an impact on its economic performance as well as its inter-ethnic relations between the Tamils and the Sinhalese. The high population growth experienced in the 1940s is of importance to in the development of economic development plans. The population growth rate in this period was considered an important aspect of the welfare state policy pursued in the following three decades. From 1975 to 1999, the average population growth rate was estimated at 1.4 per cent, and from 1999 onwards it had a sharp decline to 0.8 per cent (Pieris 2006: 7). As per the most recent statistics, it has declined further to 0.06 per cent in 2019 (Central Bank of Sri Lanka 2020).

What is important to note of the demographic information, sliced along various categories, is its political expediency to elites' identity politics. Those who take a critical look at the impacts of colonial intervention, introduction of ethnic identity categories in the official colonial census, liberal-inspired governance systems and dynamics in post-colonial political and state-building often point out to the role these variables played in creating communal tensions (Spencer 2008: 619). As an externally imposed framework of governance, the Westminster style of parliamentary democracy as established by the British colonial rule has been criticised for aiding the tyranny of the majority in the multi-ethnic society of Sri Lanka. Further, this particular system of governance has been criticised for providing very few safeguards for protecting minority rights. As David Scott claimed, the various policy and institutional measures exerted by the British colonial rule in all its colonies, under the guise of democracy and sovereignty, have ended up paving the path for many challenges for politics and post-colonial state-building (Scott 1999). Some scholars alluded that the lack of competency among the local political and administrative elites, the national elites' play of identity politics, the underdevelopment of political agency of the rest of the population and the absence of broad-based support for elites' rule from the masses and for the political institutions are other explanatory variables of weaker democracies in the former British colonies (Bose 2004: 111; Shastri and Wilson 2001: 6).

MAKING SENSE OF DIFFERENT APPROACHES TO STATE, SOCIETY AND POLITICS

With regard to the broad body of academic work on the themes of Sri Lanka's politics, society and state, both Uyangoda (2010: 67) and, more recently, Perera (2021) have lamented that they suffer from poor conceptual grounding and theoretical application. The eager adoption of dominant liberal approaches to studying the state, elites, state-building, politics and state–society relations means that ideology has been viewed as the driving force of politics, with a dominant set of analytical lenses developed around identity politics. The central importance assigned to identity politics in most such accounts is that they tend to reinforce a view of identities as particularistic and essentialised, and of ideology as 'reflecting' communal identities. The implicit comparisons with what is presumed to be a more inclusive, universalist and multicultural form of Western political life constantly reinforce the misleading impression of the 'bad local' and 'noble global' (Zarkov 2015: 126). Therefore, these studies fail to connect local political dynamics with economic, political and cultural globalisation, as well as with geo-politics and structural inequalities and exclusions. Instead, domestic political dynamics and state-in-society relations are disconnected from such conditions, viewed as 'external' and of marginal relevance in explaining the 'internal'.

One disturbing outcome of many written works is an unquestioning developmentalism of 'stages' and an accompanying essentialist understanding of political life, which is viewed as almost wholly a manifestation of ethno-nationalist variables. In other words, ethno-nationalism ends up being viewed both as the defining characteristic of Sri Lanka's post-colonial society and state, and as the 'driver' behind state-building and elite dominance. The primacy assigned to cultural–ideological differences between Sinhalese elites and Tamils is one of the main features of most such studies (Kearney 1985; Brow 1988; Tennakoon 1988; Kapferer 1998; Jayawardena 2003). As Zarkov observed in her broader studies of countries experiencing civil wars and communal violence (Zarkov 2015: 123), studies on Sri Lanka too since the early 1980s tend to reinforce a belief in a dominant liberal episteme and set of assumptions. The result is that Sri Lankans often appear external to the 'global', and to the major transformations in the global economy and contemporary forms of capitalism. Yet such structural transformations matter for understanding localised violence, state-building and Sri Lankan elites' political strategies. The dominance of liberal-ideology-inspired scholarship also factored in with the general decline of application of alternative frameworks of analysis and explanations of post-colonial societies experiencing larger-scale group violence. The gradual disappearance of the application of Marxist-inspired scholarship to the study of state, society and politics, which is critical of external factors, should be noted in this regard. The decline of Marxist-inspired scholarship is not wholly a local phenomenon, but is a global one, especially observed since the fall of the Soviet Union in 1989. Therefore, this dominance of liberal-inspired scholarship and the parallel decline of alternative approaches, such as the Marxist state theory and politics, also corresponded with other developments in international politics and scholarship. Two of these developments are internal to the Marxist theory of state, and the others are related to specific theoretical developments during this period (Jessop 1990: 2). The internal development is the failure of international academia to distinguish between Marxist politics and the Marxist epistemology, and the external is the heavy inroads made by right-wing hegemonic politics – in global and local spheres, whose political advocacy mainly relied on liberal theories of the state (that is, institutionalist and pluralist approaches) (Jessop 1990). A handful of scholarly works on Sri Lanka were undertaken by Amita Shastri, Sunil Bastian, Newton Gunasinghe and Kumari Jayawardena – a few scholars who managed to bravely brace the liberal whirlwinds of this period. Most recently, the works of Kadirgamar (2020, 2017, 2016, 2010) have been able to reopen some promising avenues to revive the Marxian line of inquiring into Sri Lanka, where global–local capitalism, economy, class, state and politics are being brought back to attention.

In addition, the written works on Sri Lanka have been long dominated by political scientists, whose primary interests lie in chronicling and interpreting major political events and studying the degree of functionality of democratic institutions. This orientation has left a few gaps in linking the micro with the macro picture, as their analyses were often getting caught in the fast-unfolding dynamics in electoral and elite politics. There is also a good number of social anthropological studies in which the culturalist, society-centric and micro-political events were central to their inquiries. The most contribution to this strand of literature comes from British and American scholars whose works are inspired by the long-term understanding of Britain as the European Centre for Sri Lankan studies, and American scholars who are eager to continue on their curiosity originally sparked by Indologists. Therefore, these studies show a greater interest in the history of culture, language and literature on the Indian subcontinent, as a subset of Asian studies, where Sri Lanka finds a place for inquiry as well (Rogers 2005: 8). The links between cultural transformation, state (institutional) transformation, functions and inventions of religious rituals, and cultural symbolism in electoral politics and ethno-nationalism have been their main lines of inquiry. With the intensification of the civil war, works of these scholars have begun to increasingly lean towards investigating the processes of cultural hegemony-building by the Sinhalese majority and examining the processes of Sinhala-Buddhist hegemonic state formation. Some critics of these works opined that the ethno-centric orientation of their work has been instrumental in the advancement of ethnic essentialism in studies on Sri Lanka (Hennanyake and Hennanyake n.d.). The most recent work undertaken by Anoma Pieris further challenged such notions by situating her work in the rather unfamiliar territory of architecture. Her work offered a critique on the heavily spatialised notions of violence and civil war that were produced by ignoring the multiple intersecting spatial scales, registers and units mobilised by both the state and extra-state agents and the significant transformative forces in politics (Pieris 2019).

Among others, historians and scholars with an interdisciplinary background situated in critical social science perspectives have contributed immensely to these debates. Their works offered a more promising, grounded and contextually rooted understanding of the complexities and a wide range of issues and challenges shaping Sri Lanka's state-building project.[11] The main inspiration underlying their work can be traced back to the 'Subaltern Studies project' conceived in the mid-1980s.[12] This project was pioneered in the Indian subcontinent by Partha Chatterjee, Sudipta Kaviraj, Ranajit Guha, Gayathri Spivak and Edward Said (McGrail n.d.; Ludden 2001: 2). Although initially the subaltern project was conceived in India, it also had a noteworthy impact on studies of post-colonial state-building in Sri Lanka. This project's influence and its critical approach, derived from the intellectual affinity with the works of Foucault, Scott, Gramsci, Derrida and Thompson, are explicitly reflective of the works of local scholars of cultural studies and social history (Wickramasinghe 1995a; Ismail and Jeganathan 1995; Abeysekara 2002; Ismail 2005; De Mel 2007). Their most important contribution to the study of Sri Lanka's state-building and politics is the subalternising of the elitist understandings of politics and state by applying the key concepts of domination, subordination, hegemony, resistance and revolt.

Although inspiring and influential, by the late 1990s, the Subaltern School had lost its academic momentum in India due to internal splits within the initial core group (Ludden 2001: 26) and in Sri Lanka, thanks to the effects of global structural adjustments undertaken by the Washington Consensus which not only introduced structural changes to state institutions but also altered the ways in which subalterns and society at large relate to the state and elites,[13] and vice versa, politically (Dunham and Jayasuriya 2001; Gunasinghe 1996c: 114), hence diluting subalterns' agency in politics in many inquiries. Such developments coincided with the inroads made by internationally driven (mainly European) scholarship on Sri Lanka, where constitution, institutions, markets and elite politics became the main topics of investigation (Ludden 2001: 27) and with the increased adoption of liberal frameworks in scholarly work (Roberts and Peters 2003: 1). As a result, subalterns' relative worth in politics was seen as a mere object of inquiry and limited their appearances to 'footnotes' to elite politics.[14]

These different strands of written work on Sri Lanka's state (building) and politics were quite useful in capturing and clearly exposing the prevailing trends in the country's state-building and political dynamics, in spite of their numerous limitations, mainly identified along essentialisation of ethnic nationalism, civil war and the notion of ethnic conflict. As mentioned previously, some of these limitations can be traced to global dynamics. As Zarkov has argued based on her observation of the phenomenon of ethnic conflict, many of the studies on Sri Lanka undertaken since the early 1980s are a reflection of the neo-colonial knowledge-production project and the effects of aggressive pursuing of the neo-liberal economic agenda by powerful global political-economic actors which pushed many scholars to turn their attention to topics such as internal ethnic strife and local violence (Zarkov 2015). Albeit remaining marginal to the mainstream ethnicised discourses on Sri Lanka's politics, state and society, the equity and growth debate focused extensively on the links between economic reform and distributional consequences; the political reactions to these reforms still managed to supply some breath of fresh air (Dunham and Jayasuriya 2000: 97). At the time of writing of this monograph, the dominant story of ethnic conflict in Sri Lankan studies is rapidly fading into the background, while some of its key properties are struggling to neatly fit in with the emerging post-war political dynamics – populism and authoritarianism, in the larger background of intensifying geo-strategic rivalries between major global and regional powers, namely the United States, India, Japan, Australia and China in the Indian Ocean region. These emerging dynamics are not without consequences in shaping Sri Lanka's internal political, state and societal dynamics, hence needing a fresh set of tools and lenses that go beyond the long-dominant internalised 'ideological and ethnic' gaze on politics, state and society.

STATE-BUILDING MEETING HEGEMONY-BUILDING

The foundation of Sri Lanka's colonial state-building was laid during the British colonial period (1815–1948). Prior to the British, the Portuguese (1505–1658) and the Dutch (1658–1798) had a presence on the island. However, compared to the British rule, the contribution of the Portuguese and the Dutch colonial rule for colonial and modern state-building was ad hoc and insignificant.

In 1931, with the granting of universal franchise to the island's population, British rule directly influenced the trajectory of democratic state-building in subsequent decades (Wilson 1988: 11; Wickramasinghe 1995b: 229–36; Spencer 2008: 613).[15] As Scott noted of the various colonial liberal democratic practices and tools, universal franchise was an important tool of organising colonial power and a way of imposing and demonstrating colonial political rationality to produce certain effects on the colonised population (1999: 25). Even before introducing universal franchise, way back in 1815, British colonial rule had already taken some other steps to lay the foundation for building a modern state by bringing the previously separately administered regions under a centralised administrative system. Some believe the idea of the unitary and centralised state pursued by the dominant Sinhalese political elites in post-independence politics has roots in this historical British template of centralised state system. Some scholars even go further to argue that the fractionised elite conflicts and elite disunity began with this state institutional design imposed by the British rule

(De Silva 1987: 222, 2007: 1; DeVotta 2005: 142). This was first manifested in the event of Sinhalese political elites rejecting a legislative proposal made in 1937 by G. G. Ponnambalam, a Tamil political elite serving in the national legislative council that demanded a 50:50 representation of the Sinhalese majority vis-à-vis the minority groups, aimed at devolving political power in the national legislature (Wickramasinghe 2006: 144). Some argue that the elites' temporary solidarity demonstrated closer to independence did not last very long as the colonial governing arrangements and the divide-and-rule policy of the British had already done damage to their unity (Wickramasinghe 2006: 150).

In the post-independence period (1948 onwards), the aforementioned initial tensions among the elites around the organisation of the state, society and politics were influential in carving out political mobilisation strategies of the masses. They were keen to capitalise on the identity differences between the groups (caste, ethnic and otherwise). Such strategies have derailed the democratic state-building or developmental state-building in this period (Shastri and Wilson 2001: 6; Thiruchelvam 1984a: 192; Wilson 1988: 7). As the capacity of state capital accumulation hit a low point in the ensuing period, political mobilisation of the masses to national politics and towards the political parties dispensing material incentives became difficult; hence, they opted for ideological- and identity-based mobilisation strategies (Wilson 1988: 7). These early political developments are often identified as responsible causes of the Sinhalese national affirmation that is based on the uniqueness of the Sinhala civilisation, which remained closed to political demands for a federal state and an ethnic power-sharing arrangement by the minorities (Wickramasinghe 2006: 149–50). Over time, these dynamics laid a weaker communal foundation for realising the liberal democratic institutional structure as established by the British (DeVotta 2005: 152).

Elite political infighting for political domination and securing alliances with the lower-class masses using identity politics have shaped and reflected on much of Sri Lanka's post-independence state-building efforts (Shastri and Wilson 2001: 6; Brow 1990a; Abeyratne 2008: 394). Resistance to this direction of politics and state transformation was challenged not only by the Tamil political elites but also by the political elites representing other minority ethnic groups (Thangarajah 2003: 17).[16] In spite of this overly identity-centric tone in the elites' political mobilisation strategies, as some scholars argue, for a nuanced analysis of elite political strategies and behaviours in the early post-independence period, understanding the broader context pertaining to Sri

Lanka's economic development and rural poverty is of paramount importance (Pieris 1978: 611–12; Dunham 1982: 46).[17]

In the early 1970s, the dominance of the Sinhalese political elites was confronted not only by the minority ethnic groups but also by the marginalised youth groups within the majority Sinhalese community who launched an anti-bourgeoisie state and anti-elite armed insurrection. The anti-state struggle was first launched as an armed insurrection in 1971 and again in 1987–91. During both these violent episodes, the ruling Sinhalese political elites resorted to the state's coercive force (Moore 1993: 593).[18] Parallel to the Sinhalese youth armed insurrection, in 1972 some segments of the Tamil youth also launched a sophisticated military movement demanding a separate state (Uyangoda 2003: 55). Yet again the ruling elites resorted to the state's military might to deal with them (Hoole and Thiranagama 2001: x). These two armed youth movements rapidly transformed Sri Lanka's image from being a successful model democracy in the 1960s to a brutal state (Kapferer 1988: 29). As one scholar remarked, 'Sri Lanka is arguably one of the most violent of modern states' (Kapferer 2001: 33).

As a way of dealing with the demands of the two Tamil and Sinhalese youth movements, the ruling regimes began exploring some solutions. For example, agrarian reform laws enacted in 1972 were mostly intended towards the Sinhalese youth. As Gunasinghe argued, although the insurgent Sinhalese youth were not landless peasants, but educated, unemployed youth, many of them came from rural areas and hence warranted the elites' attention to the rural agrarian issues (Gunasinghe 1996a: 55). Although these rural youth did not constitute an agrarian class or have their grievances and economic interests solely based on agrarian relations, the agrarian law reforms of 1972 acutely tapped into their grievances based on their common class position as school teachers, Ayurveda physicians, members of the lower level monastic order and shared cultural sensibilities (Gunasinghe 1996b: 62). To address the grievances of the Tamils, the introduction of District Development Councils (DDCs) from 1971 to 1981 was notable (Matthews 1982: 1118; Wriggins 1982: 171; Hellmann-Rajanayagam 2009: 78). Among other notable examples was the introduction of the provincial council system based on an executive agreement called the Indo-Lanka Accord of 1987, signed between Indian Prime Minister Rajiv Gandhi (later assassinated by the LTTE) and Sri Lankan President J. R. Jayawardena as a solution to the ethnically based grievances of the Tamils. The main goal of establishing the system of provincial councils is to devolve a greater share of political and administrative power at the provincial level (Shastri 1992: 723; Hellmann-Rajanayagam 2009: 78).

Likewise, from 1994 to 2006, the intermittent phase of Norwegian-mediated political negotiations carried out between the LTTE and the Government of Sri Lanka is of special significance for resolving the ethnicity-based grievances (Schaffer 1999: 131–34; Uyangoda and Perera 2003). Several plans unveiled during different phases of the negotiation process – such as the World Bank–led plan named 'Regaining Sri Lanka, the Vision and Strategy for Accelerated Development' unveiled in 2002 (Government of Sri Lanka 2002); the United Nations (UN), World Bank (WB) and Asian Development Bank (ADB)-steered 'Triple R framework' (2002) that targeted relief, rehabilitation, reconciliation and socio-economic development in the conflict-affected areas of Sri Lanka; and the Post-Tsunami Operation Management Structure (PTOMS) proposed in 2005 – inform related other examples. The external character of these plans and the suspicions raised on the possible damage they have caused to Sri Lanka's sovereignty, as often orchestrated by the hard-line Sinhala nationalists, did not help in the intended outcome materialising (Goodhand 2010: 342). The All Party Representative Committee (APRC), initiated by the Mahinda Rajapaksa government in 2006, and the recommendation of the Lessons Learnt and Reconciliation Commission (LLRC) report are other recent examples of local endeavours. However, these local elite-led initiatives often backed by the Sinhalese hard-core nationalists are seen by the external actors as extensions to the Sinhalese hegemonic state-building (Edrisinha 2008, video interview available on www.groudnviews.org; Wickramasinghe 2008: 197, 2010: 160).

Since the end of the civil war in May 2009, according to some observers, Sri Lanka's state-rebuilding has taken a disturbing turn under President Mahinda Rajapaksa (Wickramasinghe 2009: 1045–46). The main foundation of the post-war state-rebuilding project is President Rajapaksa's political manifesto: *Mahinda Chinthana: Emerging Wonder of Asia, Vision for the Future*. Reviving the indigenous culture, establishing the ancient glory of Sri Lanka and introducing a locally conceived economic system to guarantee food self-sufficiency are the main points of the manifesto (http://www.treasury.gov.lk).[19] It is not only that; the manifesto also assigns key roles to the Buddhist clergy – the Sangha – the military elites and the cultural-intellectual elites in the post-war state-rebuilding plans. By allowing major functions to these specific actors, the post-war state-building project is again empowering as well as disempowering a number of social groups in society (Wickramasinghe

2010: 160). Explicit integration of military elites for state-rebuilding departs from Sri Lanka's long tradition of the conventional path of civilian-led state-building to a civilian–military or semi-militarised state-building one (Rajasingham-Senanayake 2011a). This particular post-war state-rebuilding is now being carried forward even more vigorously by the elder brother of Mahinda Rajapaksa, the war-time defence secretary Gotabaya Rajapaksa, who won the 2019 presidential elections. The civilian–military state-rebuilding formula matches the president's previous military carrier.[20] Although President Gotabaya Rajapaksa's main supporters are drawn from the lay Buddhist professional groups that endorse the president's claimed approach to governance based on meritocracy, expertise and efficiency (DeVotta 2021), its failure to deliver is becoming apparent with the increasing slide towards an authoritarian style of governance and in addressing political questions, which became especially apparent in its handling of the COVID-19 pandemic.

In many ways, the various twists and turns in Sri Lanka's politics, society and state (building) from colonial to post-war times have been located along the high political events and the dynamics in the elite political scene. Although there is a substantial body of literature in political science, political sociology and anthropology pointing to the importance of taking 'everyday politics', 'politics as usual' and politics of the margins seriously into any account of the state, society and politics (Chomsky and Foucault 2006: xiv; Migdal 2002), much of the recent written work has fallen short in some respect in presenting a coherent narrative of Sri Lanka's state-building that provides an explanation of the key mechanisms (beyond Sinhala-Buddhist nationalism) through which the elite and subaltern politics are connected.

In order to fill this gap, this monograph relies on several key and interrelated concepts – state-building, hegemony and state-in-society relations – to shed light on these missing links. There are a number of ways of defining state-building, so are there different approaches and assumptions underpinning these numerous understandings of (state) building. In general, the scholarly work on state-building can be located along the liberal to Marxist, and from institutional, economic or developmental to cultural theories of the state and state-building (Jessop 1990: 21–14; Migdal 2001: 236–50). According to Fukuyama (2011: 81–86), investigations on state-building are inspired by different factors, such as social contract (Hobbes, Locke and Rousseau), irrigation (Wittfogel), population pressure (Boserup and Malthus), war and violence (Tilly) and circumscription (Carneiro). In spite of the availability of many approaches and emphases paid to different factors, Fukuyama lamented that 'while we know a lot about state-building, there is still a great deal that we don't know about state building' (2004: 17). However, a simple and narrow definition of state-building points to exogenous and endogenous processes and strategies to restore or rebuild institutions and apparatuses of the state, which can be broadly identified as state-building. Although largely reductionist, even this simple definition reminds us of the fact that state-building is a process by which new governmental institutions are created and existing ones are strengthened (Fukuyama 2004: 17). Disaggregating his view on state-building following his generic definition of it, Fukuyama also draws attention to two important aspects of the state: functions and effectiveness of state institutions. What seems rather implicit in Fukuyama's works on the state and state-building is the relevance of politics, and hence power.

Based on his observations made on the European state-making process, Tilly claims that state-building is not always an innocent process, as it is imbued with tactics of coercion. According to him, the use of coercive power by internal and external actors to create new, or strengthen, governmental institutions facilitates the processes of war-making, state-making, protection and extraction. As he suggests, state-making occurs in parallel to war-making and vice versa, succinctly observed in the European modern state-building. According to Tilly, war-making is an important ingredient of modern state-building and is also a key function of the state (1985: 15). Joel Migdal's work on state, society and politics also affirms Tilly's observations, but mostly in relation to the non-European state-formation and state-building (2002: 11). Migdal is of the opinion that, at least, there are three components to state-building: relations of states to their populations on the input side; creation of intra-state coherence; and a relationship between states and their population for the delivery of services (2002: 40). Tilly's take on the war-making aspect in state-building can be directly identified along the first two functions of Migdal's scheme. Considering the strengths in Migdal's approach (2001), which seems to be a fine blend of the major theoretical works undertaken so far on state-building by Fukuyama, Tilly and Weber, in this monograph I view state-building as constituted with dynamic and formal and informal political processes. This allows me to integrate Weber's ideas on sociology of the state that he developed thinking along the notion of domination. Weber captured all these elements in an institutional matrix explaining modern politics, which he also called 'the state' (Dusza 1989). In Weber's analogy, the state is a historically and structurally conceived phenomenon. Given the nature of the state embodied in the actions of specific individuals and groups, some dynamics in the behaviours of these entities manifest as temporal processes. However, such temporal manifestations should not rule out the possibility of analysing the state, owing to its underlying structural determinants (Dusza 1989: 73). According to the aforementioned specific aspects of the key works on the theorising of the state, state-formation and state-building, I mainly view the state and the state-building processes as not only illuminating the shifting linkages between the state (or state institutions) and society (Migdal 2001) but also showing a structural trait in the long view. In this monograph, I take an explicit process-oriented approach to state-building, but also treat the ever-dynamic political relationships between different social groups as crucial ingredients of state-building and that over time give it a particular structure. To capture the dynamic political relationships and the processes of politics, next, I mainly rely on Gramsci's work on hegemony with the aim of further disaggregating politics, which I find useful in the analysis of Sri Lanka's case of state-building (see later in this chapter).

I assume that my approach to state-building also resonates with South Asian scholarship on this topic, which investigates South Asia as a subcontinent where the modern state emerged under the influence of European colonisation. As Bose points out, the uneven impact of British colonialism has led to a situation of non-linearity of state-building, even within the same continent (2004); hence, it demands taking differences in the processes of state-building into account. Further, Bose and Jalal find that, although India, Pakistan and Sri Lanka were all formerly under British imperial power, they show different patterns of political development and state-building that were shaped by uniquely local circumstances (2004: 95). Shastri and Wilson remind us of the fact that, while direct European colonialism has ended many decades ago, the legacies of the Western-inspired state-building models have left a profound impact on their former colonies (Shastri and Wilson 2001: 2). Similarly, Jeffrey Herbst, a political scientist who has focused on Africa's experiences of state-building, argued that 'the fundamental problem facing state building in Africa, be they colonial kings, colonial governors, or presidents in the independent era, has been to project authority over inhospitable territories that contain relatively low densities of people' (Herbst 2000: 11). Meanwhile, by comparing and contrasting the experiences of state-building in China, Europe and India, Fukuyama noted several unique factors underpinning state-building in these contexts. As he summarised,

> unlike China but like Europe, India's institutionalization of countervailing social actors – an organized priestly class and metastacization of kinship structures into caste system acted as a brake on the accumulation of power by the state.... China's default political order was a unified empire punctuated by periods of civil war, invasion and breakdown, whereas India's default mode was a disunified system of petty political units, punctuated by brief periods of unity and empire. (2011: 94)

Next to the academic literature on state-building, which strives to paint a dynamic picture of it, the grey literature from international policy entities – namely the Development Assistance Committee of the Organization for Economic Co-operation and Development (OECD/DAC) guidelines of 2008 and 2011, the works of the Overseas Development Institute (ODI) in London and the *World Development Report* of 2011 of the WB – presents a prescriptive model and paths of state-building (OECD-DAC 2008, 2011; World Bank 2011). A few criticisms are levelled against this externally led state-building often undertaken by international organisations. Among others, dismissal of the unique historical and cultural contexts and modelling contemporary exercises of state-building on a short-cut version of European state-building are notable (Fukuyama 2007: 13). Albeit various limitations identified in externally led state-building, more or less the European-inspired model of state-building, which dates back to the 16th century, remained the dominant model or the main source of inspiration to state-building from the 20th century onwards (Jalal 1995; Shastri and Wilson 2001; Sharma and Oomen 2001; Bose and Jalal 2004).

Currently, there is also a mix of nation-building and state-building projects that have been undertaken in Afghanistan, Iraq, Somalia, Haiti, Sierra Leone and Liberia (Fukuyama 2011: x, Migdal 2004: 20). In these projects, a clear distinction is made between nation-building and state-building; the former refers to the processes leading up to the construction of a national identity, and the latter implies the building of a functioning state. In the literature, there is a considerable level of disagreement over what functionalist means and what yardsticks are to be used to get a sense of the state's functionality. In spite of the enormous financial investment that went into the externally driven state-building projects, especially in the post-war contexts, the end results of these projects point to their limitations in addressing the complexities surrounding state-building. This rather unimpressive account is also blamed on the external powers' changing commitments towards their own state-building projects, which they pick and drop as their foreign policy and strategic interests change (Fukuyama 2011: 17–18). Despite these mentioned limitations in the current body of literature, the good news is the renewed commitment to exploring the diverse, non-linear paths of state-building in which the everyday and endogenous processes of state-building are assigned great importance in their own right and in parallel to the externally driven state-building (Richmond 2014). I hope my intervention with this monograph can contribute to these renewed debates.

Hegemony is the next key concept I have used in this book. It is applied to paint a more dynamic approach to politics and the politics of state-building, where ideological–material and high elite and mundane subaltern politics can be held together. I have mainly used the Gramscian notion of hegemony, which he initially used to bring together his theory of politics and the state.[21] Hegemony, as Gramsci defined, is the supremacy achieved through domination[22] (Hoare and Nowell-Smith 1971: 12). One of the key points he wanted to convey with this formulation is that the ruling class cannot rule through force alone, but needs ideas as well (Bates 1975: 352). In addition, the hegemonic relationship between the dominant and the subordinate groups is established by the dominant classes by winning active or passive consent of the latter. Gramsci states that consent is driven historically by the prestige (and consequent confidence) that the dominant group enjoys from its position and function in the world of production (Hoare and Nowell-Smith 1971: 12). This is a very relevant point that I find applicable to the case of Sri Lanka, especially when it comes to unpacking the development of the elite–subaltern political relations and specifically the discourses and ideology of Sinhala-Buddhist nationalism. In Gramscian sense, hegemony is not about simple alliance formation

> but about complete fusion of economic, political, intellectual and moral objectives brought about by one fundamental group or groups allied to it through intermediary of ideology when an ideology manages to spread throughout the whole of society determining not only united economic and political objectives but also intellectual and moral unity. (Mouffe 2003: 25)

This way, I find Gramsci's contribution essential to understanding the nature and role of politics and ideology from a radically anti-economistic perspective and to understand the material–ideology interface in Sri Lanka's politics of state-building.

In his famous work titled *Prison Note Books*, Gramsci used the concept of hegemony to analyse a wide range of issues pertaining to Italian history, politics, intellectuals, philosophy, literature and cultural problems by using the concept of hegemony (Hoare and Nowell-Smith 1971). Although hegemony was originally applied to advanced capitalist states (Hall 1996: 416; Urbinati 1998: 373), its applicability to other contexts is still being widely recognised, especially in post-colonial contexts (Mouffe 1979: 1; Sen 1988: 32), where state-building has come to be juxtaposed with hegemony-building by dominant classes or allied groups, including the intellectuals of urban and rural origins. The role of the intellectuals acting as the dominant group's 'deputies', according to Gramsci, is crucial to realise the dominant class's hegemonic ambitions in society, politics and in the state (Hoare and Nowell-Smith 1971: 12). As will be discussed throughout this book, the role of the organic intellectuals, who hail from a subaltern class and speak on behalf of this class, in hegemony-building has been crucial. Their role was instrumental in the promotion of Sinhala-Buddhist nationalism, the ideology of the ruling class, the ruling ideology and the ideological foundation of the modern Sri Lankan state. This way the concept of hegemony is deployed to trace the various practices of the dominant classes in relation to other subaltern classes and in the evolution of complex relations of social forces at any given moment in history (Mouffe 2003: 24). There are three principal levels at which such relations of forces exist: when they are linked to the structure and dependent on the degree of development of the material forces of production, the degree of consciousness and organisation within the different social groups and, last but not least, in relation to the military forces, which Gramsci alluded to as the 'decisive moment' (Mouffe 2003: 25). Gramsci's notion of politics and state is closely connected to the attributes he assigned to hegemony by offering a richer notion of the state by paying serious attention to politics, how political power operates at all levels of the society, the ideological struggles and the material foundation of the ideological struggles at the same time.

Gramsci also stressed the importance of the material-institutional structure (also referred to as the ideological apparatus) for elaborating and spreading the ideology of the dominant classes that are fundamental for realising hegemony. Next to that, in terms of actors, Gramsci also emphasised the importance of civil society, which he referred to as all the 'private organisms' – churches, parties, journals and media, and the intellectuals – in achieving hegemony. He grouped the intellectuals into two branches, organic and traditional, whose role is to mould the social and political consciousness of the dominant class among the led (Bates 1975: 353). Organic intellectuals constitute the classes that are linked to the fundamental classes, whereas traditional intellectuals are made of the classes expressing previous modes of production. The processes of domination led by a particular class in society are what lead to hegemony. This particular class coordinates the interests of various groups and the life of the state as a whole, in the course of which the political, intellectual and moral leadership of a particular historical bloc with a 'collective will', which is also called the 'the national popular', gets established (Hall 1996: 423).

What is interesting to understand is how subaltern groups become hegemonic and dominant groups (in Sri Lanka, Sinhala-Buddhists) through different historical phases of hegemony-building by defeating their enemies (real and perceived) and by lending support to the dominant groups, actively or passively (Mouffe 2033: 39). Once hegemony is established through such a process, it can be seen in the intellectual, political, economic, cultural and moral life of the population. Formation of common sense among the subalterns is another aspect relevant to my discussion on Sri Lanka. Common sense comprises the diffuse and uncoordinated features of a general form of thought common to a particular period or a popular environment (Gramsci 1971: 330n). Despite the fact that common sense is neophobic (abnormal fear, especially of anything new) and conservative, it at the same time has a healthy basis of good sense that keeps everyone united and coherent (Gramsci 1971: 328). In Gramsci's words,

> Its most fundamental characteristic is that it is a conception which, even in the brain of one individual, is fragmentary, incoherent and inconsequential, in conformity with the social and cultural position of those masses whose philosophy it is. At those times when a homogeneous social group is brought into being, there comes into being also, in opposition to common sense, a homogeneous – in other words coherent and systematic – philosophy. (1971: 419)

By drawing attention to the concept of common sense, Gramsci draws a clear distinction between feeling, knowing and understanding – three important attributes that he finds lacking among subalterns already exposed to the hegemonising process led by the dominant classes (Patnaik 1988: 2). I find this distinction very much apparent in all four hegemony-building processes that I present in this monograph and try to engage with the following three points in my analysis of these processes:

1. Hegemony is a particular, historically specific and temporary moment in the life of a society based on a particular constellation of social forces. It is a rare moment in history and is unlikely to persist forever as it needs to be actively constructed and positively maintained.
2. It is a multi-arena and multi-dimensional phenomenon that needs to be constructed using a variety of subordinated alliances at the same time. In other words, the construction of hegemony requires mastery, which is created through winning a substantial degree of popular consent across the society as a whole.
3. Hegemony is a representation of many social entities and does not belong to only one, such as the ruling class. It constitutes a historical bloc led by one class or by the dominant faction that exercises its leadership over subaltern and dominated classes and wins them over with specific concessions and compromises (Hall 1996: 424).

This book also relies on Migdal's approach to the state and state-building. Migdal's approach is considered a middle-level theory of the state and is helpful in situating the state as a unique phenomenon within a specific historiography, where the interactions between the state and society can be closely examined (Migdal 2001). Migdal's conceptualisation of state-in-society relations also complements the Gramscian concept of hegemony, where different actors from the political, civil and subaltern groups are brought closer to each other (1971). Tracing the way they relate to each other and their interaction helps in understanding how power operates among them as well as their struggles for domination and resistance, which contributes to shaping the processes of state-building and the nature of the state, later in its structural properties, visible over a long period of time.

In the state-in-society model, the state is defined as a field of power, marked by the use and threat of violence and shaped by the image of a coherent and controlling organisation in a territory, which is a representation of the people bounded by that territory and the actual practices of its multiple parts (Migdal 2001: 15–16). The state is constructed and reconstructed, invented and reinvented through its interaction as a whole and its different parts. Importantly, it is not a fixed entity – its organisation, goals, means and partners and operative rules change as it allies with and opposes others inside and outside its territory. In other words, the state continually evolves or continually morphs (Migdal 2001: 23) resulting from struggles for domination and change from multiple centres of power. Although Migdal does not explicitly use the word 'politics', the processes of domination and change he refers to are essentially political processes concerned with the 'power dynamics' that is essential for understanding the trajectories of state-building and creating and maintaining distinct ways of restructuring day-to-day life and the rules that govern behaviour. These rules determine who benefits and who is disadvantaged by the rules, and what rules unite and divide societies. Further, Migdal's model draws attention to the role of human agency in figuring out rules and patterns of domination and subordination, and in constantly challenging and changing them (Migdal 2001: 11). In the end, it is the nature and outcomes of these ongoing struggles that give societies and the state their distinctive structure and character (Migdal 2001: 12). By applying the state-in-society approach to the case of Sri Lanka, I want to trace the nature of the evolution and transformation of the state and state-building in a highly contextualised manner with attention to its unique internal complexities and the complexities in the broader political context. Further, as Migdal emphasises, I am also interested in retaining my focus on the multidimensional aspects of the state-in-society relations and alliance formations (as in the Gramscian notion of hegemony), where image and practices of the state as well as the symbolic and the material aspects are given equal importance in analysis. 'Symbolic' could signify a particular set of interests and practices through which a particular image of the state is promoted by certain dominant societal forces, which could be challenged by some others but dealt by the former using coercion and force (Migdal 2001: 17–18). The various manifestations of the image of the Sri Lankan state, such as a Sinhala-Buddhist hegemonic state, ethnic state, violent state and, more recently, security, militarised and authoritarian state, lend useful insights to capture specially the symbolic aspect of the state. The symbolic nature of the state can be materialised through the routine performances by state actors, state agencies and their various practices, which could lead to reinforce or weaken symbolic images of the state, which are also useful in understanding the underlying complexities and vulnerabilities of the state and state-building projects (Migdal 2001: 18). Overall, owing to these various aspects in Migdal's state-in-society model, which I find relevant for the case of Sri Lanka's state-building, my aim is to shed light on the structured patterns of state-in-society relations, their different manifestations and dynamics that inform and shape the seemingly scattered and ad hoc political strategies, actors and the alliance formations to trace how they have led to Sri Lanka's state-building cum elite hegemony-building.

STRUCTURE OF THE BOOK

This book consists of seven chapters. Following this introductory chapter (Chapter 1), Chapter 2 is based on my personal-professional reflection on working in and on Sri Lanka, where I have my roots as an insider and as a member of the everyday life of the community. This chapter is a personal reflection in which I revisited the choices, especially the methodological choices that I made during my doctoral studies, which this monograph is based on, and an explanation on why and how I made these choices. One important point I wanted to draw attention to is the relevance and importance of engaging with researchers' subjectivities and incorporating the personal-social ontology of the researcher to his or her investigation. To put it differently, the main message I tried to convey is the unavoidability and futility of being completely objective when researching and writing on highly sensitive and emotional topics dealing with violence and wars. Rather than shunning my own life trajectories as subjective and irrelevant or, at worst, unscientific, by embracing them I show how they can be sources of inspiration and empowerment.

From Chapter 3 to Chapter 6, I have presented the four key hegemony-building processes that explain Sri Lanka's trajectories of state-building to a greater extent. In Chapter 3, I discuss Sinhala-Buddhist nationalism, one of the key hegemony-building processes. This chapter also delves into the historical evolution of the the Sinhala-Buddhist nationalist ideology, tracing it back to the class relations and the dynamics in the relations of production in 19th-century Ceylon. This chapter points to the material base of the evolution of the Sinhala-Buddhist nationalist ideology and the relevance of capitalist economic transformation during the British colonial period in understanding it. The class roots of ethno-nationalism, which is usually not dealt with satisfactorily in more recent literature, is addressed here as well. By examining class roots as the main material foundation of Sinhala-Buddhist nationalism, I map out how gradual transformations in class relations under the changing political and economic conditions since the early 19th century have turned into a toxic form of ideological Sinhala-Buddhist nationalism in contemporary times. Although I acknowledge the importance of Tamil nationalism in its own right and in relation to the developments related to Sinhala-Buddhist nationalism, I have deliberately kept the discussion on Tamil nationalism short to avoid falling into the usual trap of interethnic rivalries and pitting the two nationalisms against each other, which I find distracting me from my main task of looking into the historical trajectories of state-building from an intra-community, precisely, majority Sinhalese intra-ethnic, politics viewpoint. One of the grim realities presented in this chapter is the use and abuse of Sinhala-Buddhist nationalism by the right-wing[23] elite factions and their allies to manipulate and distract the Sinhalese subalterns from demanding and making binding claims to a deep democratic state and demands for the improvement of the subaltern's real material living conditions.

Chapter 4 of the book delves deeper into patronage[24] politics conceived and operated at the national political party level as another key hegemony-building process relevant for understanding state-building. This chapter begins with a presentation of the historical evolution of the political-party-based patronage system among the Sinhalese political elites and their subaltern supporters. The main discussion here is around the question of how the birth of the political party system during the British colonial rule was closely tied to the elites' nurturing of the political patronage system in everyday and high politics, which effectively combined the elites' struggles for political power and domination with the material struggles of the Sinhalese lower classes in the peripheries. One of the outcomes of this interaction between elites and the subalterns through the passage of patronage politics is the underdevelopment of political consciousness among the majority of the Sinhalese, which stands in the way of them developing the capacity to make binding claims on the state and to their rights. While trying to gauge a more coherent picture on the evolution of the party-led patronage system, I also present how this patronage system has undergone changes over the decades as a result of continually adjusting to deal with the new material, economic conditions globally and locally. My main argument is that the primary beneficiaries of the party-led patronage system have been the majority Sinhalese who over time have become increasingly protective of the system, despite the decrease in the material patronage they receive, due to the gaslighting effects of the Sinhala-Buddhist ideology and nationalism, which the party-led patronage system also runs on. These dynamics were key in realising an overt right-wing political culture in politics and the capturing of the political space and processes by right-wing forces in the ruling class and in society.

Chapter 5 delves into the institutionalisation of the patronage system in the state apparatuses. The main argument I present is that institutionalisation of patronage politics across state institution was invented by the Sinhalese ruling elites as a permanent guarantor for financing the party-based patronage system for political mobilisation and elite instrumental coalition-building strategies against a backdrop of dwindling state accumulation. By analysing a number of key state reforms undertaken by different political regimes in state power since the 1950s, where the party-led patronage system came to be established, nurtured and sophisticated at all levels of the state bureaucracy and the state institutions during the implementation of socialist and liberal state policies, I bring evidence to my argument. One of the key aspects that I am trying to draw attention to is the changed nature of the state bureaucracy from a professional bureaucracy to a politicised one and the ruling elites' sacrificing of the longer-term benefits of creating an equitable system of resource distribution to instead nurture a short-sighted system to benefit themselves. This chapter also shows how the shrinking of patronage benefits and the concentration of patronage benefits among a small circle of elites go hand in hand with the elites' increased appeal to extreme forms of Sinhala-Buddhist ideological sentiments to keep their lower-class alliances ideologically manipulated and subordinated to the elites, who have abandoned the alliances to fend for themselves.

Chapter 6 focuses on various discourses of war-making and peace-making in Sri Lanka from the early 1990s to 2009, hence presenting them as another hegemony-building process. This chapter is inspired by Charles Tilly's analogy of the European war-making and state-making process, Gramsci's work on war of position and Clausewitz's famous dictum of 'war as politics by other means'. This chapter tries to offer a systematic analysis of the linkages between these discourses and the elites' and subalterns' struggles for political power and socio-economic uplift, respectively. The main argument presented is that the various discourses of war- and peace-making are nothing other than part of the elites' hegemony-building project that co-opted any serious democratic state-building project. I also trace the specific roles and functions the various discourses had for the factionalised elites to overcome their personal-political struggles with each other over political domination and hegemony. The mainstream discourses of war and peace – first, from 1994 to 1999; second, the discourse of 'Peace by peaceful means' under President Chandrika Bandaranaike Kumaratunga (People's Alliance [PA]) from 1999 to 2002; third, the discourse of co-existence of political peace and limited war during President Chandrika Bandaranaike Kumaratunga's second term (PA) from 2002 to 2003; fourth, the discourse of neo-liberal peace under Prime Minister Ranil Wickramasinghe (United National Front [UNF]); and, last but not least, from 2006 to 2009, the cumulative discourse of war against terrorism, war for peace, total war and humanitarian war under President Mahinda Rajapaksa (United People's Freedom Alliance [UPFA]) – to show the various linkages of war, peace, politics and hegemony-building are discussed in length.

The last chapter captures the salient developments in the post-war period. Contrary to the popular belief that the end of the civil war and the defeat of the LTTE would complete the elites' hegemony-building project by establishing the Sinhala-Buddhist state, this chapter shows how far it is from being realised. The absence of war and the LTTE from the picture only helped throw a sharp light on the expanding cracks in the elites' hegemony-building project, especially under the two Rajapaksa regimes, which increasingly resorted to populist and extreme right-wing appeals to gain legitimacy for their rule. This happens in parallel to the deepening of the socio-economic struggles of the masses living on the margins of the society. This chapter ends by placing Sri Lanka's ongoing efforts of post-war state-rebuilding and hegemony-building, both led by the same right-wing forces, against the larger background of geo-strategic hegemonic competition among global and regional powers in the Indian Ocean region. The latter developments warrant further investigations in any future research to map out the possible implications they have on shaping the ruling elites' and regimes' political strategies and the overall direction of state-building, which could also help in shaping national and global policies by bringing attention back to politics in the national–global material–ideological encounters, at both high and mundane levels, and prioritising the 'issues of political' over 'technical'.

NOTES

1. For a critique of Western donor funded non-governmental organisation (NGO) operations in Sri Lanka since the 1980s and the claim of their contribution in the 'ethnic conflict', see Susantha Goonathilake's book titled *Recolonisation: Foreign Funded NGOs in Sri Lanka* (New Delhi: Sage, 2006).
2. This concept was introduced by Mary Kaldor to characterise wars in the post–Cold War order. These wars are different from old wars in terms of the nature, methods of warfare and how they are financed.
3. One of the major criticisms of the liberal peace paradigm is its ignorance of the interplay of the complex factors in conflicts and its simplistic solution for peace offered via promoting liberal market policies.
4. As other researchers working in war and violence have found (Fujii 2010: 239), I also found many silences and strategic ambiguities around some sensitive issues and hence left the interviewee to decide to what extent they wanted to share this information.
5. In Scott's framework, both public and hidden transcripts have effects on everyday politics of power. As he notes, public transcripts are only skin deep and take place in the gaze of the power holders, whereas hidden transcripts tackle a much deeper level of consciousness and are much closer to the reality of lived experiences and give insights on the political behaviour of the dominated – a better basis for understanding their political behaviour.
6. In the past, elections for the local governments and provincial councils were held on the same day. This practice has been changed recently. The elections are often conducted in a piecemeal manner surrounding major political events that are considered beneficial for the ruling party in state office.
7. Almond found it useful for comparative purposes.
8. There is also a large number of Sri Lankan diaspora population, mostly constituted of Tamils living abroad. They are mainly concentrated in Germany, Switzerland, the Netherlands, the United Kingdom, Malaysia, Australia, France, the United States, Italy, Norway, Denmark, Sweden, New Zealand and Canada. Canada alone is home to about 200,000–300,000 Tamils who fled due to the war (Crisis Group Asia Report, May 2010: 2).
9. Refer to Bryce Ryans (1953) for a detailed account of the Sinhalese and Tamil caste systems.
10. Not all Sinhalese are Buddhists; there is about 6–7 per cent of Christians among the Sinhalese.

11. Roberts (1995, 2001, a historian), Abeyratne (1998, an economist), Bandarage (2009, a political scientist) and Wickramasinghe (2006, a social historian).
12. Gramsci first used the term 'subalterns' instead of the classical Marxian term 'proletariat' to avoid getting into trouble with censorship conditions in the prison while he was writing *Prison Notebooks*. He used the term to refer to a broader category of people in the margins of the society, who otherwise fall outside of the classical Marxian class hierarchy at that time in Italy. The Marxian scheme of class was more suitable to capture the class relations in the large industrial structure (in the north) but could not capture a large number of peasants, the most exploited in the pre-industrial agrarian sector that was in the south. This was also the case in India and many other countries in the Indian subcontinent, including Sri Lanka; hence 'subaltern' is a useful term to apply to speak of this population and capture their political agency and strategies that are dynamic.
13. Based on Roberts' categorisation, in this book political elites are referred to as a social group that has control of and access to political power, and are holding public offices that are socially valued and which yield considerable authority (1974: 11).
14. One factor that needs mentioning is the dynamics in the regional politics in this period, marked by tensions between India and its smaller neighbouring countries, which influenced the local scholars to distance themselves from 'anything Indian' to avoid the attention of the vocal nationalists, who could accuse these scholars as traitors to Sri Lanka's own Sinhalese-dominated nationalist political project and as collaborators of the Indian hegemonic project.
15. Refer to David Scott (1999)'s *Refashioning Futures: Criticism after Post-coloniality* for a critique of the political rationality underpinning the introduction of universal franchise to the colonial society by the British in 1931. Based on Michael Foucault's work on governmentality, Scott convincingly argues that modern democratic processes introduced to colonial territories by the Western colonial powers were a strategy to reorganise power and conditions conducive to extending colonial power. Scott points to the fact that the liberal democracy introduced to the colonies by using various instruments (such as universal franchise) meant modernising transition from the rule of force to the rule of law that never yields political equality between the colonial rulers and the colonised. This argument of Scott can be equally applied to the local political elites who assumed state power in the post-colonial period by using the same instruments introduced by the British to

reflect on the continued inequality of the political relationship between the local political elites and the subalterns. In a similar fashion in his seminal work, *Politics of the Governed*, Partha Chatterjee (2004) calls attention to the underlying colonial political rationalities exerted through universalist ideals (that is, through instruments of modern universalist governance such as universal franchise) to recognise the contemporary life of politics.

16. In the early official census and statistics, Eurasians were categorised as a separate identity group. In the recent past they have been counted under a category called 'other'. For more on Eurasians in Sri Lanka, see Jayawardena (2009, 2010) and McGilvray (1982).
17. The Sri Lankan voter base comprises a large percentage of rural population. Rural population is estimated to be at 81.4 per cent (World Bank 2019).
18. Moore has speculated that about 6,000 were killed in the 1971 insurrection and about 40,000 during the second uprising (1993: 593).
19. The first part of *Mahinda Chinthana* was presented with the same rhetoric during Rajapaksa's campaign for the 2005 presidential election.
20. Following the incident of the Easter bomb attacks in April 2019, this particular model of state-rebuilding was an easy sell to the Sinhalese voters.
21. It is often noted that, before Gramsci, the idea of hegemony was reflected in the works of Coerce and Marx. However, the terminology they used differs from Gramsci's. Coerce and Marx used the term 'leadership' but with similar elements that Gramsci encapsulated in his term 'hegemony'.
22. Although there is no clear consensus on the distinction between domination and coercion among the Gramscian scholars, they identify two important ways in which supremacy of a social group or class could manifest.
23. The working definitions in this book of the terms 'right' and 'right-wing' are adapted and modified from Betz (1994: 4).
24. In this book, the term 'patronage' is used to denote a supportive exchange between two parties – patron and client – in an exchange of services that are beneficial for both parties. In this relationship, the patron provides inducements and rewards to clients and, in return, expects varying degrees of loyalty (Bearfield 2009: 67).

2

POLITICS OF JUDGEMENT*

> When I write, I do it to change myself and not to think the same thing as before.
>
> —Michel Foucault (2000: 240)

LOCATING THE SELF

Since the early 1980s, with the official beginning of the civil war, scholarship on Sri Lanka has been dominated by the question of identity, especially ethnic, linguistic and religious identity. In parallel to this, at a personal level, escaping the ethnic reality is almost impossible for a Sri Lankan. I recall very well from different time periods of recent political history how dramatically people identified each other and how rapidly these forms of identification could change. I draw from personal experience, having been born in Colombo but spending my early childhood years in a rural village in the North Western Province,[1] where the main livelihood was toddy tapping

---

* This chapter is a republication of an earlier book chapter (2015) of mine with some minor adjustments. The original work is titled 'Sri Lanka's Civil War: What Kind of Methodologies for Identity Conflict?' in *Conflict, Peace, Security and Development: Theories and Methodologies*, ed. Helen Hintjens and Dubravka Zarkov (London: Routledge, 2015). This chapter was a personal–academic reflection on the research methodology of my PhD research, which this monograph is based on. The title of this chapter now is inspired by Jolle Demmer's quote and her take on the 'politics of judgement'.

and minor agricultural work,[2] and where nearly 80 per cent of the population were Catholic.

Around the mid-1980s, the emphasis on my own social identity changed, and switched from class background as the main distinguishing feature to ethnic identity. I remember passing through the entrance of my primary school, where my fellow schoolmates often gathered and would look at my clothes and shoes,[3] calling out loud as I passed the entrance: 'Sub eke lamaya enawa' (which can be translated as 'the child from the substation is coming').[4] Sometimes they referred to me as 'e mahaththayage lamaya', or 'Sir engineer's child'. These two names characterised me because of my father's occupation and the class background of my family.

After a couple of years, I attended another school, a Catholic convent, in a nearby town.[5] Compared to the previous school, here the gap between the rich and poor was less striking. However, after the events of Black July in 1983, the way we identified one another suddenly switched from class to 'ethnic' identity.[6] I recall walking home with another student who declared she was Tamil. She explained how upsetting the demise of a Tamil politician was for her family and the entire Tamil community. I remember taking a long look at her and trying to see what differences there were in terms of her physical attributes that could help me distinguish her as Tamil and me as Sinhala. Until then, I had no clue I was Sinhala[7] and she was Tamil. With this kind of encounter, I began to wonder what 'ethnicity' actually meant. After Black July 1983, it was common to hear people speak of the Liberation Tigers of Tamil Eelam (LTTE), and my parents started referring to some of their friends as Tamils. In my childish imagination, the LTTE were a bit like aliens, with red eyes and in silver suits; I drew this strange comparison from a musical show I watched with my parents in a nearby town.[8] Simultaneously, the physical conditions surrounding me began to change.

From 1983 onwards, following the event of Black July, my family lived with stronger security measures. This included an army checkpoint and a massive barbed wire fence around the entire compound in which we lived. We were not allowed to ride bicycles beyond the army checkpoint at the entrance of the compound. Like the state authorities, my parents imposed a daily 'home curfew' on us, 6 p.m.[9] During university days,[10] I came across a lot of literature in which ethnic identity was always a prominent – and usually the dominant – theme. More than ethnic identity, however, I felt that my class identity defined me as a student. To me, the Janatha Vimukthi Peramuna (JVP)[11] student politics that engulfed the entire university system seemed much more about highlighting class inequalities than about ethnic identities. A great gulf was opening up between the rich and the poor, between rural and urban Sri Lankans and between the English-speaking and the Sinhala-speaking. Most of us judged one another by the clothes we wore and our mode of transportation rather than by our ethnic identity.

However, by this time I was beginning to realise that although ethnic identity was only one of the identities in Sri Lanka, my personal experience of having lived and travelled widely within the country was not common to all Sri Lankans, and maybe my privileges being a Sinhalese made my ethnic identity only a small part of the picture that defined me and others around me. I found the constant and exclusive reference to ethnic identities in much of the literature about Sri Lanka not doing justice to Sri Lankan people's many levels of existence, and the complex range of issues people face in everyday life. These issues moved not only through 'ethnicity' but also around and well beyond such one-dimensional identifications.

As a postgraduate student, I was trained as a 'reflective practitioner' in conflict and peace studies.[12] I was a student of John Paul Lederach, the founding father of the school of Conflict Transformation. Through this education, I learned to focus on the whole ecology of human relationships, issues, systems and sub-systems, which are viewed as embedded in one another and cutting across many other social fault lines. With this training experience, I started to think that I and others might need to start recovering some of the muted and lost identities that had been marginalised as 'ethnic' issues had come to the fore.

The oft-repeated and sometimes almost exclusive emphasis on ethnicity in literature and the media started to become one of the most defining characteristics of public life amidst Sri Lanka's civil war. All this left me feeling frustrated, and I became more openly critical of literature that paid attention mainly to ethnicity, since it seemed to discredit or leave out other pieces of the complex 'identity' puzzle in Sri Lanka and neglect other possible explanations of violent conflict. Perhaps this is because, as Demmers observed, '[w]e cannot escape ideas on power, knowledge and subjectivity.… [S]tudy of peace and war is political … situated in and shaped by highly political practices of categorising, naming and coding … "politics of judgement"' (2015: 237), which I find equally applicable to scholars working on Sri Lanka, whether they are of Sri Lankan origin or not. Later, as a doctoral researcher, I became fascinated with methods of critical and Foucauldian discourse analysis, as the chapter epigrah suggests, and to some extent this enabled me to trace the personal and political trajectories that reinforced a tendency towards ethnic essentialism in the literature about the conflict in Sri Lanka, politics and post-colonial state-building.

While attempting to unpack previous scholarly work on Sri Lanka's civil war, which for the most part was constituted of the literature dealing with the history and politics of the post-colonial state, by employing critical and Foucault-inspired types of discourse analyses, it became clear to me how studies by many researchers had influenced public discourses about the civil war and reproduced the reality of 'ethnic conflict', even in Sri Lanka itself. I understood how public, political and academic discourses reinforced one another, serving to reproduce and repeat the notion that 'ethnic' identity was the key explicator of civil war and the post-colonial state and society relations in Sri Lanka or how the notion of 'ethnicity' tends to be ignored in other places.

In the public domain, there were many occasions when I observed that people were unable to express themselves or identify themselves in any other way, going down the slippery slope of ethnic identification as the line of least resistance, as it were. My prolonged engagement as an educator in the field of conflict transformation,[13] particularly with hundreds of people who lived and worked in local civil society and with community-based organisations from most parts of Sri Lanka, made me reflect more deeply on the meaning of these apparently endless and unavoidable discussions around 'ethnic conflict', 'ethnic civil war' and 'ethnic' identity.

Being acutely aware of the main mandates of organisations exclusively dedicated to issues of peace and conflict, this overwhelming focus on ethnicity and the use of a language of 'ethnicity' was hardly surprising to me. There were, it seemed to me, individual and organisational motivations and economic imperatives embedded in the ethnic discourse. It could prove useful for securing funds, especially from Western donors. When, during the period 2006–2007, many organisations changed their original mandates from economic development issues to working on peace and conflict issues, this was in part what enabled them to receive large sums of foreign funds being allocated at that time specifically for peace and conflict-related projects and programmes in Sri Lanka. It was sometimes quite sad to listen to the stories of how local organisations and their members had wanted to build a community toilet or needed money to buy ten cows for the community so that they could have a stable livelihood, only to find themselves struggling to express their need for material support in terms of ethnic conflict and the need for peace.

These stories did bring me and my colleagues a lot of laughter, yet they also generated discomfort. Only during private discussions could staff members from these organisations express freely their material and developmental priorities, without camouflaging them as a means to overcome or alleviate the effects of 'ethnic conflict'.

These direct lived and field experiences with Sri Lankan people from many parts of the country made me realise the need for a broader and somewhat different approach to identity and analyse the full circle of trajectories of post-colonial politics and state-building. I wanted to capture the daily realities of life and of existences beyond what the 'ethnic conflict' and inter-ethnic driven theoretical frameworks could convey and explain. Initially, sticking with the dominant jargon of ethnicity, I was determined to explore the challenge of what was meant by ethnic identity, ethnic conflict and ethnic civil war in Sri Lanka in more depth. Soon, however, I sensed that this was not the right way, since by asking these questions I could only ever arrive at equally 'ethnic' answers. I felt momentarily defeated once I realised my own stake in reproducing the ethnic discourse myself; this was also what was expected of me. I then sought other ways to engage with identity politics, and broadened my vocabulary to find more suitable problem-spaces (Scott 1990: 8)[14] that could meaningfully connect the different levels of realities I had been exposed to in growing up and working in Sri Lanka, and of which, over time, I had come to be aware.

With warnings from my doctoral supervisory team on the dangers of broadening my conceptual vocabulary, and therefore broadening the area of my research, I stubbornly posed a broader set of questions than originally anticipated. When the context of ethnic conflict appeared to demand answers, I decided to frame my questions in a way that left out altogether the term 'ethnic' or even 'identity'; hence, I decided to look at the broader issue of post-colonial state-building, politics and state-in-society relations. It was this decision that finally enabled me to capture the many different levels of existence that people experience in practice, even in the midst of a conflict seen by many as being about identity. By doing this, I was making it possible for myself to challenge the constructed ontology of ethnicisation of Sri Lanka's civil war, as well as of scholarship on Sri Lanka. Paying due regard – but no more than that – to the (limitations of) conventional PhD research process, and bearing in mind some of the restrictions a conventional PhD structure imposes on any student's imagination and creativity, I pushed ahead with what I thought was necessary.

The main challenge was to come from the unfolding developments taking place in Sri Lanka itself. During the second year of my doctoral studies, in May 2009, I had just arrived back in the Netherlands from fieldwork when, contrary to scenarios predicted by experts, the civil war in Sri Lanka ended with a complete military defeat of the LTTE and victory for government military forces. As in 1983, after Black July, in public, political and academic discourses the military defeat of the LTTE made 'ethnic identity' and the notion of ethnic conflict and ethnic war even more prominent. With victory, the popular Sinhala-Buddhist nationalist discourse seemed to gain a new lease of life, and ethnic identity politics as popularised by the Sinhalese political elites appeared to be in full swing. Pronouncements of President Mahinda Rajapaksa's government reproduced and officialised this ethnic conflict discourse, indeed in a manner that almost no one could previously have imagined. I heard the news about the ending of the war and the accompanying hype about the 'ethnic-humanitarian' victories and defeats.

The way civil war ended further strengthened an already powerful notion that the underlying cause of the war was a violent clash between the Sinhalese majority and minority Tamils. The Mahinda Rajapaksa government kept the focus on ethnicity strong in the aftermath of the war. At this time, I made another visit to Sri Lanka and witnessed the apparent inability of Sri Lankan society at large, and of scholars and international policy makers in particular, to move in any significant way outside the official discourses of ethnicity and the notion of ethnic conflict. I began to feel uneasy about the implications of these developments for my own research and future. It appeared that with the renewed power of ethnic discourses I would have fewer career prospects (and more personal and professional unpleasantness) given my determination to pursue 'non-ethnic' theoretical research agendas. If I had simply stuck to examining ethnic identity, contentious inter-ethnic relations and 'the' ethnic conflict, things might have been easier. By trying to paint a different picture of the civil war in Sri Lanka, I started to feel like the 'black sheep' in the wider family of Sri Lanka scholars.

Genuinely worrying were the dangers of the reductionist ethnicised identity-based views of politics and public life in post-war Sri Lanka. On the one hand, my approach contradicted the official political discourse and agendas of hard-line Sinhalese nationalists. On the other hand, it could also be read – at least superficially – as something like an act of sabotage, which could equally hurt the cause of the Tamils by ignoring their own identity-based grievances and claims. From both angles, my identity as a 'Sinhalese' researcher made it look worse than I had initially feared. I was concerned that I could be branded a traitor by the Sinhalese for failing to unconditionally support the Sinhala-Buddhist nationalist discourse, and for challenging their position by pointing to the larger political picture. However, I was also aware that for Tamils struggling for recognition, I could be accused of conveniently ignoring ethnic identities or not making them explicit enough in my work because of my privileges as a majority Sinhalese. By not solely depending on the ethnic factor, I could be labelled as a (frowned-upon) 'Leftist' or 'Marxist'. At least, the latter labelling could give me solace and even make me feel proud, given my family's background in the Marxist youth uprising in the 1970s and the contribution to Sri Lanka's trade union movement. Considering the bizarre configuration of Marxist principles within the Leftists political scenario in Sri Lanka, I was not much bothered about any potential Marxist label. In retrospect, in addition to my carefully considered and academically judged choices, I have now come to think that perhaps these events, incidents and personal experiences might have had a subconscious-level influence in finally situating my research in the Gramscian tradition of work. Yet the political sensitivity of my work meant that whatever direction I took, I could imagine negative personal, political and scholarly consequences for myself and those I associate with. I witnessed other scholars having been labelled as enemies of the government just for speaking out about the interests and deeper issues behind Sri Lanka's civil war and the whole trajectory of post-colonial state-building and politics. So as I struggled to demarcate the methodological boundaries of my research, I was also careful to control my emotional responses to criticism and to anticipate what these criticisms might be.

Against this backdrop, I reconfirmed my methodological choices to broaden the analysis beyond the discourses of ethnic conflict and adopt an approach much more capable of grasping the complexities of politics and the civil war. I felt greater pressure and responsibility than I had expected since I had to both meet the criteria of academic rigorousness and mastery of methodology, as required by the doctoral research process, and design the methodology of my research with a 'double obligation'[15] in mind (Ross 1996). My first obligation was to be able to see all things as interconnected, without specifically privileging ethnicity. The second was to dedicate myself to re-connecting the parts of my own identity, the parts of myself, to everything around me and to each and every activity of the day. I treated methodology as both a strategic act and a powerful responsibility; methodology had implications for my own and for others' existence.

SITUATING THE PRESENT AND ENGAGING WITH OTHERS' AGENDAS

In much mainstream scholarship on Sri Lanka's civil war, the declared and undeclared agenda seemed to have played a part in promoting the ethnicised conclusion of the conflict itself by essentialising the notion of ethnic identity. I traced these agendas to several domains: the personal, the political and the scholarly, using the method of discourse analysis. There were instances where elements of religion were seeping into discussion of ethnicity, yet these were not sustained as a separate discussion. I took note of how religion tagged alongside the subject of ethnicity.

One reason as to why religious identity fault lines and ethnic identities might have become prominent was because of a particular historical moment within which a majority of the researchers carried out their work. During the 1980s and 1990s, ethnic identity was first made an 'interpellation', or an issue that claims people's attention (Althusser 1970: 11).[16] Ian Goonetileke's widely consulted bibliography, completed in 1984, marks the beginning of this process (Goonetileke 1984). The bibliography is in two parts: the first is on the national question, and the second contains general historical works on Sri Lanka. My first encounter with the bibliography made me wonder about the need to split Sri Lanka's history into two branches, general and ethnic. Even a cursory look at Goonatileke's bibliography shows that the majority of scholarly literature produced in this period involved moral and political responses to the violence of Black July 1983, as experienced by scholars working in and on Sri Lanka at that time. The research questions these studies posed seemed to be confined to ethnicity and cultural identity, even though Goonetileke did acknowledge the limits of such approach: 'The communal problem, though crucial, is only one of the many-sided consequences of the national crisis which is still unfolding' (Goonetileke 1984: 161). It was most disturbing, however, to find that ethnic identity was largely taken for granted. The 'ontology of the ethnic' was not seriously reflected upon, with the result that ethnic essentialism appeared almost a necessity at this time. Subsequently, many researchers appeared to take on the ontology of this crisis period, centred on 'ethnic conflict', as their main point of departure.

During and after the event of Black July,[17] and the experience of direct and indirect violence, some Sri Lankan scholars voluntarily and involuntarily migrated to the West. The first wave of emigrant scholars was mostly of Tamil origin. The violence they experienced empowered them with epistemic privilege and the undeniable authority to pursue their personal moral and political agendas and aspirations. They became the voice of the entire Tamil community and its intellectual representative. Their agendas sought individual and communal justice and demonstrated resistance to the dominant Sinhala nationalism. Their primary audience were governments and citizens in western Europe and the United States. The personal-political agendas of these migrated scholars joined in a timely way with the emerging global agendas of human rights, political recognition and democracy. Consequently, those scholars reproduced the ethnic frame that already existed in Sri Lanka, albeit with different political agendas and emphases (Rogers 2005).

A new generation of scholars among my contemporaries are just as saddled by the essentialising process as I have been. This new generation of scholars who work, for example, for foreign-funded non-governmental organisations (NGOs) in Sri Lanka and whose research projects are driven by the agendas of Western funders (including embassies), seem to limit their scope of engagement to a set of issues viewed as 'topical'. Quick explorations of such issues tend to fit in with ethnic identity conflict models, civil war, human rights and conflict resolution as used for fulfilling the background notes for short-term policies. The scholars of Sinhalese origin are divided into two camps. There are those who oppose and those who support the discourses on ethnic identity conflict and ethnic civil war. Yet both sides appear to have ended up contributing to the essentialising of ethnicity. The works produced by both these camps seemed to be caught up in an action–reaction mode with each other and with the contending discourses of political elites. The continued use of the term 'ethnicity' as the main analytical category has helped to reproduce the ethnic conflict paradigm in political and academic discourses. The implications include an inability of either side to broaden or question the vocabulary for personal and political reasons whether within or beyond the academic hallways. The works of each side were thus used to shore up the political agendas of contending sides: the political elites in power and the LTTE.

Western scholarship on Sri Lanka has been often driven by the dominant thinking about conflicts in non-Western contexts, which tended in any case to over-emphasise aspects related to identity and to view ethnic identities as somehow primordial. I have found it hard to distinguish, in terms of discourses, the academic agendas of much Western scholarship from the agendas of powerful global political and economic actors, and the agendas pursued by Western governments since the 1980s. The fall of the Soviet Union in 1989 and the redefining of policy agendas of Western governments around so-called liberal democratic political principles and institutions, including the market economy, were very striking. However, some Western scholarship, guided for example by standpoint epistemology, did take seriously the responsibility to represent voices of oppressed people, including the Tamils and other minorities in Sri Lanka. The narrative these accounts gave was, however, incomplete and did not enable an escape from the ethnic paradigm; rather, it pitted two ethnicised communities against one another once again. There was no explicit acknowledgement of the subjectivities involved in the research agendas.

As a student of Lederach, and the conflict transformation school of thought that he founded, when I was reading through the pages of such work that solely focused on ethnicity, I could not help thinking of a lesson about simplicity and complexity (Lederach 2005: ch. 4).[18] Lederach taught us, through Japanese haiku, how to capture simplicity in complexity, and vice versa. He made us write a haiku, and I remember failing miserably. The doctoral research process was a second chance to try again to recover a sense of simplicity, following the failed haiku. The challenge was to bring the lost complexity to light, no matter how painful and frustrating the process might be: to complexify before simplifying.

WAYS OF AND FOR KNOWING

Deciding on the epistemological position of my work was not an easy task. Choosing one approach meant excluding others that had their own strong points. There were times when I seemed unable to explain anything I was researching. For a long time, I was unable to make up my mind about how to be clearer about my epistemological approach. In earlier chapter drafts, there was an obvious flirtation with Marxist epistemology. In other drafts I had decided not to take any clear position. I was sending mixed messages, and eventually one of my doctoral supervisors asked me: was my approach Marxist, or did I prefer a broader political science approach? I remember struggling to find a clear-cut answer on the spot; I wanted to do both. I did not see why I had to choose, and wondered how an issue as complex as 'war' could be explained based on just one set of assumptions.

My critical readings of previous works, my fieldwork interviews and personal experiences had all suggested that a range of epistemological positions were needed. I was convinced that people's multiple experiences and multiple realities could not be captured and explained by a single epistemological perspective. Thus, having to state a single, clear position was uncomfortable and even seemed disrespectful, as I believed it was reducing peoples' real-life experiences to a single framework. For me, epistemology was also politics, so choices had real consequences for people's lives.

After a long battle and careful evaluation of various philosophical debates and reflecting on my own location(s) in the research, I came to the conclusion that my perspective was a post-positivist one. Many previous studies, including those of De Silva (1985), Tambiah (1992, 1986) and Spencer (1990a and 1990b), had all adopted a positivist epistemology, which seemed to almost invariably end up illuminating the 'ethnic origins' of civil war in Sri Lanka, at the expense of other issues. I hoped that a post-positivist approach could instead emphasise multiple causes and dynamics of war. My hope was that the post-positivist approach would highlight the limitations of different ways of theorising and of different methodologies, and could complement triangulation of data across multiple sources. A post-positivist position opened up space for dealing with human subjectivity, while allowing for possible biases I carried as a Sri Lankan and as a researcher, approaching the country, as it were, from both inside and outside. Post-positivism eventually helped me understand and analyse Sri Lanka and the civil war beyond the 'ethnic conflict' model, without denying completely the salience of identity issues during the war. By defining my location in a social constructivist approach, I placed myself as a social scientist and a human being squarely within the research process.

My post-positivist-constructivist stand proved a challenge to some dominant literature produced in the field of conflict and civil war studies about Sri Lanka, including work by cultural and social anthropologists in the 1980s and 1990s.[19] For a long time the domination of Sri Lanka's conflict studies by anthropologists maintained the focus on culture and cultural 'differences', with ethnic identity as a basic ontological category. Over time, as the dynamics of the conflict and the civil war changed, epistemological stances have become more ambiguous and merged with each other. For example, Bruce Kapferer (1998) was a well-known cultural anthropologist, whose work initially sparked quite a controversy by presenting ethnic identities in Sri Lanka as ahistorical and almost unchangeable. Later, Kapferer included elements of constructionist theory in his approach, and paid much more attention to the discursive construction of identity, illuminating the discursive logic, the strategic action of elites and the strategic actions of the masses.

Scholars have thus shifted their epistemological positions at times, making adjustments and eventually moving from more primordialist, essentialist or positivist positions to more constructivist perspectives. Their initial lack of reflection may still have meant that at some key points, uncritical academics were responsible for feeding the ongoing violence (Brass 1991).[20] Amidst the epistemological controversies among 'big names' in the field, I imagined the fate of my own work like that of someone walking forwards into an academic-political minefield.

SPEAKING OF DATA

The epistemological approach I chose meant needing several sources of data. One source could not do justice to the topic or peoples' lifelong experiences of conflict and war. It was paramount to include as many epistemic communities as possible to understand how the meta-narrative of civil war and its sub-narratives were produced and reproduced, and especially how ethnic identity politics was constructed and dismantled. Thus, I spoke to people who belonged to very different political and economic groups, to local elites, to academics who were in favour with the government and those out of favour, and to former and current political, administrative and community leaders.

I conducted my interviews amidst the final phase of the civil war. I was also fortunate to have discussed with some of the same people several years before, in 2005 and 2006, whose physical, political and symbolic presence have been eliminated since the end of the brutal war. During and in the aftermath of the war, the government of Sri Lanka came under heavy attack by human rights groups in the local and international community for committing war crimes, and the government's policy of banning journalists from travelling to the war zone to investigate those accusations sparked serious controversies.

Against this backdrop, the government launched a sophisticated surveillance system to prevent people who had first-hand experiences of violence, members of the civil society and journalists from passing on information related to the last phase of the war outside the country.

There were many cases reported where the people who attempted to pass information were subjected to threats, intimidation, disappearance, had to go into exile and were even killed. Given this situation, many people with whom I had previously talked were now unwilling to share any information. Their body language suggested they were coerced into self-censorship. For a while, I wondered whether I should include these sources and how. As much as an issue of methods, this was also a question of taking a decision about including and excluding sources that could affect theirs and my personal security.

Finally, because of the importance of the voices of these communities in different historical moments,[21] I decided to include such materials gathered from them. Dangers remain in bringing public attention to these sources and to my past engagements. Yet I still believe including information – whilst protecting people's anonymity – has a great relevance regardless of potential risks. These sources helped fill gaps and weave together a longer-term view of different trajectories of discourse production about civil war under conditions of both war and peace. Without such a painstaking route, my sample would run the risk of being rigid and exclusivist.

During document analysis, there were many instances when I noticed the author's enthusiasm for jumping to the present and omitting any but a passing reference to the past. This applied not only to events but also to structures, voices and people who lived in that past. I found this a complete contradiction to what I had learned from Lederach in one of his classes, where we learned about an African proverb that says: 'the past that lies before us'. Thus, my reading of the political history of Sri Lanka and the civil war would not begin with a short reminder of Sri Lanka gaining independence from Britain in 1948, or with the horrors of Black July in 1983, or with the killing of the LTTE leader Velupillai Prabakaran on 19 May 2009. If one takes 1948 as the main point of departure, one would frame and focus on the ills of the British rule and hold the British and the colonial institutional structure imposed on Sri Lanka as the causes of the current 'ethnic conflict'. If one chooses Black July as the starting point, the focus shifts to the atrocities of the LTTE and the role of the government. Taking 2009 would lead one to focus largely on the military clampdown on the LTTE. In all these cases, clear villains and heroes, victims and offenders are identified. But choosing the starting point depends on the personal preferences of the researcher and the ethics that he or she is bound by. And, of course, how convincingly one gets to make his or her case in the 8,000-word limit usually allowed by scientific journals. Instead, my reading of the political history of Sri Lanka went not to a specific event, but to historical processes of the pre-modern period, or before the advent of European colonialism in the island.

In addition, I decided to engage with the 'grey' or non-academic literature and unconventional sources. To me, Sri Lanka has always demonstrated the power of gossip (Foster 2004),[22] and non-academic sources have greatly contributed to wider discourse construction. As Fujii wrote based on her research work in Rwanda after the genocide, I was also determined to include and capitalise as much as I could on the meta data into my work as I found them not extraneous to any other datasets (Fujii 2010: 231). I agree with Fujii's take on the meta data as indicators of how the present conditions shape what people are willing to say about violence in the past, why they embellish or minimise, and what they prefer to keep to themselves (Fujii 2010: 231). As an insider with a substantial level of cultural fluency, I have seen that the so-called grey and unconventional sources and meta data sometimes have a power and currency that supersede more conventionally gathered data and the publications based on such data. By assigning value to such sources more or less equal to academic sources, I was determined to fill some serious gaps in the popular narratives. More importantly, I tried to contribute to a levelling of the playing fields of research. Gathering meta data also gave me a sense of relief and the confidence that I could finally include the marginal voices expressed directly in vernacular languages (in Sinhala) and capture the multiple meanings that my interviewees assigned to different events in their everyday lives that are embedded in the events in high politics. What I did was in line with both personal belief and the obligations I wanted to shoulder in this research.

There are many thorough interdisciplinary and multidisciplinary studies on Sri Lanka that have been labelled by some of my informants as too 'flimsy', 'wishy-washy' and even 'post-modernist'. The works of Wickramasinghe (2006), Jayawardena (2000), Ismail (2005) and De Mel (2007) have been described this way at times, perhaps not necessarily as an academic critique but simply due to their world view differences with these scholars' work and due to the fact that their works diverge from the personal-political interests of some of my interviewees. Yet I have learned to appreciate the contributions of these particular researchers, sometimes more than the studies done within strict disciplinary boundaries where Sinhala-Buddhist ideology and nationalism are idolised. I especially found them useful in explaining the complex, messy topic of civil war which, in my view, cannot be located in one specific discipline or subject area and without a serious critique of the mainstream and the popular.

I was also determined to take a step further, towards the principles that Voss named 'transdisciplinarity' (2002). My specialised training and field experiences working on issues of trauma and psychosocial recovery meant that I could recognise linkages between diverse disciplines, from psychology to biology, from ecology to theology and spirituality, and from metaphysics to sorcery and sociology. By pushing my research in the direction of transdisciplinarity, I suppose, a weaker form of transdisciplinary according to Max-Neef's classification (2005),[23] I was finally able to bring together and draw on traditional subject areas such as history, sociology, political science, psychology, law and anthropology together with international relations, development studies, conflict and peace studies, and gender and feminist studies. I was consistently trying to go beyond my academic comfort zone. Perhaps at some point my reading was unintentionally influenced by some form of transdisciplinarity and the diffraction method of reading. The latter, as Karen Barad puts it, 'involved paying attention to the specificity of the argumentations and the finer details of the underlying theories and assumptions of the texts aligning them horizontally' (2007: 93).

Research produced under different time periods, especially during times of threats, intimidation or killing and amidst involuntary disappearances, has its own limitations. By conducting field interviews amidst the height of civil war, personally witnessing, observing and 'sensing' the environment of war and military victories were painful yet all serendipitous encounters. The period I spent in the field allowed me to collect valuable data on the subjective human relations affected by the war. The last phase of civil war coincided with some strategically planned provincial elections as well. Being on the ground to witness first-hand these events helped me dig deeper into the 'realities in the making'.

During fieldwork, I felt I was moving inside a gold-mine of data, and on the other hand I also often felt distracted and pained. At times, I had a Zen mind[24] and absorbed the environment as I felt it physically and emotionally, without analysing or reflecting on it too much. Yet most of the time spent in the field brought feelings of shame and sadness, personally and as a Sri Lankan. For the sake of the research, I engaged and listened to people I would not usually interact with in my personal life, including people with very different and often radical nationalist political views. It was risky and also against my personal preferences; yet by doing this, I practised an inclusive ethics and tried to put into effect a more cross-cutting politics where everyone counts: the perpetrators as well as the victims, those alive and even those who have died.

BEING CRITICAL INTERPRETATIVE

At times, while writing my doctoral dissertation, I felt uncomfortable about my own findings. Several times I wrote and rewrote chapters, producing many different versions. Initially, I always sought a balanced interpretation, which was very hard to achieve. Over time, following post-war developments, sitting in The Hague and reflecting on data, I tried to look at what I had found from every possible angle and to reflect on my own life experiences. It was inevitable that I would have to take a more critical stance. I no longer felt I should try to be neutral or balanced; instead, I finally felt free to justify the methodological approach I had employed and declare my position and location as openly as I could. In one of the seminars where I presented my research, a discussant attempted to counter my arguments, unhappy with the interpretative aspect of my research. But this interpretative approach was both critical and – for me – unavoidable. War and peace are about politics. Politics is subjective, and subjectivity is shaped by many levels of existences of both the self and others. Sometimes, these layers cannot be separated; fortunately, they can always be interpreted.

As I was getting ready to defend my doctoral thesis against the backdrop of post-war Sri Lanka, I was relieved to have taken a critical approach in my theoretical framework, and to have translated this into a methodological eclecticism. This gave me the level of confidence I needed to be able to speak to the power, the authority of the dominant metanarrative of ethnic conflict, and to challenge this narrative on firm ground. By taking a critical approach, I was able to integrate both my personal and my professional selves in the research. This helped to place my own life experiences and training into the practice of research, and this meant I did not have to place myself somewhere outside the context or hide behind researcher 'neutrality'. I took on my share of responsibility for what had happened in Sri Lanka, and I wanted to make my small contribution to transforming the situation for the better of the country, in the future. Clearly these priorities are more than questions of methodology; they are questions about the ethics of scholarly research.

Dating back to Weber, today any standard social science textbook on methodology has a lot to say about the neutrality of the researcher (Shils and Finch 2011). However, I have realised that, when dealing with complex human affairs like violence and injustice, it is not only impossible but may even be undesirable for researchers to seek neutrality. Principles of neutrality may be fine for humanitarian work but are not practicable in social science. After all, researchers carry the baggage of social location whether they are insiders or outsiders, and are also under moral obligation to consider how the sufferings of people can be eased. In situations of war and violence, one has to take greater risks in exposing unjust moral and dubious political agendas. The urge and determination to challenge popular and dominant discourses of ethnic identity in conflict were part of my ethical agenda and the primary motivators for my own doctoral studies. My idea of being an ethical researcher was served by trying to paint a 'bigger picture' of the civil war and by rejecting the exclusive, ethnic identity–based politics that was part of its manifestation. I strived to bring ethics and politics together, instead of keeping them apart. The methodology I chose helped me reconstruct a terrain for research where politics was informed by the ethics of scholarly responsibility.[25]

In conclusion, by taking a risky methodological trajectory, my doctoral research on Sri Lanka, which this book is based on, challenged popular metanarratives that this was an 'ethnic conflict', pure and simple. By departing from the repeated emphasis on ethnicity, and consciously building a more inclusive methodology in terms of sources and epistemologies, I was able to recreate a long lost and more complex picture of Sri Lanka, especially how the country had arrived at the point of civil war. This picture included language, religion and identity, of course, but it also included class, caste, gender and age in relation to the rural and urban divide, patronage, clientelism, and different elite and popular struggles for controlling the state and the country's economic resources, and different groups of population, across territories and communities. As Helbardt, Hellmann-Rajanayagam and Korff cogently presented, undertaking this research project was neither an accident nor an adventure in a world of research on wars and violence where danger has become 'interesting' and maybe even alluring to some researchers (2010: 351)

Contrary to most current social studies research on Sri Lanka's civil war and the post-war situation, my own research rejects the thesis that ethnic identity was the main cause of violence and conflict. Instead, I painted a messier picture, where roots, manifestations and realities of conflict and violence were embedded in one another, and overlapped with many social processes and identities, traversing fault lines of class, political party affiliations, caste and marked regional identities. Because of the methodology I employed, the popular master narratives of ethnic identity and ethnic war were revealed as products of specific methodological and epistemological choices made by many previous scholars and researchers. Methods that came to be fashionable and were sustained from around the early 1980s to the present meant that ethnic essentialism came to be moulded into a powerful set of public, political, cultural and academic discourses. So many previous studies on Sri Lanka's civil war and trajectories of post-colonial state-building had claimed to take a neutral or objective position, and yet came up with similar findings.

The bigger question remains: what does one do with the ethnicised conclusions of the still dominant theories, and how can essentialising of ethnic identity in Sri Lanka's politics, state and society leave any room for manoeuvring towards a socially just transformation of the society? I conclude with Albert Einstein's famous words, 'We can't solve problems by using the same kind of thinking we used when we created them.' I continue to think that to break an impasse, more than anything else, as researchers we need imagination and creativity. These are the keys to the methodological choices of my research, and I propose that to take a step in the direction of 'imagination' is to leave behind some of the old assumptions that can perpetuate war. In retrospect, what I have tried in this chapter is to paint a more subtle vision (Haraway 1997: 273) than undertaking a full-fledged exercise of reflexivity of my doctoral journey, by assigning myself a great deal of self-accountability and a critical and responsible engagement.

NOTES

1. The village was called Bolawattha. The biggest nearby town is called Dankotuwa, which is famous for clay and porcelain tableware production.
2. Toddy is an alcoholic beverage made by fermenting the sap of the coconut flower. In English usage, it is popularly known as palm wine. In the coastal belt of Sri Lanka, toddy tapping is mostly associated with one caste, Durava. In these areas, many people used to work in the paddy fields as casual labourers.

3. I happen to be the only child who came to school wearing socks and shoes.
4. My father served as an Engineer-in-Charge in one of the biggest electrical substations in the area. The substation was adjoining the official compound where we lived.
5. The town is called Wennappuwa. In terms of electoral politics, this area is dominated by the United National Party. It was the electoral seat of the former cabinet minister and the parliamentarian Mr Festus Perera (deceased 2013), who was on friendly terms with my father.
6. Black July refers to the anti-Tamil pogroms and riots carried out by Sinhalese mobs in the month of July in 1983. It is estimated that about 4,000 Tamils were killed during the seven days of pogrom. This incident is also often referred to as one of the turning points of the civil war in Sri Lanka.
7. Looking back to my past, perhaps it is because I was privileged to ignore my majoritarian ethnic identity, which could not be a choice for someone from a minority ethnic group in Sri Lanka, who is constantly reminded of his or her ethnic identity when navigating through everyday life in a majority Sinhalese-dominated context.
8. I painted this image of the LTTE based on a background performance to a song titled 'Kurumitto', sung by the popular music band Gypsies at the venue.
9. I also recall during this turbulent time period that my father had to leave us for a six-month training programme in Sweden. According to the new security measures, he had to obtain a special permit to travel to the airport if the travel had to take place during the curfew hours. These measures also restricted the number of people who could accompany the main air passenger to the airport. This meant one of us had to stay back as a family of five we exceeded the number of accompanying travellers allowed (including the driver). But our parents managed to take all three children to the airport by smuggling my older sister under a seat to avoid detection at the military checkpoint. I remember we were so fearful of getting caught when the soldier at the checkpoint started counting the passengers by directly pointing the flash light on each of our faces.
10. To obtain my bachelor's degree, I attended the University of Colombo, Sri Lanka (1996–2000). I graduated in 2000 and continued to work at the university as a research assistant and later as a junior lecturer.
11. JVP (translated as Peoples' Liberation Front) is a political party founded in the 1960s. Its party ideology is based on Marxist-socialism. The cadres of the JVP, including its leadership, were primarily drawn from the lower

caste, rural, petty bourgeoisie and the proletariat class. Unfortunately, more than for its declared Marxist-socialist ideological stand, JVP is popular as an extremist political party of Sinhala-Buddhist nationalist orientation.
12. I studied at the Eastern Mennonite University, Virginia, under the Fulbright fellowship program.
13. This was drawn from my experiences working as an advisor for capacity-building for conflict transformation and peacebuilding for Sri Lanka's civil society organisations with the German Technical Cooperation/Facilitating Local Initiatives for Conflict Transformation (GTZ/FLICT) project in Sri Lanka.
14. I borrowed this term from David Scott. Scott defines problem-spaces as conceptual-ideological ensembles, discursive formations or language games that are generative of objects and therefore of questions.
15. I borrowed this term from Rupert Ross.
16. I here used Althuser's term 'interpellation' to mean how the institutions and discourses created the 'ideology of ethnicity' and was able to condition their minds to effortlessly or unconsciously respond to an ethnic 'hailing' in their everyday social interactions.
17. Also known as ethnic pogroms.
18. This lecture was based on chapter 4 of John Paul Lederach's book, *Moral Imagination: The Art and Soul of Peacebuilding* (2005).
19. Here I am specially thinking of the work of Spencer, *Sri Lanka: History and Roots of Conflict* (1990), and the work of S. J. Tambiah, *Sri Lanka: Ethnic Fratricide and the Dismantling of Democracy* (1986), and the work of Bruce Kapferer, *Legends of People, Myths of State: Violence, Intolerance, and Political Culture in Sri Lanka and Australia* (1998).
20. This has been argued by Brass, who represents the constructionist discourse that claims that ethnic identity is constructed, fluid and multiple, and he has attempted in this book to deconstruct ethnic essentialism. His view, unfortunately, did not stand much chance among the powerful positivist anthropological work being carried out.
21. Here I am referring to the discussions I had with a number of members of the LTTE in regional commanding positions who were in charge of relief and development work in Jaffna district after the tsunami disaster in December 2004. During this time period, peace talks were taking place between the Government of Sri Lanka and the LTTE.
22. I take gossip to reveal the power relations, political actions of resistance, and social change.

23. A weak transdisciplinary is applied following traditional methods and logic, which essentially remains practical in a research process. Whereas the stronger transdcisplinarity is aimed at tackling an epistemological challenge where the researcher works with quantum logic, as a substitute for linear logic, and breaks with the assumption of a single reality, and deals with three levels of Reality, the Axiom of the Included Middle, and Complexity.
24. In Zen Buddhism, having a Zen mind means having a mind of a beginner and an empty mind. Both empty and beginners' minds are considered to be fresh, uncluttered and without having pre-conceived thoughts and notions.
25. I became more aware of this relationship reading Michael Foucault's work.

3

FROM NATIONALISM TO ETHNIC SUPREMACY

While I acknowledge the relevance of the ethno-nationalism discourses for understanding Sri Lanka's past and present politics and state-building, in this chapter I want to draw attention to the importance of class-based roots of ethnic-nationalism. By examining the class roots of Sinhala-Buddhist nationalism, it becomes possible to shed light on how gradual transformations in class relations under the impetus of changing political and economic conditions have come about since the early 19th century. The importance of historical legacies of class relations in forming the current toxic form of Sinhala-Buddhist nationalism can thus add something to the more usual ethno-religious accounts of political transformation and state-building. A more nuanced analytical account of class conflicts within the Sinhalese majority population can help to explain and illustrate how class conflict paved the way for the galvanising of Sinhala-Buddhist nationalism as a profound hegemony-building tool in its current exclusionary form.

THE STRANGE STORY OF CLASS ORIGINS OF SINHALA-BUDDHIST NATIONALISM

The genesis of Sinhala-Buddhist nationalism can be traced back more or less to the second half of the 19th century, with the first emergence in Sri Lanka of something like a Sinhala 'identity' or consciousness (that is, the Sinhalese became aware that they were a distinct group of people) (Jayawardena 1987b: 2). During late British colonial rule, this vague notion of collective ethnic and religious identity was transformed into a distinctly

Sinhala-Buddhist form of nationalism. In its early form, it was described as 'religious nationalism',[1] reflecting the way that certain politically significant events were expressed in Sri Lanka prior to the country's independence. This phase of late colonial history is commonly described as a period of anti-colonial and 'first generation nationalism'.[2]

However, in the post-independence period, ethnic identity formation became a more important element in overall Sinhala-Buddhist nationalism, alongside religion and anti-Western sentiments (Wickramasinghe 2006: 45). It was in part the result of the British colonial power's systematic categorisation of colonial 'subjects' that ethnic and religious identities were mobilised in such a rigid and exclusionary manner. Numerous identity labels were used, involving caste, race, ethnic and religious groupings. All these were an attempt to 'describe something that had practical and conceptual coherence ... for outsiders and observers rather than for Sri Lankans themselves' (Wickramasinghe 2006: 48). Varying entitlements and rights were then attached by the colonial administration to these identity categories, contributing to their hardening. Identity categories were both instrumental and politicised in this way, and ceased to be only about cultural and social differences (Wickramasinghe 2006). Some observers stress how formation of a self-conscious collective 'Sinhala consciousness' by some local leaders towards the end of the 19th century lay at the origin of the later denial of the multi-ethnic character of Sri Lankan society. They argue that the question of how the nation was 'imagined' thus became early on a major point of tension among Sinhalese and Tamil Sri Lankans (Jayawardena 1987b: 2). Nesiah claims that conditions for the emergence of ethnic-identity-based consciousness among the Tamil population did not exist until much later, because of the greater hold of caste divisions and other forms of fragmentation among Tamils (Nesiah 2001). Compared with the majority Sinhalese, divisions among Tamils thus hindered the early development of the kind of shared ethnic consciousness or awareness of incipient nationalism that formed among the emerging Sinhala-Buddhist elites (Nesiah 2001: 12).

Many of those interviewed for this study viewed the emergence of Tamil nationalism in the early 1900s as arising mainly in reaction to Sinhala-Buddhist nationalism. This reaction-based nationalist discourse can be framed from within the grievances thesis as a form of contestation of injustices and social exclusion.[3] However, a quick glance at the popular discourses of both Sinhala-Buddhist and Tamil nationalism suggests that today both express similar grievances, based on claims of historical injustice, and surprisingly similar and competing claims of shared ethno-religious victimhood. The entanglement of such grievances-based national claims is particularly illuminated by political discourses, where both Tamil and Sinhala elites appear to be motivated by directing attention away from their hegemonic and counter-hegemonic claims. While there is a lot written about the ethnic and religious foundation of Sinhala-Buddhist nationalism and the rival inter-ethnic relations, what is mostly missing from the story is the class foundation of the Sinhala-Buddhist nationalist ideology, and its start as a carefully crafted class-based project of the local bourgeois class in colonial Sri Lanka, who used their class identity instrumentally in national politics. The absence of class analysis in many historical analyses has been noted by other researchers (see, for example, Jayawardena 1985a: 36). In this way, as the Gramscian notion of hegemony stresses (Gramsci 1971), class conflict and class relations played a crucial part in Sinhalese hegemonic state-building. Going further in illuminating the class foundation, I will first start illuminating the role of class in the 19th and early 20th centuries to show how one social class was able to acquire the dominant class status in the society and manipulate societal value systems for its own purposes by shaping a particular worldview and (ethno-religious) nationalist ideology. Given this background, it is fair to suggest that contemporary manifestations of nationalism as ethnic nationalism are an extension of the dominant petty bourgeoisie elites' past political project for economic and political hegemony-building during the colonial period. From there to the present right-wing ethno-nationalism and the development of the ethnicised image of the state, this class-rooted political project has passed through various intended and unintended consequences while concealing the many significant tensions within each 'component part' of Sri Lankan society in the processes of constructing hegemony- and state-building. Arguably, without examining the class origins of Sinhala-Buddhist nationalism, no analysis of contemporary discourses on Sinhala-Buddhist nationalism or state-building is complete. This is especially relevant for unpacking the phenomenon of hegemonic state-building and to unravel the tension between hegemony-building and democratic state-building which have effectively concealed the emergence of right-wing politics and the domination of right-wing forces in shaping the paths of state-building.

An important connection between present nationalist discourses and the 19th-century nationalist ideology is the material basis of popular loyalties to the local (petty) bourgeoisie in the British colonial period (1815–1948) and in the years since the start of the civil war (1983–2009). Such historical resonances can best be explained by examining the economic basis and the corresponding class interests of the emerging petty bourgeoisie during the British colonial period. Ruptures and fissures in local power dynamics were brought on by colonial rule and various interventions by the British. In this way, the islanders' social, cultural and economic relations, and traditional structures and dynamics of power between numerous local communities were completely transformed by colonial rule. During this period, the local bourgeoisie embarked on a primitive form of 'passive revolution' against colonial interventions and dominance.[4] Colonial rule in Sri Lanka – as elsewhere – upset the economic basis of the local elites' powerful positions. For the British, to realise their own colonial and capitalist interests, it seemed necessary to first dismantle the pre-colonial or feudal economic and social structures on which local elites depended. As in many late colonial contexts, Sinhala-Buddhist nationalism thus developed in response to threats by the colonial authorities to elite control over feudal economic structures, which the colonial power sought to transform into a more capitalist and trade-oriented economic system, introducing institutions and labour relations that shattered the previously privileged economic and social positions of the local elites[5] (Pieris 2006: 156).

These structural changes began a phase of reordering of the economy and the society previously based on a complex system of service tenures and operated within a framework of feudalistic societal relations (Pieris 2006: 3). To put it simply, the means through which people obtained access to resources and to the 'social products' produced by these resources changed fundamentally. Caught in this unravelling system, beset by threats but aware of new opportunities, the elites (who were becoming petty bourgeois instead of feudal) struggled to preserve elements of their traditional social-economic order, while making efforts to derive benefits from being attached to the newly emerging economic order. This required a convincing political strategy and formation of alliances within the local community. What emerged was a threatening economic situation and damaged social relations among Sinhala Sri Lankans that then justified an appeal to a nationalist ideology that papered over the breakdown of traditional relations of domination and subordination between upper and lower classes. The political strategy of economically well-to-do upper classes involved both popular mobilisation and alliance-building with lower class-masses. Both manipulative and coercive strategies were used to ensure that elites that had lost much of their previous assurance were able to retain overall dominance of an emerging bourgeois class, even as economic, political and social conditions were completely transformed.

The main strategy that the bourgeois class pursued was initially based on the new colonial capitalist economic structure and the unified administrative structure supported by the British. These two changes provided the traditional local ruling class or the bourgeoisie ample space and opportunity to launch various attacks on British rule, in the form of rebellions, conspiracies and armed struggles. Most of these anti-colonial attacks were strategically crafted to mobilise local communities of all social, cultural and religious backgrounds, for example, in revolts against new taxes imposed by the colonial rulers (Jayawardena 2010: 63). Such revolts and disturbances can be seen as symptomatic of a period of transition (Jayawardena 2010: 147). These incidents testified to the profound ways in which colonial measures disrupted the feudal economic basis on which the traditional elites' dominance had been built. In resisting new measures, elites were joined by the rest of the population, across community divides.

To mobilise the masses, an appeal to the lower classes was required, which could be formed out of elements shaping the ontological conditions of the poor and their perceived or imagined realities of life. At this stage, the locally emerging bourgeoisie highlighted the cultural differences between local inhabitants, the 'native' people of 'Ceylon', and foreign colonisers. By highlighting the immorality of Western rule, and the need to preserve local culture from external influences, common forms of identity among Sri Lankans were emphasised during this phase. In anti-colonial mobilisation strategies, differences between the locally emerging bourgeoisie and lower classes were kept out of the framing of nationalist politics. By implanting and kindling anti-colonial cultural and ideological sentiments, the locally emerging bourgeoisie was able to gather support from lower classes while also preserving and further legitimising their own domination and privileged positions. Considering the pattern of traditional land holdings, Moore suggests that changes brought about by British rule affected the economically dominant position of the local feudal elites most directly (Moore 1989: 180). What is interesting to note about the coalition-building between the lower classes and the economic elites of this period was the largely unquestioned support rendered by the lower classes to the upper class. In Gramscian terms, this can be interpreted as a primitive stage of the development of the 'national popular'.[6] Several conditions facilitated this development. Of particular significance was that the poor masses were mostly peasants, readily influenced by the ideologies of local chiefs, landlords and monks. Their ideological manipulation accompanied a promise by such elites to restore a pre-colonial status quo, a kind of 'Golden Age' (Jayawardena 2010: 45) that also corresponds with the existence of the precondition of desire for common change by both classes. As summed up by another scholar,

> the peasants yearned for the old society, the only one they knew and understood and desired to return to their norm of life. And although it may not have been a very happy one, they readily accepted traditional society with its manifold defects as part of man's fate, in contrast to foreign rule and the new form of society ... which brought unfamiliar distractions but no compensating advantages. (De Silva quoted in Jayawardena 2010: 45)

When taking the structural transformations, changes and the struggles experienced by local communities during the British colonial period into account, it is plausible to suggest that the first seeds of anti-Western nationalism were a result of the threatened economic interests and the traditional sources of social power of the bourgeois and petty bourgeois classes in the colonial society. Their economic, social and political frustrations (a degrading of their position as subordinates of an imposed colonial power hierarchy in the island) were translated into a language of cultural and anti-colonial nationalism.[7] The birth of cultural nationalism and its anti-Western manifestations thus signal an emerging class-consciousness and the class-for-itself of the local emerging bourgeoisie. Class awakening was eventually translated into the language of an all-encompassing 'nationalist interest'. However, the ideological, cultural, moral, economic and intellectual leadership remained with the local upper classes, who influenced the consciousness of the lower classes in their struggles to restore the ancient glory of the pre-colonial society. In effect, the emerging local bourgeoisie had managed to forge a political alliance with the masses. Yet the logic of such struggles was mainly to protect the narrow economic interests of the emerging bourgeoisie by staged expressions of anti-colonial sentiments and struggle.

The interesting question that remains to be answered is: Why did the oppressed and exploited classes in Sri Lankan society not revolt against their local exploiters in the pre-colonial period, even before British colonial rule, and why with Western colonial rule did the lower classes remain loyal to their local oppressors, rendering them subordinate in the anti-colonial and nationalist struggles led by elites? One reason might be that the complex governing of pre-colonial society, under overlapping layers of local chiefs (Swaris 1973), made mass mobilisation unlikely, making conditions difficult for the formulation of a 'national popular' political project. Perhaps, as Dewasiri has argued, another reason can be found in the policies of the previous colonial rulers, notably the Dutch, who maintained traditional power hierarchies in place, reinforcing pre-colonial hierarchies, and strengthening the elites' hold by reinforcing the privileges and economic power of local chiefs (Dewasiri 2008: 211).

Based on these accounts on the nature of the pre-colonial society and the symbolic relationships painted about a 'past' image of the society, what this suggests is a certain rationalisation of the ontology[8] of local rural masses by the upper classes. This gradually developed into a coherent anti-colonial ideology based on an image of a 'glorious past' and local culture. This became an important element of the local petty bourgeoisie's strategy to safeguard their own economic interests under late colonialism. Mobilising rural peasant masses to actively defend the economic and political interests of the upper classes was thus the foundation and first impetus for an emerging form of nationalism. From the perspective of the state-in-society model (Migdal 2001), by linking their class identity with discourses of a glorious past, the emerging bourgeoisie invented a set of practices in politics that would lay the foundations for later ethnic nationalist discourses and elite hegemony-building.

EARLY TAMIL NATIONALISM

Any mainstream account of anti-colonial nationalism in Sri Lanka is incomplete without looking into early Tamil nationalism. It is mostly given a subordinate position in the literature on late colonial and early post-independence politics in Sri Lanka. The evolution of Tamil nationalism can be viewed as a resistance movement and a counterweight to Sinhala-Buddhist nationalism. Yet it is also important to acknowledge the relatively independent dynamics of the rise of Tamil nationalism in its own right. The pioneering works of Arumuga Navalar (1822–1879) in Saivite-Tamil marked the start of a cultural renaissance movement. This movement was begun by Tamil graduates who wanted to demonstrate the distinctiveness of Ceylonese Tamils from Tamils in south India. The latter were brought as indentured workers to the island, mostly to work on plantations, during British colonial rule. Indeed, the origins of the Tamil cultural revival can be dated to at least fifty years before the Buddhist revival in the south of the country (Wickramasinghe 2006). Later, at the end of colonial rule, and in the early post-independence years, Tamil nationalism gradually came to be conceived in opposition to Sinhala-Buddhist nationalism, but this was not always the case. This transformation of the Tamil cultural revivalism project tended to lead to a reactive reassertion of the Sinhala-Buddhist nationalist ideology. The mutually reinforcing effect of Tamil nationalism and Sinhala-Buddhist nationalism was especially apparent in the lack of a strong, united independence movement.

Studies on Tamil nationalism are few and far between. Cheran suggests this lack of scholarly interest reflects the generally marginalised position of Tamils in Sri Lanka (2001: 3). Tamil nationalism was imagined both in the works of Tamil scholars and in the imaginaries of Sinhalese scholars who often over-emphasised the reactive nature of both Tamil and Sinhala nationalism.[9] In the beginning, Tamil nationalism was articulated by the literature elite of the Tamil community (Roberts 2005: 4). S. V. J. Chelvanayagam, Ponnanbalam Ramanathan and Ponnanmbalam Arunachalam were people of special importance. Not only were they of bourgeois origin, they were also all from the Tamil upper caste, the Vellala. In a way that was similar to our account of how Sinhala-Buddhist nationalist discourse emerged, over several decades, as Tamil nationalism was made and remade, the elitist and caste-based roots of Tamil nationalism were gradually forgotten (Cheran 2001; Roberts 2005). The contribution of the Jaffna Youth Congress, the main counteraction to the elitist Navalar-Ramanathan tradition, and the anti-caste social movement in the 1920s that became active in the 1940s and reached its zenith in the 1960s mark some of these important erasures (Cheran 2001: 6). As Cheran further notes, 'it is ironic that the conventional Tamil narrative that often begins by recollecting events in the 1920s – the rift between the Tamil and Sinhala elite has completely ignored and erases this subaltern trend by privileging the Tamil elite discourse on nationalism' (2001: 6). These observations made on the Tamil nationalist discourse is very similar to what were observed on the Sinhala-Buddhist nationalism discourse, in particular the class roots, as discussed earlier. Nevertheless, these omissions can be interpreted as discursive practices and as an extension to the Tamil elites' political project that successfully gathered the necessary support and legitimacy from the lower class segments in the Tamil community. The literature written by Tamil scholars on the early period of Tamil nationalism provides evidence of inter-ethnic elite solidarity of leaders of both nationalist projects during the early colonial, which only began to disintegrate in the late colonial and worsened in the postcolonial period (Thiruchelvam 1984a; Wilson 1988, 2000; Thangarajah 2000, Nesiah 2001: 20).

EARLY ANTI-COLONIAL LEADERSHIP: BOURGEOIS POLITICS UNDER BRITISH RULE

The following section further explores the class[10] basis of the birth of cultural nationalism in the 19th century that has important bearings on understanding hegemony-building through history and contemporary times. Any examination into the circumstances surrounding the birth of cultural nationalism requires looking into the early leadership of the anti-colonial nationalist movement. It shows how important linkages were between the political engagement of the bourgeoisie and the petty bourgeoisie in constructing the Sinhala-Buddhist nationalist ideology and the underlying dynamics of class-based interests pursued under the banner of nationalism. An example is used to illustrate this argument, namely the background and legacies of the country's first and main architect of cultural and Sinhala-Buddhist nationalism, Anagarika Dharmapala (1864–1933).

In developing his nationalist ideological project, Dharmapala drew inspiration from his father, a furniture manufacturer and a dealer and member of the traditional local petty bourgeoisie. Having started his own working life as a clerk at the education department (Rambukwella 2018: 51), Dharmapala believed in a rigid work ethic for the development of the country, the reform of institutions, and the application of science to modernise the economy. Dharmapala drew inspiration from a Calvinist-like ethos of self-restraint and self-discipline to transform Sinhala Buddhism into an urban middle-class creed, a merchant spiritual ideology and field of practices (Obeysekara quoted in Uyangoda 2007b: v). He also envisaged two seemingly contradictory projects as conjoined: an industrialised society based on the development of trade, combined with maintaining the virtues of traditional society, including its oppressive forms of class, caste and gender structures (Jayawardena 1985a: 9). In the process of reinventing Buddhism for the purposes of 'modern' economic development and the restoration of Buddhist morality and righteousness, the urban Sinhalese may have learned some significant lessons from Protestant Christianity (Seneviratne 1999: 49).

As Chatterjee has observed, similar contradictions between the desire for modernity and rejection of 'Westernisation' frequent occur in 'eastern types of nationalism' or early anti-colonial ideological projects (Chatterjee 1986: 51). The tension between simultaneously imitating and being hostile to alien models of social and economic change arises from the contradictory forces that make for the emergence of anti-colonial nationalism in the first place (Chatterjee 1986: 51).[11] Taking this into account, it is fair to state that Dharmapala's anti-colonial Western nationalist project was also an attempt to square the circle, by securing the narrow interests of the local bourgeoisie. As a member of the petty bourgeois class, Dharmapala seemed to have sought to retain his class privileges in the traditional social and economic order, while claiming to envision forms of development that would benefit all – rich and poor alike – and lead to the end of British economic and political dominance. Thus, while Dharmapala's nationalist ideology was based on Buddhism, it was also resolutely modernist. It drew on the ideal of a peasant-centric glorious past, and in this way sought to safeguard the country's local cultures and traditions from the perverse effects of Western colonial rule. Overall, however, this contradictory ideological project tended to serve the narrow class interests of the emerging bourgeoisie.

Seneviratne's account of New Buddhism as it emerged in Sri Lanka portrays Dharmapala's efforts as genuinely aimed at reviving the social and religious morality of Buddhist society and ending the poverty and ignorance of the masses in a colonised society (1999: 35). However, this rather rosy view is the least convincing part of Seneviratne's overall argument. From some of Dharmapala's public speeches,[12] for example, it is evident that he advocated both violence and looking down on other non-Sinhala, non-Buddhist communities. It happened to be those non-Buddhist communities that were most successful in trade during the late colonial era, however. His vicious verbal attacks especially against the Moor community, who were successful traders and the main competitor to the petty bourgeoisie's economic interests, stand as strong testimony to this effect (Rambukwella 2018: 65). One could say Dharmapala's overall political vision was not all that resonant with the teachings of Buddha or that he displayed the ideal characteristics of a Buddhist. An excerpt from one of Dharmapala's public speeches can make this point more clearly:

> Aliens are taking away the wealth of the country and the sons of the soil where [are] they to go? The immigrants who came here have other places to go to; the Sinhalese has no place to go to. It is just that the sons of the soil should suffer while alien enjoys... the ignorant helpless Sinhalese villagers is made a victim by the alien sharper who robs his ancestral land. (Guruge quoted in Jayawardena 1985a: 12–13)

And again, as he said on another occasion:

> ... from the day that the white man set foot on this soil, the arts and the sciences of the Aryan customs of the Sinhalese have gradually disappeared and today the Sinhalese have to kiss the feet of the dastardly Tamils. (Quoted in Dharmadasa 1993: 138)

In Dharmapala's brand of anti-colonial cultural nationalism, Buddhism is chosen as the primary ideological ingredient, a peculiarly 'protestant' form of Buddhism linked to the emerging ethos and economic interests of the class-based proponents of nationalism. Puritan values of discipline, hard work, punctuality, and so forth, were preached by Dharmapala and had already been accepted by a rising middle class during this period (Seneviratne 1999: 34). These norms and values tied the early anti-colonial nationalist project to a set of economic interests tied to class. Interestingly, Dharmapala's economic vision of 'Calvinist Buddhism' was never fully embraced by the majority of Sinhalese of lower-class background, most of whom lived in rural areas. However, this ethos was attractive to the emerging urban middle class (Seneviratne 1999: 57). As Srinati suggests, to accept leadership of dominant political leaders, the values, reasoning and interests of the subordinated classes should be presented by elites as their own (Strinati 1995: 166). What was remarkable about Dharmapala's ideology was his ability to simultaneously find resonance with the ideological sentiments of the lower classes in the rural areas through his exclusive nationalist vision, and to appeal to the urban middle classes through his appeal to 'economic Buddhist' form of modernity.

Seneviratne implies that both admirers and followers of Dharmapala, and he himself, genuinely believed in contributing to the moral and economic development of all Sri Lankans. Yet it was specifically the Sinhala that Dharmapala believed were most vulnerable to losing their values under Western influence. In this regard, by choosing Buddhism and the Sangha monastic order[13] as the prime agents of cultural nationalism, Dharmapala could not have been unaware that he was contributing to a sectarian form of political nationalism. While successfully mobilising the lower classes and rural masses against the colonial order, his ideological project also posited the preservation of the economic dominance and class interests of the bourgeoisie and petty bourgeoisie over these same rural masses. In other words, his political program represented the perfect union of the class interests of economic, political and social upper classes, embarking together on a national mission in the face of an overwhelming threat to their shared class position, their status and their privileges in the face of rapid social and technological changes.

The image of an ideal local culture drawn from the pre-colonial past, which Dharmapala painted as a 'righteous culture', was itself dependent on a prevailing culture that justified continued subordination of the lower classes, lower castes and women to the authority of local chiefs, upper classes, upper castes and patriarchy (Jayawardena 1985a: 9). This message came across clearly in Dharmapala's eight-point proposal[14] for improving rural development, in which the intention to preserve existing social hierarchies, legitimising the role of the Sangha monastic order, and consolidating the class position of a rural petty bourgeoisie were central ingredients of the 'ideal' painted for rural life (Seneviratne 1999: 57–58). Even at this stage of early or proto-nationalist thought, there is enough evidence to suggest that it could later take distinctly right-wing, sectional forms, though it was still too early to predict how far certain conservative, right-wing political and cultural agendas would later be pursued in the struggle for political hegemony of state elites.[15]

From the quotations included earlier, it is apparent that Dharmapala's brand of nationalism stated with an explicit focus on the Sinhalese as descendants of the 'pure Aryan race' (Jayawardena 1985a: 9; Tambiah 1992: 131). At a later stage he directly included Buddhists in his projected vision of the nation. But why Buddhism? Dharmapala, like his father, had received his education at a Christian missionary school. Despite his exposure to Christian theology, over years he became increasingly preoccupied with Buddhism. In his own brand of cultural and economic anti-Western nationalism, Dharmapala explicitly based his position on Buddhism. This strategic decision was his way of trying to address the ruptures and fissures that had opened up in Sri Lankan society with the rapid spread of Western Christianity, which he sought to counter, along with Western customs and lifestyles introduced into the island society with colonial rule. By this time, many in the colonial society were feeling these transformations; therefore, it was easy to mobilise them in favour of his project.

Dharmapala's nationalism reinforced the cultural values of a colonised, Christian social strata, imitating Western and Christian-inspired economic models of national development. At the same time, this nationalism was romantic about the pre-colonial past, and implicitly hostile to these same 'modern' models proposed as worthy of imitation. This mix of imitation and hostility was likely the result of the impossibility of reconciling the desires of the petty bourgeoisie to reap the possible benefits opened up by colonial role for themselves as economic actors, and the priority of maintaining their increasingly precarious, previously largely unquestioned, authority within local power hierarchies, previously based on the feudal system still dominant in rural areas. Bringing Buddhism in as a central ingredient in this mix of elements in anti-colonial nationalism undoubtedly enabled the bourgeoisie to demonstrate their cultural distinctiveness vis-à-vis the British, while undermining emerging local practices within the Sinhalese community that followed Western lifestyles and Christianity and sought to widen the distribution of benefits from capitalist economic structures. By reinforcing cultural and religious forms of identity, Dharmapala was able to mobilise lower-class masses, but of course precisely not along any explicit class lines. Initially it was not the poverty-stricken rural poor who endorsed Dharmapala's revivalist nationalist project, but the well-to-do Western-educated urban elites, who saw their economic interests as being under attack by British colonial policies (Seneviratne 1999: 49). His project was supported by prominent figures of the day such as Hikkaduwe Sri Sumangala (Dharmapala's teacher and mentor) and initially from the members of the local and international theosophical movement, for example, Henry Steele Olcott, Annie Besant and Helena Blavatsky. As economic and cultural associations started to be formed among emerging local comprador classes[16] and colonial rulers, these associations were used as a criterion to exclude some segments of society (notably Tamil elites, and Tamils in general) from the nationalist project, or morally oblige them to join in to prove their anti-colonial credentials. Interestingly, the class underpinning of Dharmapala's political project couched in the language of Buddhist and narrowly conceived nationalist revivalism appeared not to have bothered to liaise with the broader social justice movements underway in the Indian subcontinent at that time. Dharmapala's notable distance from the greater social justice movement of Ambedkar in India (Rambukwella 2018: 52) and even from Sri

Lanka's pioneering trade union movement led by A. E. Gunasinghe's broader cross-class-based mobilisation for greater economic justice stands as striking evidence to this claim. Although one could argue that compared to India, caste oppression was less rigid in Sri Lanka, hence the need for a caste centric social justice movement was less important in the Sri Lankan context, given the exploitative economic character of the caste hierarchy, which works in the favour of the dominant social and economic classes in pursuit of their interests, Dharmapala's distance from such broader solidarity movements can be alluded to his motivation of preserving the local social and economic order of the day.

Taking a radical theological position based on Buddhism was a way to counter the emerging local Anglo-Saxon colonial capitalist class and its influence in transforming the traditional socio-economic and political hierarchies of the island (Obeysekara quoted in Uyangoda 2007b: v). In classical Theravada politics, the Sangha were inter-class mediators. Giving primacy to the Sangha in Dharmapala's revivalist project and the anti-colonial struggle reinforced their position; so, indigenous leaders – both the bourgeoisie and the rural petty bourgeois leadership – came to accept the Sangha as a mediating force between them and lower-class masses in colonial society (Seneviratne 2007: 89). In this new nationalist ideology, the Sangha's role of the caretaker of the people opened up floodgates for hostile relations between religious communities. Sangha monks were inspired to think of themselves as empowered political activists, even as entrepreneurs, becoming active facilitators of transformations in the social order (Seneviratne 2007: 27; de Silva Wijeratne 2006).

A number of studies point to the significance of this role of the Sangha as an agent of social change, historically speaking (Obeysekara 1979: 288). Archaeological discoveries from the pre-colonial period also support the institutionalised power of the Sangha and reveal their considerable influence in the traditional social order and their dominant status in the island's pre-colonial affairs (Warnapala 1993: 217; Kiribamune 1999a: 205). Various accounts of pre-colonial society in Sri Lanka make reference to the strong patron–client relationships that existed between members of the Sangha. However, with the spread of Christianity, the privileges enjoyed by the Sangha and the traditional local bourgeois class were equally threatened (Gunasinghe 1996e: 237). In such circumstance, an alliance between the two for mutual gain became part of Dharmapala's nationalist vision. Over time, this transformed the Sangha from a mainly cultural and moral leadership role to a more economic, material and political role as part of a powerful hegemonic bloc behind anti-colonial nationalism. During colonial rule, the Sangha weakened as an institution of the rural Buddhist moral community as it allied itself with agrarian landlords (Gunawardena in Uyangoda 2007: v). With elaborate landholdings, an extensive bureaucracy to administer the land and peasantry, and the forging of close links with ruling families and sub-ruling strata, the Sangha could be likened to a form of monastic landlordism. A symbiotic relationship emerged and was reinforced in the 19th-century nationalist project, in which the Sangha, in return for patronage they received from the upper echelon of the Buddhist laity, were obliged to render services and help secure these elites' political authority, and to act as brokers in the religious and secular affairs of the lower-class masses to the benefit of the elites, landlords and emerging bourgeoisie.[17]

Since the material well-being of the Sangha was dependent on state patronage and donations offered by the local bourgeois and petty bourgeois classes, their mutual interests were considerable (Wickramaratne 1995: 192, 216). During the precolonial and colonial periods, the upper-class lay elites were the primary alms givers (*dayaka*s) for the urban Sangha. Together, these two privileged groups became interdependent on each other and played an increasingly important role in the everyday lives of the lower-class Buddhist laity as well. Under Dharmapala's nationalist project, a strategic partnership emerged between these social forces. After the end of colonial rule, their combined economic, social, intellectual, cultural and moral authority almost guaranteed their dominance not only over the rest of Buddhist society but over society as a whole. The Sangha had for some time already operated a very different approach to Buddhism to the approach commonly adopted by monks of the Vinayankalara School of Buddhism. Vinayankalara monks generally continued to reside in villages and engaged in village development work, with a notably selfless attitude for the most part, remaining rooted in the ideal of service to others and the relief of suffering (Seneviratne 1999: 57).

Applying Gramsci's ideas on hegemony and the conditions he pointed out as requirements for hegemony formation – a combination of balance of force and consensus, without force subverting consensus too much and instead making it look as if the force is the consent of the majority (1971: 103) – this early phase of alliance-building between various forces of upper-, middle- and lower-class background around cultural revivalism not only entailed elements of manipulation, consent creation and consensus-building but also entailed the use of subtle coercive strategies or threat of use of coercion for non-compliance. Branding certain social groups as 'non-authentic' (Rambukwella 2018: 72) and 'non-native', and thereby subjecting them to a form of social ostracisation was an integral part of such coercive strategies.

Eventually all those who wished to become involved in national politics or had higher ambitions of winning political office, embracing Dharmapala's political project was almost unavoidable. In most instances, this embracing was more rhetorical than real. The urban, Westernised local elites, faced with the long-term exclusion from Dharmapala's nationalist project, and considered a comprador 'alien' class, were obliged to join this project, a project of nationalism that had explicitly labelled them 'non-national'. It might have been obvious to these classes that under the changing state-in-society relations set in motion by colonialism and Dharmapala's counter project of cultural revivalism, they ran the most risk of losing many of the economic privileges they enjoyed in the past. In the long run, in order to secure and maximise their economic and social benefits, the new comprador class opted to join the nationalist bandwagon. Under the prevailing political conditions, changing the direction of loyalty might have been the most logical and strategic option available for them.

The reinvention and reproduction of nationalism by Dharmapala set the direction for its consolidation in subsequent decades as ethnicity gained prominence over religion. In Dharmapala's ideology, ethnicity was a secondary element, but was present nonetheless, as quotations selected from his speeches show. Towards the beginning of the 19th century, increasing resource exploitation by the British, continued expansion of foreign trade, and the near-monopoly of non-local groups (immigrant communities) over trading raised the spectre of takeover aroused by national leaders. The prospect of a south Indian invasion was especially invoked, leading to a gradual strengthening of ethnic factors of Sinhala identity and Buddhism within the nationalist discourse (Dharmadasa 1992: 2; Uyangoda 2007c: 4). The implicit emphasis on ethnicity became more explicit under changing socio-economic conditions, and was later enshrined in the right-wing ideology devised by the local bourgeoisie within the broader nationalist movement. Seeing their economic interests directly threatened by immigrant or minority-controlled trading groups, identified as 'Indian' or 'Muslim', the Sinhala bourgeoisie that was emerging was also squeezed from 'among its own' by an emerging economic and political cross-class alliance of

Sinhala-Christian forces, often more open to Western influences and education, and advancing in the conditions created by colonial ruptures in history.

Currently, it is important to problematise nationalism and develop historical interpretations capable of exposing the narrow political and economic interests pursued by political elites. Robert's work (1982) on caste in Sri Lanka sought to tease out the political implications of caste inequalities but did not deal with inter-bourgeois and inter-elite conflicts of interests to the same extent. The class-based underpinnings and economic interests of cultural and economic elites in the early nationalist project have not yet been fully explored. David Scott's (1996) critical review of the story of how Buddhism was transformed during colonial times, itself a response to arguments of Malalgoda (1976), open up different interpretation of nationalism by illuminating the way class interests played a part (Scott 1996: 7).

In narrating nationalist history, the birth of nationalist ideology has often been viewed in simplified terms as resulting from a struggle for dominance between British colonial rulers and local people (Wickramaratne 1995: xii). In this kind of narrative, a homogeneous category, 'local people', struggles as one, more or less, and the other politically significant divisions among Sri Lankans, of class and status, and relationships of domination and subordination among them are overlooked. In this way the historical precursors during the colonial period of post-colonial hegemony-building, state-building and elite consolidation are also overlooked. Class relations and various kinds of entrenched social inequalities in society are of remarkable significance, however, for understanding nationalism, including during the colonial era, and as this discussion has showed. A reductionist understanding that *a priori* considers political nationalist discourse to be national rather than class based, tends to reinforce the intellectual and moral authority of dominant and state-based interpretations of local history.

When accounts of history that are written and views that are expressed by political elites in upper-class discursive communities that successfully influence the minds of the majority of the Sinhalese, it leaves little room for alternative interpretations of nationalist history to emerge. Critically questioning dominant Sinhala-Buddhist nationalism means questioning a hegemonic project (Rampton 2011), something sacred and almost by definition so, and therefore not to be questioned. During interviews carried out for this research, which happened to coincide with the last phase of the civil war (May 2009), most Sinhalese I spoke to expressed a renewed sense of Sinhala-Buddhist nationalism, which they tended to justify as necessary for their own secure existence and also as simple 'common sense' (R.1; R.16; R.18), the latter in Gramscian terms a heterogeneous belief or self-evident truth arrived with no critical reflection (1971: 347).

As shown thus far, class interests have determined how religion and ethnicity have been mobilised, and it is class conflict that can be viewed as the founding principle of other elements in Sinhala-Buddhist nationalist ideology. Michael Mann's observation on ethnic nationalism (2005) applies, since he suggests that by elevating ethnicity, the class origins of nationalism are often obscured. He therefore proposes class as an important preliminary point of departure for any analysis of nationalism, since class conflicts and power dynamics will inform the nationalist basis for political hegemony formation by the elites and the masses alike. Similarly, when discussions of nationalism focus on the content of nationalist discourses in symbolic terms and at the level of superstructure, pursuit of narrow class interests by bourgeois nationalists in 18th- and 19th-century Ceylon is being concealed. In this way, the powerful self-interest of contending local political elites are tacitly endorsed by those in academia who accept the dominant Sinhala-Buddhist nationalist account of the politics of decolonisation.[18] One early positive gain of nationalism was that it for some time brought together vertically divided classes, castes and regional communities within the Sinhalese community by mobilising them against colonial rule. During this mobilisation process, the unequal and exploitative power relations between foreign colonial rulers and all locals were exposed. However, since similar unequal power dynamics and relationships also existed between locals of different castes and classes, the manipulation of anti-colonialism for factional, elite political and economic gain was a part of the picture from early on in the anti-colonial nationalist movement. This chapter has suggested that Sinhala-Buddhist nationalism was at times used to paint a picture of a *seemingly united local people against the British rule*, but at other times was itself used to exclude some Sri Lankans from the definition of 'nation'. Despite its arguably Sinhala-Buddhist character, support for early nationalism extended to Tamils who engaged in this project as one anti-colonial and inclusive enough to unite all Ceylon islanders (Nesiah 2001: 9). In this way, early on, the local bourgeoisies or upper classes were able to pursue their ambition of establishing overall cultural, ideological, intellectual and moral leadership over the lower classes of all communities, so long as inequalities and exploitative relations between all locals and all foreigners could be highlighted. The nationalist project gained this unity, however, only by glossing over or ignoring inequalities at vertical and horizontal levels within Sri Lanka, and exploitative relations within the Sinhalese community in particular.

CLASS, ETHNO-RELIGIOUS NATIONALISM AND HEGEMONY

Following Sri Lanka's independence in 1948, the mainstream political and intellectual discourse on nationalism began to be dominated by the subject of 'ethnic' nationalism, in which Sinhala and Tamil nationalisms came to be pitted against each other. This conforms to the overall trends in ethno-nationalist literature written around the world since the 1980s, in which ethnicity has been used as the main point of departure for analysis of violent conflict. Overall, the literature on ethno-nationalism is compartmentalised into four overarching categories: primordialist (historical and biological), constructivist (sociological), instrumentalist (elite and rational choice) and institutionalist (DeVotta 2005: 145). Since the early 1980s, the term 'ethno-religious nationalism' has become popular in the local academic vocabulary in Sri Lanka (Hettige 2000: 21), which can be understood in terms of collective interests of creating (or preserving) the optimal conditions for the existence of a group and maintenance of its identity (Hass 2000: 27). In Sri Lanka, it was both the existence and maintenance of group identity that was seen as critical, and the manipulation of such ethno-religious sentiments by dominant classes by concealing their underlying class and economic interests tied to these ideological sentiments.

Since the early 1980s, ethno-nationalism has been linked directly to inter-ethnic tensions between Sinhalese and Tamil ethnic groups. Kapferer (1988), for example, observes that nationalist forces during the 1980s involved processes of personal and collective reaffirmation and rebirth, processes that ultimately influence selective readings of historical events, by creating national mythologies. As Kapferer expresses this: 'the powers and dangers of representation in nationalist discourse in which the myths made into reflections of reality were also invested with a force for the remaking of the reality' (1988: xxi). Reinventing the past became an important strategy in the hegemony-building process. As pointed out by Gramsci, hegemony is not built on an accurate record of historical events; it is built instead on discourses about the past that help to bring selected experiences closer to people's daily life. From the vantage point of hegemony-building, myth-making and re-enacting past events, whether real or imagined, was a strategic act pursued by Sinhala-Buddhist dominant elites, for the purposes of nation-building. The period from 1983 onwards has been characterised by onset of 'inter-ethnic political conflict' between the majority Sinhalese run Sri Lankan state and indigenous Tamils, leading to civil war that officially began in 1983. With the onset of war, in a fiercely competitive Sinhalese electoral political arena, mainstream discourses of ethnic nationalisms became susceptible to more extreme political manipulation. This manipulation was of course not entirely new to the island's high politics; already in the late 1920s, debates in the legislative council revolved around issues of universal franchise, and can be considered historical precursors in this regard to ethno-religious discourses of later decades (Jayawardena 1985a: 41).

During civil war, the benefits of mobilising nationalist arguments, as a means of consolidating political capital to benefit political elites, became more apparent, however. Earlier developments in politics underpinned openly competitive ethnic outbidding[19] as a political strategy (DeVotta 2005: 143). Sinhala (and Tamil) elites gradually strengthened and propagated myths of the past, constructing and reproducing new ethno-nationalist realities as political circumstances demanded. Rather that awakening a spirit of common Sri Lankan nationalism, through finding an inclusive tone or more civic forms of secular nationalism, the elites opted for mass political mobilisation through hegemonic alliance-building. For this they drew on the construction and reproduction of ethnic nationalist discourses based on selective events and symbols, and competing misinterpretations of history.

The overall body of literature on the discourses of nationalism in Sri Lanka presents varying interpretations on the subject. This multiplicity is based on the origins, nature, agencies and functions of nationalism in politics and state-building. Despite subtle variations, taken together, there seems to be a tendency at placing the ethnic fault line at the heart of these interpretations. By so doing, they have directly or indirectly endorsed the political discourse of ethnic nationalisms. At the same time, these discourses have also diverted the attention away from the big picture of emerging state-in-society relations that were steadily falling short in realising egalitarian values. Although there are some studies that captured various political uses of nationalism for hegemony-building and state-building, especially in contemporary times, revisiting these issues seems important (Rampton 2011). Because all these processes and their contexts are dynamic, they could expose different propensities of elite politics and in the elite-driven state-building project over time, whose political interests cannot be fully divorced from their bourgeois class roots, class consciousness and (petty) interests. I suggest that historically nationalism was used by political elites, including during the colonial period, as an instrument to pursue their own hegemonic ambitions over Sri Lankan society. Both for short-term political gains and for longer-term state-building, this was to prove a decisive 'turn' in local politics in the future. What this brings into the light is the bigger picture that state-building and the most important ideological and political divisions in national politics arise from class tensions embedded within hegemony-building and state-building projects from the start. These tensions help to account for the significant deviations from the path of democratic state-building hoped for at independence. It is also important to note that deepening inequalities in Sri Lanka's society – both horizontal and vertical – and the persecution of marginalised and minority groups have long-lasting implications for social-democratic processes, involving inequalities between ethnic and religious groups, as well as within ethnic groups, between classes,[20] between genders[21] and between urban and rural[22] places and people, with profound implications for democratic state-building in Sri Lanka.

Although ethnic nationalism seems to be the commonly suspected cause of such inequalities, the real roots of these inequalities lie along non-ethnic factors. Further, these non-ethnic roots and the signs of vertical and horizontal inequalities can be traced back to colonial times. The documentation carried out by Jayawardena on the labour movement from 1890s to the 1930s provide important evidence in this regard. Her work suggests there had been important periods when class-consciousness and class-related grievances took precedence over ethnic and religious emotions, albeit the chauvinist propaganda that was popular since the 1880s (1985b: iv). Despite the availability of such evidence, by narrowly focusing on the ethnic factor, most written accounts since the 1980s have successfully reproduced the ethnic-nationalist discourse and painted the image of the state as a hegemonic-ethnic state. Besides, these discourses have also brought inter-ethnic relations to the forefront of the analysis. This has led to meagre appreciation of the nationalism discourse and the nexus and tensions between hegemony-building and state-building and the issue of deepening inequalities (vertical and horizontal) in the society.

The question that has remained unanswered so far is how and why the majority in the Sinhalese society did accept this exclusive ethnic-nationalism discourse and become an important ally of the hegemonic project that is perceived to be benefitting the economically dominant classes and the political elites sprung out of those. There is a number of ways this state of affairs can be explained. From the perspective of hegemony-building, the element of manipulation by the dominant class in making ethnic nationalism a reality in life and using it as a powerful force of mobilisation of consent is an interesting point, and provides one such explanation. Besides, the use of sanctions and threat and coercion for not complying with the hegemonic project pursued by the dominant class is another plausible explanation. Also, the utilitarian effect of nationalism in meeting the material, ideological and symbolic needs of the Sinhala-Buddhist masses whose social status was being elevated to a position of privilege and entitlements vis-á-vis the other minority ethnic communities could explain this further. As Gramsci indicated, the belief, acceptance and participation of the wider society in consolidating ethnic nationalism could be the result of an ideological bond established between the rulers and the ruled that gives natural legitimacy to the rulers (explained later in this chapter).

Further unpacking what Nigam calls the 'twists and turns' in nationalist debates and discourses with attention to class dynamics, in the following section I discuss how the cultural revivalist movement started by the local bourgeois and petty bourgeois classes during the British colonial period over time has given rise to an explicitly right-wing form of Sinhala-Buddhist nationalism, which not only continues to shape intra-Sinhalese relations of domination and subordination between different classes, but also constitutes the main ingredient of the state-building cum hegemony-building project undertaken by the dominant elites. Contrary to the popular belief that the island's nationalist movement was instrumental in winning independence, there is enough evidence pointing to the fact that Sri Lanka's independence was not a direct outcome of the elite-led nationalist movement. It was rather a by-product of the neighbouring vibrant Indian nationalist movement and the British decision to relinquish formal colonial control (Nandi 2000: ch. 8). My interviewees who identified as Sinhalese nationalists, representing nationalist-oriented political parties such as the Janatha Vimukthi Peramuna (JVP) and the Jathika Hela Urumaya (JHU) (R.1; R.20; R.21), were of the opinion that Sri Lanka's civil war was the real struggle for freedom and sovereignty from the Tamil invaders, almost resembling a 'second independence movement' along Dharmapala's nationalist ideology, in which Sinhala-Buddhist domination and the image of a victorious Sinhala-Buddhist nation state will be reproduced eventually.

The 'nationalist movement' in Sri Lanka was a fairly lethargic movement under the leadership of local upper classes (Wilson 1975: 7). Initially, this movement included two main components: the cultural revivalist movement, associated with Dharmapala, and a political reform movement. Opposed to the earlier cultural revivalist movement spearheaded by the petty bourgeoisie and the traditional bourgeoisie (Dharmapala and his successors), the political reform movement was largely spearheaded by the bourgeoisie previously defined as comprador and was resolutely modernist and secular in outlook. Out of these two movements, the combined creation of a single and unified nationalist movement was an important venture of the bourgeois leaders of both movements. As Swaris argues, such a merger was aimed at securing continued protection of class-based interests and was geared towards securing overall legitimacy for the continued moral, intellectual and political domination of the existing elites over the rest of Sri Lankan society (1973: 32). The merger arose alongside an unfavourable image painted by the cultural movement of the leadership of the reform movement, criticised as being too close to the British colonisers and insufficiently anti-colonial. Such criticisms generated a desire to shake off a 'culprit' image on the part of the reform movement leadership, increasing their sense of urgency in joining forces with the cultural movement leadership. This merger helped to redress the public image of the reform movement, previously labelled as alien and foreign to the interests and culture of local people (Swaris 1973: 2). As they travelled along the road towards representative democracy, such an image could be electorally damaging to the reformists.

Given this context, for mutual survival elite solidarity brought together a united front to confront the British, as the leadership of the two movements declared a 'truce'. In Gramscian terms, this confluence of different social forces arose because each faction had reasons of their own to come together and form an alliance, which he termed as 'a historical bloc' (1978: 462). It can be safely assumed that for the leadership of the cultural revivalist movement this merger became as important as for the leadership of the reform movement to maintain the unity of the already mobilised masses. This mutual need for each other felt by the leadership of both movements was able to temporarily or superficially overcome their real and perceived differences. From the point of view of class relations, this merger also highlights their common goal of securing class domination and the common interest in establishing a bourgeois-elite leadership over the rest of the society. However, this confluence of different social forces and class interests did not mean a complete washing away of all other underlying tensions among the elites based on ethnic, religious, class, and caste, regional and urban–rural divisions. Importantly, what this situation suggests is that, when and where necessary to defend the class and other related interests, the various divisions among them can be muted strategically. However, if political competition and other underlying tensions among the various groups representing the dominant class affect their preferred balance of power in national politics, they are not hesitant to use the Sinhala-Buddhist nationalism as the bandwagon to on one the hand conceal their tensions and on the other hand justify and gain legitimacy to rule over the lower-class masses.

FROM MODEL DEMOCRACY TO FACTIONAL POLITY

During the transfer of power from the British to the native population, local elites consisted of several sub-classes and ideological-political factions. There was the traditional bourgeoisie, the colonial or comprador bourgeoisie, Tamil elites, Sinhala, Marxist and conservative – together, they successfully claimed political-intellectual, moral, cultural and economic leadership of the country as the British withdrew their formal colonial control. By then, by using an inclusive form of Sinhala-Buddhist nationalism, they had already established an alliance that reinforced their shared dominance over peripheral communities. Comparing Sri Lanka and Malaysia in terms of the nature of inter-ethnic bourgeois harmony at the time of Sri Lankan independence, Horowitz observes,

> ... no comparable mono-ethnic elite institution existed in Ceylon. Instead, a variety of elite colleges was established, largely in Colombo where both Sinhalese and Tamils were educated. As a result, although the two countries had approximated the same populations, the Malay and the Chinese political leaders in Malaysia were not on intimate terms, whereas the Sinhalese and Tamil leaders in Ceylon frequently knew each other well, having been to school together. It is fair to describe the Ceylonese elite at independence as genuinely intercommoned, sharing many common values. The same description would not apply to the Malayan elite at independence. (1993: 2–3)

By the time of independence, Ceylonese elites had developed a bargaining culture in local politics, which had advantages over a culture that put a premium on personal relations (Horowitz 1993). What should be remembered, however, is that there were those who paid the price for this friendly, bargaining political culture among the elites. The implied 'progressive' culture involved in politics based on bargaining was the erosion of the possibilities for realising an egalitarian society, an open political culture and a democratic state in the years to come. Since the introduction of universal franchise in 1931, Tamil political elites of bourgeois class background were increasingly finding themselves marginalised by Sinhalese political elites in these bargains and compromises. This situation was aggravated by the way the British handled looming factional conflicts, and the way the British simply left, placing the fate of Tamil political elites in the hands of rival Sinhalese elites (Wickramaratne 1995: xi), whose dominance was also institutionalised during the constitution-making process with a majoritarian bias, as the British were preparing Sri Lanka for independence (Coomaraswamy 2003: 152). This political model encouraged local political elites and political parties to view democracy as a winner-takes-all system, akin to the Westminster model, rather than a process of power-sharing and bargaining (Coomaraswamy 2003: 152). To take a lead against rival factions, and given the overall ethnic composition of the Sri Lankan population, the new era of representative democracy started on a fiercely competitive institutionalised foundation for future politics. According to the dominant majoritarian logic of electoral competition, dominant Sinhalese elites were drawn towards more exclusively Sinhala-Buddhist forms and right-wing nationalism in their efforts to appeal ideologically to the numerically largest electoral constituency, the Sinhala-Buddhist majority. This way, Sinhala-Buddhist nationalism became a key mechanism through which the lower classes in the Sinhalese majority community were incorporated into national party politics. Also, by making repeated promises to make Sinhala-Buddhist identity and Sinhala-Buddhist nationalist ideology the state and national ideology, ruling elites managed to keep them politically mobilised successfully. As political parties competed around the mobilisation of ethnic nationalism, they went overboard and fell prey to the 'dark side' of democracy – majoritarian democracy – in the 20th century (Mann 2005).

During the early years of post-colonial national politics, political power and social prestige were based firmly in control of economic capital (Fernando 1973: 364). After independence, economic capital was not the sole determinant of political power and social prestige, as numerous attempts were made to capitalise on the material resources accessible through public office and state bureaucracies. This led to overt inter-elite factional conflicts, as the relatively superficial and instrumental elite solidarity of the late colonial period started to fall apart. By the time of independence, with twenty years of electoral politics behind them, not to mention the Second World War, the emerging ruling class consisted of various sub-fractions of the bourgeois class and other middle-class sub-fractions. This alliance could be further broken down into two main sub-factions: colonial and traditional local bourgeoisie (based on class), Sinhalese and Tamil (based on ethnicity), Goyigama, Salagama, Karava (based on caste), up-country–low-country (based on regional origin).[23] Among all these various sub factions, the two class-based factions played an important role in party politics in the ensuing period. These two factions took centre stage in forming the political party system in Sri Lanka, where the present culture of Sinhalese electoral politics came to be rooted. In this regard, an elaboration of the evolution of these factions, the nature of their struggles in politics and the various strategies they devised and how these strategies influenced the path of hegemonic state-building in the subsequent decades is important.

The colonial bourgeoisie faction[24] represented liberal conservatism in politics. By engaging in new opportunities opened during the long period of Western colonialism (Portuguese, Dutch and the British), this faction triumphed economically. In Marxist terms, this faction could be called the comprador bourgeoisie[25] (Paulantzas 1973) and the local version of the *nouveau riche*. Their economic prosperity was mainly reliant on lightweight industries such as arrack renting, mining in the graphite industry and trade. The new wealth they acquired helped them to overcome their previous secondary or inferior position in the island's traditional socio-economic hierarchy (Roberts 1982; Jayawardena 2007). Furthermore, members of this class mainly came from the southern parts of the country and specifically from the coastal regions. During the three phases of Western colonial rule, these regions came to be commonly alluded to as 'spoiled'.[26] Also, in the contemporary, everyday perception of people, those who come from these regions are not considered 'authentic' Sri Lankans or authentic representatives of the island's cultures. For these reasons, the colonial bourgeoisie was often looked down upon, especially by the people from 'up-country' regions who claimed to be more authentic representatives of the island.[27] The close connection the colonial bourgeoisie class had with the British, their public admiration for Western values and practices and their mimicry of Westernised dress and behaviour raised questions about their political legitimacy and ability to lead the masses towards independence. These attitudes persisted during the period of the nationalist movement too.

Amidst such social taboos and criticisms, the last years of colonial rule generated many economic opportunities for social promotion, with new economic policies introduced, and rapid economic expansion. In this context, the colonial bourgeoisie achieved a remarkable degree of upward economic mobility, investing their hopes in gaining upward political mobility as well. Inevitably, these transformations affected the economic, social and political privileges of the previously dominant traditional bourgeoisie and rural petty bourgeoisie. These changes and transformations created various ruptures and fissures in the traditional order and upset the established patterns in the balance of power among various social classes. Eventually, these developments began to manifest in the post-colonial national political sphere and set the stage for aggressive exploitation of Sinhala-Buddhist nationalism by both factions to mobilise the masses on their behalf. At the same time, the ways in which national politics was developing, with strong ideological underpinnings, meant that their economic prosperity was not enough of a basis to enable the colonial bourgeois class to successfully claim the leadership of nationalist political movements and parties.

The history of the development of the political party system on the eve of independence reveals important dynamics of national politics (see Chapter 4), the main political agencies and state-building in Sri Lanka. Many of these dynamics noted in the immediate post-colonial period are still prevalent and reproduced under various political-economic circumstances even today. In 1947, under the leadership of the colonial bourgeois faction, the United National Party (UNP), the first national political party, was established. As a political party, the UNP was based on conservative political ideology[28] and liberal economic ethos. In Sri Lanka, all these elements are closely identified with Western colonialism and imperialism. The Western educated (neo) colonial bourgeois class, entrenched in the colonial economic structures and financial capital, had been the main local beneficiaries of these structures and had pursued their higher education in the West. As Fernando observes, in general, the Westernisation embraced by the colonial bourgeoisie included radical changes in lifestyle and a universalistic worldview, invariably producing social distance and lack of identification with the masses, still steeped in traditions, poverty and parochialism (1973: 366). This undermined any expectations the colonial bourgeoisie might have had of leading the masses to independence and thereafter.

Despite the UNP leadership and ideology, its creation as a national party was hailed as a symbol of national unity, capable of retaining the loyalties of the Tamil bourgeoisie alongside the Sinhalese (Horowitz 1993: 4).[29] At the time of the UNP's founding, it represented an amalgamation of a number of explicitly communal parties (Arsaratnam n.d.: 44). Besides being committed to inter-communal unity, the UNP was also representative of the common interests of the new, modernising bourgeoisie of all ethnic groups in Sri Lanka/Ceylon. From the perspective of hegemony-building, the breaking away of Tamil elites from the upper-classed inter-ethnic elite political coalition is an indication of future resistance from this breakaway group to the hegemony-building attempts of the Sinhalese political elites.

From the 1930s to early 1940s, when mere ideological slogans fell short in addressing the economic grievances and the widening vertical and social inequalities among the socially marginalised and lower-class masses, whose main form of power was the power to vote, the impoverished majority sought any strategy, actual or rhetorical, that would guarantee their upward economic and social mobility. However, in real life, the dominant elites were unable to address the long-term materially rooted grievances of the masses of rural and agricultural backgrounds. In the long term, it was the inability of the political and economic elites to generate enough capital that threatened to undermine their support base. In distributing state revenues, principles of inclusivity and equality were sacrificed to the politics of favouritism and exclusion, entrenching and reinforcing existing vertical and horizontal inequalities. As horizontal ethnic-identity-based inequalities intensified, so too did the gradual exclusion of most Tamils and other minority ethnic groups from political life come to be justified, reinforced by appeals to Sinhala-Buddhist nationalist slogans. Vertical inequalities in this emerging relationship between Sinhalese political elites and the Sinhalese majority slowly cemented into a right-wing political culture based on forms of ethno-religious identity.

Initially, the main political opposition to the colonial bourgeoisie came from the more traditional or local faction of the same class. Following Jayawardena's approach to social stratification at that time, I suggest the traditional faction as those who earned their wealth and property, and owned means of production through economic activities not related to colonial economic expansion. This group was constituted of upper castes and the country's traditional land-holding class. In contrast to the colonial faction, members of the traditional or local bourgeoisie stemmed mostly from up-country regions[30] and considered themselves to be 'authentic' representatives of the country's Sinhala-Buddhist majority. Many notable members of this class belonged to the aristocracy and were 'title' holders of various kinds during the colonial period. In many cases, their power and authority were highly localised, being confined to certain villages and rural areas, where around 90 per cent of Sri Lanka's population was still living. Before the colonial capitalist economy expanded, this faction of the upper class benefited from feudal agro-economic structures and from prevailing patterns of social relations of production embedded in feudalism. As the island's main landholding class, this faction became the most dominant local economic force too. Further, over a long period of time, through the use of the feudal economic structure and the associated social and cultural practices, this traditional bourgeoisie had cultivated a vast network of patronage relationships with the local communities under their tutelage: the rural peasantry and the rural petty bourgeoisie. Therefore, the economic prosperity of the rival colonial faction of the bourgeoisie and the alterations taking place in the economic sphere threatened the previous power relations and this group of traditional power wielders.

Despite such differences in class and economic background, by the eve of Sri Lankan independence, this traditional upper class had entered into a seemingly cordial relationship with the colonial faction of the bourgeoisie under the umbrella of the UNP. However, within a few years of independence, this relationship fell apart. This disintegration was the result of limitations faced by the traditional bourgeois class in achieving further upward mobility in the emerging political and economic opportunity structures. This situation was in part triggered by the overall approach to political and economic organisation pursued by the UNP during the immediate post-colonial period of state building. They sought to build the post-colonial state on the liberal economic model and the ideology of political conservatism. Obviously, this approach was inspired and tied to the UNP's and its leadership's economic base that disregarded the power base of the traditional bourgeoisie.

For both factions, the brewing political conflict over capturing state power and establishing one's political legitimacy and domination over the other, and mobilising lower classes and the fellow bourgeois factions were important. Until the early 1950s, the use of Sinhala-Buddhist nationalism in popular politics was largely an affair of the traditional bourgeoisie. The rising powers of the traditional bourgeoisie and the ability it demonstrated in mobilising the various groups under the indigenous petty bourgeoisie's control made the Sinhala-Buddhist nationalism appealing to the rival Sinhalese political elite factions as well. The kind of indigenous socialism[31] the Sinhala-Buddhist ideology was embedded in became a point of attraction for rural masses at election times. The credibility claimed by the traditional bourgeois faction by using Sinhala-Buddhist nationalism encouraged its main competitor, the UNP, to openly appeal to Sinhala-Buddhist ethnic sentiments as well (Horowitz 1993: 4). Learning from the Dharmapala era, the Sinhalese elite political leadership of both class factions was convinced of the power and robustness of Sinhala-Buddhist nationalism in mobilising the masses. Therefore, the cultural aspect of nationalism constituted of Sinhala-Buddhist nationalism is believed to have come into great ferment during the 1940s, which has continued and reproduced until now in national politics under different constellations of power (Seneviratne 1999: 56).

In 1951, the political solidarity formed among Sinhalese political elites under the UNP started to fall apart further. A more traditional faction broke away from the UNP and formed a new political party, the Sri Lanka Freedom Party (SLFP), built on a few distinctly localised political goals around the class-based interests of the traditional bourgeoisie and their rural petty bourgeoisie allies. The founding father of the SLFP, Oxford-educated Solomon West Ridgeway Dias Bandaranaike (S. W. R. D. Bandaranaike), was a former senior member of the UNP. From the very beginning, the UNP's intentions in establishing a 'Senanayake dynasty' in politics were apparent (Jayaweera 2001: 6).[32] Undoubtedly such a move would facilitate retaining party leadership and importantly state power in the hands of the newly rich colonial bourgeoisie faction. This emerging culture of dynastic politics led by the UNP upset Bandaranaike and damaged his personal political ambition to become the UNP party leader and capture the limelight of post-colonial political power. Although Bandaranaike was not the most direct economic beneficiary of a petty-bourgeoisie-defined political party and a political culture,[33] the political capital he could harvest by using the Sinhala-Buddhist identity of his main support base was enormous. Despite factional conflicts among the elites, under Bandaranaike political, economic, cultural and class power came to be finely blended into a force close to national popular. As witnessed in 1951 when Bandaranaike formed the SLFP, the party immediately became attractive to many who were excluded in national politics in the past. Importantly, his political coalition brought the Buddhist monks (Sangha), other radical nationalist Sinhala-Buddhists and the

Marxist–socialist political forces of this period together.[34] In the 1956 general elections, by claiming 39.5 per cent of the total number of votes casted (www.lankanewspapers), they defeated the conservative Western-oriented UNP. The SLFP's party ideology was based on promotion and encouragement of local, indigenous cultural values. The spiritual philosophy of Buddhism and the Sinhala language, the religion and language of the majority population, were all given prominence in the party's manifesto. Meanwhile, the SLFP promoted exclusively 'pan-Sinhala-Buddhist nationalist' solidarities, over other forms of class or locational solidarity within the Sinhalese community.

Bandaranaike's victory is often seen as a 'success story', for having brought the formerly divided Sinhalese political elites together and reconciling some elite factions of Sinhalese society (Jayawardena 1985a: 68–69; Roberts 1995: 298). There is some truth in this interpretation, yet Bandaranaike's electoral victory was primarily based on an appeal to Sinhala-Buddhist constituencies, with predictably divisive effects on Sri Lankan politics. In 1959, when Bandaranaike declared his willingness to accommodate the interests of the Tamils into this political project, the same forces he had gathered together decided to assassinate him. He had 'gone too far' for his more right-wing allies. Bandaranaike's leadership was defined by symbolic politics and, in some ways, laid the ground for later dominance of traditional bourgeois factions and their close ally, the petty bourgeoisie, in Sri Lankan politics.

Following the UNP's electoral defeat, blamed largely on the conciliatory strategy of Bandaranaike, the UNP began to appeal to the same narrow ideological and cultural sentiments as the SLFP, thereby aiming to counteract the effect of Bandaranaike's inter-class coalition. By so doing, the UNP ensured Sinhalese elite domination in Sri Lankan politics for some time to come. This development marginalised Tamil elites who had become involved in electoral and party politics through the UNP. These changing dynamics of electoral politics also paved the way for a shared pan-class ideology among the political leadership, based on narrow Sinhala-Buddhist ethno-nationalism. Horowitz explains that

> after the resounding victory of an SLFP-led coalition in 1956, the Sinhala Only legislation was passed, and Tamil civil servants were discriminated against on linguistic grounds. Rebuffed at the polls, the UNP responded by becoming as ethnically exclusive as the SLFP. When Prime Minister S.W.R.D Bandaranaike attempted to diffuse the Sinhalese–Tamil tension by making a compromise agreement with

the Federal party leader, SVJ Chelvanayagam, the UNP campaigned against it. (1993: 4)

By adopting Sinhala-Buddhism as their chosen ideology, the ruling bourgeoisie leaders of both the main political parties deconstructed their previously negative public image in politics, overcoming the difficulties they had faced in identifying with the lower-class Sinhala majority. The evidence can be traced back to political debates in the 1920s and 1930s in the legislative council, when legislative councillors from among the Ceylonese bourgeois sought to implement a set of policies concerning land, peasant colonisation and state welfare provision. In these ways, the bourgeoisie sought to restore their image among the masses, whose economic plight could be directly attributed to the actions of that same bourgeoisie class. For instance, in addition to British capitalists, during colonial times, the local capitalist class also profited from the colonial land sales policy. In other words, the local capitalist class had a stake, if not an equal one, in the forced landlessness of the poor rural peasantry (Roberts 1977: 447). Roberts notes that nationalist leaders realised the importance of improving the peasantry's well-being for the sake of political development (Roberts 1977: 446); therefore the nationalist leaders also began to focus on the poorer peasantry, enfranchised since 1931. The same bourgeoisie that was at least in part responsible for the plight of the peasantry and the rural masses used Sinhala-Buddhist nationalism to woo them and build the much-needed winning political alliances. Since the majority of the peasantry and rural masses were Sinhala-Buddhists, this political strategy largely worked to repeatedly return Sinhala-Buddhist-led parties to power.

Political debates in the legislative council from the late 1920s onwards about the welfare state policy were another convincing example supporting this argument here (Roberts 1977: 476). In the late 1920s, it was largely migrants working in plantations who benefited from welfare provisions under British colonial administration. They also enjoyed exemption from the poll tax. Under the Minimum Wage Ordinance of 1923, detailed criteria were laid down for wage levels for different categories of immigrant Indian workers. This ordinance also required plantation owners to provide specified quantities of rice to plantation workers at a subsidised price (Roberts 1977: 477). In national politics, the trade unions and the Marxist political parties represented this highly organised and unionised segment of workers. The leaders of the reform movement foresaw the dangers of granting universal franchise to Indian migrant workers, who were inclined to vote for Marxist parties as their class champions. The disenfranchisement of Indian immigrant workers in 1948 and the demand for a welfare state policy for all therefore can be related to this fear of a Marxist threat. Consequently, regardless of the underlying political motives, the behaviour of the political-economic elites on both these occasions were attempts to redress the past ills caused by their actions and a way to get closer to the Sinhala-Buddhist masses.

During colonial rule, for economic as well as social reasons, many among the Sri Lankan bourgeoisie converted to Christianity (Jayawardena 2007: 249). Their conversion brought about obvious changes in lifestyles, distinct from the lifestyle of the masses. The aggressive launch of Sinhala-Buddhist nationalism in Sri Lanka reinforced the identity dilemma of the local comprador bourgeoisie (who suffered from the brown *sahib* syndrome).[35] By highlighting their own more authentically Sri Lankan approach, the traditional bourgeoisie in the SLFP hoped to appeal to the voters and defeat the more Western-oriented comprador classes represented by the rival UNP. In the light of this, Bandaranaike who led the SLFP was compelled to carve out a new political coalition, combining elements of the structure and superstructure of Sinhala-Buddhist nationalism. This phase of national politics renewed a pattern of alliance-building initially launched during the Dharmapala period and built upon ever since.

Taking a Sinhala-Buddhist nationalist stand in politics, Bandaranaike and the leadership of the UNP embarked on a dangerous path of promotion of exclusion of other communities. As Elie Kedourie pointed out in his seminal work on nationalism in Africa and Asia, the period of early anti-colonial nationalism was in most former colonies a project mainly of the left (1960: 91). Given the origins and the interest pursued by using nationalism in national politics in Sri Lanka, the various phases of development of Sinhala-Buddhist nationalism and nationalist rejuvenation, including the Bandaranaike period, I would suggest that, uncharacteristically for a colonial and early post-independence setting, dominant modes of nationalism in Sri Lanka were generally part of the political project of the right, rather than that of the left.

As a result, Tamils and other minority communities became increasingly isolated and the subject of state persecution. As a number of self-identified politically moderate Sinhalese I interviewed stated, during the 1950s, Bandaranaike used Sinhala-Buddhist nationalism in politics in ways that were 'not all that bad' and seemed like a 'necessary step' towards overcoming inter-elite schisms. This reasoning was grounded in the belief that Bandaranaike sought to bring the deeply divided Sinhalese together under one umbrella, and thereafter to open up to a coalition or consensus with Tamils. However, by using exclusive and parochial Sinhala-Buddhist nationalism as his main political mobilisation strategy, he even contributed to elevating the image of the Sri Lankan state as a Sinhala-Buddhist state. There resulted the exclusion of the Tamils and other minority groups including the Sinhala-Christians. It was quite apparent that Sinhala-Buddhist nationalism successfully drew attention away from the poor living conditions of the masses, and also from the widening inequalities in Sri Lankan society. Even before the SLFP was created, deep divisions existed within Sinhalese society. There were certain economic groups such as small-scale craftsmen and the petty bourgeoisie who often felt politically alienated by post-independence national politics (Gunasinghe 1996c: 174) and who were later incorporated by Bandaranaike into national politics by elevating their cultural and ideological significance in the postcolonial state-building.

THE LEFT'S RIGHT-WING POLITICS

Bandaranaike's election campaign in 1955 indicated the changed direction of nationalist ideology in Sri Lanka. His style of political campaigning rekindled ethnic, linguistic and religious awareness among the majority Sinhalese, eventually leading to 'ethnic outbidding' in politics (DeVotta 2005: 141). The rural as well as urban Sinhala petty bourgeoisie were eager to embrace this political culture and ideology based on ethno-religious identity as they were closely aligned with their class-based interests. The revival of local culture, local economic development, the restoration of the Sinhala language to prominence, and the reformation of the old educational system, which was based on English, replacing it with a vernacular form of education – all these were popular and attractive policies for the Sinhala electorate. Meanwhile, the Sinhala-Buddhist petty bourgeoisie class acted as the organic intellectual force behind realising Bandaranaike's vision as state policies. Symbolic and emotional rhetorical appeals overshadowed appeals to economic self-interest, within an overall demand for the restructuring of state institutions to give priority to vernacular educated classes. Their list of demands also included establishing Sinhalese supremacy over the Tamil people, a move justified by the perception that Tamils were privileged during British colonial rule and had reaped economic rewards.

These demands were not purely rhetorical, but were translated into public policy and constitutional provisions that sought to institutionalise Sinhala-Buddhist dominance over non-Sinhala-Buddhist communities eventually. For example, the 1956 Language Act as introduced by Bandaranaike (known as Sinhala Only Act)[36] became the ultimate expression of the hegemonic project pursued through Sinhala-Buddhist nationalism. When the first republican constitution was introduced in 1972 by Bandaranaike's widowed wife, as prime minister, it bestowed privileges on Buddhism rather than other religions in the country, yet another example of the continued pursuit of hegemony by Sinhala political elites (Coomaraswamy 1984: 4).

Ever since Bandaranaike, ruling Sinhalese political elites have successfully employed the 'ethnic card' in politics (Jayatilleke 1991). This became especially visible as economic conditions deteriorated in the early post-independence years. At the same time, conflict and competition over access to state resources began to intensify, as state resource distribution was increasingly mismanaged by ruling elite factions. As well as scarcity of resources, there was also a scarcity of political imagination and vision on the part of the dominant Sinhalese political elites. Further, this direction of politics, having shaped the post-colonial state-building project to establish Sinhalese domination, also forced the old and newly emerging rival political forces of left-wing orientation to embark on symbolic politics of right-wing propensity. In other words, albeit the self-identified image of being left and right, regardless of the other identities the various elite factions carried in politics, they together practised one form of politics, that is, right-wing politics.

Overall, the direction of politics after Bandaranaike raises several important questions as to why he did not opt for a clear left-wing and class-based political strategy. Given the brand of indigenous socialism he espoused in politics, this would have seemed to be his logical course of action. It also seems likely, had he opted for a class-based strategy, that he might well have gained support from both less privileged Sinhalese and the lower classes of other ethnic communities. During the early post-independence period, class-based grievances had considerable currency among the majority of the Sri Lankan population, regardless of their ethnic identity.[37] Party politics could have worked out quite differently, with a real left-wing alternative to Sinhala-Buddhist nationalism. However, the ethno-religious strategy that Bandaranaike followed was mainly for convenience, since it mobilised a majority of the electorate, and brought Sinhalese political elites together, across their divisions.

Indeed, Marxist–socialist groups were dominant in early post-independence politics. Their pioneer, the Lanka Sama Samaja Party (LSSP), was formed in 1935, and gave birth to a number of other breakaway Marxist and leftist parties. Out of these came a left movement, bringing together the LSSP and the Communist Party. At that time, with global economic crisis deepening, these left-wing parties attracted members from across the Sri Lankan bourgeoisie and the lower classes. The organisational basis for this socialist-inspired movement was the militant labour and trade union movements, dating back to the 19th century and the establishment of plantation capitalism in Sri Lanka. As Jayawardena explains, that period (the 1930s) was one in which class-consciousness was able to take precedence over ethnic and religious emotions (2003: 17). Perhaps it was precisely the growing strength of class-based left-wing demands, after the Second World War, that made appeals to ethno-national sentiments more attractive for Sinhala elites. Also in line with other political developments in the post–Second World War period, the left had to be counter-balanced to gain political legitimacy for rival non-left parties and the UNP.[38]

The bourgeois leadership of the reform movement were less left-wing in their overall agendas than the labour movement. While the bourgeois leadership advocated for limited voting rights, the labour movement advocated voting rights for all Indian and migrant workers in Sri Lanka, and supported universal suffrage early on. Further, it also advocated voting rights for Indian workers in Sri Lanka (Jayawardena 2003: 21; Shanmugaratnam 2007: i). Given the nature of these potential new constituencies, advocating for voting rights of these underprivileged economic forces by the labour movement was perceived by the reform movement leaders as a threat of expanding the support base for the leftist parties. Despite their early positive track record, after 1929 they also succumbed to the allure of communalist politics. Although the labour movements claimed to be left wing, its political leanings got clouded with right-wing tendencies since then.

From the 1920s to the mid-1970s, traditional Marxist forces were present in Sri Lankan politics, and were an important force that claimed to represent the interests of the proletariat, across ethnic and religious divides. The left also saw themselves as the real liberators of Sri Lanka both from imperialism and in terms of class liberation of the oppressed proletariat (Wickramaratne 1999: 252). Some scholars agree that the Marxist parties deserve a part of the credit for securing Sri Lanka's independence (Wilson 1979: 1132). The Marxist left parties were the only major ideological alternative to the dominant postcolonial political parties: the UNP and the SLFP (Fernando 1973: 371). Contrary to the UNP and the SLFP, however, in the popular political arena, the Marxist–socialists openly campaigned for rights and welfare for urban working-class Sri Lankans and for rural plantation workers, including plantation workers of Indian Tamil origin. Although the Marxist parties were small, they were able to secure a decent number of votes in parliamentary elections in the post–Second World War period. For instance, in the 1947 general elections, the LSSP, the Communist Party and the Bolshevik Leninist Party together secured 21 per cent of the votes cast (Moore 1985: 294), which allowed them to secure 19 parliamentary seats (Moore 1985: 242). Despite some electoral victories, their influence in politics remained mainly confined to the urban working class and the southern coastal belts, the most commercialised areas of the country (Jayawardena 1974: 3). Given the still largely feudal nature of social and class relations in rural areas, where up to 90 per cent of Sri Lankans still lived in the early post–Second World War years, their success electorally was quite impressive. The colonial capitalist plantation sector and the urban light industry were relatively small sectors of the economy (Hettige 2000: 20).

These structural features in the economy did not favour socialist and Marxist parties retaining their 'left', class-solidarity oriented identity for long. In the years after 1931, the left gradually started drifting towards the right, politically speaking. A new constitution was introduced in Ceylon in 1931, which marked the start of self-governance and universal suffrage in legislative elections to the state council. In the 1930s, Sri Lanka was hit by the worst economic crisis in its history, and in 1934 by a serious malaria epidemic. Combined, these two crises resulted in large-scale unemployment, leaving many workers impoverished. As left-wing historians have shown, these two events further shaped the previously vibrant trade union and labour rights movement in the island (Jayawardena 2003: 27). The global recession of the 1930s thus hit the emerging working class the hardest, those who had formed the support base for left-wing parties. As also in Europe, the overall impact of the economic crisis of the 1930s was to move left-wing political parties to the right.

As competition between the UNP and the SLFP for state power intensified, Marxist–socialist forces decided to join with the SLFP, convincing themselves that the SLFP represented the only political alternative to the capitalist class, and that the SLFP was both progressive and anti-imperialist in character (Jayawardena 1974: 4) and was the main challenger of the pro-imperialist UNP (Shanmugaratnam 2007: i–ii). This way the entire spectrum of political ideologies came to be subsumed under a single Sinhala-Buddhist nationalist ideology. As one veteran politician remarked, 'upon securing ministerial portfolios in the MEP government that was led by the SLFP, the traditional Marxist parties simply abandoned class politics' (R.13). According to contemporary critics of the traditional Marxist parties I interviewed, the pro-capitalist bias of the UNP was a simply good enough reason for the traditional Marxist parties to support the SLFP and to jump on its ethnic bandwagon. Leftist parties subscribed to ethnic politics from a fear of becoming completely isolated and left out of popular politics altogether. What can be noted is the shared bourgeois background of the leadership of almost all Sri Lankan political parties (Jayawardena 1974: 6).

Since the gradual demise of the influence of the traditional Marxist political parties, a number of smaller radical nationalist political parties have gained an important voice in national politics.[39] Among these, the Janatha Vimukthi Peramuna (JVP) and the Jathika Hela Urumaya (JHU) are the most prominent. The prominent figures in these two parties resemble the organic intellectuals whose role in the hegemony- and state-building project was instrumental. At the time of its birth in the mid-1960s, the leadership of the JVP promised to fill the vacuum left by the traditional left parties. Since its formation, the JVP has worked from within to achieve its main goal of establishing a Marxist–socialist state. The JVP also continues to advocate a change to the post-colonial political system captured by the bourgeoisie and their capitalist state-building project.[40] Clearly, until the early 1980s, the main competition to the JVP was the perceived pseudo-nationalist project of the bourgeoisie (Samaranayake 1987: 273).

Compared to the leadership of the UNP, the SLFP and the traditional Marxist political parties, in terms of class origination, the JVP leadership belonged to the rural non-bourgeoisie class and was inspired by the claim to represent the 'oppressed classes' of all communities (Uyangoda 2006a: 6). In its electoral propaganda, the JVP spoke of being the voice of landless peasants living in the rural areas, and being a mobilising party for them. However, upon the introduction of the open economy from 1977 onwards, and with significant changes in traditional class structures, there has been a gradual vanishing of a sizable part of the agrarian population. In the light of these economic changes, the JVP has fine-tuned its strategy to appeal to members of newly formed underprivileged classes, the precariat labourers[41] in urban areas, whose economic and social fate is as much dependent on global as on local processes. The launching of the open economy policy in 1977 significantly expanded the private sector and service industries, enabling the JVP to penetrate into a voter base of emerging casual labourers. Through its anti-neoliberal rhetoric, the JVP was able to attract these new class segments to its political coalition, despite their primary economic identity and economic fortunate being entirely dependent on the neoliberal economic policies.

Given the uneven impact of the roll-out of the liberal economy in different parts of the country, it was mainly in the southern parts of the island that the JVP found support. The JVP's electoral strategies adjusted the party's ideological orientation to the material and ideological needs of their new-found constituencies, many of whom were also Sinhalese. Although the JVP proclaimed itself as a Marxist political party, succumbing to ethnic politics only favoured the building of narrow ethnic solidarity over class solidarity (Samaranayake 1987: 277). For these reasons, the majority of the respondents I interviewed who belong to other political party affiliations raised questions on the JVP's continued self-declared identity as a Marxist–socialist political party. In their view, the JVP did not stand by any Marxist–socialist ideals; highlighting the JVP's confused political identity, one respondent, a leader of a traditional left political party, remarked: 'JVP is a peculiar animal.'

Compared to the privileges enjoyed by the dominant bourgeois ruling factions in politics who have also established themselves as gatekeepers to state resources, the JVP lacked ready access to the state's resource base. Since the party had no access to public funds or networks of state-sponsored patronage on which to build political coalitions, to reach the rural youth who constituted the majority of the JVP's electoral base, the party needed a way to prevent its electoral base from drifting towards the two main political parties. In 1971 and again in 1989–1992, the JVP led two anti-state protests in the name of 'saving the nation'. During these two events, JVP protestors were attacked by the coercive forces of the state. These defeats seem to have persuaded the JVP leadership to gradually join the hegemonic ideologies of the two main parties. After 1992, the JVP leadership largely abandoned their previously progressive political ideology in order to accommodate an ideology that would enable it to win elections. Ironically, the JVP adopted an even more explicit and aggressive ethno-nationalist ideology than the UNP or the SLFP. What this illustrates is that the hegemonic position of Sinhala-Buddhist ideology was already firmly established in Sri Lankan politics and have taken roots as the ideology of the ruling class, the ruling ideology and the state ideology. The JVP felt obliged to work within this framework, taken as 'common sense', forming part of the broader discursive practices that link Sinhalese political elites and with the Sinhalese majority.

Already in 1971, Tamil youth and others in the Tamil community were excluded from the 1971 insurrection organised by the JVP. This represented a failure to imagine a broad and inclusive political programme with a firm left-wing foundation. This exclusion of Tamil youth from JVP activism can also be linked to the way in which post-colonial electoral and political competition in Sri Lanka has been conceived as a zero-sum game from independence onwards. Anti-Tamil prejudices within the JVP's historical perception is similar to that of the UNP, where Tamils are viewed as having been historically privileged during British colonial rule in spite of their evident impoverishment during the civil war (Moore 1989: 180). During one interview, one present youth leader of the JVP party shared this comment:

> According to my opinion, there are no grievances for the Tamils. Their grievances are based on their interests. I agree with the root causes of this conflict before 1987. And I must say that as I think, there are no other new grievances after 1987. So I question, what are their new grievances? If there are new grievances then we should start discussions. There is no need for any discussions, because there are no new grievances. (R.1)

In accordance with this sanguine view, another interviewee, a JVP member of parliament, suggested that 'Tamil separatism is a distraction for realising the important class struggle and there are no ethnic-based grievances'. In his view, realising class struggle will automatically take care of the so-called ethnic conflicts. As another JVP respondent pointed out,

> Tamils demands are based on Tamilness and historical grievances, both are unacceptable. If one is to accept the Tamils' right to self-determination and recognise the armed struggle for a separate state, people from the Monaragala District[42] who are equally underprivileged in terms of access to state resources should also be fighting for a separate state.

Although in these two statements class was emphasised as the main preoccupation and the basis for resolving the ongoing conflict, in the arena of electoral politics the issue of class domination and class struggle was already overtaken by fiery ethno-nationalist JVP propaganda. In its campaigning and rhetoric, the JVP hardly distinguishes the Tamil community as a whole and the LTTE in particular. As Jayawardena points out, they make little effort to distinguish Tamils on a class basis or even on the basis of being Sri Lankan or Indian Tamils. In Jayawardena's view, these characteristics are synonymous with the ideology of Sinhala chauvinism, or even racism, which regards all non-Sinhala, regardless of class, as aliens to Sri Lanka, redefined as 'Sinhala-land' (1985: 88).

By taking a Sinhala-Buddhist chauvinist stand, the JVP's degree of subordination to the ideology of the bourgeois faction in the ruling class and their hegemonic right-wing politics becomes evident.[43] Bopage, a former JVP active party member, pointed out in a recent interview,

> In my view the JVP should not have campaigned to elect Mahinda Rajapaksa the President, in 2005. That harmed the party. They should have taken into consideration the history of Rajapaksa and his family. The JVP contributed a lot towards promoting nationalistic communalism. Even today the JVP has not been able to recover from the blame for that wrong decision it made to promote racism then. I think it has realised its mistakes. I think its decision to accept positions in the Kumaratunga government, too, was counterproductive. They should not have done that, because after taking up ministerial posts, they would not be able to carry out their agenda. (*Counterpoint* 2019)

These different views on the JVP's transformation over time suggest that the more the JVP attempts to differentiate itself from the SLFP and the UNP in rhetorical terms, the more it subscribes to a hegemonic right-wing ethno-national politics. By doing so, the JVP has effectively closed the space for realising egalitarian politics and has itself become part of the wider obstacles to establishing a genuinely democratic state in Sri Lanka. Considering the gaps between what the JVP claims as an under-class-oriented party and an alternative to the prevailing bourgeois and elite politics and what it actually practises in electoral politics, it is reasonable to suggest that the extreme nature of the JVP's Sinhala-Buddhist nationalism makes a sham of its proclaimed intentions to protect the unitary state in Sri Lanka from the Tamil secessionist movement, and from both Indian and Western forms of neo-imperialism. Instead, the JVP is mainly concerned with ideals that can serve in its strategy to muster as many votes as possible in competitive elections by hiding its true colours as a 'name board party'.

The JHU is a political party of more recent origin, established in 2004. In national politics the JHU has adopted a militant Sinhala-Buddhist stand. The Buddhist monk faction in the JHU claim to be the 'bearer of Sinhala-Buddhist heritage' and the 'sons of the soil' and are supported by a powerful faction of Sinhala-Buddhist petty bourgeois laity. As Seneviratne has observed, the monks in the JHU have become

> strident nationalists, not pragmatic nationalists whose social priorities could have been economic rather than ideological ... in the end, that pragmatism and sober preoccupation with the economic were dethroned. Ideology was enthroned, holding the scepter of Sinhala Buddhist hegemonism. (1999: 336)

The JHU claimed to represent the interests of the majority Sinhala-Buddhists. The direct role they play in politics to realise the 'Sinhala-Buddhist hegemonic state' is a force that redefines the problematic of Buddhism in contemporary Sri Lanka (Uyangoda 2007a: ix). The JHU's imagined state-building project included a detailed programme for the re-establishment of the ancient glory of precolonial Sri Lanka and its values based on the principles of Buddhism and Sinhalese culture (Roberts 2001: 21; Uyangoda 2006a: 7).[44] This vision gave prominence to the country's rural peasantry and identified them as the main agents of state-building.

As a general characteristic of the Sri Lankan nationalist elites (Moore 1989: 180), from the very beginning, the JHU seemed to suffer from the problem of locking into a particular interpretation of history in which the peasantry is treated as the historical and moral core of Sinhalese society. Also, in the mainstream national political debates often conducted via the mass media (televised debates and discussions in state and private television and radio stations), the JHU made strong claims to vast areas of land in the eastern and northern parts of the country inhabited by Tamils. While Tamils regarded these areas as their Tamil homelands, the JHU claimed the before colonial rule, these lands were sacred possessions of Buddhist temples and therefore part of the Sinhala-Buddhist cultural heritage and the Sinhala-Buddhist cultural triangle. This idea seems to be based on arguments made by the early nationalist leaders, particularly Walisinha Harischandra, who opined that this territory was part of a sacred city granted by King Devanampiyatissa for future Buddhist temples and monasteries known as *viharagam* (Nissan 1997: 37).

As a Tamil scholar and a political observer I interviewed mentioned, 'with parties like the JHU and the JVP the country is back to original Sinhala-Buddhist nationalism' (R.19).[45] In his view, the major involvement of a powerful segment of the Sinhala-Buddhist intelligentsia[46] with the JHU is a dangerous trend in recent politics. As many respondents shared, their role in promoting such chauvinist politics was not only altering the state's ideological path but also distorting the teachings of the Buddha. For example, by providing manufactured Buddhist doctrinal justifications for killing and for the end goal of establishing a Sinhala-Buddhist hegemonic state through the means of violence, war and killings, they have ignited tensions in society (Uyangoda 2007b: 2). The confluence of religious, economic, intellectual and political forces under the JHU leadership can be seen as a renewal of the traditional hegemonic bond during the Dharmapala and Bandaranaike periods between the same historical forces. As one respondent noted (R.19), as was the case during Dharmapala's times, despite their minority status in politics, the JHU (along with the JVP) is effectively manipulating the sentiments of the majority Sinhalese by using Sinhala-Buddhist nationalism that has an ideological and material underpinning. Reflecting on the structure of the political system and the nature of competition and cooperation between large and smaller political parties, the same respondent opined,

> When the main political parties have to rely on extremist Sinhala political parties to secure a parliamentary majority, they cannot offer concessions to the minority ethnic political parties.... The problem in Sri Lanka is everyone wants mainstream politics, not peripheral politics. Therefore there is a tendency to use nationalism rhetoric to be part of the mainstream.

Another respondent marked, 'Without an element of nationalism, today no political party or leadership can mobilise people.' Regardless of the JHU's ideological overtone in national politics, a few respondents of Sinhala-Buddhist background maintained that Sangha leadership in the JHU is both the most corrupt and the least nationalistic. Another Sinhalese respondent was disappointed that

> there are no true Sinhala-Buddhist nationalists in politics. But we witness true Sinhala-Buddhist nationalists are being used in politics as 'curry leaves'. This is equally true for the Tamils too. Once the goals

of the competing political parties are achieved, true nationalists are ignored. Today there are people like Champika Ranawaka and some people in the JVP who are identified as nationalists by some in the Sinhalese community, which is not true.

Although the Sangha has been an integral part of constructing and maintaining the moral and cultural leadership underlying Sinhala-Buddhist nationalism, today there seems to be a growing disapproval from the lay community of the central role the Sangha has assumed in contemporary Sri Lankan politics. Instead of cultural and moral leadership (functioning as a part of the organic intellectual force), there are struggles for domination and resources between various Sinhala-Buddhist elite factions and the Sangha. These dynamics point to the urgency of realignment of forces within the Sinhala-Buddhist hegemonic coalition, in which the lay and non-lay segments have to redefine their roles and responsibilities in reproducing the Sinhala-Buddhist hegemony-building project under new political and economic conditions. This is especially applicable to those members of the Sangha whose direct moral and cultural leadership come under increased critical scrutiny given their growing economic power.

The transformations in the broader political landscape since the late 1980s due to the diminishing influence of the traditional left politics marked the revival of the JVP in the national political scene, and also the direct entrance of the Buddhist Sangha into mainstream politics via the JHU. The JHU in particular adopting an extreme form of Sinhala-Buddhist chauvinism is another indication of the continued appeal that hegemonic Sinhala-Buddhist nationalism has for the political elites in contemporary Sri Lankan politics. Where necessary, they were not reluctant to re-enact the imaginations of an authentic Sinhala cultural identity comprised of 'weva, dageba and yaya', which was popular during major development initiatives undertaken in the post-colonial period and during the Mahaweli Development Scheme launched by the J. R. Jayawardena regime in the 1980s. In the past, this formula was proven to be highly successful in the regime-building efforts of J. R. Jayawardena (Jayawardena 1992: vii), which the current and aspiring future political regimes hope to reproduce.

In the post-war period, the strength of the Sinhala-Buddhist nationalism as a hegemony-building process is still unfolding. In this period, the muted form of the Tamil nationalist project and the absence of the LTTE, the long-time arch-rival of the Sinhala-Buddhist hegemonic project, may trigger the unveiling of new strategies to continue this project with no serious counter-hegemonic forces. The bounce back of the Sinhala-Buddhist nationalist rhetoric has been a trademark of Sri Lanka's politics during the times of drastic changes to the economic, social and political context. Therefore, in the post-war period, the introduction of a rejuvenated form of nationalism may not target an internal enemy, but rather an external one. Targeting Sri Lanka's Muslim community, especially in the post-war period, as the new internal enemy of the Sinhalese-led hegemony-building project that was supported and led by some radical Buddhist monks under the banner of 'Bodu Bala Sena' (DeVotta 2018; Imtiyaz and Mohamed-Saleem 2015) is only the tip of the iceberg of what is to come and an indication of the future directions of finding a long-lasting double enemy from inside-outside (that is, the global jihadist movement). To contain the internal forces immediately following the military defeat of the LTTE in May 2009 and to deal with likely anti-hegemonic forces under the current Rajapaksa regime (since 2019), already a number of pre-emptive measures have been put in place. The latest is the introduction of the 20th amendment to the constitution which grants supreme power to the executive president. To a lesser extent, the continuation of the hegemonic project lies in the ability of the Sinhalese political elites to spread their hegemonic influence over minority communities and dissidents in the majority community..

TAMIL NATIONALISM AND SINHALA-BUDDHIST POLITICS

The tendency in post-colonial political discourses is to view Sinhala-Buddhist and Tamil nationalisms as competing and mutually reinforcing each other (Uyangoda 2000: 64). This view stresses the antagonistic relationship of these forms of nationalism, and tends to obscure the numerous factional and class conflicts within each group – the Tamils and the Sinhalese. These divisions and internal inequalities are sidelined in this overall analysis of ethno-nationalisms (De Silva 2005: 454–55). The focus is instead on actual and perceived cultural differences, and perceived irreconcilabilities. Mainstream Tamil nationalist narratives are generally articulated through an emphasis on their defensive and protective nature, focusing to a large extent on the victimhood of Tamils historically (Kearney 1985: 904). Since these discourses often refer to the intimate ties with south Indian Dravidian and Sri Lankan Tamil nationalism, they tend to generate fears among the Sinhalese (Kearney

1985: 903; Krishna 1999: 61). One politician captured these fears, playing with the fear of being swamped, when he said,

> In this country the problem of the Tamils is not a minority problem. The Sinhalese are the minority in *Dravidastan*. We are carrying on a struggle for our national existence against the *Dravidastan* majority. (Parliamentary debate quoted in Kearney 1985: 903)

Meanwhile, the idea of Tamil victimhood, the issue of territoriality, and the nexus of Tamil militancy and 'Navalar centrism' are a few recurring themes often highlighted in Tamil nationalist debates (Cheran 2001: 37). The victimhood narrative has been especially helpful in understanding the post-colonial origins and manifestations of Tamil nationalism and confers a sense of moral legitimation through references to a shared identity reinforced by the blood sacrifice of those who fell in war (Cheran 2001: 3–4). This notion was also emphasised in the written work oriented towards a global readership, another major player in Sri Lanka's political conflict (Roberts 2005: 5).

As one respondent who attempted to trace the subaltern elements of Tamil nationalism shared,

> later in the years, Tamil youth took up arms against a particular system that maintains public power for the benefit of a few. The Tamil youth were fed up with Tamil elites who played a double game[47] with them. The Bandaranaike–Chelvanayakam pact, the Dudley–Chelvanayakam pact could not stop them. They thought the Tamil elites are playing a double game. They go to Colombo and say one thing and once they secure power or win elections, they say something else to the people there. There is a saying 'idle mind is devil's playground' which was the case with the Tamils. Amirthalingam, Sivasumbramaniam[48] lost their credibility, and then the fight began.

Despite these less popular elite and caste roots of Tamil nationalism, the eventual transformation of Tamil nationalism as witnessed in contemporary politics and LTTE militarism has roots in the actual experiences of the Sri Lankan Tamil community – their continued systematic marginalisation from mutually acceptable political power-sharing and resource-sharing mechanisms in the postcolonial phase of politics (Shastri 1990). According to one Sinhalese scholar,

Sinhala nationalism is born out of the past, Tamil nationalism is born out of the present. But this does not imply that because it has emerged recently, Sri Lankan Tamil nationalism may be ephemeral. History cannot be reversed, the sequence of traumatic events since independence cannot be undone, and the nationalism that has emerged from such a cauldron cannot be put back. (De Silva quoted in Nesiah 2001: 20)

In the mid-1970s, a more forceful articulation of Tamil nationalism with separatist themes emerged with the launching of a systematic armed resistance movement against Sinhalese dominance. This transformation was caused by the changed direction of Tamil internal political dynamics during this period, as the traditional Tamil political leadership was taken over by the LTTE and an overtly military form of nationalism was launched. The forceful embarkation of the LTTE into the Tamil political scene removed the influence of educated Tamil elites in Tamil politics almost totally. As widely observed, Tamil youth militancy was not only a factor that altered the path of Tamil nationalism, it also altered Sinhala-Buddhist hegemony-building and the overall political landscape of the country. On the birth of Tamil militancy, renowned Tamil scholar Professor Sivatamby identifies three important junctures in the rise of Tamil militancy: as a resistance force against the leadership of the Tamil United Liberation Front (TULF),[49] as a reaction to the oppressive acts of the government and as a response to the repressive acts of the security forces (2004: 15). Further, refuting some established notions of the origins of Tamil militancy in Sri Lanka, Professor Sivatamby also notes that Tamil militants learned their lessons from the post-colonialist, anti-imperialist and various liberation struggles of this period across the world, not from any nationalist organisations based in Tamil Nadu, hence qualifying as a militant movement of Marxist rather than racial roots (2004: 15). Others who agree with this interpretation suggest that the very concept of Eelam[50] and the main goals of the LTTE were derived from the material conditions that pushed the LTTE to advocate for a more socialist equilibrium model for a new state where the material needs could be met (Shastri 1990: 74).

However, among the majority Sinhalese, the most popular discourse is that Tamil militarism changed the course of Sinhala-Buddhist nationalism, and that Tamil nationalism had played an influential role in the militaristic transformation of the state and society. However, when looked closely, since early 1980s there are other political and economic conditions that facilitated the dynamics and transformations of both nationalisms in Sri Lanka. As observed by Hardt and Nergi, the military character of nationalism is a manifestation of its status as a part of 'Empire'[51] (2000: 43–45). In Hardt and Nergi's thesis of empire claims, forces of globalisation generate a massive degree of political and economic deregulation, a marked decline in social and economic planning, and political fragmentation alongside more centralised authority structures, accompanied by rising numbers of incidents of state and civil violence (2000: 3). Nationalist movements were part of the forceful expression of a new neo-colonial dependency, and a reliance on debt. In Sri Lanka, for example, the 1970s and 1980s were marked by global economic changes that resulted in a major economic downturn and considerable hardship for ordinary people, both Tamil and Sinhalese (Bastian 2001: 2). Embarking on an aggressive path of Sinhala-Buddhist nationalism was a way of countering the emerging anti-hegemonic Tamil military and political forces such as trade unions, repressed by Jayawardena in 1981. In some ways, the emergence of the nationalist-military Tamil forces of the LTTE was a 'political bonus' for the Sinhala-Buddhist elites in charge of the state, since it legitimised their authority and their use of force to protect their own hegemonic power.

Since the late 1970s, in a general political context marked by deteriorating social and ethnic relations, subscribing consciously and unconsciously to the mainstream political discourse on nationalism become a profitable project for the Sinhalese elites and the Sinhalese subalterns. Writing on the intellectuals' subscription to this project, Roberts has emphasised the inter-ethnic nature of nationalisms of this period as a legitimisation exercise embarked on by certain members in the mainstream intellectual community who did not wish to be seen or treated as traitors by their ethnic communities (2005: 3). This brings us back to the point of Gramsci's work on hegemony that emphasises that it is not only the manipulation, but also coercion and the presence of threat of use of coercion playing a role in hegemony-building. What is important to note in this regard is the lasting impacts left by the intellectual community by making certain choices under various dynamics in state-in-society relations of this period, especially on reinforcing a binary view of Sinhala and Tamil nationalisms and justifying the forceful political use of it in the elites' political strategy. Over time, as the Tamil military struggle for self-determination entered into a violent path, these discursive versions gained organic legitimacy and made common sense to the majority in the

Sinhalese and Tamil communities. The military events after the late 1970s were interpreted applying this inter-ethnic framework. As I argue, the ethnic essentialism[52] articulated in Tamil and Sinhala nationalisms gained immense currency because of the utilitarian effect it has in politics and scholarship. In the interviews I had with the younger generation of scholars from the Sinhala community, there is hardly any willingness to understand nationalisms outside the inter-ethnic framework or to see it as a hegemony-building project of the elites.

After the May 2009 military victory of government forces against the LTTE, the main anti-hegemonic force capable of confronting Sinhala-Buddhist hegemony had been wiped out. Post-war politics was marked by the absence of meaningful opposition among progressive Sinhalese forces due to the excessive militarisation of daily life across Sri Lanka. There was virtually no direct challenge to the right-wing Sinhala-Buddhist parties. The charges of war crimes against the current regime (raised by a number of political parties from all ethnic groups and ex-LTTE cadres) are increasingly being used by the ruling political elites to gain a new momentum for Sinhala-Buddhist nationalism in local politics that is likely to advance their edge in politics and hegemonic-authoritarian state-building that seeks legitimacy largely through ideological hegemony.[53] This new strategy pursued by the right-wing forces in state power now has to search for new enemies for the survival of their project, where the Tamil diaspora and the Western liberal international community are projected as the new enemies of Sinhala-Buddhist nationalism and the rightful Sinhala-Buddhist hegemonic state. Even minor forms of opposition to this dominant political project are brutally cracked down upon by the coercive apparatus of the state. Conversely, those who comply with the hegemonic project are rewarded with state patronage. There are enough incentives built into the state system and state practices for those who comply, and enough sanctions and negative consequences for those who do not comply and consent, to ensure the system's almost continuous reproduction.

In conclusion, the discussion I presented so far clearly identified how Sinhala-Buddhist nationalism became a critical tool for the mobilisation of the Sri Lankan Sinhala masses by the dominant economic classes from the 19th century onwards until after independence. As the upper classes sought to secure their flailing economic dominance amidst colonial interventions, they resorted to a Sinhala-Buddhist nationalist ideology associated with Dharmapala and the legacy of his uneasy alliance of a nostalgic longing for the past feudal order and an embracing of economic modernity. To fulfil their narrow class-based interests and obtain consent for their unquestioned ideological, cultural and moral leadership, as well as control over the expanding colonial and post-colonial economy, the Sinhala-Buddhist upper classes built cross-class alliances with the subaltern masses during the colonial era, establishing a sense of legitimacy that would persist into the post-independence period.

On the one hand, Sinhala-Buddhist nationalism has been a means of constructing hegemony by bringing the Sinhalese together in the face, first, of the colonial enemy and, then, of other, non-Sinhala minority communities and electorates. On the other hand, this process itself generated some perverse effects in that it pre-empted the more inclusive national goal of constructing a more egalitarian, decolonised society and a more democratic state in the post-independence period. As both vertical and horizontal inequalities were institutionalised, growing ruptures emerged in state structures and in state-in-society relations. The emphasis has been on the need to view historical development of Sinhala-Buddhist nationalism through the lens of class relationships and class power struggles, beyond the more usual ethno-religious frame.

It is clear that by using Sinhala-Buddhist nationalism and giving a prominent place to ethno-religious identities within their nationalist discursive practices, dominant Sinhalese political elites successfully manipulated the class-based economic and social struggles of the masses for upward social mobility. Any challenge to the exploitive and manipulative relations between Sinhalese elites and masses were put on hold, and side-stepped. This led to the creation of a form of synthetic class solidarity, not among the masses, but among the Sinhalese upper class, as a class-for-itself, inward-looking members of the ruling class and horizontal divisions among subalterns. In these ways, relationships of domination–subordination, manipulation and coercion were successfully perpetuated well beyond independence by Sinhalese political elites. Cross-class coalitions, formed on the basis of shared ideologies of justice and freedom, soon collapsed, and instead party politics and ideology worked in favour of a narrow elite that was determined to protect its political primacy over subsequent decades and marginalise other elite groups. The trajectory of post-colonial politics has thus been profoundly shaped by explicit Sinhala-Buddhist identity politics in which the lower-class Sinhalese were intellectually, economically, morally and politically subordinate to the bourgeoisie.

Appealing to Sinhala-Buddhist mobilisation strategies, Sinhalese political elites were able to establish this form of nationalism as 'common sense' among lower-class Sinhala-Buddhists as well, by tying their imaginaries to the state. Embracing this majoritarian notion of the state, Sinhalese masses drew ideological satisfaction from their identification with elites, while the elites drew on the state for significant political and economic benefits. By surrendering their consent to hegemony-building strategies of reward, manipulation, coercion and threat, the majority of the Sinhalese came to actively participate in creating the conditions for further ethno-religious control over state-building, producing social polarisation and setting conditions for future violent conflicts in Sri Lanka. Popular moves towards more inclusive and democratic forms of state-building were arrested, since the Sinhalese masses were led to believe that the Sinhala-Buddhist hegemonic state elites would serve their interests.

As suggested in the discussion on Tamil nationalism, where the hegemonic project pursued by Sinhalese political elites has been challenged or perceived to have come under threat, elites do not hesitate to unleash the state's coercive powers to deal with opposition using force. In relation to theories of hegemony-building, in Sri Lanka manipulation and coercion go hand in hand, and are applied simultaneously not only to suppress and to gain consent to the dominant political order, but also to quash and delegitimise any social, economic or political oppositional forces to the state among ethnic minority groups. Force is also used against 'dissident elements' within the Sinhalese community.

Taking stock of what Sinhala-Buddhist nationalism has achieved in terms of improved real living conditions for the masses, this chapter identified both Tamils in general and the majority of poor Sinhala-Buddhists as losers in this nationalist state-building project. By enshrining principles of inequality, Sinhala-Buddhist nationalism has left neither the room needed nor the capacity within or outside the state to address compelling issues of poverty and deepening of democracy in Sri Lanka. So long as the Sinhalese masses can be manipulated electorally, and assimilated to the dominant hegemony-building project, through a combination of coercion, threat and selective bribery, the state will be increasingly captured by a right-wing bourgeoisie espousing ethno-nationalism. For the future, the broader nature of the state is being moulded in this image, with state practices and discourses being fashioned to meet the needs and interests of right-wing political elites, moving the political conjuncture and state-in-society dangerously in the direction of an authoritarian-populist and ethno-nationalist state. Only by exposing the deep-running class interests underpinning the now almost sacred hegemonic Sinhala-Buddhist state-building can a more democratic state and a more inclusive society and economy be constructed in future. As the war recedes into history, Sinhala-Buddhist nationalism seems to have gained a new lease of life, with the almost total absence of opposition parties among the Sinhalese a testimony to the success of their hegemony-building mix of consent-based and coercive state-building.

NOTES

1. Understood as a relationship of nationalism to a certain religious belief or dogma. In the context of 19th-century Sri Lanka, this relationship was often made between nationalism and Buddhism.
2. Often identified with the nationalist struggles or struggles for independence waged in the colonial territories under Western colonialism.
3. Grievances theory focuses on ethnic and religious divisions, political repression and inequality as the basis of ethnic violence (Collier and Hoeffler 2002).
4. Passive revolution refers to a situation whereby molecular changes progressively modify the pre-existing composition of forces and hence become a matrix of new changes (Gramsci 1971: 109).
5. In the colonial context and to a certain extent in the post-colonial context of Sri Lanka, the bourgeois class does not possess the same amount of wealth and ownership of the means of production of a bourgeoisie in western Europe. For this reason, sometimes the Sri Lanka's bourgeoisies are compared to the petty bourgeoise class in western Europe. In this book, the term 'bourgeoisie' is simply used to denote a wealthy class that owns means of production (that is, land and capital).
6. In the non-Marxian vocabulary, national popular would mean collective will. According to Gramsci, there are several preconditions required for the emergence of a national-popular collective will. The desire for a common change by individuals and mass incorporation of peasant farmers burst simultaneously into political life. The participation of the masses in political life is of vital importance for the development of a national-popular collective will (http://neogramscian.blogspot.com/2011/01/what-is-national-popular-collective.html, accessed on 20 March 2011).

7. Cultural nationalism means giving prominence to cultural factors (as opposed to civic nationalism that gives primacy to a 'general will') to fashion the nationalist ideology.
8. Borrowing from Kapferer, this research understands ontology as an orientation to the world and to existence by which these make sense, where ideology is understood as a reasoned, rational and conscious process: the deliberate taking up of ideas about the world and the systematic ordering of these ideas as logically coherent bodies of interpretation (Kapferer 1988: 79).
9. For a detailed comparative analysis of their work, see Michael Roberts' 2005 book, *Narrating Tamil Nationalism: Subjectivities and Issues*.
10. Class model is defined by reference to a shared position in the organisation of production and a solidarity deriving from a consciousness of that shared position (Roberts 1974). For an elaborated scheme of the elite model, consult Roberts (1974).
11. Chatterjee defines eastern nationalism as nationalism that is drawn into a culture alien to it. In his words, 'peoples recently drawn into a civilization hitherto alien to them, and whose ancestral cultures are not shaped to success and excellence by these cosmopolitan and increasingly dominant standards' (1986: 23).
12. For the full volume of his public speeches, refer to Ananda Guruge's 1965 book, *Return to Righteousness: A Collection of Speeches, Essays and Letters of the Angarika Dharmapala*.
13. Sangha is the Buddhist monastic order in Sri Lanka.
14. For details of Dharmapala's rural economic development proposal, see Seneviratne (1999: ch. 3).
15. This point can be later elaborated by bringing examples from contemporary times as well.
16. Dharmapala constantly referred to them as idiots, meat-eating, whisky-drinking, superstitious people (see Seneviratne 1999: 35–36).
17. Some argue that this is because the kings of Sri Lanka traced their lineage to India. Therefore, having a firm social base to their authority was derived from the Sangha and extending state patronage to the Sangha.
18. I do not wish to claim that there are no genuine Sinhala-Buddhist nationalists in the country.
19. Ethnic outbidding refers to an auction-like process in which Sri Lankan politicians strive to outdo one another by playing on their majority communities' fears and ambitions (DeVotta 2002).

20. In this research the definition of class is based on the simplest notions in Marxism. In Marxism class is mainly defined in relation to the ownership of means of production (land, capital). The broadly identified two classes are the bourgeoisie, who owns the means of production, and the proletariat, who provides the labour.
21. Refer to De Mel (2001) for a profound elaboration of the linkage between gender and nationalism in Sri Lanka. On the one hand, her work challenges the dominant gender-blind lenses applied to the nationalist discourse in Sri Lanka and, on the other, questions how gender is mediated though the intersections of cultural productions such as Sinhala-Buddhist nationalism and politics.
22. Galtung identifies eight such social fault lines.
23. For the various schemata employed to stratify the colonial society and the Ceylonese society until the end of the 1950s, refer to Roberts (1974).
24. The colonial bourgeoisie is the class whose economic wealth is directly linked to colonial expansion.
25. The comprador bourgeoisie is a fraction of the bourgeois class whose interests are constrictively linked to foreign imperialist capital and whose loyalties are completely bound politically and ideologically to foreign capital (Paultanzas 1973).
26. During the Portuguese (1505–1658), Dutch (1685–1798) as well as British (1802–1948) colonisations.
27. This regional distinction is still prevalent in Sri Lanka. People in the Kandyan areas (known as Nuwara Kalaviya) consider themselves superior to the people from the rest of the country. This is an important factor that is considered in politics as well as in marriage and the hierarchical ordering of the Sangha.
28. Here meant the non-interventionist stance they take in the economic sphere.
29. More details on the Tamil faction will be discussed under the section on Tamil nationalism.
30. The founder of the SLFP, S. W. R. D. Bandaranaike, is of low-country origin. His marriage to Sirimavo Ratwatte of up-country aristocratic origin elevated his low-country position. In Sri Lankan politics, strategic alliances through marriage are common as a way of enhancing social status.
31. Indigenous socialism is a sub-form of socialism of the mainstream and universal notion of socialism that is being adapted and adjusted to suit local conditions.
32. The Senanayake family belonged to Sri Lankan aristocracy from the time of British colonial rule of Ceylon.

33. This electoral political coalition was called the Mehajana Eksath Peramuna (MEP) and consisted of five social forces, that is, Sangha, *weda*, *guru*, *govi* and *kamkaru* (monks, indigenous Ayurveda physicians, teachers, peasants and labourers).
34. The MEP coalition constituted of the Sri Lanka Freedom Party, the Bhasha Peeramuna and the Viplaavakaree Lanka Sama Samaja Party (VLSSP).
35. Refers to the local bourgeoisie who act like their British masters. The literal translation of the term is the Brown British.
36. The Sinhala Only Act is a law that was passed in the Sri Lankan parliament in 1956. The law made Sinhala, which is the language of Sri Lanka's majority Sinhalese community and is spoken by over 70 per cent of Sri Lanka's population, the only official language of the country.
37. For statistics see Snodgrass in Hettige (2000).
38. Some argue that since the time Tamil elites left the Ceylon National Congress two years after its establishment as a future mode of representation, the structure of political competition and the pattern of political party formation has been exclusively ethnic. This had resulted in the party system revolving around competition between the two main Sinhalese parties for Sinhala votes on the one hand and the two main Tamil parties for Tamil votes on the other. This pattern continued until 1972 when the Federal Party and the Tamil Congress merged (Horowitz 1993: 4).
39. After the 1971 insurrection the JVP was banned by the ruling regime, which led them to operate underground. In 1988 the Jayawardena government lifted the ban.
40. This research understands that the fundamental interest of the ruling class is to reproduce its exploitative relations vis-à-vis the producing class. The JVP joining the ruling class is marked by an important change in the overall structure of the ruling class as it created a non-bourgeoisie faction within its membership.
41. According to Guy Standing, 'the precariat' is people living and working precariously, usually in a series of short-term jobs, without recourse to stable occupational identities, stable social protection or protective regulations relevant to them. He describes them as a dangerous class (2011).
42. Monaragala district, located in the Uva province, is inhabited by the Sinhalese, and is identified as one of the most underdeveloped and poverty-stricken districts of Sri Lanka.
43. I am grateful to Dr David Dunham, who pointed this out during a personal meeting.

44. It is important to note that the Sangha is not a monolithic entity in Sri Lanka. Especially in the Sri Lankan political realm, the Sangha is divided on a range of issues concerning secular life. One such issue is the participation of monks in politics (Seneviratne 2001).
45. By 'original', this respondent meant the Bandaranaike period.
46. They were Gomin Dayasiri, Champika Ranwaka, Suriyapperuma and Nalin De Silva.
47. By double game, this respondent referred to what these elites say to the people in Jaffna being one thing (promising to address the issues of the Tamils by using all the necessary means) and what they say to the Sinhalese political elites (appeasing and collaborating) in Colombo being another thing.
48. Amirthalingam was a leading Tamil politician, member of parliament and the leader of the opposition. In 1989, he was assassinated by the LTTE. Sivasubramian is a contemporary of Amirthalingam and another leader in Tamil politics.
49. The Tamil United Liberation Front (TULF) is a political party organised in 1972 by several Tamil political groups, including the All Ceylon Tamil Congress. In 1976, the TULF, or TUF, was joined by the Federal Party. The TUF changed its name to the TULF and adopted a demand for an independent state to be known as the 'secular, socialist state of Tamil Eelam'.
50. *Eelam* in Tamil means a 'separate state'.
51. Empire is attempts to theorise an ongoing transition from a 'modern' phenomenon of imperialism, centred around individual nation-states, to an emergent postmodern construct created among ruling powers which the authors call 'Empire' (the capital letter is distinguishing), with different forms of warfare (Hardt and Negri 2000).
52. Refers to making belief that ethnicity is the underlying and unchanging essence in nationalism.
53. For a detailed discussion of this relationship, refer to Sim (2007) that analysed the case of Singapore.

4

POLITICAL PATRONAGE

UNDERBELLY OF EVERYDAY POLITICS

This chapter presents a historical and contemporary account of patronage politics as an important hegemony-building strategy of the ruling elites in Sri Lanka. It sheds light on how the birth of the political party system during British colonial rule was closely tied to the elites' nurturing of the political patronage system in everyday and high politics that effectively combined the struggles for political power and domination at the centre and the material struggles of the lower classes in the peripheries.

THE ROOTS OF PATRONAGE POLITICS

The roots of contemporary manifestations of patronage politics in Sri Lanka can be traced back to the pre-colonial era (Swaris 1973). Pre-colonial patronage relations were transformed by colonial interference and administration, but strong elements of pre-colonial patronage survived through three long phases of European colonialisation (Portuguese, Dutch and British) and through the extraversion of economic exploitation, as well as the modernisation of state and society (Jayasundara-Smits 2010: 31). By the end of colonial rule, as in other former colonies, the trust of traditional authority structures in modern liberal political institutional structures implanted by the British was low. Uneven capitalist development in the country ensured that most Sri Lankans remained tied to the largely rural remains of the traditional agrarian society, where provision of needs was fashioned and negotiated through a web of well-established patronage relations that ran through the agrarian economy. The perpetuation of these relationships of patronage was not significantly altered during the years of British colonial rule, and even grew stronger after independence. The absence of a developed market economy and the lack of formal institutional mechanisms to mediate the affairs in the large agricultural sector are identified as factors that facilitated the strengthening effects of these networks in the post-colonial period, which was not unique to Sri Lanka (Archer 1990: 19; Boone 1994: 109).

According to one respondent, the contemporary dynamics of patronage politics rooted in patronage relations in the pre-colonial era is the result of people's experience with colonialism itself (R.1). As he opined further, although these institutions were embraced by the elite political leaders as pillars of the modern state and symbols of modernity, the rest of the society's ways of political communication, incorporation and participation were largely based on traditional and feudal means. These networks were instrumental in interest aggregation and satisfaction. Wickramasinghe observed, closer to independence, how negligence of peasant agriculture under British colonial rule enabled local elites to incorporate these neglected masses into formal political processes through a state-sponsored patronage system (2006: 303–04). In an era of representative democracy, the political future of the emerging elites largely depended on the successful inclusion of the greater segment of the peasantry into national politics. State patronage thus offered a promising strategy for political alliance-building between the ruling class and the lower-class masses, particularly the peasantry. State-sponsored land settlement projects carried out in the dry zones from the 1930s onwards was one example of this (Wickramasinghe 2006). For the Sinhalese nationalist politicians, especially those who are from low-country backgrounds, carrying out dry zone settlements was important and a matter of urgency as such a scheme would enable them to build a politically beneficial relationship with the Kandyan peasantry who perceived themselves to have had been treated unfairly under British policies that favoured their Tamil counterparts (Peebles 1990: 37). The continuation of dry zone land settlements in the subsequent period became an attempt by the Sinhalese elites to integrate the majority Sinhalese into the society in the absence of effective local institutions for doing so (Peebles 1990: 30). As Peebles further noted, these land settlement schemes are part and parcel of a form of welfare and preferential policies by the Sinhalese political elites targeting the Sinhalese peasantry and their votes to maintain their power (1990: 30).

Even after gaining independence, agriculture remained the main source of livelihood of many people who continued to live in the interiors of the country (Moore 1989: 180). Since pre-colonial times, the Goyigama caste (cultivator caste) enjoyed a privileged social and economic position as the dominant caste group, and capitalised on the traditional social relationships they had cultivated with lower social groups (Jayawardena 2007: 192). The only contender for their power was the *nouveau riche* (colonial bourgeoisie) from Karava (fisher caste) and Salagama (cinnamon peelers) castes. En route to independence, particularly from the 1920s onwards, with the power of wealth, traditional high-caste individuals began to enter into electoral politics (Jayantha 1992: 5). Despite their rhetorical support for local culture, values and traditions, most were more attracted to Western culture as essential to their own upward social mobility (Houtart 1976: 16). The introduction of universal suffrage to both men and women in 1931 made these Westernised elites depend on lower-class and low-caste masses to realise their own political ambitions.

A political strategy that combined ideology and economy was a necessity, and was secured by relying on traditionally cultivated networks based on kinship, caste and land-based village-centred social relations of production (Jayewardena 2007: 196). In the 1930s and 1940s, the colonial treasury was still under the tight control of the British, which pushed these new political elites to tap into traditional patronage routes as a means to mobilise the masses, given the lack of material resources available to distribute through patronage networks. Moore's work on the rural consciousness of the Sinhalese peasantry provides significant evidence for this claim (1985: 187). In contrast to India, Moore (1985) claims, the use of pre-colonial structures allowed for the non-antagonistic integration of rural populations into Sri Lankan national politics. The result was to reinforce the submissive relationships between elites and the peasantry in the early years of electoral politics (Moore 1985).[1]

The new political elites' exploitation of traditional patronage networks that had survived and were renewed through the Vidane, Muhandiram and Mudliyar systems, which were established by the Portuguese in the 17th century, mainly in the coastal areas based on pre-colonial caste-feudal social order (De Silva 2015: 1), was later turned into a pre-requisite for entry into the political party system (Peebles 1973: 64–65). The official demise of the Mudliyar systems in 1946 did not end the influence of such patronage networks for post-independence politics. Mudliyar families retained a major influence over people in rural localities, as the only ones with the requisite means to satisfy the material needs of the local population (Obeysekara 1967:

101). Even after been stripped of their titles, their amassed wealth and social power provided a useful foundation for the claim to represent local people. The Mudliyars remained in the rural sector and successfully mobilised the rural masses, transforming them into loyal supporters of newly formed national political parties. Among those who entered national politics were Illangakoon, Dias Bandaranaike and Obeysekara, from the traditional landlord class, alongside representatives from the new bourgeoisie, Jayawardena, Senanayake and Jayawickrama. All were from notable Mudliyar families and entered the national political scene using the former connections and influence implied by their positions (Peebles 1973; Roberts 1979; Jayawardena 1987a).

The Mudliyars, both traditional and new, were able to offer employment and other fringe benefits to workers on their estates. They undertook infrastructural projects, building schools, hospitals and temples. They also donated large sums to local charities run by the same elites and offered protection to village society (Jayantha 1992: 199). The influence of the *nouveaux riches* among the Mudliyars, those who had accumulated wealth during the colonial period, also termed the 'colonial bourgeoisie', went beyond the influence of the traditional Mudliyar class. This was because during British colonial rule, the new rich started to monopolise landholdings, wealth and administration posts, enabling them to emerge as the major dispensers in local patronage networks. One respondent confirmed that in post-colonial politics, the former power relations of the Mudliyar class were successfully translated into cultural, social and political capital in national politics (R.14). In urban areas, where there was no Mudliyar system in place, the new entrepreneurial classes created their own patronage networks (Swaris 1973: 77–78). Urban business-centred patronage networks incorporated the urban working class into urban sections of political parties, mobilising the mass of urban voters on behalf of bourgeois political leaders. These political mobilisation strategies, founded on old and new patronage networks, together formed a hybrid political system, based on the mass political participation of lower-class rural and urban voters in national politics.

Caste has also been identified as a primary shaper of the initial phase of post-colonial electoral politics, at least until 1977 (Jiggins cited in Jayantha 1992: 4). Perhaps this was stemming from the Portuguese and Dutch rules that had given a firm lease of life and injected social aura in terms of titles awarded to certain economically useful caste groups then (De Silva 2015: 2). Alongside other types of patronage networks, caste-based patronage was probably a small element in the entire web of patronage networks during this period.[2] Gunasinghe claims caste ideology having been used for political gains, as caste was presented as a protective cushion for poor peasant and agrarian labourers (1996b: 109). As he further argues, keeping caste consciousness alive proved a useful political-economic strategy for elites seeking to distract the peasants from the exploitative class relationships they were subjected to, especially in rural areas (Gunasinghe 1996f: 159). Caste can thus be said to be mobilised to mask unequal and exploitative economic and social relations of production. As one veteran observer of Sri Lankan national politics suggested, 'people choose their political representatives and alliances by considering a number of complex factors; therefore there is no single factor such as caste that we can point out as the most important factor for voters to make their electoral decisions' (R.14, also confirmed by R.13, R.14 and R.1). As one social historian also noted, modernity in Sri Lanka successfully eroded the traditional caste order, so that caste became a somewhat abstract notion in political discourses (Wickramasinghe 2006: 332). Complementing the work of Jayantha and Gunasinghe, a few respondents shared that the outcomes of elections in the post-independence era were not entirely dependent on caste identity, but on several factors (R.23; R.1; R.13; R.17; R.19).

PARTY-SPONSORED PATRONAGE

In a democratic political system, political parties are conventionally viewed as channels for interest satisfaction, arenas for new types of associations, and providers of communication and information networks (Weingrod 1968: 385). Patronage is often regarded as a 'traditional' political mobilisation tool (Thiruchelvam 1984a: 189–89; Thangarajah 2003). It was expected that, around the world, patronage would diminish with the effects of state and socio-economic modernisation in the 20th century (Roniger 2004: 353). However, as the work of Brow (1988), Dunham (1983), Spencer (1990) and Swaris (1973) on Sri Lanka has shown, the political salience of patronage in contemporary national politics has not diminished. Patronage systems in Sri Lanka were also investigated by other authors (Goodhand and Korf 2005; Korf 2010) more recently, in relation to 'tsunami politics.'[3] These latter studies explored linkages between local patronage politics and international disaster aid distribution.

However, the functions of patronage in politics extend beyond simple instrumental electoral mobilisation. In Sri Lanka, the pervasiveness of patronage systems is captured in everyday expressions such as 'politics as usual', or 'that is the way we are and that is how things are', common when corrupt practices arise on a daily basis. Gramsci encapsulated such 'common sense' notions as an intrinsic element in hegemony-building (1971: 419), and a similar notion is expressed by Bourdieu in his concept of the 'doxa'. This denotes 'what goes without saying and therefore goes unquestioned' (Bourdieu 1977: 166). Despite a common sense that patronage politics is 'natural' in Sri Lankan society, I claim that patronage politics is a relational place where hegemony-building strategies of the Sinhalese majority and their ruling elites frequently met at a seemingly innocent place that continued to nurture the material–ideological entanglements underlying patronage relations with a serious dose of ethno-nationalist and right-wing political culture.

Political parties function as mediators and integrators between society and the state, and tend to devote resources to encouraging the political mobility of previously demobilised constituencies. Yet where traditional patronage networks are widespread, and at the forefront of the governance of everyday associational life, patronage in politics can lead to a concern with the 'politics of development', rather than 'political development' as such (Weingrod 1968: 398). Weakly institutionalised political parties, relying on forms of patronage networks for their support, can have serious negative impacts on the governability of society, and on the quality of democratic representation (Epstein 2009: 338).

In Sri Lanka, the Donoughmore Constitution (1931–1947) paved the way for formal development of political parties (De Silva 1987: 221). Despite initial attempts by the local bourgeoisie in the legislative council to scrap proposals for franchise rights to lower-class members of the society, in 1931 the Donoughmore Commission granted universal adult suffrage. This move extended the voting rights to rural inhabitants and created a new power base for the Ceylon National Congress (CNC), whose leadership consisted of British loyalists. In this way the Donoughmore Commission's extension of the vote served to undermine an emerging urban labour movement and forms of class politics arising from labour protests and left-wing anti-colonial and socialist political organisations, mainly in urban areas (Wickramasinghe 2006: 204). The bourgeoisie in the CNC were brought closer to the rural masses through the universal franchise, and they depended on the rural votes to win elections. At the same time, earlier communal systems of indirect representation (the Mudliyar system and others) were abolished. As a result, bourgeois elites started to openly compete against each other in their efforts to secure political power. Previously established patronage networks along ethnic lines came to be the most obvious means of mobilising voters, and so were incorporated into party political 'machines', integral to building support for political parties through ethnically oriented alliance-building.

By 1946, shortly before independence, six major political parties took part in national elections. Of these, the Ceylon Labour Party (CLP), formed under the leadership of A. E. Gunasinghe, was the oldest, having been founded after the First World War in 1928. It represented a wide range of issues from calling for political independence, universal suffrage, political rights for all, regardless of race, religion or sex, to the recognition of trade unions and the right to strike along with minimum wages, pensions and other social legislation for the working class (Jayawardena 1974: 7). The most popular political party at this time, shortly after the war, was the Trotsyist Lanka Sama Samaja Party (LSSP), established in 1935. The leftist and Marxist orientation of the LSSP appealed mainly to lower-class and urban working-class voters. Dating back to the catastrophic economic depression of the 1929–1935 period, the LSSP at that time had carried out an impressive task of bringing relief to unemployed urban working-class communities, which were the most affected by the depression. LSSP party cadres also carried out a tremendous amount of grassroots work to alleviate poverty in the dry zone and in coastal fishing villages that were frequently hit by malaria and extreme weather conditions. This made the party very popular with communities living in these areas, who overwhelmingly expressed their appreciation in election periods around this time. Some scholars claim the Donoughmore Constitution was explicitly intended to undermine the influence of the LSSP and other leftist parties, who were able to mobilise to protect people from the worst effects of natural disasters and ill health (Jayawardena 1974: 8). Left-wing and Marxist parties were originally formed to provide leadership for anti-imperial struggles and were able to build a strong working-class movement across the island and between communities (Jayawardena 1974: 9). This movement became a nuisance for the British colonisers. The militancy of the LSSP, which organised frequent strikes in urban areas, had become a headache for the British. The LSSP manifesto demanded national independence, abolition of social and economic inequality and oppression, abolition of differences based on class, race, creed and sex, as well as socialisation (nationalisation) of the means of production, distribution and exchange (Jayawardena 1974: 29).

Political dynamics set in motion by the Commission's reforms eventually obliged the LSSP and other left-wing parties to more or less abandon their class-based ideological position, and succumb to strategies of political mobilisation that enabled them to compete with the rising conservative political parties such as the United National Party (UNP) and the Sri Lanka Freedom Party (SLFP) (R.13).[4] De Silva, an intellectual with a broadly right-wing outlook, suggests that urban-based Marxist and left-wing-oriented political parties could not have competed in rural areas because of their mostly secular attitude, which viewed religion as backward-looking and typical of the traditions of rural areas. The left-wing parties not only were not sympathetic towards religion, but also dismissed the linguistic and cultural aspirations of Sinhala-Buddhist nationalists, who were to replace English with Sinhala as the main official language shortly after independence, in 1956 (De Silva 2005: 610).

Leftist parties too bear some responsibility for their own demise, given the frequent in-fighting and party fracturing that took place. This tendency was not understood by most of their working-class supporters, for whom internal political schisms and divisive ideological stances and alliances simply weakened their faith in these parties (Moore 1997a: 1012). Political anxieties and uncertainties for the left could also be attributed to the emergence of largely rural-based competing political parties. The outcome was that some of the left-wing leadership started to rely on more traditional patronage relations, entering into new networks and alliances with more conservative, rural elites for electoral reasons. This rendered the majority of lower-class voters' subordination to the bourgeois elites at the top of the hierarchy of patronage. By 'selling out' to seek their fortunes in a new political game, the left also abandoned the politics of class solidarity, which had been so attractive to a growing and mainly secular urban working class. As one scholar lamented: 'the trajectory of the left, as a movement and as an idea can also be read as the gradual decline in ideological terms of a democratic and secular project unable to sustain the assault of the hegemonic forces of Sinhala-Buddhist exclusivism' (Wickramasinghe 2006: 202).

The United National Party (UNP) was the other political party contesting in the elections. It was the first non-Marxist political party established in Sri Lanka (Jayantha 1992: 5) and was formed shortly before the elections in 1946, just two years before gaining independence from the British. The

UNP is a blend of the colonial and traditional bourgeoisie classes. The UNP was supposed to be a political party representing the majority Sinhalese community, but at the same time acceptable to the minorities (De Silva 2005: 602). The founding father of the UNP, D. S. Senanayake has been a minister in the CNC (De Silva 1987: 222). Until the UNP's birth, there were no other political parties that took the lead in organising the majority Sinhalese in these segments of the society to enter into the political arena (Gunasinghe 1996d: 60). However, from the time of the party's creation, the leadership of the UNP was concentrated in the hands of the colonial bourgeoisie.[5] Although there were some initial signs of intra-party factionalism, in general the birth of the UNP could be considered a success story since it mobilised different bourgeois factions across caste and ethnic divides (Gunasinghe 1996d: 56). However, the elitist party leadership lacked deeper ties with ordinary people, especially those in rural areas. By including the Sinhala Maha Sabhas (Sinhala Higher Gathering), links were established with the rural peasantry. These were loosely organised cultural networks, pioneered by one of the UNP leaders, S. W. R. D. Bandaranaike (De Silva 1995: 532). Despite the party's humble beginnings, the UNP gradually became an elitist political party (Uyangoda 1993: 7). One left-wing respondent opined that the UNP could even be seen as 'notoriously imperialist' (R.13). In theory the UNP is an internally driven political party,[6] as it was founded by elites who occupied positions within the prevailing regimes (Shefter quoted in Piattoni 2001: 19).

The UNP's programmatic appeal was formulated around the development of the agricultural sector and addressing issues concerning the peasantry, which it still does today. Even more recent election manifestos promise to continue long-standing UNP commitments to promoting rural agricultural development (UNP Election Manifesto 2000; Pieris 2006: 202). Given the prevailing structural composition of Sri Lanka's economy, the rural agricultural sector remains significant, with a substantial share of the population being impoverished rural peasantry (Venugopal 2011: 72). The UNP's continued embrace of an agrarian-oriented reform programme is not surprising in the light of this. To overcome its elitist reputation, the UNP was keen to tap into popular patronage networks and become more socially connected. The UNP's consistent outreach to rural peasantry through various subsidies has played a major role in making Sri Lanka almost 90 per cent self-sufficient in food (Wickramasinghe 2006: 304). Intra-bourgeois factional conflicts often led to the questioning of the legitimacy of the UNP leadership, given their colonial bourgeoisie background. Meanwhile, while the UNP voiced the plight of the peasants, another political challenge came from Marxist political parties. They successfully integrated the marginalised urban working class into mass politics through loosely organised trade associations (Gunasinghe 1996d: 59–60). Around the same time, the plantation Tamils were integrated into the colonial national politics through trade unions specifically set up to channel their grievances.

In the first general election, as the urban-based Marxist political candidates voiced the rights of the neglected urban labourers as well as the Indian-origin Tamil plantation workers (De Silva 1995: 533), the UNP pushed further to voice the plight of the peasantry (Jayawardena 1985a: 47–49). This trend came to stay in national politics in the following decades, as mass incorporation of the peasantry into national politics through political parties became ever appealing due to the electoral strength of the rural society (Bastian 2003b: 203). However, compared to rival political parties, the UNP had an upper hand in mobilising the peasants as the UNP leader D. S. Senanayake was a respected figure among the peasantry due to his services as the chairman of the Land Development Ordinance Committee of 1935, under the British (De Silva 1995: 457). The various projects carried out by his office, under his direct supervision, such as the works of the Land Development Board and various land settlement schemes, showed his distinct bias towards the peasants (Samaraweera 1981: 150). Such state-sponsored projects in the peripheries formed a pool of powerful legitimising instruments and symbols for the elites in the centre (Shastri 1990: 62).

Table 4.1 illustrates the major occupational groups in Sri Lanka, indicating the numerical strength of each group in electoral politics. Until 1970, more than half of the working population was involved in agricultural occupations.[7] According to the International Labour Organization (ILO), approximately 80 per cent of Sri Lanka's population lives in rural areas and the agriculture sector is the largest employment provider, with more than 2.3 million employees (ILO Laborsta 2008).

In 1951, the UNP was split between Senanayake and his peasant-centric patronage network on the one side and S. W. R. D. Bandaranaike and his cultural networks on the other. Bandaranaike, who was of low-country origin and the traditional bourgeoisie class, became increasingly dissatisfied with Senanayake who tightly controlled the party and favoured the colonial bourgeois faction in the party. Bandaranaike grew even more disillusioned when he became aware of Senanayake's intention to promote his son Dudley

Table 4.1 Major occupational groups in Sri Lanka, 1921–1970 (% working population)

Occupation	1921	1946	1963	1969/1970
Farmers, fishermen, hunters and related	62.4	52.9	52.6	50.8
Draftsmen, production process	11.5	9.9	19.8	20.2
Sales and clerical	6.8	7.9	10.4	11.2
Service and recreation	6.5	9.0	8.2	7.4
Professional, technical, managerial and related	2.1	2.9	5.5	6.0
Transport and communication	3.5	3.6	3.2	3.7
Miners, quarrymen and related	0.2	0.3	0.2	0.5
Other and unspecified	7.0	13.3	1.2	0.2

Source: Roberts (1979: 443).

as his successor to lead the party (Gunasinghe 1996a: 234; De Silva 2005: 611). Bandaranaike left the UNP to form his own political party, the Sri Lanka Freedom Party (SLFP) (De Silva 1987: 223; Sabaratnam 2001: 165–66). In addition to personal ambitions, it is believed that Bandaranaike was motivated by the Westernised UNP leadership, whom he thought were unsympathetic to the cultural sensitivities of the majority of the rural Sinhalese (De Silva 1987: 223; Sabaratnam 2001: 167; De Silva 1987: 223). Bandaranaike's own political base was drawn mainly from his previously established networks within communal organisations, such as the Sinhala Maha Sabha, the Eksath Bhikku Peramuna (United Buddhist Front) and the Sinhala Jathika Sangamaya (Sinhala National Councils) (Sabaratnam 2001: 161–62). Yet the SLFP was more centre-left than right in its economic orientation, and this leftist element was probably a response to the party's impoverished rural base. The SLFP has often been identified as socialist-leaning, but as this account shows, its ideological and electoral base remained firmly founded on Sinhala-Buddhist nationalism, even if of a socialist variety (De Silva 2005: 610). Perhaps it is most realistic to suggest that Bandaranaike's new party occupied the centre ground between the UNP and the left-wing parties. As a strategic move by Bandaranaike, this represented a sought-for alternative to the political ideology of both the UNP and the left-wing parties, giving the SLFP its own brand of state-building and hegemony-construction.

Since left–right distinctions among political parties can appear quite confusing over time, it is perhaps useful to consider Table 4.2 which summarises self-descriptions provided by contemporary party leaders of the

Table 4.2 Party profiles of UNP and SLFP

Name of Party	Founded	Self-description	Support Base	Splits
United National Party (UNP)	1947	Nationalist Pragmatic	Entire population	1951, no major splits afterwards
Sri Lanka Freedom Party (SLFP)	1951	Socialist Nationalist	Teachers, doctors, farmers and workers	No splits

Source: Adapted from IDEA (2007: 72).

two main political parties. This helps to highlight their own perceptions of what the primary ideological divisions have been. The table is presented with the proviso that such self-perceived descriptions of the ideologies of the two major political parties cannot be equated with these parties' actual practices in electoral politics, which can tell a different story.

The SLFP's combination of nationalism and left-wing economics produced a political ideology capable of mobilising many previously marginalised forces in rural Sri Lankan society, particularly the rural petty bourgeoisie. Members of this intermediary class included rural power mediators with large established patronage networks in the interior of the country (Moore 1997a: 1011). Any political strategy mobilising this group required two elements: a material reward and an ideological appeal. The material component of the SLFP's strategy mainly operated through distribution of state-sponsored social and economic welfare provisions. This is what is meant by 'socialist'. Thanks to the influence of the Buddhist revivalist movement during the resistance to British colonialism (see Chapter 3), Sinhala-Buddhist ideology was already successfully internalised by the rural lower classes. This made it easier for the SLFP to appeal to the same ideological sentiment as part of its own political strategies. Upon assuming office as prime minister in 1955, Bandaranaike's first task was to deliver on promises he had made during election campaigning. 'Mass clientelist benefits' were offered to the Sinhalese, particularly through the controversial Sinhala Only Act of 1956. This was in many ways an example of 'pork barrel legislation', defined in ethnic terms, and paving the way for opening up employment opportunities in the state sector for those who spoke Sinhala, rather than English.

Not surprisingly, from the moment of its enactment and implementation, the Sinhala Only Act became a major point of contention between the Sinhalese and the Tamils. In subsequent decades it sowed the seeds of inter-ethnic animosities and consolidated a sense of collective grievances among Tamils, which would help bring about the onset and then would prolong civil war in the island (Sabaratnam 2001: 161–79). By passing the Act, Bandaranaike was responding to Sinhalese grievances that dated back to the British colonial period. By reversing the British policy of favouring Tamils, who more often spoke English, Bandaranaike justified new grievances among the Tamils, who now felt excluded by the formal advantage for Sinhala in public policies, reinforced by subsequent right-wing UNP governments' more open appeals to Sinhala-Buddhist nationalism.

The Language Act of 1956 also demonstrated Bandaranaike's political shrewdness in identifying and linking struggles from the periphery with his own struggle at the centre. His ambition was to forge dynamic alliances that could break the domination of the UNP. In the literature, it is the Sinhala Only Act of 1956 that is primarily regarded as an ethnically motivated policy (Jayawardena 1985a: 59; Thangarajah 2003: 21; Wickramasinghe 2006: 271). However, the Language Act was offered to the working and peasant class of Sinhala society and also had strong 'ethnic' appeal as a form of mass clientelism or pork barrel legislation. Wickramasinghe remarks that the Language Act was targeted towards capturing a specific social group of low-caste and low-class background (2006: 243). This way, the language legislation can be seen as a political incorporation strategy targeting the rural Sinhalese voters which helped the factionalised elites to expand their narrow political bases, and, from the vantage point of Gramsci's hegemony, to form a new historical bloc[8] (Gramsci 1971: 418).

For the first decade after independence, a mass political mobilisation strategy enacted through selectively redistributive legislation was becoming a winning formula for Sinhalese elites to pursue political domination and hegemony-building with the Sinhalese lower-class segments. Some respondents commented that the path the SLFP and its ruling political elites adopted at this time was capable of achieving only short-term political gains (R.11; R.14; R.16). A mass patronage strategy embarked upon by the SLFP, and infused with Sinhala-Buddhist ideology, also provoked growing anti-hegemonic agitation, especially across the minority Tamil community, which became united in opposition to the preferential populist measures for Sinhalese Sri Lankans. In time, this created a permanent chasm in the political party system, with a party-based patronage system distributing on an ethnic basis, and an opposition system based on a sense of grievance and alienation of the Tamils from mainstream party politics (IDEA 2007: 39).

The emergence of a Tamil armed movement in the early 1970s coincided with violent anti-bourgeois uprising by Sinhalese youth in 1971. Both exposed the shortcomings of the elites' manipulative strategies geared at gaining consent, but mainly incorporating rural groups at the margins of society, and not engaging sufficiently with the urban working class or Tamil communities.

The mobilisation of the law and social policy for exclusionary ends did not start with Bandaranaike. Before Bandaranaike, already in 1948 the UNP had passed a Citizenship Act, and the following year the Indian and Pakistani Residents Citizens Act and the Parliamentary Elections Amendment Act were also passed (De Silva 2005: 605), denying citizenship to more than 700,000 people; about 11 per cent of the population were denied citizenship and made stateless. These laws were enacted to safeguard the interests of a group of Sinhalese known as Kandyans (De Silva 2005: 605) who had lost most of their lands when the British introduced the plantation economy into Sri Lanka. The UNP's fears of an 'imbalance' between the Sinhala-Kandyan voter base and Indian-origin Tamil citizens led to the reform of the law.[9] Granting citizenship rights and the franchise to plantation workers of Indian Tamil origin was not a favourable or profitable project for the ruling political elites (De Silva 2005: 605) until the nationalisation of the foreign-owned plantations in the mid-1970s was completed. Nationalisation of plantations released this population group from the political and administrative control of foreign plantation owners, the main patrons of plantation workers. Nationalisation provided a unique opportunity for President Premadasa. He later led a UNP government and enacted a new law in November 1989 that finally granted citizenship rights to a large number of Indian Tamils in the plantation sector. This helped him win a large number of votes, mobilising a new political alliance with plantation Tamils. Premadasa, who was of lower-class background, was thus able to stand up to the Sinhalese elites who tried to bully him.[10] This specific case of Premadasa granting franchise rights to plantation Tamils of Indian origin suggests the willingness of Sinhalese political elites to invent new strategies of political inclusion, depending on the nature of their own personal and political struggles. Since 1989, when Tamil plantation workers received franchise rights, in all elections they tended to vote as instructed by their leader, Saumiyamurthi Thondaman.[11] He had served under four governments since 1978 and remained as the party leader of Ceylon Workers' Congress (1939–1999), which represents exclusively the plantation Tamil workers. His strategy was to jockey between the two main political parties, the UNP and the SLFP, in order to obtain as many personal and group benefits as possible. He controlled millions of votes in the plantation sector, located in the up-country. Under Thondaman's direction, plantation workers often voted for the UNP, though this voting pattern shifted after political factions emerged in plantation sector politics in the background of growing political rivalry between Thondaman and his rival, Chandrasekaran.

Standardisation of university education under the Bandaranaike government had clear electoral goals. University education was free from the 1940s, although with great disparities in school facilities and the quality of education in different regions of the island. As Bandarage observed, traditionally schooling in Sri Lanka was designed for the bourgeoisie (2009: 61). However, the standardisation policy had ethnically sensitive effects on the Tamils, whose education opportunities were now curtailed compared with in the past. In this way, educational reform in the higher education sector became another form of pork barrel politics – the ruling party channelling public money to particular constituencies based on political considerations, at the expense of broader public interests in search for new political alliances with the Sinhalese ruling elites across the Sinhalese community (Bastian 1985: 231). The main beneficiaries of such changes were the younger generation of the Sinhalese bourgeois class, who could now enrol in greater numbers in university science faculties, previously dominated by the offspring of the Tamil upper classes. The positive effects of this policy were limited to the children of upper-class families, because pursuing a science curriculum at university level was only possible for these children who attended schools with better state-sponsored science facilities (Bastian 1985: 231). Bastian interprets this as a move to expand opportunities for upper-class Sinhalese, rather than an attempt at wider redistributive justice for the entire Sinhalese community. The class-based motivation of the standardisation policy is crucial to understanding its effects on the ruling Sinhalese elites' hegemony-building strategies, which required continuously striving to retain the support of the upper classes and the educated.

Next, Buddhism was given a prominent place in the first republican constitution of 1972. It says, 'The Republic of Sri Lanka shall give to Buddhism the foremost place and accordingly it shall be the duty of the State to protect and foster the Buddhism, while assuring to all religions the rights granted by Articles 18 (b)' (Constitution of Sri Lanka, 1972). This can be seen as another measure to woo the majority Sinhala-Buddhists by the ruling regime that was under serious pressure from the rural Sinhalese youth. This constitutional measure is primarily presented as a cause for ethnic divisions between the majority Sinhala-Buddhists and the Tamils (Coomaraswamy 2005: 157). The special status of Buddhism in the 1972 Constitution can be seen as a strategic response of Sinhalese political elites to the Sinhalese youth, who openly challenged the elites' dominance over political affairs. By the 1970s, state-led capital accumulation was running into serious trouble, and this made it more difficult for the ruling elites to reproduce the previous strategy of simply extending patronage networks by dispensing material benefits to their allies and supporters. The constitutional measure may have been calculated to undercut the mainly rural Sinhala-Buddhists youth, who had taken up arms by this time against the Sinhalese ruling elites. Capturing these ethnic implications of the new constitution, Jayathilake sums up as follows:

> ... faced with the loss of political support due to unfulfilled promises and economic hardships, it is not surprising that Sirimavo Bandaranaike's government already elected on a Buddhist-Sinhalese nationalist platform chose to 'play the ethnic card' even more strongly. Policies that equated Sinhalese nationalism with Sri Lankan nationalism [were] legally enshrined in a new Republican Constitution. (1999: 68)

Although the new constitution could not address youth demands for upward social and economic mobility, by making a serious ideological appeal to this group, it took a step in the direction of advancing Sinhalese ruling elites' overall political hegemony. Some radical economic and social reforms were implemented after the 1971 Sinhalese youth insurrection, such as the land reform laws of 1972, and nationalisation of plantations from the mid-1970s onwards. The state increased its control over trade and industry, establishing what looked like a socialist state. Yet political factions remained divided, and economic conditions were about to be hit by the OPEC crisis[12] and the first global economic recession since the Second World War. Agrarian reform in 1972 was a direct response to the 1971 insurrection, which placed the land question and priorities of rural development at the forefront of political power struggles.[13] These reforms enabled ruling political elites to address some injustices in agrarian property structures, tackling traditional elites' positions of dominance. In the first phase of implementation, from August 1972, the new land law was to take over individual plots of land exceeding a ceiling of 50 acres. In 1975, during the second phase of implementation, the SLFP government nationalised all foreign- and company-owned estates (Gunasinghe 1999: 55). In Herring's view, these land reform measures were motivated as much by the need to increase resources available for the everyday politics of patronage and partisan manipulation tied to election processes as by concerns for social justice in the rural areas (Herring 1987: 327).[14]

HEGEMONY OF THE RIGHT

In the late 1960s, new political parties entered the political stage, generating a new set of dynamics in the previously comfortable post-independence bipartisan party system. Almost inevitably, a struggle ensued in which the two dominant political parties vied to retain their established political clienteles. The Janatha Vimukthi Peramuna (JVP) was created in the late 1960s (also discussed in Chapter 3), and soon was seen as a hindrance to the dominance of bourgeois elite politics and the overall hegemonic political project of Sinhalese elites. The JVP[15] was an odd combination of Marxist ideology and Sinhala-Buddhist nationalist orientation, professing a radical brand of socialism based on liberation of the oppressed masses, while at the same time strongly influenced by Sinhala nationalism (Pieris 2006: 340).

JVP cadres and the leadership were primarily drawn from the lower castes, and from the rural petty bourgeoisie (lower middle class) and the urban proletariat. The JVP was associated with armed insurrections against elites and the bourgeoisie state in the early 1970s, these uprisings expressing the grievances of unresolved class contradictions in Sri Lankan politics, and resentment at continued bourgeois domination of the state and state resources. During two insurrections, the JVP gained considerable electoral support from the rural youth belonging to oppressed caste communities at the margins of Sinhalese society. The 1971 insurrection in particular exposed cracks in the ruling elites' hegemony-building efforts, and exposed a level of political disintegration and vulnerability within the Sinhalese political leadership, which had ignored sharp class contradictions in the past (Jayawardena 1985a: 84; Wickramasinghe 2006: 235, 240). Violent suppression of the insurrections by the army and police under the SLFP was accompanied by a subsequent ban on the JVP, which forced the party underground until 1988. A brutal crackdown against leaders of the uprising showed the readiness of the ruling Sinhalese elites to deploy violence when their own ideological manipulation and consent-building measures started to fall apart.

As a new political party, the JVP struggled to compete with rival political parties who already had established political dominance via their long-cultivated and sophisticated patron–client networks. The JVP's political leadership did not belong to the traditional land-owning class and was unable to cultivate the kinds of networks the landlord class could rely on. Nor did any JVP leader have access to the kinds of state or economic resources needed to dispense the patronage required to mobilise voters beyond their own constituencies of the marginalised (Chandraprema 1991: 74). In comparison to the old left, the Marxist political parties led by members of the comprador and traditional bourgeoisie class, JVP leaders had few advantages that would enable them to thrive in a world of politics still dominated almost entirely by competing bourgeois political elites. As Pieris observed,

> JVP's social base, which stemmed from the poorer strata of the rural society, was of great significance. JVP cadres are also distinctly from the torturable class and are accustomed to physical hardships that have built their capacity to live frugally. (1999: 168)

Based on these strengths, the JVP chose to awaken class consciousness as their main political mobilisation strategy, entering the national political scene by attempting to appeal to a wide spectrum of the oppressed, and threatening to fracture Sinhalese society along class lines. The legacy of the Sinhala-Buddhist nationalist mobilisation, however, meant that appealing to class sentiments alone was not easy. Due to tutelary, custodial and paternalistic attitudes towards the lower classes, especially the peasantry, administrative and political elites had ensured a virtual lack of effective representation of these classes and their occupational interests. In sum, mobilising class consciousness was an uphill struggle, since any sense of a 'class for itself' among this segment of the population had been co-opted through clientelistic forms of politics (Moore 1985: 3, 5).

Under these circumstances, the JVP resorted to an extreme form of Sinhala-Buddhist ideology, which it attempted to marry with raising class consciousness among the most marginalised sections of the Sinhalese population. This chauvinist Sinhala-Buddhist stance of the JVP affected the tone of national politics, not in the direction of class, but by provoking the other main Sinhalese political parties (the SLFP and the UNP) to elevate their ideological pitch, transforming the outlook of the state into forms of renewed ethnic chauvinism (Chandraprema 1991: 99). Despite this, or perhaps because of this unsustainable competition, the JVP's performance over the decades in national politics was lacklustre, suggesting their continued inability to appeal to an identifiable winning block of the Sinhala electorate. And as the JVP elites came to find ways to extend their own networks of personal patronage, the top cadres of the JVP became progressively most anti-Tamil in their stance, and softened their former anti-bourgeois tone considerably.

Since the early 1990s, the JVP has been a coalition partner in various SLFP-led governments. As a result, party elites were able to access state resources and dispense material benefits and build their own political alliances. This enabled the JVP to survive as a party, but only just. As Tamil and Muslim political parties increasingly started to take part in coalition governments, often led by either the UNP or the SLPF, the JVP's relative advantage as a minor partner began to diminish. The JVP splintered, and this resulted in the creation of the National Freedom Front (NFF), further undermining the party's overall bargaining powers with the main parties. Despite becoming even more strident in their ideological pronouncements, the JVP was in decline.

Similar observations can be made with regard to the Jathika Hela Urumaya (JHU), another new political party (launched in 2004) that was discussed in Chapter 3. Its support base consisted of Sinhalese middle-class conservatives who felt threatened by rapid economic change, and mainly Buddhist youth. In terms of its political ideology, the JHU adopted an even more extreme form of Sinhala nationalism than other political parties (Deegalle 2006: 238). The party leadership was publicly critical of contemporary state structures, the culture of Sri Lankan politics and the corruption of Sinhalese political elites (Deegalle 2006). Their highest priority seems to have been establishment of a renewed, 'pure' Buddhist state. The newest creation on the political scene, the ideological path taken by the JHU was a worrying signal for the direction of future state- and hegemony-building. Although small, the JHU had a significant impact in changing the direction of Sinhalese elite politics overall. The role played by Buddhist monks in the new party, by openly promoting right-wing politics, reinforced the idea of Sinhala-Buddhist hegemony over the state, popularising and legitimising this tendency more broadly in Sri Lankan society. During the 2004 general elections, for example, the JHU secured 6 per cent of the total votes and obtained just five seats in the national legislature. This posed a serious threat to the JVP, which relied on a similarly dissatisfied voter base, using similar political mobilisation strategies loaded with Sinhala-Buddhist nationalist sentiments. As one respondent in this study stated,

> JVP and JHU both appealing to the ideological sentiments is not surprising, because the people have already developed strong affiliations with the UNP and SLFP. And these people hardly shift their party loyalties. These loyalties are formed on a mixture of material and symbolic patronage. In Sri Lanka there is about 20% of floating voters, so the entire political competition is about winning this 20 per cent of floating voters. Winning this 20 per cent is crucial for winning elections. (R.10)

By participating in coalition governments, both the JVP and the JHU have been able to disproportionately influence political reforms, introducing major variations in political party systems (IDEA 2007: 60). A number of respondents pointed out that such alliance-making between larger and smaller parties has been increasingly dependent on the exchange of material benefits between political parties and established political elites, for example, through the distribution of ministerial portfolios with lucrative opportunities for patronage, through diplomatic postings, and key posts in public sector ventures. Sometimes money is simply given to individuals within the parties their parties, denoting a strengthening of horizontal patronage systems.

Alliance-building through coalitions of political parties became much more evident after proportional representation (PR) was introduced by J. R. Jayawardene in 1978. Initially this measure was introduced to enhance the participation of minority Tamil and Muslim political parties in politics. However, PR effectively prevents pendulum-like swings during elections and tends to undermine permanent ideological commitment to any one political party. The PR system can be seen as having a positive effect in the sense that it obliged all political parties, large and small, to seek consensus and form coalitions in order to share power and form a government (Coomaraswamy 2005: 167). On the flip side, the number of small parties grew within these political coalitions and their demands for a larger share of patronage benefits led to a deepening of corruption, as coalitions became more costly to form. This marked a worrisome aspect of PR-based politics, and suggests a scenario for the main political parties of declining opportunities to generate the growing finances needed to sustain alliances with multiple smaller parties. As in a number of other South Asian countries, in Sri Lanka, the rising costs of coalition-building are largely met by using state resources and involve the wider dissemination of corrupt practices throughout the local economy. This conclusion was validated by almost all respondents of this study (around 90 per cent) as well as by a report released by IDEA (2007: 60).

As demands made by coalition partners to major political parties increase, the number of cabinet ministerial portfolios and the number of state-sector employees also rose. Both these elements of governance form the major issue in deals negotiated between allied parties, involving bargaining for specific awards for key party cadres and their networks of supporters (R.1; R.2; R.10; R.11; R.13; R.14; R.16; R.23; R.24; R.25). With the rising cost of coalition-building, there was almost inevitably a decline in the overall material benefits the state could offer to other social groups outside the political party system. For those in business or without significant political affiliations, there was very little opportunity to obtain public funds. A prominent Sri Lankan constitutional lawyer summarised the situation:

> Today in Sri Lanka, politics is no longer about contest of ideas. There is a great deal of power of political patronage where the interests of some and few are looked after by political actors. This system of patronage politics has undermined the ideals of politics. (R.12)

Distinctly negative outcomes of this deepening of political patronage between party elites included a distinct tilt towards more right-wing discourses and policies, and a deepening of social and economic inequalities between classes as well as between urban and rural Sri Lankan society. Those who failed to consent to the dominant political arrangements and systems were faced with the coercive use of state security forces to ensure compliance. Elimination of oppositional actors through the use of violence was no longer ruled out. These conditions deepened the democratic deficit and led to the malfunctioning of democratic institutions even before the onset of civil war. As the main mechanisms setting the rules of the political game, democratic institutions tended to feed into intensifying factionalism among the smaller political parties that survived. Such divisions and splintering were furthermore encouraged by the larger, traditional political parties, in the hope of reducing the costs of building coalitions. As smaller political parties split, traditional political parties could offer individual patronage to splinter groups, instead of to the entire party leadership. In the arena of electoral politics, such manipulative political dynamics tended to increase political, social tensions, and party fragmentation was frequently accompanied by violence. Some examples come from fragmentation of minority ethnic-identity-based political parties, such as the Sri Lanka Muslim Congress (SLMC) dividing into several factions resulting from intra-party leadership struggles between Rauf Hakeem, M. H. M. Ashraff, and the National Unity Alliance (NUA), the latter led by Ms. Ferial Ashraff, the widow of the late M. H. M. Ashraff. Among the Tamil political parties, the Tamil People's Liberation Tigers (TMVP) split into the Karuna and Pillaian factions and the JVP gave birth to another faction, the National Freedom Front (NFF)[16]

This fragmented picture of political parties is also key to understanding the ruling elites' increasing reliance on the ideological manipulation of their constituencies. As the intra-elite competition to secure the biggest share of material benefits to a political party, smaller parties like the JVP and the JHU's use of Sinhala-Buddhist nationalist ideology is noted. The ability of the main political parties to include or exclude the JVP and the JHU depends on the scale of the political sacrifices they have to make to accommodate or exclude other non-Sinhalese minority ethnic political parties. As the recent trends in politics of coalition-making in Sri Lanka suggest, deals with minority ethnic political parties help exclude the JVP and the JHU, hence increasing the value of ethnic-based minority political parties. Further the minority political parties can easily opt for soft bargaining that will undermine the often hard bargaining positions of the Sinhalese minority political parties, thus pushing these parties to elevate their ideological drumbeat of Sinhala-Buddhist nationalism and chauvinistic slogans for their own political survival. The JVP and the JHU's ideological propaganda can be easily sold to the voters who are faced with declining trickle-down effects of material benefits from the political elites in power. Therefore, they can be also easily mobilised against granting any material concessions to ethnic minorities by other Sinhalese political elites.

FROM WELFARE TO WARFARE

In Sri Lanka the state welfare policy is known as the sacred cow of policymaking, denoting its untouchability and the danger electorally of attempting to remove or cut welfare in the political agenda of any political party or alliance of parties in government (Kelegama 2000: 1484). Against the backdrop of ethnic conflict, some would argue that despite its limitation in promoting economic growth, a welfare-based set of policies made it possible to maintain the social peace for some decades (Dunham and Jayasuriya 2000: 97).

The history of state welfare policies can be traced back to the Donoughmore reforms of 1931. Indeed, until the late 1970s, Sri Lankan welfare programmes continued to be greatly influenced by pre-war British social policy norms, concerned with countering rapid declines in the local population's living conditions as a result of the economic depression of the 1930s. The near-collapse of the plantation system was also of great concern at that time, alongside scarcities in essential goods, widespread unemployment and a malaria epidemic in the mid-1930s. All these crises combined to slow down economic recovery, and resulted in the decision to introduce state welfare policies. In addition, the Second World War plunged the economy into crisis, disrupting external trade and led to diminishing resources as the British siphoned out funds to support the war effort. Under such conditions, rescue and relief became a priority in the areas of education, health care, food supply and peasant agriculture (Pieris 2006: 147).

Even after independence, colonial-style state welfare policies remained in place and were continued by Sri Lankan political elites. In addition to distribution of essential items, such as a universal rice ration, welfare packages included opportunities in the educational sector, land grants, and subsidised seed and fertilisers for peasant producers. Although state welfare policies did not target any particular community, the focus was especially on certain vulnerable and underprivileged occupational groups such as the peasantry, most of whom were Sinhalese (Wickramasinghe 2006: 303). There are contending views as to why such marked welfare policies continued to be pursued by the ruling elites after independence. Pieris summarises that these debates represent two different paradigms, the first the 'third world development paradigm' and the second concerned with varying commitments of local party politics (2006: 148). In analysing this issue, McCourt emphasises the noble goals underlying Sri Lankan welfare policies, and warns against reading social welfare as little more than a euphemism for mass distribution of state patronage (2007b: 434). To quote McCourt,

> It seems plausible to suggest that altruism combined with the ideology of Fabian socialism that dominated the formative independence period to produce a not wholly self-serving welfarist conviction that the State should provide, irrespective of the electoral benefits of so doing, which

has at least contributed to the impressive basic human development statistics, such as life expectancy. (2007b: 434)

This positive evaluation is not shared by all analysts, however. Others point to the politicisation of state welfare policies under the party system as an ineffective tool of genuine political mobilisation (R.1). The basic orientation towards a state welfare policy has generally as its rationale the aim of contributing both to social equity and economic efficiency (Abeyratne 2000: 20). Yet a more dynamic view of Sri Lanka's post-colonial politics suggests that political goals started to supersede these more noble economic and social goals at some point around the 1950s or so. One scholar who supports this kind of argument is Kearney, who shows how welfare policies were used by the ruling class to strengthen pre-existing patronage networks on which they depended electorally (Kearney 1973). As Swaris (1973) also suggests, the Sri Lankan welfare state was used paternalistically from the colonial period onwards by a (colonial) bourgeoisie keen to legitimise their newly acquired political status as the leaders of Sri Lanka and counter the accusation that their outlook was neo-colonial. Since their rule was socially and culturally contested by competing local political forces, welfare policies remained an important form of government legitimation after independence (Kearney 1973: 77). Bastian views the ideology behind welfarism as tied from early on to popular politics targeting the Sinhalese peasantry (1993: 11).

Overall, whatever their original motivation, it seems clear that strong welfare-based state policies reinforced existing cultures of dependency between patrons (the political elites) and their clients (the lower classes, and society at large). Over time, such dependency could be shown to politicise state institutions, and resulted in budgeting and state policies being centred on the principle of equity in resource distribution for the majority of Sri Lankan society. As one respondent of this research observed,

> from the beginning, the state was politicised in Sri Lanka, people voted for welfarism as they gained material benefits out of it. Since 1931, upon receiving the universal franchise, the political identities were created based on 'what we receive and what we get by giving mentality'. (R.1)

As in many other parts of the post-colonial world (Hopkin 2006: 16), state welfare policies originated in the 1930s, were adopted by the post-colonial ruling elites, and soon transformed into a strategy that dispensed benefits to secure mass clientelism, which was intended to benefit the least privileged in society. The 'clients' in turn had little more to trade besides their votes. As Shanmugaratnam points out, welfare-inspired nationalist economic policies of successive Sinhalese-led governments, including the regime of Jayawardena from 1977, not benefitted the Sinhalese alone, whatever the ethno-nationalist ideology proclaimed. In his view, for example, the import-substitution policies of 1970 to 1977 significantly benefitted Tamil farmers in the north as well as Sinhalese farmers (Shanmugaratnam 1993: 11, 13). Table 4.3 provides some statistical evidence for the claims made regarding the overall improvement of the quality of life as a result of state welfare policies at individual and economic levels.

This begs the question with regard to state welfare policies in Sri Lanka: have short-term benefits of welfare policies outweighed their long-term costs on democracy and democratic state-building? It is safe to argue that, at the beginning of its implementation, intended welfare benefits reached the least underprivileged sections of the society, hence denoting a vertical pattern of state resource distribution. During this initial period, no other Asian country went as far as Sri Lanka in the direction of funding universal welfare provisions in the form of free health care and education, as well as welfare provisions targeted at the poorest (Gunasinghe 1996d: 55). However, as competition for government positions and access to state resources began to intensify among the ruling elites since the early 1970s, and with an ailing economy, the dynamics of operationalising state welfare policies underwent a metamorphosis. Sinhalese political elites who captured state power mainly by using state resources to distribute resources through their patronage networks, started to use these same resources to benefit their close political allies, leading to growing misuse of public funds. Perhaps in the Marxian sense of the word, one can interpret this transformation among the ruling

Table 4.3 Improvement in physical quality of life in Sri Lanka, 1946–1981

Year	1946	1981
Population (in 1,000s)	6,657	14,487
Crude death Rate (per 1,000)	20.3	5.9
Life expectancy (at birth, years)	42.2	69.9
Infant mortality (per 1,000 live births)	94	30
Adult literacy (%)	57.8	87.4

Source: Adapted from Pieris (2006: 149).

elites that began to be composed of different class backgrounds as 'class for itself' or, as Gramsci suggested in his work on hegemony, the emergence of a new historical bloc under the tutelage of a dominant group whose dominance has been already established over a very long period, which can be traced back to the transformation of the economy during the British colonial period. Decades of welfare-based policies imposed an increasing tax burden on the local economy, and although in this way the state accumulated wealth, it was mostly spent to pump prime the welfare system and systems of nationalist economic government control.

As Waldner notes, resources are increasingly distributed more thinly, between welfare-based coalition-building with the masses, and a parallel transformation of state institutions and budgets, gradually redeployed as artefacts of coalition-building, neither of these strategies being able to promote economic development (1999: 3). In the light of his analysis, one can suggest that also in the case of Sri Lanka, state welfare policies and state patronage as a tool of coalition-building entrapped political elites in a scheme of their own making, one that impoverished a heavily taxed economic base. The highly competitive inter-elite conflicts have compelled each government to continue this double-edged expenditure strategy, which was renewed over time in different ways under alternating elite control. This two-pronged strategy to gain support from the masses and to buy off contending political elites set in motion a set of dynamics that sowed the seeds of longer-term rising inequalities, right-wing politics, economic underdevelopment and under-investment, amidst a rising trend of elite predation of state resources.

The rise and gradual demise of welfare policies for the least privileged were determined by global as well as domestic economic conditions. When the UNP proposed a mixed economy in 1947 and introduced the Six Year Economic Development Plan (1947–1953), the world policy paradigm was broadly supportive of such mixed-economy initiatives (Kelegama 2000: 1480). This plan entrusted the state with a large share of total expenditure, mainly for social welfare, free education, food subsidies and free public health services. As Kurian points out, the plan included a commitment to develop economic infrastructure and overcome the structural weaknesses of the colonial economy, but little was done to address these two issues despite these commitments (Kurian n.d.: 2). Instead, until the mid-1960s, the substantial amount of wealth accumulated by the national treasury by continually exploiting existing economic activities were distributed as welfare benefits by the ruling regimes, with a gradual expansion of existing welfare provisions over time (Kelegama 2000: 1477). In the early 1950s, certain global conditions resulted in sudden positive economic conditions, notably the unexpectedly favourable price of rubber because of the outbreak of the Korean War (1950–1955).[17] As prices rose in the world market, so did possibilities for taxing rubber exports (Lakshman 1987: 11; Gunatillake 2000: 134). The Korean War also led many import restrictions imposed on Sri Lanka during the Second World War to be removed, giving a boost to international trade, which provided another source of tax revenue (Pieris 2006: 179).

Then in the 1970s, Sri Lanka's economy experienced a series of mostly negative global economic shocks. The first was the 1973 oil crisis, which had an adverse effect on the overall financial situation of the country (Jayathilake 1999: 61; Central Bank of Ceylon quoted by Pieris 2006: 180). High interest rates and inflation followed, interrupting the smooth operation of state welfare policies and constraining the scope and scale of distribution and the size of the target population reached.

As shown in Table 4.4, from as early as the late 1950s, the Sri Lankan trade-based economy began to stagnate in terms of growth, and to decline markedly in terms of its significance in per capita terms (Lakshman 1985: 18; Jayawardena 1985a: 84; Wickramasinghe 2006: 243). The country's reliance on the old colonial economic infrastructure and primary resources, which continued to be exploited, was soon insufficient to ensure that the booming population could be fed adequately. Economic decline coincided with a steady increase in population in the late 1950s, 1960s and 1970s, as shown in Table 4.5.

Table 4.4 Change in external resources, 1945–1975

Year	USD Million	LKR Million	Per Capita (LKR)
1945	379	1,260	189.3
1950	280	1,100	147.6
1955	258	980	115.1
1960	114	422	42.7
1965	92	312	28.0
1970	68	197	15.7
1975	108	133	9.8

Source: Adapted from Abeyratne (2000: 28).

Note: The rupee values are in constant rupee values, deflated by import price index (1945 = 100). These figures are also adjusted for changes in import prices and the increase in population (Abeyratne 2000: 28).

Table 4.5 Population size and rate of growth in Sri Lanka, 1871–1981

Year and Date of Population Census	Average Annual Growth Rate (%)
1871 March 27	-
1881 February 17	1.4
1891 February 26	0.9
1901 March 01	1.7
1911 March 10	1.4
1921 March 18	0.9
1931 February 26	1.7
1946 March 19	1.5
1953 March 20	2.8
1963 July 08	2.6
1971 October 09	2.2
1981 March 17	1.7
2001 July 17	1.2

Source: Department of Census and Statistics (2010); Population and Housing Survey (2010: 2).

As welfare expenditure struggled to keep up with this growing population, the results are shown in Table 4.6. This shows that state welfare expenditures declined from around 30 per cent to around 20 per cent of total expenditure between 1955 and 1975. That such priority was given to maintaining a high percentage of welfare expenditure in total budget allocation was partly because of previous political choices to focus on health, education and food as priorities, and partly because this provided political advantages for political patrons who sought to be re-elected into office.

In 1971, according to a report released by the ILO, Sri Lanka was living far beyond its economic means (Abeyratne 2000: 34). This was not only due to the dedication of a large share of national earnings to providing welfare benefits and social expenditure but also because of the overwhelming attention paid to rural agriculture and various government subsidies to this sector of the economy. Significant expenditure on agriculture was not only a reflection of the peasantry's importance for island electoral politics (Moore 1985: 5), it was also spurred by advice from the World Bank and personal and political preferences of the ruling parties. On the one hand, agricultural subsidies were publicly proclaimed to be aimed at achieving food self-sufficiency for the country, an important goal in itself. On the other hand, state support of agriculture can be viewed as a means of maintaining the vast

Table 4.6 Government expenditure on social welfare, 1955–1975

Year	All Social Services	Education	Health	Food Subsidies
1955	29.1	13.1	8.4	3.4
1956–1960	25.4	12.8	7.7	8.0
1961–1965	24.7	13.7	6.8	14.1
1966–1970	21.5	12.0	6.0	17.1
1971–1975	19.5	10.9	5.3	15.2

Source: Adapted from Abeyratne (2000: 30).

patronage networks forged by political elites and their parties with the rural – mostly Sinhalese – peasantry.

As noted elsewhere, giving primacy to agriculture over and above industry can be read as a carefully crafted effort to forge alliances with the agrarian elites as well as undermine the formation of a common front between agrarian and industrial elites, who together could damage the control and power of the political elites (Waldner 1999: 30). In Sri Lanka too, the focus on agriculture might have represented an effort to pre-empt conditions favourable for the re-emergence of class consciousness back in politics and agitations of blue-collar working-class movement in a growing industrial sector, who could no longer be controlled by neo-traditional patron–client relations (Waldner 1999). This suggests that Sri Lankan political elites' early aversion to industrialisation was part of a wider political strategy to keep lower-class masses under their influence and control, perhaps while protecting them from uncontrollable global economic forces for the benefit of elite politics. Gunatillake notes that the ruling regimes' general shared aversion to supporting the industrial sector was identified by the World Bank mission to Sri Lanka in 1951, which also supported delaying industrialisation processes until the country had reached its maximum potential in agricultural modernisation (Gunatillake 2000: 135). This advice nicely juxtaposed with the ruling elites' distinct preferences and political strategies to continue with state welfare and focus on the rural agricultural sector that formed the vast majority of the electorate. Meanwhile, there were some efforts to offer state patronage to the private sector through various quota systems, import tariffs, and granting of permits and licenses to local industries. However, these concessions were handed out to supporters of the ruling parties (Gunasinghe 1996g: 184) who acted as intermediaries between the elites and the working-class segments under their control. Even the steps later taken for nationalisation of private assets and introduction of various state controls with regard to foreign trade in the 1970s, especially during the period of socialist economy, could be viewed as part of the ruling elites' clientelist political strategies aimed at keeping their control on the entire economy and the different social forces in them (Herring 1987: 327).

The political elites' overall lethargic approach to supporting private industry can perhaps also be interpreted in the light of their continued concern with eliminating support of the urban and rural industrial working class for Marxist parties and left-wing political forces. Since most governments until 1977 were short-lived, rarely holding office for more than five years continuously, this further mitigated against a concern on the part of those in government to develop longer-term, well-planned industrialisation strategies for the country. Meanwhile, without new avenues for capital accumulation, and the state's tax base, and with considerable pressure to maintain high welfare expenditures, the tax burden on the local industrial economy grew markedly (Abeyratne 2000: 34). Increasingly, foreign exchange reserves earned from export booms were used to pay for imported consumer items (Abeyratne 2000: 35). The country's elaborate, expansive – and expensive – welfare policies, which were notably disproportionate to per capita income levels, led some in the international development community to label Sri Lanka a case of 'premature welfarism' and this started to be viewed, in an era where the post-War Keynesian consensus was under attack, as a 'negative development model' (Herring 1987: 325).

Meanwhile, any attempt made by the ruling regime to cut state welfare provisions became an act of political suicide. As early as in 1953, the UNP government headed by Dudley Senanayake sought to cut subsidies on rice, adversely affecting his popularity and sparking widespread protests, which eventually forced his resignation (Herring 1987: 326; Abeyratne 2000: 34). These incidents of 'rice politics', or what is sometimes called 'belly politics' (Bayart 2009),[18] arise in relation to a 'welfare induced dependency syndrome' observed to operate in Sri Lanka. Such a syndrome corresponds to the elites' ideal scenario of political clientelism driven by both supply and demand (Piattoni 2001: 13). During the first three decades of independence, political elites started to use state resources to dispense mass patronage, in the hope of securing political support networks in elections. Temporarily capturing state power, each party acquired access to state resources and continued, like its predecessor, to compete in dispensing the benefits of state patronage to the population as a whole, and to politically loyal groups in particular. These forms of expenditure in turn became a push factor in inter-elite struggles for political and economic hegemony.

Underlying the increasingly clientelistic nature of politics in Sri Lanka is the unequal treatment received by those who did not conform and were largely by-passed in this system of welfare expenditure. As people perceived the situation, a 'fixed national pie' (Wilson 1988: 49) was distributed along the lines of identity politics to secure a higher voter turnout from one's own 'constituencies'. Higher voter turnout did not so much reflect greater civic engagement or civic-political consciousness, but was mainly attributable to the increased need of some voters to identify with whichever ruling party was in power, and consequently had acquired the authority to distribute material resources. High voter turnouts in Sinhalese-dominated areas, especially in the countryside, were not a sign of the resilience of parliamentary multi-party democratic government, but a sign that patronage networks functioned well to 'deliver' the vote to the two dominant parties of the post-War era (Pieris 1999: 191). These dynamics of Sri Lankan electoral politics have restricted the political agency of various social and economic actors, as confirmed by a number of respondents. Even today, the expectation of obtaining the benefits of selective state patronage significantly motivates the Sinhalese majority community to vote in elections (R.1; R.2; R.3, R.4, R.5; R.10; R.11; R.16).

In line with Waldner's findings of a number of transitional economies in post-Soviet states (1999: 34), in post-colonial Sri Lanka, welfare policies were used by political elites at least in part to better control and manage class relations in a volatile political context. This allowed the ruling elites to reward a politically submissive and dependent majority electorate, and reproduce favourable conditions for elite domination and hegemony, despite alternation in the fortunes of individual political parties. Welfare provisions and support for free provision of public-service at the point of access were popular among the poor. These policies eliminated many problems of excess mortality and illiteracy associated with mass poverty, an impressive result gained at considerable cost to economic growth and budgetary balance. Even so, some of the root causes and the structural imbalances in the economy went unaddressed as welfare payments were not accompanied by deep-rooted structural economic reforms (Abeyratne 2000: 20). With structural causes of poverty remaining in place, rural poverty continued to be generated systemically, both among the peasantry and in the plantation sector. Rural poverty drove people towards patronage politics, suppressing the democratic functioning of state institutions and organised political action. Malevolent linkages emerged over time between poverty, patronage politics, low levels of political development, economic underdevelopment, and elite hegemonic strategies based on a culture of submissiveness and consent combined with periodic violent coercion of opponents.

As in other developing countries, so too in Sri Lanka the poor bore the long-term economic, social and political costs of debts accumulated by the ruling elites in the process of consolidating their own power base (Grindle 2001: 345). At the same time, the Sinhalese poor in particular were manipulated through welfare-based policies into giving up voluntarily most of their fundamental rights to political agency, in exchange for a slight reduction in the daily misery of their lives for some decades. From the perspective of political elites' hegemony-building this relinquishing of their power by the Sinhalese poor produced ideal conditions for continued predatory state-building by the alternately ruling political elites in the first few decades after independence.

AFTER 1977: FROM JAYAWARDENE TO RAJAPAKSA V.1.0 (1977–2015)

JAYAWARDENE REGIME (1977–1988)

Developments since 1977 have not only transformed patronage politics from how it operated in the previous era (through welfare-based spending) but also produced further barriers in the way of more democratic state-building, with the increasingly solid hegemony on the part of right-wing political parties strengthened by the springboard of emerging social and political violence, rising horizontal and vertical inequalities and elite state capture. As Flynn's (1973) seminal piece of work on clientelism argues, such major transformations in context traditionally marked by strong patron–client relations and patronage ties tend to be heightened during the transition to political independence. The year 1977 has been noted as a turning point with regard to Sri Lanka, when a number of major structural changes began in the economic and political fields (R.13).

By the late 1970s, state accumulation was under severe stress, as financial resources available to sustain the elaborate state-sponsored welfare cum patronage system dried up. This situation demanded the ruling elites to bring significant changes to the way state and party political machinery were run. Unemployment rose to over 20 per cent, and social service provision was deteriorating, with periodic shortages of essential food items and rationing combined with black marketeering of essential goods. All this contributed to the landslide victory of the UNP, which had been out of power during the previous few years (Matthews 1978: 92; Dunham and Kelegama 1994: 8). In the UNP's 1977 election manifesto, the party promised, 'We will ensure that every citizen, whether he belongs to a majority or minority, racial, religious or caste group enjoys equal and basic human rights and opportunities' (UNP election manifesto 1977). UNP leader Jayawardene captured the mood of alarm felt by people facing appalling economic conditions, and seized the moment politically to pursue one of his long-standing personal and political visions – the vision of a united Sri Lanka.

The 1977 general elections secured a two-thirds majority for the UNP in the national legislature, giving them for the first time in history a comfortable majority in all legislative votes. This huge majority was unique and in popular discourse, the UNP's victory was referred to as *badagoastharavaadaya*,[19] or the 'theory of the stomach'. This victory took place amidst the backdrop of scarcity of essential food items, rations imposed on food items and long food queues during the previous government, and the UNP's promise of open economic policy was appealing to many. Some of the UNP's rivals interpret pro-UNP voter behaviour as 'voting for the grain or a lentil' (the Sinhala phrase is *parippu eteta chande dunne*).

This sweeping electoral victory enabled the regime to introduce drastic changes, including the new constitution of the second republic of Sri Lanka, introduced in 1978, which introduced an executive presidential system for the first time, and switched the dominant economic focus from socialism and economic nationalism to a more open economy (Jayathilake 1999: 65; R.13; R.1). Jayawardena's victory signified his realisation of the incapacity of existing economic and political elites to reproduce their hegemonic position, without opening up to supplementary sources of finance and credit available in international markets (Jayathilake 1999: 29). Also known as the 'Gaullist constitution' (Wilson 1980: xvi; Bandarage 2009: 95), the 1978 Constitution of the Second Republic involved a mixture of institutions and powers from both the French Constitution and the British parliamentary system, with elements borrowed from the Constitution of the United States of America.

The executive presidency became a powerful instrument that would be used by successive office-holders for both good and bad, depending on the personal qualities and circumstances of the president elected (Coomaraswamy 2005: 153; R.12; R.9). Under the powers rendered to the executive president in the second republican constitution, he or she was no longer primarily answerable to parliament, and enjoyed a number of immunities while in office. He or she would no longer be subject to the long list of checks and balances that had applied to the head of state in the previous political system. President Jayawardene was both the chief architect of the new constitution and its main beneficiary. He justified new executive powers as opening up a more definite pathway to speeding up economic growth, attracting foreign investment and improving the workings of an open economic system without the impediment of parliamentary constraints on the president (Edrisinha and Selvakumaran 2000: 105). In 1982, still in power, it was Jayawardena who introduced the system of proportional representation (PR), which as was discussed earlier served to transform the entire political landscape and the functioning of the political system in Sri Lanka.

Alongside economic justifications for introducing this new constitution, Jayawardene also argued that it would facilitate the mechanisms needed to bring an end to the inter-ethnic conflict that was disrupting the economic, social and political life of the island (Shanmugaratnam 1993: 7). As some observed, such 'institutional choices are never made in apolitical and economic vacuum; they are often tailored to suit the narrower political and economic agendas of those making them' (Bastian and Luckam 2003: 307). The changes did not arise out of nowhere, and were part of a cherished political vision Jayawardene had advocated for some time (Bastian and Luckham 2003: 197). Various reforms were introduced after 1977, establishing new patterns of resource allocation and redefining how state budgets should be spent. The net effect was also to secure the UNP's own political domination and to settle many 'old scores' with its political rivals[20] (Dunham and Jayasuriya 2001: 3).

By continually referring back to the overwhelming mandate of the 1977 election, Jayawardena was able to implement his personal institutional vision of the state and society, and completely transform the political system.[21] He did this in ways that lacked public legitimacy and had little perceived relevance to meeting the concerns of most ordinary Sri Lankans (Coomaraswamy 2005: 153; Bandarage 2009: 95).[22] He sought to justify this overhaul of political institutions in line with his own wishes, by repeatedly emphasising the potential economic benefits of such a system. However, in practice the new institutions did not change the underlying and long-standing practices of patronage politics and it being an appendage to the ruling elites' hegemony-building efforts. Under the new institutions, the old system continued, allowing the UNP to now gain full control of the political machinery of the state. As has been observed, being able to push through substantial reforms usually requires a broad range of underhand political tactics (Jenkins cited in Venugopal 2011: 70), and in this respect the Jayawardena regime left little to imagination. As Jayawardene pursued his authoritarian fantasy, many remaining democratic mechanisms of parliamentary control and oversight were dismantled as the new state architecture emerged. In parallel with this reinvention of the state, a growing tendency was observed, of recourse to significant – and unapologetic – misuse of coercive and judicial state institutions to repress, contain and punish opposition leaders, trade unions and minority and human rights activists.[23]

Jayawardene's open-door economic policies soon brought foreign investment and aid into Sri Lanka, and this quickly became the main basis of revenue with which he could distribute patronage benefits to his political party and personal loyalists. The large sums of money from external sources also encouraged corruption on a previously undreamt-of scale. Meanwhile, Jayewardene readily used his own self-appointed executive presidential powers to reward himself and his loyal supporters, replacing SLFP-appointed bureaucrats with new presidential appointments to higher public office, as provided for under Chapter VII, Article 33 of the new constitution. Judges to the Supreme Court were appointed by the president, as was the chief justice and all diplomats. In effect, any remaining SLFP-oriented high-level public servants were removed from state employment during Jayawardene's presidency.

The new president further reinvented the traditional patronage system by creating a new landowning class of loyal politicians (R.2). One respondent described this process as follows:

> President J. R. Jayawardene himself also acquired the best coconut land in the country by manipulating the Land Reforms Commission. He also permitted his political loyalists to exchange their worthless lands for valuable lands and permitted his landless ministers and MPs to acquire valuable lands at a nominal price. This system has been followed by a greater or lesser degree by every governing party, which has come to power thereafter. (R.2)

According to another interviewee, this situation led to open land grabbing by politicians and their political subordinates in several parts of rural and urban Sri Lanka during this time[24] (R.25). The resulting new institutional structures made it much easier for politicians to openly engage in other economically advantageous activities and transactions. As one describes the situation, anecdotally,

> Jayewardene's political system [was] designed on the rules of Napoleon's war, under which a bonus system (*prasaada deemana*) was introduced. Under this system, whoever ... wins a territory is entitled to use the resources as [he or she] wishes. In other words, this implies that, when a political candidate wins an election from a certain electorate, the winner can use the resources of that area as they please. Jayawardene turned this system into a durable political strategy to make the president and his party to retain control of the territory over a long period of time. (R.2)

Moreover, ministers were given the sole authority to issue licenses to various highly profitable businesses such as radio stations, television stations, private transport facilities and liquor stores in their respective electoral constituencies. According to some observations, none of the 25 radio stations operating in Sri Lanka today obtained their licenses through formal processes. All had to go through networks of political affiliation and use the services of political intermediaries and fixers to obtain their licenses, compromising their integrity and independence as media (R.2). Such rampant corrupt practices steadily cut into important sources of national taxation and revenue generation, increasing the economic price of political interferences in business affairs across Sri Lanka (R.2; R.13; R.14). One respondent estimated that around 90 per cent of the intended state tax revenues probably failed to reach the national treasury (R.2).[25] Although some may believe that political clientelism and corruption can help avoid bureaucratic red tape, facilitate rapid economic decision-making and even accelerate economic growth (see for example Nye 1967: 421), during the Jayawardena period in Sri Lanka, such practices mainly channelled finances into luxurious imports for personal consumption of the political elites and their close supporters and to generate resources needed for (re)election.

Apart from the patronage benefits distributed among close political allies, there was also an element of vertical redistribution under Jayawardene's regime, thanks to large-scale public sector investment programmes (PSIP) undertaken. These PSIPs allowed Sri Lanka's government to borrow large sums of money in the form of long-term bilateral and multilateral international development loans, and obtain larger grants from multilateral aid agencies.

Much of this funding was supposed to be dedicated to the Accelerated Mahaweli Development Project (AMDP of 1977–1984), an extensive housing development programme, and other projects involving resettlement. In effect, the AMDP provided housing and employment to political loyalists of the UNP (Herring 1987: 331; Moore 1990: 352; Dunham and Kelegama 1994: 16; Spencer 2008: 623; Bandarage 2009: 84). To quote Spencer, who accurately sums up the situation at that time,

> ... huge aid inflows mostly directed the big development projects discussed earlier and easily transferred into jobs and contracts which could be handed out to political supporters along the usual channels of party-based patronage. In other words, beneath the rhetoric of liberalism and rolling back the state Sri Lanka experienced a minor Keynesian boom based on public works and bank- rolled by international aid flows. Because of the aid subsidies this expansion of public works – and public spectacle-politicians and the politically connected – prospered as never before. (2008: 623)

Such mega development projects have been associated with intensifying ethnic antagonisms between the Sinhalese and the Tamils, as well as a growing sense of collective grievance among Tamils in relation to resource distribution. The main beneficiaries of the AMDP projects were the Sinhalese, but not all segments of Sinhalese society benefited. Those who gained were mainly UNP loyalists and activists. Dunham and Jayasuriya have pointed out that the way investments were channelled was less the outcomes of any opening up of the economy, and more along well-worn, pre-existing channels of socio-political relations of party patronage (Dunham and Jayasuriya 2001: 2). These authors agree that most new development projects launched during this period of opening-up, under Jayawardene, benefited the middle- and lower-level UNP supporters, who were offered employment, grants for small businesses and lucrative government contracts (Dunham and Jayasuriya 2001: 5).

A well-known example, the *chit* system, operated solely on the basis of small, handwritten notes issued by members of parliament (MPs) (Thiruchelvam 1989a: 189; R.19). A *chit* could be issued by any MP of the ruling party, and issued to any public institution, including public schools. Publicly run organisations could be ordered to recruit political subordinates for employment or, in the case of schools, to admit the children of political loyalists.[26] These clientelist practices were often difficult to detect, and soon created new networks of patronage, which were eventually fully integrated into formal state institutions. In return, political beneficiaries of such state-sponsored schemes were expected to demonstrate their political loyalty by voting for the party, and helping the UNP's election campaigns. To this end, they mobilised family members, neighbours, caste communities, their own institutional colleagues and communities in specific locations. Next to such forms of manipulation, the UNP also sponsored entire trade unions, such as the Jaathika Sevaka Sangamaya (JSS), which was deployed to deal with oppositional trade unions and groups. In 1983, JSS members were even mobilised to carry out ethnic pogroms against Tamils (Hoole and Thiranagama 2001: 152–61). Table 4.7 describes some key differences between political brokers before and after 1977.

As the central government and all organs of the state increasingly came under the direct control of the UNP, a larger share of the benefits of state-managed projects reached UNP supporters (Gunasinghe 2004: 100). The LTTE was violently barred from holding elections and voters were prevented from casting their ballots in Tamil areas. These developments resulted in the deepening of the horizontal inequalities between the Tamils and the Sinhalese, in general, as well as growing vertical inequalities among the Sinhalese along the lines of political party affiliation. Overall, the new situation solidified the domination of the Sinhalese community over other

Table 4.7 Differences between traditional and broker clientelism

Forms	Scope	Durability	Intensity	Type	Reach	Resources
Before 1948 (Traditional)	Extensive (all inclusive)	Very high (generational transfer)	Very high	All kinds	Vertical	Personal
After 1948 (Welfare state)	Selected essential goods and services	Medium (regime oriented)	High	Votes for collective welfare benefits and ideological	Mostly vertical	State patronage
After 1977 (Broker managed)	Restricted (mostly electoral)	Low (one or more elections)	Low to high	Votes for personal favours	Mostly horizontal	Political party managed state patronage

Source: Adapted from Archer (1990: 34).

communities, and markedly increased party political consciousness among the Sinhalese. During the Jayewardene period, a new precariat emerged within the traditional class hierarchy of Sri Lanka, and high numbers of unemployed were incorporated into the UNP's political alliances and many were rewarded with low-paid public sector employment (see Chapter 5). Other new forms of patronage arose, facilitated by the growth of a more 'liberal' market economy, for instance, to the small-scale business class, which started to arise from the recently promoted precariat. Their distinctiveness was a particularly strong political orientation towards right-wing, ethnically chauvinist attitudes. They were allowed free use of government property, occupying public roadsides and pavements for their small-business premises, without paying any form of tax. In return, these small-business people ran errands for the regime, putting up election posters on behalf of their 'bosses', and removing the posters of rival political candidates, as well as engaging in election canvassing, intimidating opposition voters, and gathering people to attend UNP election meetings. In the long run, these routine tasks enabled this new category of small-business people to identify with particular ministers and certain local electorates as their own domain of (petty) power (Uyangoda 2008b). In most cases, members of this class indirectly exercised the authority of the local UNP MP, and there was an increase in violence around election times. Some Tamils based in the capital, identifying themselves as UNP loyalists rather than on the basis of ethnicity, were also rewarded under this system (Shanmugaratnam 1993: 11, 13; Gunasinghe 1996g: 189; Bandarage 2009: 80). However, their rewards were very minor compared to the patronage extended to Sinhalese formal and informal business establishments under UNP patronage (Gunasinghe 1996g: 189).

Within the state administration, Jayawardene's regime introduced decentralisation reforms (which are discussed further in Chapter 5). Under the reformed administrative structures, District Development Councils (DDCs) were introduced in 1981, ostensibly to address ethnic grievances and deal with growing inter-regional disparities (Coomaraswamy 2003: 157; Bandarage 2009: 73). However, along the way, the DDCs also became political tools of the ruling party and the ruling class (Bastian 2008: 158; Spencer 2008: 615). DDCs, established in 24 districts, each had a decentralised budget that enabled those elected to these bodies to deliver patronage in their own areas, through various development initiatives (Coomaraswamy 2003: 157). Elections to the decentralised councils were supposed to assuage Tamil grievances (Wriggins 1982: 171), or at least that was the stated intention of the president. However, DDCs soon became a point of contention between the upper ranks of the UNP and the president (Bastian 1993a: 17) because the decentralisation of funding to Tamil-controlled DDCs was adamantly opposed by the UNP elites. They saw no political or electoral advantage in granting Tamils access to state resources through the DDCs. By this time, ethnic politics was already the dominant narrative across national political parties. Gunasinghe observes that by the end of the 1970s, whatever might be their political leanings or popularity, no Tamil candidate would be able to win an election in in areas where the Sinhalese formed the majority. Reciprocally, no Sinhalese candidate, however committed to the local constituents, could hope to win an election in a Tamil-majority area (Gunasinghe 1996f: 159). In his effort to decentralise, Jayawardene was looking, perhaps in vain, and all too late, for ways to include Tamil Sri Lankans in his ambitious national political project.

When the system of PR was introduced in 1978, the aim was to replace the cumbersome majoritarian first-past-the-post (FPTP) system of elections inherited from the British. This FPTP system was also seen as imposing too many restrictions on the unfettered development of the economy in a more liberal, capitalist direction (Bastian 2003b: 196). PR was considered a complete break with past political traditions (Bastian 2003b: 213), and replaced a system that was seen as sclerotic, favouring only established political parties (Warnapala 1979: 181). The initial cut-off point for representation was 12.5 per cent, lowered to 5 per cent in 1982. Minor political parties were initially kept out through this high cut-off point, depriving them of parliamentary experience (Bastian 2003b: 211–12). The PR system did encourage coalition politics in Sri Lanka, as discussed earlier in this chapter, especially between larger and smaller parties. However, another consequence of the PR system was to increase electoral expenditure, a burden for smaller political parties who could not raise the amount of money needed to contest highly competitive elections. Lists of candidates were controlled by each political party, and so the PR system encouraged intra-party rivalries as candidates vied for position. Moreover, the system encouraged more authoritarian party leadership styles within political parties and greater intra-party clientelism, with those closest to party leaders often being favoured with more promising electoral possibilities. The PR system therefore was plagued by the diminished accountability of individual politicians who no longer represented their individual constituencies. Party discipline also seemed to suffer as a consequence of the diminished sense of accountability to specific publics, with a sort of free-rider problem emerging in politics. The counterpart of such free-floating MP competition was an effort to increase control by political parties over their candidates. These broad observations made in Sri Lanka are similar to findings of research conducted about the effects of PR systems in other developing countries in Asia and Latin America (Persson, Tabellini and Trebbi 2003: 959; Kunicova and Rose-Akerman 2005: 573; Chang 2005: 716).

In subsequent elections, after 1977, Jayawardene's politically motivated grand design did deliver the anticipated electoral victories to the UNP, consolidating its position of political dominance. With increased politicisation of trade unions, and party penetration of other large-scale trade unions in transport and port services, for example, the remaining elements of class solidarity among the Sri Lankan working class were all but destroyed (Moore 1990: 366, Dunham and Jayasuriya 2001: 6). In Spencer's view,

> it (UNP) had established its control over key trade unions: it had enmeshed a substantial stratum of potentially influential people – from new business elites to more humble village school teachers and minor officials – in a skein of patronage and obligation. (2008: 617)

Gunasinghe observes how implantation of bourgeois ideology and right-wing political propaganda among the working class progressed in ways that transformed Sinhalese chauvinism into a feature of working-class organisations, marking the end of inter-community class solidarity not based on ethnic ties or identities. The result was an even more complete subjugation of the Sinhalese working class to bourgeois class domination (Gunasinghe 1996c: 176). Over the years, with their politicisation, trade unions became a mere appendage of the regime, used to garner votes and punish opponents. The UNP established small juntas in various trade unions that acquired a monopoly of official positions in these unions, preventing action on various issues and dealing with internal opposition to the UNP. Leaders and members of these juntas were often promoted or rewarded with bonuses from state funds, in return for their loyalty to the party. In parallel to strategies of political domination within institutions, through a mix of consent, manipulation, rewards, and threats or use of force to suppress and intimidate opponents, the path of state-building also began to tilt distinctly further to the right under Jayawardene's presidency.

The political machine had been controlled by the UNP for 17 years, and by Jayawardene for 11 of these 17, and had extended its material rewards to significant groups in Sinhalese society as a means of maintaining and extending control over the electorate. As Scott cautions in his own findings on practices of political clientelism in the United States of America (1969: 43), the widespread corruption generated by Jayawardene's sophisticated state machine should not be mistaken for random greed; it was a well-oiled machine that delivered more than personal reward for the rulers; it also maximised electoral support and provided the state elites with a control mechanism capable of suppressing political opponents. One effect of these measures in Sri Lanka was the intensification of ethnic tensions and entry of the country into a civil war, which pitted the LTTE against the largely Sinhalese-controlled army and state, which were now 'fattened' by having absorbed most of the surplus investment and state-accumulated wealth brought about by structural changes in the economy and a more liberal and extraverted set of economic policies (Venugopal 2011: 69).

PREMADASA REGIME (1989–1993)

Premadasa was the first high-ranking political figure in post-independence Sri Lankan political history to challenge the symbolic monopoly exercised by the Westernised English-educated Goyigama political elites over local political and intellectual life (Uyangoda 1993: 6; Keerawella and Samarajiva 1994: 169). Premadasa was regarded as a shrewd political innovator with tremendous organisational skills (R.4). In the arena of Sri Lankan party politics, his lower class was something he explicitly used to appeal directly to the masses of lower-class background Sri Lankans. Premadasa's position on the margins of established political elites enabled him to approach the hegemony-building UNP project from a different angle, by confronting head on the problem of poverty, and the concerns of poor Sri Lankans. Considering his low caste and class background, this political strategy proved popular. Once in power, he oversaw several large-scale pro-poor projects, including a major housing project building affordable homes.

The Premadasa regime (1989–1993) was a time of several large-scale publicly funded infrastructure and pro-poor welfare-oriented programmes, including the Gam Udawa ('village awakening') project, the Janasaviya ('strength of the people') and the National Housing Scheme (its main slogan was *hisata wahalak – hithata nivanak*: roof for the head – relief for the heart).

All were launched shortly after his election to the presidency, and took place in an entirely different political context. During this time there was a second JVP armed uprising and a sharp escalation of armed conflict also in the northeast around Jaffna and other Tamil-dominated areas (Uyangoda 1993: 6). By consciously targeting and benefiting the poorer segments of Sinhalese society, Premadasa and the ruling party (UNP) managed to contain powerful anti-hegemonic forces arising across Sri Lankan society, from the poor stratum across the whole society.

Once again, the benefits of Premadasa's state-funded projects were largely distributed to loyal party members and their political subordinates across class differences (Moore 1990: 352; Dunham and Kelegama 1995: 21). However, the very nature of these projects was pro-poor and this made it easier for the benefits to reach the intended lower-level political supporters of the UNP. Before he became president, Premadasa had been appointed head of the National Housing Authority, established in 1979 when he had been prime minister. Premadasa initiated the construction of 100,000 living units, completed before the end of 1983. This goal was extended after Premadasa became president in 1989, after which a further 1 million housing units were built through direct construction and state-aided self-help building programmes. In addition to these, he launched a project to construct 155 houses with electricity per electoratal constituency. He also bet on establishing 500 garment factories targeting employment opportunities for the rural poor.[27] These local projects were popular with UNP politicians for whom they provided opportunities for kickbacks or 'skimming' (Herring 1987: 331). The cost to the treasury was substantial, sending shock waves through the ranks of the government's economic advisors, alarmed at the extent to which housing and construction were being politically prioritised (Bastian 1993b: 13).

Through such consistently pro-poor development projects and welfare programmes, Premadasa was able to build a steadily stronger power base in Colombo itself, and in many Sinhalese-dominated rural constituencies (Keerawella and Samarajiva 1994: 169). This deep penetration into lower-class support in the geographical peripheries of the island disturbed the balance of power among political parties, and in Uyangoda's view,

> Premadasa was more farsighted than any other politician in the UNP, who knew how to distribute immense state resources and even honours among loyalists as well as proletarian recruits in order to turn them into a solid and devout support base. (1993: 7)

According to political observers, he further reinforced his power base by using other state-funded programmes to make a contribution to the welfare of the poor (Dunham and Kelegama 1995: 10). Most importantly, such redistributive programmes helped ensure President Premadasa's individual political survival and consolidated a solid base of support for his regime, extending to the further rural areas. His leadership was challenged more from within the UNP, for example, in his attempted impeachment in 1991 (Uyangoda 1993: 5; Bastian 1993b: 13; Dunham and Kelegama 1995: 21). Premadasa interpreted the impeachment charges as an upper-class conspiracy against him (Uyangoda 1993: 7), citing it as further evidence of the ongoing class conflict affecting Sinhalese politics. His political mobilisation strategy hit the JVP's power base the hardest, and to survive among hostile elites within his own party, Premadasa did not hesitate to do deals with JVP dissidents. He even extended his political strategy to survive in office to having talks with the LTTE (Hoole and Thiranagama 2001: 247). Unfortunately for him, the outcome of his opening up to ties with the LTTE was his assassination, apparently by an LTTE suicide cadre, in 1993.[28]

During Premadasa's regime, the UNP experienced a political crisis in relation to its long-standing class composition (Uyangoda 1993: 6). This crisis within the party renewed long-standing political rivalries between the UNP and the SLFP. The effects of this internal crisis in the UNP could be seen at several levels. First, the old rivalry between elites was expressed in a revival of party competition between the UNP and the SLFP. Second, under Premadasa's leadership, splits emerged between upper-ranking, upper-class UNP party members. Finally, splits emerged between both the UNP and the SLFP as elite-oriented political parties and the popular class-base of the JVP. At the broader societal level, this triple crisis in politics brought suppressed class-consciousness to the fore once more in Sri Lankan politics and brought intra-Sinhalese social inequalities back into public view, and centre-stage once more in the public theatre of party politics. This resurfacing of class-consciousness and vertical class conflict was a reminder to party elites in the UNP and the SLFP of the fragility of their political dominance and the ongoing need to constantly innovate new strategies of mobilisation and mass incentives in order to remain in power. In such a challenging context, President Premadasa could no longer rely on subordination of his rivals through support from the poor alone. The scale of fragmentation pushed him to resort to coercion, and even to extreme forms of violence in the hope of regaining overall control and re-establishing his political authority and the UNP's political pre-eminence.[29] Instead, although Premadasa came to be known as a particularly ruthless political leader who used state violence and even paramilitary forces to deal with his enemies, his popular pro-poor programme and his patronage systems that ensured that benefits did 'trickle down' mainly to the poor and low-class groups in society meant he was still viewed in a largely positive light by the Sri Lankan, and especially the Sinhalese, poor.[30]

KUMARATUNGA REGIME (1993–2004)

Upon securing a landslide victory against the UNP, Chandrika Kumaratunga came to power in 1994. Her People's Alliance coalition government (PA) was made up of seven smaller political parties, under the overall leadership of the SLFP (Bastian 2003b: 216). This coalition came to power by promising to accelerate economic development and improve welfare provision for the poor. The PA election promises included free cash for unemployed youth, cash income supplements for low-income households, interest-free farm loans, producer subsidies, a reduction in the price of fuel and abolition of income tax for private sector employees. The PA electoral victory was especially significant in areas where the majority of the population was predominantly rice-growing Sinhalese farmers. The manifesto promised restoration of the fertiliser subsidy for rice growers (withdrawn in 1990 due to World Bank pressure) and other measures of mass patronage. Outstanding farm loans to banks would be written off by the new regime, and interest-free loans from banks to farmers would be supported by the government (Samarasinghe 1994: 1028). These pre-election promises wildly raised expectations among farmers, the poor, and indeed across the society, placing the new regime under intense pressure to deliver.

The PA presented itself as a party with a fresh-faced, youthful leadership that stood for radical change and a renewed 'social contract' between the state and citizens. Citing the deepening democratic deficit under successive UNP regimes, the PA leaders expressed their commitment to good governance and democracy. On the economic front, Kumaratunga and others in the new regime accepted the need to continue with an open-market economy, and promised to make improvements by avoiding political favouritism in the privatisation process, or the common UNP practice of granting contracts only to political loyalists (Samarasinghe 1994: 1022). In short, the new regime promised to be more efficient, less corrupt and more accountable than the old regime. State accumulation of resources would be improved by reducing corruption and avoiding waste in the public sector and tax evasion by private businesses.

Immediately after assuming office, President Kumaratunga and the PA leadership devised the attractive proposal of reducing the number of cabinet ministers. The newly established government also expressed sincere hopes to end the prolonged civil war and channel resources being spent on fighting towards economic and social development. President Kumaratunga expressed optimism about future peace dividends that would come from the international community and help the PA government achieve its stated objectives and fulfil its campaign promises (Samarasinghe 1994: 1033). Not surprisingly, given the long list of sometimes incompatible commitments made, the regime could not live up to the expectations it had raised. It did not take long for the PA to be accused of political favouritism and large-scale political corruption, especially since the PA was counting largely on privatisation of state enterprises as a key resource accumulation and extraction strategy, rather than, for instance, insisting on higher business taxes. Due to the bad reputation of privatisation under the previous regime, the PA used the term 'peoplisation with a human face'. Under this second phase of privatisation, a large number of profitable public sector ventures were sold off to political subordinates of the regime. Not only this, but as Dunham and Jayasuriya observed, rapid privatisation of public ventures, including the national airlines, telecommunications, plantations and ports, enabled all kinds of rent-seeking behaviour on the part of the regime under the cover of economic reform (2001: 15).

A parliamentary committee that was later appointed to investigate the level of fraud and corruption in public enterprises and in vital public utility institutions, including the Ceylon Electricity Board, Ceylon Petroleum Cooperation, their subsidiaries, and financial institutions such as the Central Bank and the Sri Lanka Insurance Company, reported that all these cases of privatisation involved mishandling of the process by the PA government. The committee reported instances of regime members and close friends of President Kumaratunga benefiting from the sale of such assets and services. It also revealed that chairpersons and boards of directors of these privatised establishments were mainly appointed on the basis of political influence and connections with the PA (Dizard, Walker and Cook 2010: 579).

Almost all respondents interviewed for this research claimed that privatisation in Sri Lanka was plagued by corruption from beginning to end, with insiders in the process, like leading politicians and their family members or high-ranking administrative officers, vying to buy what had been publicly owned companies. Among many incidents that caught the public eye was the case of President Kumaratunga granting political favours to a close personal friend, Ronnie Pieris, by allowing him to engage in an illegal land deal involving state-owned land. This deal had earned Pieris LKR 60 million (*Sunday Times* 2007b). Moreover, quoting the second commission report (*Sunday Times* 2008), another huge land deal secured by the president as a favour for a friend cost an estimated one-seventh of the total national revenue for that year (Colombopage, 2007).

In addition, it was during the PA regime, elected on the promise that it would fight corruption, that Sri Lanka was featured in international news for being involved in Asia's biggest value-added tax (VAT) scandal. This had cost the national economy a whopping USD 40 million in lost tax revenue, from 2002 to 2004 alone (*Sunday Times* 2006c). Given the bitter political rivalries among various political elites, however, the authenticity of some of these alleged incidents of corruption may be questionable. Nevertheless, enough credible evidence exists to suggest that large-scale political corruption did take place during President Kumaratunga's period in office. Indeed, without her own patronage networks, it is highly unlikely she could have remained in the presidency for over a decade.[31] Apart from such high-profile cases of political corruption and political favouritism, according to some reports, over a period of 13 years, a total of 98 state-owned businesses and service providers were privatised (Balasooriya, Alam and Coghill 2008). This benefited neither the public through lowering of costs nor the enterprises sold by increasing efficiency. The COPE findings suggest that institutions like the Lanka Marine Services Limited, Sri Lanka Insurance Company and many others were already profitable ventures at the time of their selling, and so represented short-term gain and long-term lost revenue for the state. As reported, all these transactions were closely related to politicians and supporters of the PA regime (*Sunday Times* 2007a). Under Kumaratunga, as under Jayawardene, privatisation was an attempt to raise funds for distribution through corrupt economic practices that put state insiders in an advantageous position when it came to selling off public assets. All this may have been essential to remaining in power.

Overall, Kumaratunga's economic strategies were about generating sufficient financial resources to renew and extend PA patronage networks and alliance-building, rejuvenating previous alliances of the SLFP. This was firmly aligned by the PA with a right-wing economic strategy, first launched under the UNP. In many ways, although the SLFP was historically known as a party of centre-left orientation, during the regime of President Kumaratunga it became fully aligned with right-wing politics. While she promised a more left-wing political orientation, which proved popular electorally, and a return to the 'Golden Age' of the welfare state, towards the end of her second term, she fully oriented her government's policies towards the right-wing of Sri Lankan political opinion. The trajectory of the PA government also needs to be understood, however, within the local and broader global dynamics of the years that the PA was in power.

RAJAPAKSA REGIME (2005–2015)

With the aid of Sinhalese nationalist political parties such as the JVP and the JHU, Mahinda Rajapaksa first came to power in 2005. A leadership split in the SLFP along class lines during the last phase of the Kumaratunga regime meant that President Rajapaksa was forced to rely on the backing of smaller political parties outside the SLFP. Even his presidential election manifesto, entitled *Mahinda Chinthana* (Mahinda's visions), was heavily influenced by the smaller Sinhalese nationalist political parties with an overtly patriotic tone and claiming to represent the underclasses (R.20). In this manifesto, Rajapaksa's vision for Sri Lanka's future was:

> To develop a man to safeguard his family, To develop the family to safeguard the village, to develop the village to safeguard the country, and to develop the country to win the world. (*Mahinda Chinthana: Towards a New Sri Lanka* 2005: 101)

Rajapaksa faced a schism within the SLFP, with one faction loyal to former president Kumaratunga and another faction loyal to Rajapaksa himself. This left Rajapaksa relatively isolated, and unable to trust his own party cadres or rely on their support for his electoral campaign. He therefore turned to family and close political ties that he had built up through strong social networks in the south of the country. Reliance on family members as allies in government also earned his regime the nickname of 'Rajapaksa & Company'. JVP and JHU leaders were given a prominent place in national politics, both as a result of his need for political allies in order to survive and as a strategy to incorporate marginal groups from the south, his main power base.

Drawing on these alliances, the Rajapaksa government assumed a markedly more right-wing political tone and ideological orientation than any previous government. A return to an assumed old order, a turning back to the mythical 'authenticity' of the past, all this was part of his rhetoric, which invoked the ancient governing codes of kings, and appealed to social forces left behind, on the periphery of mainstream politics. However, mere incorporation of marginal groups ideologically would not prove to be enough to mobilise support. At the same time, a strategy to distribute material benefits would be needed alongside such ideological appeals to lost glory.

Hence, under Rajapaksa, previously established patronage systems required some adjustments to ensure his political domination, and he did this by appealing to 'the little man', and invoking the centrality in his programme of the family unit, with the man as its head. Through a system that could be termed a form of nepotism, he first appointed his two brothers and a number of other family members to key positions in the government. In this way, almost three-quarters of total public expenditure, 70 per cent of the government budget, came under the direct ministerial control of the extended Rajapaksa family (*The Economist*, 7 June 2007). His regime also embarked on new projects aimed at regime-building (or more accurately, dynasty-building). These projects exploited state resources and state institutions, appointing many new ministers and officials without much justification in most cases. A 2005 Transparency International report, with the title 'Mega Cabinets in Sri Lanka: Perceptions and Implications", revealed that President Rajapaksa had a total of 26 ministries, with 108 ministers (including 52 cabinet ministers, 36 non-cabinet positions and 20 deputy ministers). Many of these positions were distributed as rewards for loyalty to the president. Indeed, the president also rewarded himself with a total of six ministries in addition to the presidency. All the expenses of these multiplying ministries and ministers were met from the public coffers (R.2).

The Rajapaksa regime was soon involved in several high-profile corruption cases, being accused of nepotism and gross misuse of public funds. The first incident reported took place even before Rajapaksa was elected and consisted of trying to 'buy off' opposition MPs in an effort to secure a majority in parliament, by offering these MPs ministerial posts and other lucrative perks (R.2; R.3; R.8; Wickramasinghe 2009: 4). Rajapaksa was also accused of corruption as former prime minister, in the last years of the PA regime. After the tsunami struck in December 2004, the international community pledged more than USD 11 billion in humanitarian and development aid to the affected regions of Sri Lanka. Rajapaksa, whose own district, Hambantota, was one of the worst affected by the tsunami, was accused of personally misappropriating at least USD 830,000 in tsunami relief funding (BBC Sinhala 2005; Reliefweb 2007). 'Helping Hambantota', a project established by Rajapaksa, administered and distributed all the money that came in aid of tsunami victims through three private bank accounts. According to numerous sources and an official report released by the auditor general, a sum of USD 724,170 that was intended for the worst-affected families was instead used to provide benefits to families loyal to Rajapaksa but unaffected by the tsunami. One prominent lawyer and the head of a leading civil society organisation, Mr Weliamuna, suspected tsunami funds were also used for party political purposes and to build new houses for those with political affiliations to Rajapaksa in Hambantota district (Reliefweb 2007).

These allegations were corroborated through reliable research carried out in the post-tsunami period in Sri Lanka, which assessed the effectiveness of aid provided following the tsunami (Goodhand and Klem 2005). First-hand information also reveals that many politicians at national, provincial and local levels used this humanitarian aid money to extend their political capital within constituencies, to bolster their legitimacy and for personal enrichment (Goodhand and Klem 2005: 58). Once Rajapaksa was elected president in 2005, investigation of these incidents was stopped, and was labelled malicious political rumours (Elhawary and Aheeyar 2008: 6). Rajapaksa's alleged theft of tsunami funds points to an important direction in recent regime- and hegemony-building efforts in Sri Lanka, shedding light on how significant development and disaster aid can become as sources of funding for local patronage systems. After exhausting internal state resources, in the wake of tightening financial controls by international donors, Rajapaksa was looking for new avenues to generate funding so he could maintain and extend his patronage networks so as to remain in power for longer. He found new opportunities after the tsunami mobilised a huge international relief effort for the victims.

Under Mahinda Rajapaksa, civil war itself turned into a golden opportunity, a new area to explore for resources for the regime's insatiable appetite (see Chapter 7). Widespread allegations that the military sector and military-centric forms of patronage were emerging are cited as evidence for this claim. One major scandal involved fraudulent military purchases linked to the president's brother, Gotabaya Rajapaksa, who was defence secretary at the time. He was reported to have signed a multimillion-dollar arms deal while deviating from standard tender procedures. In Sri Lanka, as in many other countries, military procurement is not subject to public scrutiny, and such corrupt deals can potentially go undetected. Military purchases do not even come under the purview of the auditor general, and so are a 'safe bet' for such blatant misuse of public funds. Laws such as the 1955 Official Secrets Act make it an offence to discuss publicly any suspected irregularities in the military (Transparency International 2008: 301). Such irregularities are also never publicly investigated, to avoid damaging military morale and national security.

According to several newspaper reports, after President Rajapaksa's election, all arms purchases and military procurement were channelled through a private company, Lanka Logistics, whose chairman was none other than the president's brother, also defence secretary. When Rajapaksa assumed power, all authorisations for military equipment were handled by his brother, who was also responsible for overseeing all purchases and sales (Transparency International 2008: 302). As reported by Iqbal Athas, a leading military correspondent in Sri Lanka, and according to reports by Transparency International, the president's brother had purchased four Mikoyan Mig 27 aircraft for the Sri Lanka Air Force in 2006, paying a much higher price than usual, and supposedly taking a large cut for himself in this arms deal. Various reports confirm that the regime made a payment of USD 14.6 million for second-hand MiG-27 aircraft, which Sri Lanka had already rejected in 2000 as too old and unsuitable for the Air Force (*Sunday Times* 2006a). The Rajapaksas have continued to enjoy immunity from criminal investigation of these scandals, since a high-level investigation by the Commission to Investigate Allegation of Bribery or Corruption (CIABOC) was called off (Transparency International, Cambridge University Press and Ernst and Young 2009: 302).

Apart from the above, financial scandals related to the purchase of military cannons from Israel by the Sri Lanka navy were reported to have involved a payment discrepancy of USD 7 million (*Sunday Times* 2006b). The skyrocketing military expenditure under the Rajapaksa brothers was justified under the guise of the civil war. However, interesting research by Venugopal on military fiscalism in Sri Lanka has claimed that since 1977, throughout a long period of rising inequalities and social tensions, and later during market reforms and privatisation, military employment has provided a huge number of jobs, creating conditions of relative sociopolitical stability (2011:

71). Tables 4.8 and 4.9 are drawn from two different sources and demonstrate the increases in military expenditure over time. In addition to the purchases of military equipment during the Rajapaksa regime, the rising costs of the armed forces reflect ongoing and large-scale military recruitment, which has served to construct an enormous army with a core of over 210,000 regular military troops. In 2009 alone, military troops made up 2.65 per cent of the total labour force in Sri Lanka, and the military expenditure was estimated at 3.5 per cent (as percentage of the gross domestic product, or GDP)[32] and plans were unveiled for further increase in the number of soldiers in the armed forces to 410,000 by 2015.[33]

The marked decline in military expenditure from 2009 to 2010 as a percentage of GDP was either due to an actual decline in the military expenditure after the ending of the war in 2009, or due to the growth of the GDP as the war ended. Another consideration could be that under Rajapaksa's leadership, definitional problems arose as to what was reported as 'military expenditure', a problem highlighted in the World Bank report (Mohammed 1999: 7). Besides, official reports confirm an increase in military budgets in 2011 (USD 1.92 billion) and again in 2012 (estimated at USD 2.1 billion), amounts that exceeded the total combined expenditure allocated in those years for the health and education sectors. This increase was justified by citing the need to pay off weapons bought during the last stages of the war, in 2009 (Gunadasa 2011).

It is also worth noting that after the war, Rajapaksa successfully re-incorporated a large number of Sinhalese male youth from the rural areas into national politics and into his political support base, offering them employment using state funds. This segment of the population mainly belongs to the 18–30-year age group, and strongly identifies with their

Table 4.8 Defence expenditure, 2007–2011 (in LKR million)

2007	2008 (Approved Estimates)	2008 (Provisional)	2009 (Approved Estimates)	2009	2010 (Approved Estimates)	2010 (Provisional)	2011 (Approved Estimates)
101,856	108,086	134,710	134,260	144,884	142,348	145,243	163,486

Source: Adapted from annual reports of Central Bank of Sri Lanka (2008: 136, 2010: 137).

Note: These figures should be read against the overall context of high inflation experienced during this period. From 2004 until 2012, Sri Lanka inflation rate averaged 10.3600 per cent, reaching an all-time high of 28.2000 per cent in June 2008. This figure is calculated based on the changes in the annual consumer price index (http://www.tradingeconomics.com/sri-lanka/inflation-cpi, accessed on 30 March 2011).

Sinhala-Buddhist identity. Most are rural, have a low level of educational attainment, and are concentrated in the poorer, interior districts of Ampara, Traincomalee, Polonnaruwa, Anuradhapura and Monaragala. Around one-quarter of them – 23 per cent – are based in the Eastern Province, where most Sinhalese are second- or third-generation settlers in irrigation-based colonies such as Gal-Oya and Kantale (Venugopal 2011: 73).[34]

Next to the overt incorporation of the military sector into Rajapaksa's political alliance-building and revenue-generation activities, he and his family went on to exploit state property and land. According to the second Parliamentary Committee on Public Enterprises (COPE) report, Sri Lanka lost LKR 600 million because of financial malpractices between July and December 2008. Among these are the Foreign Employment Bureau, the Sri Lanka Cashew Corporation, the National Housing Development Authority, the National Gem and Jewellery Authority, the Export Development Board, the Building Materials Corporation, the National Transport Commission, the Associated Newspapers Ceylon Limited, the Sri Lanka Rupavahini Corporation, the Consumer Affairs Authority, and the Mahapola Higher Education Trust Fund. As per various estimations, these public institutions have lost LKR 1.5 billion because of corruption and malpractices (Gunaratne 2007). Citing these recent developments, Professor Indraratne, a leading Sri Lankan economist, estimates that due to petty and large-scale corruption in the public sector, the country has lost up to 2 per cent in overall economic growth. He further notes that corruption in infrastructure projects was rampant at both the central and provincial levels.[35] In most cases, it was revealed that by giving commissions and kickbacks to officials and elected representatives, the contractors got away with substandard work, through pilfering of inputs and by not using materials of the required standard.

Despite the scale and gravity of the charges of corruption, nepotism and political favouritism, thanks to the continued euphoria of war victory and the military defeat of the LTTE, the regime seemed to have received an informal pardon in the short-term from many voters in the south who now envisaged the possibility of finally establishing a Sinhala-Buddhist state. Decisive military success over LTTE forces renewed the hold of the Sinhala-Buddhist nationalist elites' hegemony over the Sinhalese majority, which continued to support Rajapaksa after the end of the war. However, the economic situation in post-war Sri Lanka meant much economic hardship for those living in the periphery, and this challenged the regime in power to create new strategies to manage and control groups that had already been mobilised and were highly charged ideologically. A fall-out with Western donors who brought accusations of war crimes against Rajapaksa's government during the last phase of the civil war made the situation all the more challenging for President Rajapaksa. The much-awaited post-war peace dividends and humanitarian aid, which he had been counting on, did not materialise as expected.

As with other previous regimes, the Rajapaksa regime was marked by attempts to harmonise struggles at the centre for political power with struggles for economic development in the periphery. While maintaining patronage systems as before, the president and his entourage sought to reinvent their patronage networks through new sources of funding. It was the military and 'war industries' that became the most promising avenues. In the absence of other sources of funding (that is, Mahaweli funds[36] and privatisation, all having been exhausted), the military was directly integrated into his plans, a move that seemed almost inevitable. Not only for Rajapaksa but for any other future political leadership in politics, defeating the LTTE was paramount for advancing their political projects of domination and hegemony. For a long time, because of the activities of the LTTE, the Sinhalese political elites could not successfully incorporate the Tamil community into their hegemony-building projects. By defeating the LTTE, Rajapaksa overcame this obstacle. The military might he used and demonstrated in the final phase of war was used to send a clear message to the other oppositional forces.

Against this backdrop, under Rajapaksa the Sinhalese majority benefited from state patronage through different channels. The renewed Sinhala-Buddhist nationalist state project under Rajapaksa and the ideological nature of the state's patronage under his presidency are of special significance. The material patronage offered to the Sinhalese youth through military employment complemented the regime's ideological aspect of hegemony-building. Military victory against the LTTE enabled the regime to justify its own ideological path to the majority of the Sinhalese voters. As a result, even in the absence of the LTTE and its military activities, the Rajapaksa regime was able to reconstitute its support bases among the Sinhalese electorate. The latest political developments in post-war Sri Lanka suggest successful incorporation and mobilisation strategies targeting minority community factions in elite politics through an extension of personal patronage that benefited some elites from minority communities as well. This strategy was able to incorporate many elite factions regardless of their class belonging, leading them to lend their support to Rajapaksa's project of remaining in power. However, there were also those who were left behind, and who protested. For them, coercive strategies were more frequently used to repress their active opposition. In addition, self-imposed censorship and isolation became the chosen strategy of other forces within the Sinhalese elite group (political, economic and intellectual) hostile to the regime. Their resolve to overcome the pressures of coercion, and organise as a united and decisive oppositional force, would determine the next phase in the transformation of Sri Lankan politics during the post-war, post-LTTE period. Already, the excessive patronage used in the forms of ideological and material rewards has been successful in absorbing many in the political circles to Rajapaksa's nepotistic regime. The right-wing politics propagated by this alliance has moved state-building further and further away from any kind of radical or egalitarian political vision.

In conclusion, the impetus of the present political-party-led patronage system can be traced back to the pre-colonial era, when it was an important element in shaping social relations in rural areas. Despite some elements of political and economic modernisation under colonial rule, however unevenly pursued, traditional patronage relations continued to operate through six centuries of European colonial occupation. New opportunities resulting from colonial extractive economic activities paved the way for the rise of a new class, the colonial bourgeoisie, and a new working class. The colonial bourgeoisie was able to offer its own forms of patronage by offering material benefits in exchange for gaining influence over the working classes in the commercial economy. In the post-independence period, such old and more recent patronage networks were recycled and recombined, and successfully mobilised for the mass political incorporation of lower-class voters into politics. Institutionalisation of the patronage system in parallel to the institutionalisation of the political party system since the 1930s has left remarkably negative legacies on the contemporary state-in-society relations and contributed to the rise of right-wing hegemony in politics. Today, its hegemonising and the commonsensing effects are often captured in everyday expressions, such as *muttiya allanawa* (holding the pot underneath) and *pandama allanawa* (holding the torch for someone with power/a patron), *danna kawuruth nedda?* (is there anybody you know?), and *ethulen kaawahari allagannwa* (catching someone from inside).

Over the decades, consistent use of the patronage political system to incorporate Sinhalese lower-class masses has been accompanied by increasing factionalising of the Sinhalese elites' rival political projects. This has pushed minority ethnic groups to the margins in the distribution of state patronage and subjected them to unequal treatment. The expansion of the economic and social role of the state and launching of an extensive welfare state in the early 1970s further enabled the ruling Sinhala-Buddhists elites to obtain consent for their rule from lower-class Sinhala masses, who became increasingly dependent on, and subservient to, these political elites. At times of periodic economic and demographic decline, the resource base available for distributing patronage shrank, and at these times alliances tended to be mobilised through more direct appeals to the ideological element of Sinhala-Buddhist nationalism, which could be distributed at a fraction of the cost of conventional, material patronage.

The main beneficiaries in this material–ideological relationship were the majority Sinhalese, who became increasingly protective of the patronage system that underpinned this ideological system. However, their position as consenting subjects of the state aggravated their lack of capacity to make binding claims on the same state. With introduction of the open economic policy since 1977, and the emergence of a new urban underground economy, the entire patronage system and its ideological foundations experienced a tremendous transformation. A criminal underworld acted as new political brokers, operating largely in unregulated businesses and lending their loyalty to the highest bidders among the competing elites. The majority of this new broker class of urban criminal class were involved in running casinos, drug cartels, construction and hiring temporary labourers and mostly short-term workers in urban areas. Their economic survival was entirely dependent on political patronage and right-wing economic policies and ideologies supporting them. Their political expediency to the ruling elites and specific political regimes' pursuit of political domination and hegemony was indispensable. They were specifically useful for the elites for the deployment of coercive tactics when their consent-building strategies failed, and hence to silence and diffuse anti-hegemonic forces and the progressive societal forces demanding state reforms and redistributive justice. Nevertheless, people's dissent and dissatisfaction towards the aforementioned developments are frequently expressed creatively and humorously using political cartoons, memes, emojis and in both conventional and social media forums, despite the threats from the ruling elites and their supporters. These dynamics have contributed in realising a widespread right-wing political culture and aligning the elites' state- and alliance-building strategies with openly right-wing hegemony-building. This was to subsequently drag Sri Lanka into a sustained path of state and political violence involving 'dissidents' from both Tamil and Sinhalese communities.

NOTES

1. Waldner assigns these characteristics to the 'mediated state', a state where the elite rule through an alliance with local notables. An 'un-mediated state' refers to a state in which institutions replace notables to link state, economy and society (Waldner 1999: 2).
2. There are recent trends observed that suggest the bouncing back of caste politics in national and provincial council levels too. Refer to Roberts (2010) and L. De Silva (2010).
3. Refers to the ways in which politics of distribution and redistribution was conducted in the aftermath of the Tsunami disaster in the Indian Ocean region in December 2004.
4. Also ethnic politics as discussed in Chapter 3.
5. The only exception to this rule was the election of President Ranasinghe Premadasa, who became the party leader as well as the president of the country from 1989 to 1993.
6. Shefter defines externally mobilised parties as political parties that are founded on programmatic appeals to attract voters and capable of including socially excluded groups to the mass political party structure and, therefore, tending to be patronage free.
7. The significance of the agricultural sector in Sri Lanka has not changed much even after various reforms were introduced in the post-colonial phase of economic development. According to labour force statistics in Sri Lanka, in the first quarter in 2010, employment in agriculture was 33 per cent of the total labour force. This report also noted 49.7 per cent of account workers working in the agricultural sector and a total of 73.5 per cent family workers, thus making the agricultural sector the largest in the country (Department of Census and Statistics 2010: 2).
8. Gramsci defines a historical bloc in the following way:

> If the relationship between intellectuals and people-nation, between the leaders and the led, the rulers and the ruled, is provided by an organic cohesion in which feeling-passion becomes understanding and thence knowledge (not mechanically but in a way that is alive), then and only then is the relationship

one of representation. Only then can there take place an exchange of individual elements between the rulers and ruled, leaders [dirigenti] and led, and can the shared life be realised which alone is a social force – with the creation of the 'historical bloc'. (1971: 418)

9. Besides these interpretations, the link between the Ceylon Indian Congress and their left-leaning voting behaviour are also of importance (De Silva 2005: 605).
10. For details, see http://www.slelections.gov.lk/pdf/1982%20Presidential.pdf (accessed on 6 September 2011).
11. He was succeeded by his grandson Arumugam Thondaman.
12. This was initially caused by the decision of the OPEC (Organization of the Petroleum Exporting Countries) countries to peg the price of oil to gold, instead of the US dollar. This new measure was taken to avoid further decline of these countries' revenues from oil exports, as the value of the free-floating US dollar began to decline.
13. For a detailed discussion on the land reform and agrarian change in Sri Lanka in the 1970s, read G. H. Pieris (1978).
14. A handful of scholars, for example, Bastian (1985), Bandarage (2009) and Jayawardena (2005), have analysed this situation by taking the overall context into consideration.
15. It operated underground after being banned following the 1971 insurrection.
16. According to Sri Lanka's Department of Elections, there are more than 70 registered political parties as of 2019.
17. Due to the increased demand for rubber during the Korean War from 1950 to 1955, Sri Lanka experienced a favourable economic condition. This situation is known as the Korean economic boom.
18. Bayart refers to belly politics in the African context as an expression of necessities of survival and also as a complex array of cultural representations, both visible and invisible.
19. The suffix *-vaadaya* translates to 'ism' in English.
20. The 1977 elections brought the UNP back to power after 13 years. This electoral victory was used to suppress the SLFP as well as other oppositional groups.
21. This vision was a blend of the economic, political and sociocultural. In terms of the social and cultural aspects of his vision, Jayawardene was committed to the establishment of a *dharmishta samaajaya*, meaning righteous society.

22. As Fukuyama suggests, institutional reforms should have a strong demand from the society to be able to function successfully (2004: 47). Fukuyama also points to the fact that the public legitimacy (perceived legitimacy, at least) of state institutions is an important aspect for successful state-building (2004: 34). The legitimacy of the second republican constitution is still being questioned in Sri Lanka because it was brought into effect overnight (on a Friday night), which deliberately left no time for public debate on the new constitution (Coomaraswamy 2005: 152–53).
23. The full report on the 1980 strike and its aftermath is compiled by S. Nadesan, QC. The use of new legislation and the political motivations underpinning the assault on trade union action is well documented (http://www.naturesl.lk/pdf/ar/THE_1980_STRIKE_AND_ITS_AFTERMATH.pdf, accessed on 22 July 2011).
24. The latest attempts at land grabbing by politicians are being reported in the Eastern Province and the post-war areas in the North (Fonseka and Raheem 2011).
25. The percentage expressed by this respondent can be an exaggeration of the situation. The official reports and statistics released by the Department of Inland Revenue acknowledge the general challenges pertaining to collection of taxes in the country and yet are silent on political corruption and the practices mentioned by the respondent as a cause for loss of revenue (http://www.inlandrevenue.gov.lk/publications/PReports/PR2009.pdf, accessed on 2 July 2012). For most recent details that confirms accumulation of wealth through corrupt deals and initiatives launched to investigate the undisclosed wealth, refer to http://www.tisrilanka.org/?p=9646 (accessed on 2 July 2012).
26. In Sri Lanka there is major competition among parents for admitting children to a school. Although the education is free, not all schools have the same facilities. Therefore, the parents are even ready to pay bribes to the education authorities and the school principals. It is observed that newly married young couples choose to rent accommodation near a better school to make sure that their 'children to be born' have access to better education facilities.
27. However, he could only establish 300 factories.
28. For further reading on the relationship and the consequences of this relationship between the LTTE and Premadasa, please refer to Hoole (2001: ch. 17).
29. Because of the challenges that came from the various Sinhalese forces, Premadasa began to work closely with the Tamil political groups and the LTTE.

30. For a detailed account of the Premadasa period and the aspect of state violence, refer to Gunasekara (1998), Chandraprema (1991) and Hoole and Thiranagama (2001).
31. Unless these incidents are questioned in parliament by the opposition, they go un-investigated. It is suggested that since all regimes in power engage in similar corrupt practices, sometimes deals are made between political parties not to investigate each other, as they all can be victims of their own strategies.
32. See https://data.worldbank.org/indicator/MS.MIL.XPND.GD.ZS?end=2020&locations=LK&start=2009 (accessed on 22 March 2022).
33. See https://www.globalsecurity.org/military/world/sri-lanka/army-troops.htm (accessed on 22 March 2022).
34. Although this study does not extensively deal with the issue of the gendered nature of patronage politics in the military and gendered inequalities in the elites' hegemony-building strategies pursued in Sri Lanka, the statistics presented in this chapter explains the above linkages. For detailed critical studies that explore intersections of gender and war in Sri Lanka, see Neloufer De Mel (2007) and Malathi De Alwis (1998).
35. I had personal communication with a high-ranked financial officer of one such infrastructure project, called Maga Neguma (a road development project), which was also cited in a number of cases of corruption. This project was initiated and conducted under the personal supervision of President Rajapaksa.
36. International funds received for the Accelerated Mahaweli Development programme (AMP) in the 1980s.

5

STATE INSTITUTIONS AND PATRONAGE POLITICS

Politics in Sri Lanka has been described as a 'consuming passion', but a passion that may boil down to no more than the question of 'who will be employed by the Ceylon Transport Board as the bus conductor'.

—Jupp quoted in McCourt (2007b: 433)

Institutions play a central role in constraining behaviour and shaping preferences, goals and strategies, and even identities (Waldner 1999: 19).[1] Where mass incorporation into politics happens before or simultaneously with the elaboration of a national administrative system, that system is likely to be based on patronage politics and patronage appointments (Waldner 1999: 24). The case of Sri Lanka provides some compelling evidence for this suggestion. It shows how important linkages can be made between intra-elite conflicts, timing of mass incorporation of lower classes into nation politics and paths of state-building (Waldner 1999). Such interconnected elements have encouraged the ruling elites to (ab)use state institutions for purposes of political patronage. In general, state institutions play a direct role in enabling political elites to act as intermediaries between the state, the economy and society (Waldner 1999: 24). The example of Sri Lanka shows institutional changes introduced to the state apparatus being closely tied to or even completely aligned to financing an institutionalised form of patronage system to pursue faction-ridden ruling elites' hegemony-building project.

Critiques of the functioning of state institutions often point to their inefficiency in delivering basic public services, their uncontrolled expansion and the mammoth maintenance costs of public bureaucracies (Hulme and

Sandaratne 1996; Samaratunga and Bennington 2002: 87; De Alwis 2009). Similar to observations in the *World Development Report* (Evans and Rauch 1999: 748), there are numerous works on Sri Lanka that identify politicisation and widespread patronage politics as a worrisome development across state institutions (Ranugge 2000: 51; IDEA 2007; De Alwis 2009: 57). Important work on patronage politics in state institutions links this phenomenon with ethnic conflicts and civil war (Thiruchelvam 1984c; Uyangoda 1994; Wilson 1979; DeVotta 2002; Shastri 1990). Reciprocally, studies have shown how state institutional transformations can impact inter-ethnic relations adversely (Thiruchelvam 1984b: 185–95; Mathews 1986: 33; Thangarajah 2000: 127; DeVotta 2005: 145–47).

From the particular perspective of hegemony-building, this chapter shows how institutionalisation of patronage politics across state institution was invented by Sinhalese ruling elites as a permanent guarantor for financing the party-based patronage system, for political mobilisation and elite instrumental coalition-building strategies against a backdrop of dwindling state accumulation.

QUASI-PATRONAGE: THE BRITISH COLONIAL PERIOD

State structures and institutional changes introduced by the British were key in (re)shaping the state-building project in subsequent decades. The institutional structure of governance, established during the British colonial era show how a quasi-patronage system was nurtured, and later came to be finessed by ruling elites in post-independence Sri Lanka. The functioning of state institutions was turned into tools for the sustainable political mobilisation of lower classes into electoral party politics. Overall, the goal was to build a form of consent-based political alliance that could be beneficial for advancing elites' hegemony-building project.

Under British rule, centralised state structures were designed to maximise revenues and to maintain law and order in the colony. Parallel to the expansion of colonial economic exploitation, British rule in Sri Lanka institutionalised an expanding colonial bureaucracy. Periodically, waves of specialised officers were recruited into this bureaucracy as consultants and technicians. The services of these officers were crucial for implementing various projects aimed at developing infrastructure necessary for extraction and exploitation (Oberst 1986: 166). At the same time, these developments enabled a narrow segment of the local population to acquire the administrative and technical skills needed for statecraft. To systematise the functions of the colonial bureaucracy, a set of regular government agencies were established (LaPorte 1981: 581).

As Warnapala notes, the expansion of colonial administrative structures was tied to a rapid expansion of public works. Between 1850 and 1910, increasing population combined with demand for economic development led to an increase in the number of departments under different specialised agencies (Warnapala 1972: 133). A system of village committees was one notable structural variation, newly introduced to the colonial administrative apparatus in the early 1900s mainly to improve irrigation. Such institutional changes were largely tied to the machinery of the colonial extractive economy, and altered existing administrative structures, laying the foundation of a 'modern' system of local government in the island (Collins 1951: 86). Contrary to popular belief, Collins argues that village committees simply reincarnated the precolonial village committee system, known as *gam sabha*s (village councils). In the urban areas, roughly around the late 1800s a similar micro-administrative structure was introduced, which bore a notable resemblance to the local administrative structures in the United Kingdom at that time (Collins 1951: 86).

Since the early 1830s, local elites became interested in serving in the colonial bureaucracy, and demanded increased opportunities in the colonial civil service (De Silva 2007: 535). Although initially the British rejected such demands, in 1833, on the recommendations of the Colebrook-Cameron Commission (CCC), the way was opened for 'natives' to serve in the colonial civil service. The CCC report stated that

> the public service should be freely open to all classes of persons based on their qualifications, the exclusive principles of the Civil Service should be relaxed and means of education should be held out to natives whereby they may in time qualify themselves for holding some higher posts. (Collins 1951: 68)

Despite its seemingly positive consequences, this CCC recommendation implied that locals needed to acquire the necessary knowledge and skills (that is, on administrative laws and functions) in order to serve in the colonial state service, based on the same criteria already applied to colonial bureaucrats (Oberst 1986: 166). In addition, a good knowledge of politics of the colony was a requirement, and was especially handy when manoeuvring policy reforms through the parameters set by the legislative political apparatus (Oberst 1986).

Subsequently the Donoughmore reforms of 1931 marked a major shift in the previously established institutional layout, expanding opportunities for local elites to enter the British civil service. This set in motion certain local political dynamics in the island, by stimulating local managerial and technical capacities, knowledge and skills, pre-requisites for eventual self-governance (LaPorte 1970: 159). However, by demanding specific skills and knowledge, colonial rule hindered opportunities for the lower classes to join the colonial bureaucracy, further formalising inequalities of opportunity among different groups in Sri Lanka's colonial society. The new rules introduced for colonial civil service examinations ensured that local recruits were tightly controlled (Collins 1951: 100). Those who were educated at leading Western educational institutes and those from the upper crust of local colonial society were favoured during recruitment (Fernando 1973: 364). Adherence to social values similar to the British, regardless of their actual performance in office, was favoured as well (Fernando 1973).

Such conditions for employment helped to foster a notably externally oriented value system among local bureaucratic elites, nurturing a quasi-patronage system that benefited colonially minded local elites of upper-class backgrounds as well as the British. Colonial practices moulded the attitudes and patterns of thoughts of these local recruits in line with the ideas of their rulers. By the same token, however, British disregard for their own proclaimed principles of neutrality and anonymity in state service ended up encouraging quasi-patronage practices (Fernando 1973: 363).

As local recruits began to demonstrate the required levels of competency in all domains (skills, knowledge and ideological subordination to British colonial rule), the British introduced several changes to previous recruitment policies, enabling more local recruits (Table 5.1). This was done also with a view to preparing local elites for future self-governance. This meant that by 1937, the recruitment of British and Europeans to the Ceylon Civil Service was completely halted (Collins 1951: 102), enabling the British treasury to save on high costs of administering the colony using British recruits.

Table 5.1 Europeans and Ceylonese, including others, in the Ceylon Civil Service

Year	Europeans	Ceylonese and Others
1920	79	11
1930	83	55
1940	49	81
1950	10	124

Source: Collins (1951: 102).

Following the recommendations of the Donoughmore Commission (1931), the various administrative structures and the administrative culture it introduced paved the way for creating a highly centralised decision-making system in which the local elites became more powerful (Wijeweera 1989: 228) and setting certain dynamics in the state-in-society relations in the late colonial period.

As we saw in the last chapter, with the introduction of universal franchise, also in 1931, inter-elite political competition gradually fed into the politicisation of central state institutions. Such centralisation tendencies became more visible in the ensuing period, especially as local elites started to assume various ministerial portfolios under late British rule. Seven out of ten ministerial portfolios were filled through a process of competitive elections, and the rest through nominations. By using their public office local elites began to cultivate their own patron–client networks of relationships, vying for influence with the rural masses, and seeking to edge out their rivals. Rising elites also used new administrative–developmental institutional structures, such as the interdepartmental committee system meant for skills coordination for various projects, as a means to encourage party loyalties from the public that could be helpful for their re-election prospects (LaPorte 1970: 159). Having secured access to state positions, and occupying an intermediary position between the masses and British colonial rulers, these local elites successfully intervened in local resource distribution mechanisms and started to solidify their own patronage relations (Wijeweera 1989: 288). Values associated with the civil service were adhered to as ideals. Thus, one elderly interviewee who had served in the Ceylon Civil Service recalled, 'The overall quality, neutrality and impartiality of the colonial state bureaucracy was still at its best' (R.4).

USING STATE INSTITUTIONS TO FINANCE PARTY PATRONAGE SYSTEM: 1948-1977

After independence, until the mid-1950s, ruling political elites did not make many changes to the state bureaucracy and the structure of the state as left behind by the British. Their motivations for keeping the colonial state apparatus in place can be explained in two ways. First, continuity benefited those elites who had already established themselves in the upper ranks of the bureaucracy and the government in colonial Ceylon. They did not seek any changes that might undermine the privileges they were enjoying under existing institutional arrangements. Second, inter-elite political competition was relatively mild shortly after independence, as Horowitz has observed. Elites were still genuinely inter-communal at this time, and shared many common values, having established a political culture of bargaining (Horowitz 1993: 3). None of these factions wanted any drastic changes to disturb the status quo.

Gradual changes introduced during the early post-independence years mainly focused on re-categorisation of the existing departmental system into two main ones, one category dealing with the regulatory and administration functions and the other dealing with economic development (Warnapala 1972: 134). In 1948, at independence, some new departments were introduced, including rural development, information, social services, town and country planning, census and statistics and parliamentary elections. Some had branches at regional, divisional and village levels (Warnapala 1972: 134). The elected representatives were keen to expand departmental activities to make a good impression among their constituencies and thus take credit for the country's rapid social and economic development (Warnapala 1972). After 1956, the responsibilities of the state were extended further into areas of economic and social development. They included rehabilitation of Kandyan peasantry, coconut cultivation, and agricultural and cultural services. These reforms were followed by a plethora of supporting committees, at regional, village and divisional levels. Overall, the performance of this growing administrative state structure had mixed results in meeting the proclaimed economic and social needs of the population. Warnapala especially has observed that overlapping functions and roles between various state bodies led to confusion over their designated responsibilities (1972: 135).

Perhaps, as Venugopal suggests, the emerging disorder and partial dysfunctionality can be explained in Foucauldian terms, which throws light on the possible instrumentality that lay behind these chaotic institutional developments and agendas (Venugopal 2011: 69). These new administrative bodies had some positive impacts on rural economic and social development and on agricultural in general. However, an expanding administrative structure was not without adverse consequences, in the form of emerging patronage relations, especially through the granting of employment to political allies. However, some of my interviewees suggested that in the 1950s, politicisation of the state bureaucracy and political patronage were still marginal, and the main beneficiaries were local English-educated upper classes. The less-politicised character of the state bureaucracy during the early post-independence years can be explained by the political elites' sense of respect towards the legal safeguards contained in the Soulbury Constitution, which explicitly sought to prevent the politicisation of state services and of the works of the Public Service Commission (PSC) (Warnapala 1974: 165). The PSC functioned as an effective screening mechanism for all public appointments, and had the authority to consult the national legislature when appointing higher offices to the state bureaucracy. These measures helped to secure public trust in state institutions, including from local communities. The public tended to perceive government service as a route to status, social prestige and authority, raising hopes among the educated lower-class local population of securing a future job in the state bureaucracy (De Silva 2007: 535).

There are numerous different interpretations of the radical transformation of the state bureaucracy in the ensuing period, and of why patronage politics subsequently became more widespread. A majority of the people I interviewed agreed that since 1956, a stronger patronage system had emerged across state institutions. They pointed out that this transformation of state bureaucratic institutions was also associated with the increasing need felt by new political elites of bourgeois origin to adjust the colonial bureaucratic structure to meet their own political needs. Some others acknowledged that intensification of patronage politics after the 1950s related to stronger direct pressures on political elites from lower-class masses and from the youth, whose rising expectations demanded that state resources and employment be opened up to them after independence (R.7; R.14; R.17). The statistical evidence supports this claim. According to a 1953 estimate, 18 per cent of the working age population was unemployed (Politicus 1972: 260). Unemployment and indebtedness had become compelling issues in the rural sector, and given the importance of rural electorates in winning elections, the struggles of the rural population had to be addressed by the ruling political elites. Certain limits were placed on the state's basic economic structure by its heavy dependence on taxes generated by three major export crops, and revenues were stretched relative to the basic needs of a growing population (Lakshman 1987: 11). The 10-year Economic Plan of 1959 was introduced by the ruling Mahajana Eksath Peramuna (MEP) regime, and aimed to improve the economic conditions of the masses, but faced tight budgetary restrictions (Politicus 1972: 260). Constraints on the budgets were both local and international (Lakshman 1989: 107).

Among the local factors, the population boom and the massive resource demand this created was noted. In addition, state institutions were expanding in parallel to the rising political elite, and intra-elite competition for political office and state positions, especially around the birth of the Sri Lanka Freedom Party (SLFP) out of the United National Party (UNP), and with traditional Marxist parties flocking around the SLFP (Politicus 1972: 263–66). Politicisation of state institutions during this period seemed almost inevitable, given this backdrop of increasing inter-elite political competition at the centre. Lakshman has observed that providing economic benefits to certain groups during this period (1950s to early 1970s) was a part of the ruling elites' political strategy for securing political legitimacy and hegemony (1987: 12). An integral element of this legitimation strategy was a series of massive social democratic welfare reforms (Venugopal 2011: 60).[2] With highly centralised state institutions, a growing dependency was created between communities in the peripheries and those in control of central state institutions when it came to accessing public funds, providing new opportunities for political elites at the centre to exploit state budgets for their own ends. In parallel, the legacy of the institutional structures left behind by the British colonisers, based on assumptions about the Weberian rationality of the bureaucracy, still mitigated against use of state resources to further the exploitative ambitions of politicians at this time.

As political elites struggled for power, and as these struggles began to intensify, especially between the UNP and the SLFP, the state bureaucracy became increasingly politicised. State institutions and resources were increasingly changed to serve the interests of one faction or party, frustrating those in opposition and denying them access to state institutions and budgets. In the ensuing period, every regime that came to power resorted to instrumental use of the state institutions in building new political alliances and for incorporating the lower-class masses into national politics. Members of parliament (MPs) were involved in local distribution of resources, beyond any ordinary requirement of 'constituency service', as a means of gaining support. The MPs became unofficial ombudsmen in relation to resource-related decisions, politicising the role of the ombudsman in the process (Wijeweera 1989: 292). Given the central role assigned to local MPs in resource allocation, collectively and individually, local communities sought the help of their MPs whenever they wished to access state resources, whether in the form of welfare payments, employment or other resources, ensuring both a strong demand and a supply for such forms of patronage politics (Wijeweera 1989: 292).

Consequently, by end of the first decade of independence, the gradual politicisation of state institutions, representation and the bureaucracy had almost completely eclipsed any remaining notions of impartial Weberian rule or the ethos of British-trained bureaucratic elites who had run the state bureaucracy along technocratic lines (Wijeweera 1989: 291). Access to state resources had come to depend on one's proximity to an individual or a community centred on local MPs and their political party structures. One respondent, who had served in the state bureaucracy for decades and was an eyewitness to these dynamics noted, 'Since the late 1950s, the structure and the quality of the bureaucracy established during the British colonial rule have been undergoing tremendous transformation' (R.4). In the words of another respondent, who had served his entire career in the highest ranks in the Ceylon Civil Service,

> the public service has changed tremendously; it is a complete turnaround of what it was before. Today people depend more on politicians than on public servants to get their services done; political patronage is the answer to everything. (R.25)

These statements are testimonies to the genuine concerns of those who served in the state bureaucracy during the transitional period between colonial rule and post-independence. They observed the politicisation of the bureaucracy and other state institutions with concern, expressing disappointment at their own loss of power, prestige and status as bureaucrats in relation to political elites.

STRUGGLING FOR HEGEMONY: ELITE CIVIL SERVANTS AND POLITICAL ELITES

Towards independence, as recruitment criteria imposed by the British were relaxed, it became easier for upper-class men to become employed in the prestigious Ceylon Civil Service. From the perspective of the political elites, those recruited into the British bureaucracy and the local civil service during the colonial period were alien to the local society. During colonial rule, meritocracy was combined with the requirement that civil servants be ideologically subservient to Western values. These were the combined basis for recruitment of civil servants into the colonial service. For commanding superiority over political elites, bureaucrats were resented, especially since political elites could claim to have obtained a mandate from the common people (Ranugge 2000: 53). According to political elites, upper-class, fluent English-speaking bureaucratic elites had become distanced from local realities and communities, and were insensitive to their problems. Bureaucrats did not uncritically follow advice from political elites with regard to issues concerning public service delivery. This led to accusations of 'unresponsiveness' on the part of the bureaucrats from political elites who could not conceal their disappointments about these public servants' lack of loyalty to the regime in power (Wijeweera 1989: 292).

By promoting negative views of bureaucratic elites, the new ruling political elites soon portrayed the civil service mentality as a barrier to reaching out to the public. During the early post-independence years, distinct tensions thus emerged between politicians and elite bureaucrats (Samaratunga and Bennington 2002: 93). In fact, such tensions had little to do with the quality of the civil service as such. Instead, hostility to the bureaucratic elites was part of an unfolding power struggle between the two groups for control, legitimacy and authority over the state apparatuses and the masses.

Competing and shifting power relations between bureaucratic and political elites were manifested at the local community level as well (McCourt 2007b: 433). For instance, when distributing state resources and services, electorates that had voted for a particular government or political party, in the expectation of enjoying the fruits of state patronage, did not always tolerate the continued impartiality of state functionaries in the ministries and local government. Such community sentiments threatened to undermine the legitimacy and authority also of those who had assumed political power in the name of representing their constituency. Since the mid-1950s, it may have been such situations that encouraged elected politicians and regimes of this period to introduce reforms that served to establish greater domination over a more politically subservient state bureaucracy. From the point of view of Gramscian hegemony-building strategies, these reforms largely entailed consent-building, but wherever the consent-building strategies failed, the ruling elites resorted to coercive strategies. Punishing civil servants by making politically motivated transfers was one example of the underlying coercive aspect of such reforms.

As De Silva observed, after Sri Lanka's independence, political elites could no longer afford to ignore the sentiments of voters. Sri Lanka's politics – and especially the outcomes of periodic parliamentary elections – has become a matter of considerable significance for both politicians and the communities they seek to represent (quoted in McCourt 2007b: 433). In many ways, political elites were in a vulnerable position, having few resources of their own to draw on, compared with bureaucratic elites who enjoyed a more secure position, mostly in permanent jobs for life. As pressures on political elites mounted, with demands from their local communities for more resources, the continued reluctance of state bureaucrats to cooperate with them, and follow elected politicians' and ministers' instructions about resource distribution, started to trouble ruling political elites. During this period, tensions between politicians and state bureaucrats sparked numerous ad-hoc reforms in the state bureaucracy, all aimed at undermining the secure position of state bureaucrats. Pointing to the vested interests of politicians, civil servants often rejected reforms legislated by the ruling regime in power, leading to accusations of the gross politicisation of the state bureaucracy by political elites, who in turn sought to establish their dominance and authority over bureaucrats (Wijeweera 1989: 292).

The governments that came to office during the first three decades after independence introduced a total of some 30 separate reform bills affecting the state bureaucracy (De Alwis 2009). All these reforms were directed, at least partially, at reducing the independent authority of civil servants and aimed to enhance the power and influence of political elites and their control over public resources and their distribution. The Wilmot Perera Commission Report of 1961[3] (Government of Sri Lanka 1961) provides some important clues about the underlying motivations of some of the state sector reforms of this period. In addition to the justification that a conducive environment was needed for implementing the flagship Language Act of 1956, the report also underscored that the post-colonial state bureaucracy suffered from its elitist composition. Civil servants had been warned about the negative consequences of their past prolonged association of with the colonial authorities (De Alwis 2009).

Interestingly, by equating the elitism of state bureaucrats with elitism of the British colonisers, this report deliberately appealed to the cultural and moral sentiments of the Sinhalese majority. The report went even further, comparing the structures of the state bureaucracy to a fixed system of caste hierarchies (Wijeweera 1989: 289). The report also pointed out that the legacy of the colonial state bureaucracy was rooted in indigenous village headmen, a system that mainly favoured a restricted circle of local families of high social status. This kind of argument fitted well with Prime Minister Bandaranaike's argument for introducing the Sinhala Language Act of 1956. This was framed as the means to expand social and economic opportunities for about 90 per cent of those who were not educated in English, yet had to compete with the 10 per cent of the English educated who occupied 90 per cent of the positions in the colonial state bureaucracy, and remained dominant a decade later (De Alwis 2009: 140).

Officials in state institutions were dismayed that the report doubted their ability to handle the new economic ventures embarked on by the post-independence regimes, questioning the relevance of their competencies to a new developmental philosophy oriented towards the masses. In many ways the emerging scenario suggested the political elites' determination to sow the seeds for a new historical bloc where elite bureaucrats would have only a subordinate role to play in the service of the political elites, the latter having had acquired the status of the dominant class above all elite groups. By comparing the transformation of the direction of the evolution of state institutions upon the implementation of the recommendations of the Wilmot Perera Commission, a respondent who had served in the state service opined that the reforms not only abolished the Ceylon Civil Service but, importantly, it also marked the official inauguration of the institutionalisation of the patronage political system and the decline of public administration. As another retired senior civil servant anecdotally recalled,

> immediately after reforms, those who got immediately recruited into the civil service by the politicians through back channels were the ones who failed in the civil service entrance examination in the first place. (R.4)

Despite such criticisms of bias in the reforms recommended by the commission, some would support the idea that its advice helped reform the feudal character of public service and opened up public employment to a broader cross-section of Sri Lankan society (Wijeweera 1989: 289). However, those who served in the public sector expressed their scepticism of the underlying motivations of administrative reforms recommended by the commission. According to them, these recommendations had more to do with the growing inter-elite political struggles at the centre than with providing services for the masses. Different elite groups were polarised and sought to strengthen their political alliances with the lower-class majority constituted of blue-collar labourers and rural peasants. By introducing various state reforms (not only administrative but also economic and political), the underlying motivations of the ruling political elites was to turn all state institutions into promising and strategic arena of building political alliances with the lower classes and to ensure their mobilisation and consent to their rule.

SOCIALIST RHETORIC AND THE POLITICS OF STATE REFORMS

This section focuses on the institutionalisation of patronage politics during the era of socialist control over government, under the SLFP-led governments, the party that ruled for most of the period from the mid-1950s to 1977. As previously mentioned, politicisation of the state bureaucracy and manipulation of state institutions for coalition-building by political elites are linked with changing dynamics of state-in-society relations, and with inter-elite power struggles during the first three decades after independence. After independence factional conflicts among political elites intensified, compelling the regime in power to look for new ways to incorporate the masses into their alliance-building projects, in the hope of ensuring their political survival. Such alliance-building for mass political incorporation required that certain privileges and concessions be extended to the masses, notably welfare entitlements. The SLFP-led regimes sought to pursue a socialist-style set of public policies, and upheld this template to serve its left-wing objectives. However, as noted by Waldner in other, similar contexts (1999: 33), when political elites choose socialist rhetoric and socialist-oriented policy measures, they also seek to retain control over the state through electoral political power. The socialist model was critical to state transformation in many post-independence regimes at this time, and, interestingly, in the case of Sri Lanka, the SLFP was prepared to make considerable economic and political sacrifices in order to keep the state's socialist profile intact.

Considering the importance of the youth, in terms of their numerical strength and the social power they possess, the ruling regimes were keen to find ways to provide employment, especially for increasing numbers of vernacular-educated local youth.[4] For example, by 1953, 65 per cent of the population acquired literacy. However, rising unemployment (Politicus 1972: 260) meant that in one year alone, 1969, 10,000 university graduates had become unemployed after completing their tertiary education (Politicus 1972). In the English-speaking public sector, youth who were mostly educated in the vernacular (Sinhala) had very limited prospects of securing employment (De Alwis 2009: 139). For many young graduates, finding other forms of employment was difficult, since the private sector was too small to absorb the number of young people coming onto the job market. In the background of the ruling elites' socialist economy drumbeat and their deliberate attempt to paralyse the development of the private sector to keep their rival Marxist political bases under control, the local capitalist class was also not showing much enthusiasm in investing in the private sector. Introduction of the State Industrial Act of 1957 and a number of new state-managed industrial corporations established under this act, such as state banks, a public transport board, wholesale and retail import and export agencies, state insurance cooperation, aviation services, a plantation agriculture board, and an industrial production corporation, further discouraged the local capitalist class from making any investment in the private sector, which could be easily run over by state bodies (Wijeweera 1989: 289).

This situation worsened in subsequent decades as the effects of socialist economic policies further limited the space for independent, private sector activities. Instead, a growing state sector became the main agent of economic development, of capital accumulation and resource management and of distribution, as well as of employment. Lakshman suggests that it was the effect of poor economic performance,[5] improved educational opportunities, high unemployment, growing political awareness and frequent regime changes that were used as justifications for the birth of social welfarism and socialist state policies. Even so, socialist policies still could not address all these issues (Lakshman 1987: 15). Various socialist-inspired policies were enacted by the SLFP-led regimes that governed the country more or less from independence to 1977, but they did very little to satisfy the interests of the majority in the society. Nevertheless, what they actually contributed towards was to secure the bourgeois–elite domination of the state (Lakshman 1987). It was mainly the ruling elites' political objectives that were met by introducing several more reforms of state and private production structures, under an overarching 'socialist' regime. Public enterprises (PEs) were established, with the express aim of transforming colonial economic structures to better address local needs.

In line with Lakshman (1987: 10, 15), I suggest that the introduction of PEs was mainly motivated by the need to satisfy demands for advancement from segments of the capitalist class close to the ruling SLFP government. Yet it was presented to the public as a necessary initiative of the state on the path to realising a socialist system, to benefit the poor. Scholars who have contested the ruling regimes' official discourses around the PE reforms see the sole intention of such policies as being to capture the commanding heights of all aspects of the economy in the hands of the ruling party. De Silva justifies this interpretation by drawing a comparison between the outcomes of PEs and its declared objectives. For him, the overall failure of PEs to produce employment and redistribute resources towards the poorest were the result of gross government mismanagement and inefficiency, overseen by unqualified political appointees of the SLFP (De Silva 1987: 258). He further argues that public state-run companies established as PEs became places of corruption, political favouritism and even political revenge (De Silva 1987). Similarly, Warnapala notes that, by introducing the PEs and nationalising essential public services, the SLFP governments punished public servants who sought to remain neutral or supported rival political parties. They were forcibly transferred, dismissed and demoted (Warnapala quoted in De Alwis 2009: 142).

An example given by Warnapala is the nationalisation of bus transport under the SLFP that supports his claim further. According to him, it was intended to punish private bus companies that had contributed substantial donations to the election fund of the rival party, the UNP (Warnapala quoted in De Alwis 2009). The propagated socialist ideology underlying nationalisation was little more than the fashion of that era, and thinly masked an emerging and institutionalised patronage system centred on state institutions and state-run companies, amounting to little more than ideological manipulation for consent-building, and strategies of coercion – a way of punishing the opposition and their political allies.

Other examples show political parties assuming state office during this period and introducing reforms that enabled them to bypass checks and balances from public servants and to more directly engage in the dispensing of patronage and benefits from state revenues and budgets. An early example was the abolition of the examination system previously in place to recruit the *grama sevaka*s (village headmen). Under new rules, *grama sevaka*s would be appointed on the recommendations of the local MPs instead (Wijeweera 1989: 293). Given the authority of the *grama sevaka* in everyday village affairs, especially in resource distribution at the village level, appointing them on MPs' recommendations in effect allowed MPs to take control of the entire village administrative structure through appointment of those loyal to their own political party, and then using the *grama sevaka* position to mobilise village-level support during election times. In 1973, by reorganising the consumer cooperative networks, the SLFP government in power replaced the previous system of elected boards for these bodies with a system of nomination based on MPs' advice. In a similar fashion, the members of cultivation committees and agricultural productivity committees were all appointed on the recommendations issued by the minister of agriculture and lands to the local MPs (Wijeweera 1989: 293).

On the surface, all these measures of nationalisation and state control appeared to align with a socialist ideology of economic nationalism. However, they produced devastating effects on economic growth and the development of private enterprise in Sri Lanka. The growing population was increasingly dependent on the state to fulfil its material needs, especially in relation to food and employment. The SLFP regime's aversion to capitalism can be seen as justifying its own, illegitimate form of accumulation that had nothing much to do with socialism (Moore 1997b: 336). A major reason underlying the SLFP's reluctance to embark on a more capitalist form of economic development was that this would destroy the power base of its main supporters – the rural elites of the Goyigama caste and the majority Sinhala-Buddhist-originated communities (Moore 1997b: 336). Therefore, development of the private sector was consistently discouraged by attacking the principles of capitalism, even justifying a socialist economic policy on the ground that capitalism was 'alien to Buddhist culture' (Moore 1990: 374). Later, the SLFP government supported state-owned corporations with money donated from communist countries in the name of socialist solidarity. The main opposition party throughout this period was the UNP, whose alliances were mainly with capitalist countries and private enterprise.

In the face of this opposition party, joining hands with international socialist forces seemed the most strategic foreign policy available to the SLFP. Despite the hype, eventually the public companies started with donor money from the socialist bloc began to suffer from massive deficits due to being grossly mismanaged and plagued with corruption, political interference and the recruitment of unqualified personnel on the basis of party patronage (Warnapala 1974).

Under the Second Five-year Plan (1972–1976) enacted by the SLFP-led United Front (UF) government, state management was extended to public services as well as industry. The long-term objective of the plan was achieving 'socialism' or 'socialist democracy' (Balakrishnan 1973: 1155). Until the economy was opened up under the UNP government in 1977, state-owned service agencies had a complete monopoly in the service industry. Although the official aim given for establishing state corporations was now to generate revenue and strengthen state capacity for accumulation, the outcomes suggested the reverse. Those who had worked in public service tended to view such state-owned companies as deeply enmeshed with expanding relations of nepotism and political favouritism. State-owned and state-run companies became the locus of redistribution for short-term political gain. In their view, these industries suffered from lack of financial autonomy and profitability as they came under the direct control of the ruling regime. The political capital these industries brought to the SLFP was used to mobilise more support for the ruling party, enabling it to hold on to state power for so long.

In the absence of favourable conditions for state capital accumulation to finance the patronage system, abusing the state structure was seen by the ruling elites as the best option to keep their already mobilised political alliances intact and reproduce the political elites' authority. Yet this strategy also eroded the autonomy of the state sector to almost nil and implied a tremendous and continuous expansion of state budgets. Table 5.2 shows a steady increase in the number of employees in the public sector over the first three decades after independence. This suggests that expansion of the state sector was linked to a patronage political system, as was reconfirmed by several interviewees who were insider-witnesses to these developments at that time (R.1; R.4; R.13; R.14).

However, sustaining the direction of the 'socialist' politics embarked on by the ruling SLFP elites required a constant process of state renewal and reform, to expand the revenue basis for patronage. At a certain point, it even

Table 5.2 Growth of public service, number of employees, 1948–1980

Year	Population (Millions)	Government	Local Government	State Corporations
1948	7	109,854	n.a	Negligible
1958	9	222,940	15,000	n.a
1973	13	341,805	27,000	167,000
1980	15	399,840	44,427	755,558

Source: Wijeweera (1989: 297).

Note: Corporations are either government-funded or semi-government establishments.

required the elimination of the Soulbury Constitution, when in 1972, the first republican constitution was introduced, doing away with the Westminster-style system. One respondent who had worked in the health sector at that time recalled the impact as follows:

> There were many qualified assistant medical practitioners in the island, but after granting powers to the cabinet in 1972 to appoint medical practitioners, they were only recruited from the [loyal] electorate. The list of medical practitioners was selected based on the electorates and then went to the ministry. This system not only reinforced patronage politics in appointments, it also began to cultivate masters in the public offices. For instance, those who joined the service with the blessings of the politicians acted with superior status. (R.4)

Using specific provisions in the new constitution, the SLFP ruling elites granted more powers to cabinet ministers over local appointments, over civil service promotions and over the transfer of public servants between posts and locations.

THE GHOST OF SOCIALISM

Not everyone agrees that the SLFP regime based on socialism and welfare policies was used for political alliance-building through the nurturing of a system of patronage politics. However, the parallel growth of state control over the economy and the rise of patronage political networks suggests that this was the case (McCourt 2007a: 11, 2006: 234). According to the majority of the people I interviewed, including those who were first-hand witnesses to these transformations, this was largely the case (R.1; R.4; R.9; R.10; R.13).

The success of the governments in this period largely depended on the performance of the economy. Until the economic downturn experienced in the early 1970s, when an anti-state youth movement led by the Janatha Vimukthi Peramuna (JVP) started to protest, rising revenues from exports had helped to cushion the regime from disappointed hopes. Given the much less positive economic situation after 1973, it became more difficult to generate enough material resources to dispense patronage for political mobilisation and political incorporation of the masses, especially the youth from the periphery. As the economy dwindled, the reliance of the political elites on state revenues and public institutions intensified. By officially adopting a socialist set of economic policies, the SLFP governments of 1956–1959, 1965–1970 and 1970–1977 moved to capture not only state institutions, but also private economic production, using it for their own ends to dispense state patronage to their allies. The transformation observed in the entire realm of state institutions and state policies were not mere material, but with a serious ideological foundation as well, all integral for the ruling elites' overall hegemony-building project. Faced with multiple pressures resulting from the faltering economy, population boom, increasing demand for material resources and factionalising politics at the centre, the SLFP governments had brought the entire economy under state control, significantly extending the role and size of the public sector. In the process, scores were settled with political rivals and complete domination was sought over state, society and even economy.

Theoretically, in a socialist system, the state assumes a primary role in economic development. It controls the use and distribution of resources and production, and assigns various roles and functions to various state institutions in its efforts to reach its political and economic objectives. Fulfilling these roles requires an enlarged state apparatus and a matching bureaucracy. In Sri Lanka, the state's economic functions became so highly politicised that by the time of the UF government (1970–1975), the state held a near-monopoly of purchasing power and distributing capacity in relation to most essential products (Richardson 2005: 312). The Coconut Development Authority was introduced in 1971, and in 1974 a system of price controls on paddy production, which became subject to compulsory state purchase under the Paddy Marketing Board (Athukorala and Jayasuriya 1994: 18–19).

To reinvigorate their brand of socialism, the ruling regime orchestrated anti-Western slogans, such as 'economic liberation from foreign domination', as a way to divert attention away from the politicisation of state institutions under 'socialism'. Such slogans drew attention to foreign domination of the Sri Lankan economy, successfully keeping a lid on the growing internal tensions because of domination by the ruling class and subordination of the lay society. These anti-Western sentiments corresponded closely with the dominant sentiments of the Sinhala-Buddhist rural petty bourgeoisie, the main support base on which the ruling political elites relied to mobilise the electorate (Lakshman 1987: 15). The nationalist tone of the Business Acquisition Act of 1971 also appealed to anti-foreigner sentiments among the rural majority (Kelegama 2000: 1479). This Act allowed the state to absorb any private companies with over 100 employees. Private industries such as the British Ceylon Corporation and the Wellawatte Spinning and Weaving Mill were nationalised (De Silva 1987: 258). The Land Reform Law, No. 1 of 1972 was one of the earliest examples of nationalisation, and through this law the state-imposed ceilings on private ownership of land, monitored by a newly established Land Reform Commission (LRC). The LRC was vested with the authority to acquire privately held land in excess of the legally permitted ceilings (Bastian n.d.: 10). Three years later, the scope of the reform was extended through the Land Reform (Amendment) Law, No. 39 of 1975 which brought all land held by public companies under the control of the state. Once again, with nationalisation, these large-scale land ventures became sources of revenue to dispense political patronage and reward the regime's supporters. Nationalisation also provided an ever-expanding number of white-collar jobs in the public sector, but mainly for the political supporters of the ruling party. The LRC recommended that the ruling regime should commit more seriously to ensuring the efficient functioning of land-holding companies, especially by eliminating the system of political patronage and cutting 'hidden subsidies' granted to senior regime-friendly public officials (Richardson 2005: 313). Some even opined that, in spite of such recommendations, the trend of making political appointments to such state ventures was more or less unstoppable (R.1; R.4; R.7; R.10). Overall, this system ended up either issuing threats or granting rewards as ways to ensure loyalty to the regime.

Table 5.3 compares some characteristics of those who serve in classical and in welfare bureaucracies. These differences also help to convey the contrasting values and ideal functioning of bureaucrats during the colonial

Table 5.3 Types of bureaucracies

Classical Bureaucracies	Welfare Bureaucracies
Classical Bureaucrats	Welfare Bureaucrats
Professionals/Intellectuals	Professionals/Intellectuals
Corps	Social reproducers
Workers	Workers
Domination ⟶	**Subordination**

Source: Hoff (1985: 221).

period and under the 'socialist' period of the SLFP. Identifying bureaucrats under welfare bureaucracy as social reproducers helps shed light on how they form the overall hegemonic relationship of ruling elites as patrons and the welfare bureaucrats as subordinates in a chain of welfare relationships with workers and peasants.

During the period of 'socialist' state policies, the patronage networks established were multi-directional; they operated between upper levels of state bureaucrats and the ruling political elites as well as between the upper hierarchy of the state bureaucracy and those working in lower rungs of the public sector (Moore 1997b: 346–68). Patronage relationships were important as a criterion of recruitment; for public sector employees and bureaucrats, to remain outside the symbolic politics of the ruling regime was difficult. High-level state bureaucrats appointed as secretaries to ministries or heads of government departments, statutory bodies or state enterprises were all capable of influencing the organisational and political behaviour of a large number of lower-level public servants working under them. In addition, through close ties between upper-rung appointees and those with political power, their combined authority helped make peripheral communities dependent on state institutions for accessing welfare resources, helping both sets of elites to gain enormous influence over these communities' political behaviour as well. In many ways, politicised bureaucrats were able to help the ruling regimes spread their ideology of rule among social forces in the periphery. Some argue that it was through the welfare state's operations that the ruling ideology of Sinhala-Buddhist nationalism gained legitimacy among the masses in the periphery as the official state policy (Moore 1997b: 337).

In time, as senior state bureaucrats played a more instrumental role in promoting the regime's political ideology, political elites became reluctant to initiate any further state reforms that might undermine the authority of senior public officials. As Moore claims, the result was that spaces for different political opinions and ideologies started to shrink, tilting the dominant political ideology towards more right-wing political ideas and culture, which protected only the privileged few. Lakshman has observed that the officially socialist policies of the state during this period were never particularly left-wing (1987: 15). This chapter goes on to argue that the nature of politics at the end of the 'socialist' era (1970–1977) already had a tendency to further intra-elite competition and fragmentation, encouraging hasty and instrumental coalition-building, which helps to explain the fragility and short-lived nature of coalition politics during this period. Such short-lived political alliances played a part in elite politics tilting more and more towards right-wing politics, with most regimes subsequently positioning themselves somewhere between centre-right and far right on the ideological spectrum. Socialist left-wing political rhetoric, often heard during election times, was merely part of the elites' manipulative politics aimed at political alliance-building and luring the voters. The majority of the respondents pointed out that the socialist stand of the SLFP-led coalition governments was mostly to satisfy its left-wing coalition partners, whose partnership was essential for the SLFP to consolidate its hold on state power. Out of such uneasy alliances came the hegemony of right-wing politics, cloaked in left-wing political rhetoric.

As discussed earlier, the underlying reasons for the politicisation of the state bureaucracy in the period 1948–1977 correspond to numerous social and economic struggles experienced by particular social forces in the periphery and internal struggles among political elites at the centre. Migdal reminds us in his state-in-society model (2001) that the situation in Sri Lanka during the short-lived socialist regimes of the early post-independence period revolved around elites' political struggles at the centre to connect with various social struggles in the peripheries.

The use, abuse and manipulation of the state apparatus in the pre-1977 period for coalition-building and overall political hegemony of the ruling elites continued in the post-1977 era, but with a much more liberal economic ideology attached. One of the main changes noted in the elite-sponsored patronage system that operated through state institutions was its veering to the right, and the marked increase in social and political violence. The following section discusses several key areas and examples where the state administrative structure in the post-1977 period came be to abused and exploited by the new centre-right ruling regime led by the UNP.

THE GHOST OF LIBERALISM: THE POST-1977 PERIOD

A plethora of political and economic reforms were introduced after 1977 and helped the dominant Sinhalese ruling elites to build political alliances and further advance their hegemony-building project through the state and, increasingly, through the market. More coercive strategies went along with a broad shift from 'socialism' of the state to a liberal state that professed to be for more of a 'free market' economy than previous regimes (Figure 5.1).

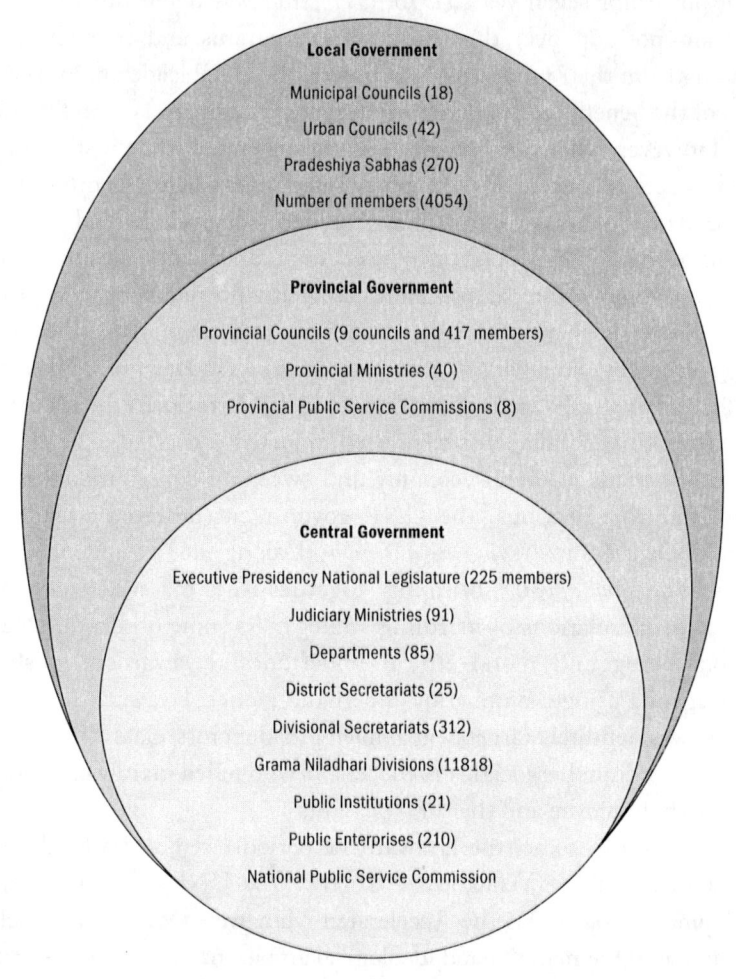

Local Government
Municipal Councils (18)
Urban Councils (42)
Pradeshiya Sabhas (270)
Number of members (4054)

Provincial Government
Provincial Councils (9 councils and 417 members)
Provincial Ministries (40)
Provincial Public Service Commissions (8)

Central Government
Executive Presidency National Legislature (225 members)
Judiciary Ministries (91)
Departments (85)
District Secretariats (25)
Divisional Secretariats (312)
Grama Niladhari Divisions (11818)
Public Institutions (21)
Public Enterprises (210)
National Public Service Commission

Figure 5.1 Structure of government (as of 2008)
Source: Based on data in De Alwis (2009).

In the post-1977 period, the political elites assuming office required a renewed and different set of expansive strategies that would enable them to stay in power. Considering the state of the economy (crisis) and the diminishing stock of exploitable resources available for maintaining the loyalties of already mobilised rural and urban forces, the ruling elites increasingly relied on the public sector to meet their narrow political objectives, which was perhaps not that surprising (ABD 2004: i). Right after the UNP came to power, they made a fresh set of political appointments to top levels of the state sector (McCourt 2007b: 432). The UNP had been out of power for seven years (1970–1977), and was determined to secure a dominant position over the entire state apparatus and over the society. Learning from their predecessors in power, the UNP leadership was acutely aware of the benefits of financing a state-based patronage system for political ends. However, when the previous UF regime ended, state institutions had already been exhausted for the purposes of patronage. Another strategy was needed. So unlike its 'socialist' predecessors, which had introduced reforms gradually, the UNP introduced some drastic changes to the entire state apparatus.[6] These changes were justified with reference to widespread public disappointment with poor economic conditions under the previous UF government. Following the overwhelming mandate the UNP received in the 1977 general elections, with a two-thirds majority in the national legislature, this mandate was then used to justify a really drastic change of course – towards a liberal economy and sweeping constitutional reforms. Soon after the elections, the UNP government declared its adherence to an 'open economy' (*nidahas aarthikaya*) alongside 'a righteous society' (*dharmishta samaajaya*),[7] bringing together the material and moral–ideological foundations of its ruling strategy. As some observed, albeit the freedom-loving and moral–ethical undertones, Jayawardene pushed its policy agenda using a number of underhand tactics. Jayawardene's political formula was definitely targeted at a much broader cross-class alliance, which was different from his socialist predecessors who relied mainly on mobilising the petty bourgeoisie and the rural peasants.

According to some, the Jayawardene period resembled a kind of 'free-market dictatorship' (Venugopal 2011: 69). The UNP's flagship economic development project was the Accelerated Mahaweli Development Scheme, an example of the material and ideological ambitions of the new government (Spencer 2008: 621). To be able to implement this huge resettlement and irrigation scheme, the UNP leadership needed to overhaul state institutions. Contrary to its predecessors, Jayawardene's government sought funding from overseas, especially from commercial banks, in the form of huge loans, along with some foreign aid grants, used to launch an ambitious development agenda. These foreign funds were instrumental not only in funding the large-scale Mahaweli scheme but also for funding institutional changes favoured by the new government, institutionalising forms of patronage politics in a renewed institutional arena that the party elites could control (Spencer 2008: 623).

The most drastic change introduced was the second republican constitution (1978), marking the desire for a clear break with the past, institutionally speaking. The provisions of the new constitution allowed the UNP to swiftly replace the SLFP-leaning bureaucracy with a UNP-leaning state bureaucracy. Another major change witnessed was the shifting of the centre of power from the parliament to the executive president's office, hence bringing what had been rather diffuse political-party-based patronage networks directly under the new office of the executive president. From most respondents' perspective, and as noted by other political observers of this period, the 1978 constitution changed both the direction of politics in Sri Lanka and the whole trajectory of state-building (Warnapala 1974: 156–58). This constitution paved the way for patronage politics to become institutionalised in new ways, within the state system, across all public institutions. Table 5.4 offers a summary comparison between the first and the second republican constitutions and the shifting direction of powers.

The second republican constitution removed various checks and balances on the executive, allowing the president to reorganise power relations more or less at whim. Using powers he had vested in himself as executive president, Jayawardene now dismantled the Parliamentary Select Committee responsible for overseeing state appointments. He then influenced appointments at the higher levels of the state bureaucracy, openly politicising these portfolios. The direct presidential appointments to high public offices completely overrode the power and authority even of the national legislature (Wijeweera 1989: 294). Such radical reforms resulted in state institutions that revolved almost entirely around the personalised rule of the president and a loyal group of MPs (Wijeweera 1989).

These changes left little room for rival political parties or other anti-regime political movements to arise. As Venugopal observes, during this

Table 5.4 Comparison between the First and the Second Republican Constitutions

Aspect	First Republican Constitution (1972)	Second Republican Constitution (1978)
Supreme Instrument of State power	National State Assembly (NSA)	President
Head of State	President (Nominated by Prime Minister)	President (elected by people)
Head of Government	Prime Minister	President
Legislative power	Parliament (bicameral)	Parliament (unicameral)
Executive power	Cabinet of Ministers	President
Judicial power	NSA exercises though courts	Courts established under the constitution
Highest judicial appellate body	Supreme court of Sri Lanka	Supreme court of Sri Lanka
Determination of Number of ministers and assignment of subjects	Prime Minister	President
Appointment of ministers	President on the advice of the Prime Minister	President
Appointment of Public Officer	Cabinet of Ministers	President (18th amendment)

Source: Adapted from Nanayakkara (2006: 426–27).

period, civil war began in the north and east; this too served the interests of the regime and was used to justify pushing forward Jayawardene's agenda of strengthening the executive and opening up the economy (2011: 70). A majority of those I interviewed considered that the president's executive powers were geared towards his numerous personal and political agendas – in particular, the cultivation of very close-knit networks of patronage around the president and the discretionary use of executive power to appoint MPs to ministries as he pleased. Most positions were 'gifted' by the president to his inner circle of party loyalists, his 'henchmen'. Jayawardene's approach to his expanded presidential powers created a renewed sense of hierarchy inside the ruling party. This was centred on his own dominant personality and worked to sanction his unapologetic 'iron fist' approach to intra-party dissent, crushing internal resistance to his autocratic rule. In many ways these developments mirror the path to Fascism during inter-war Italy (Adamson 1980) where the relative autonomy of politics and gradual detachment of social classes from the political parties tbegan to occur with the introduction of more sophisticated and systematic alliance-building strategies that were aligned with the broader cultural whole. Jayawardene too pursued similar goals in Sri Lanka by using the wholesome cultural notion of *dharmishta samaajaya* (righteous society), which was tightly aligned with Sinhala-Buddhist nationalism. Additionally, Jayawardene also manipulated the parliament by introducing a new political system and a new constitution, in Gramcian terms 'building a long life' for the UNP. Just like what Gramsci observed in the Fascist build-up in Italy, Jayawardena was keen to rope in the lower-class segments of society, most unlikely supporters of his glittery liberal economic project, without uniting them around the Sinhala-Buddhist cultural and religious symbols.

Under Jayawardene's new political dispensation, ordinary MPs took on new tasks in state administration, through the system of district ministers (1978), the Public Service Commission was also re-established (1978), and District Development Councils (DDCs) were created (1980). In the economy, PEs were privatised. Taken together, these measures institutionalised the parliamentary electorate as the base unit of public administration, while ensuring that the UNP re-incorporated and remobilised various social forces around its own political networks and priorities. Politicisation of the state bureaucracy was no longer behind the scenes, but out in the open (Warnapala 1974: 164–66). Some observed that this further enlarged the public sector, in spite of privatisation, tightening the regime's hold over budgetary decisions and resource allocation. It is interesting to note that these efforts to recentralise authority and state control appeared contradictory to the open-door, externally oriented economic policy pursued by the regime. Again, the majority of those I interviewed agreed that the public sector expanded with the start of the war and the coming of the new government, including through the proliferation of a range of quasi-government institutions. However, in terms of number of employees in the state sector, this started to decline in comparison with the previous era, given the partial and full privatisation of PEs after 1977. Employment in these industries shrank as workers who had been given jobs under the previous regime were let go of (Samaratunga and Bennington 2002: 94). Yet the Department of Census and Statistics reports confirm that after several rounds of privatisation, there was no decline in the number of employees in the semi-government sector. As some interviewees pointed out, because of the recruitment of a large number of party-friendly-unskilled political allies, the state sector performed poorly as well. For those in power, the productivity of workers was not a serious concern so long as public employees remained faithful to the party elites. Meanwhile, new recruits were tasked with diffusing any potential political unrest detrimental to the UNP's overall hegemony (Hettige 2010).[8]

The most worrisome aspect of political patronage in the state sector was the soaring financial costs of maintaining the system. In 2009, of the total state tax revenues of LKR 618 billion, more than half, or LKR 356 billion, was allocated to public sector wages and salaries (LBO 2010). Since the majority of these state sector employees had been political appointees, and productivity was low, much of this massive public spending could be classified as pure political patronage. In addition to their salaries, permanent employees in the public sector received additional in-service and after-service benefits, including pensions, housing and educational loans from state banks at low interest rates, scholarships and full health care coverage for family members. Their salaries were also tax-free. This meant that, according to the Central Bank, of every rupee collected in taxes, salaries and pensions of state sector employees were absorbing 0.576 cents, even though the public sector generated just 20 per cent of the total earnings of the economy (LBO 2010).

The expansion of state institutions and their spectacular enlargement by ruling regimes in power since 1977 have distinct gender dimensions as well. The entire political system was highly male-dominated, from the highest political office to the low-paid, unskilled government workers. Patterns of political alliance-building and patronage benefits were thus distributed along clear gender lines – mainly to men. Public and private sector employment were both highly skewed in gender terms. Tables 5.5 and 5.6 provide useful indicators of this aspect of the patronage system, which corresponds also to the gendered nature of elite politics and a wider pattern of male domination through state institutions (Kearney 1981: 729: Kiribamune 1999b: 71: Kodikara 2008).

As noted by one respondent,[9] compared to the number of male candidates, female candidates contesting in electoral politics is generally very low, hence naturally limiting the room for patronage extended to female allies (R.11). Since independence, women's participation in politics has remained quite low (Kodikara 2009: 18–19).[10] Violent electoral politics in the post-1977 period further reduced the number of women taking part in high-level politics. One respondent mentioned traditional social roles and gendered cultural expectations of men and women, as a barrier for women wishing to take part

Table 5.5 Public and private sector employment: male and female distribution, 1998–2008 ('000)

Sector and Sex	1998	1999	2000	2001	2002	2003	2004	2005	2006	2007	2008
Private Sector											
Male	1,666	1,799	1,866	1,907	1,969	2,003	2,128	2,182	2,016	2100	2,023
Female	815	818	837	874	926	920	1,022	950	976	907	924
State Employment											
Male	566	567	534	547	555	561	518	538	565	561	621
Female	310	309	311	317	320	325	331	359	390	408	449

Source: Ministry of Labour and Manpower (2009: 80).

Table 5.6 Distribution of semi-government sector employees by sex, 2001–2007

Year	Total	Male	%	Female	%
2001	370 350	256 692	69.3	113,658	30.7
2002	272 111	205 056	75.4	67,055	24.6
2003	243 891	181 099	74.3	62,792	25.7
2004	231 519	169 553	73.2	61,966	26.8
2005	236 457	172 579	72.5	63,878	26.9
2006	226 306	164 011	72.5	62,295	27.5
2007	235 441	171 394	72.8	64,047	27.2

Source: Department of Census and Statistics (2007).

Note: Decline in number in 2002 is due to the closure or privatisation of some institutions in the semi-government sector.

in electoral politics. This was even evident in a fairly recent election manifesto, where one of the main political parties stated,

> A woman provides a solid foundation to the family as well as to the society. She devotes her life to raise children, manage family budget and ensure peace in the family.... I will arrange to increase the number of nominations of women to a minimum of 25% of the total number of candidates in respect of Provincial Councils and Local Government Authorities. (*Mahinda Chinthana: Towards a New Sri Lanka* 2005: 13–14)

In the 2010 version of the same party manifesto, women's participation in public was limited to being included in community development (*Mahinda Chinthana: Vision for a Brighter Future* 2010: 23), despite clauses pledging to treat women equally. By introducing a proportional representation (PR) system, the UNP regime paved the way for establishing physically larger electorates by redrawing their previous boundaries, though it also increased the distance between MPs and their constituencies. Pressure was brought to bear on contesting candidates to reach out to those in the more marginalised areas, and this required more campaign financing. Such developments made political elites even more reliant on patronage networks than under the former majoritarian electoral system. Organising for election rallies, lobbying key individuals and bargaining for future patronage rewards all intensified under PR as part of becoming an elected MP, raising barriers for the financially poor to enter politics.

Table 5.7 shows that that the growing number of public sector employees in lower-level occupational categories was one outcome of a class-biased and gendered political culture of patronage. Furthermore, Tables 5.8, 5.9, 5.10 and 5.11 show the concentration of a large number of employees in the non-executive and minor categories of employment in the state sector, further evidence of the expanding focus of patronage in state institutions over the years.

Male bias is all the more evident in the state sector and in semi-government institutions,[11] given that in general women and girls in Sri Lanka obtain higher educational levels compared to men, across secondary and higher education, with female educational enrolment in university being 42 per cent in 1989 and rising to 52 per cent a decade later (De Soysa 2000; Gunawardena 2003).

Within the private sector, women's employment tends to be highly concentrated in a few specific sectors, including services and the garment industry. These favour women as more 'biddable', harder working and easier to exploit.[12] As Venugopal suggests, there is also a reluctance from the private sector to employ educated male youth, given the historical perception that these young men are 'trouble makers' (Venugopal 2011: 72). Sri Lanka's recent unemployment data shows a significantly lower percentage of male unemployment compared to female unemployment. With the onset of the civil war, recent accounts show, employment in the military sector rose rapidly, indicating that it was specifically the (male-dominated) military sector that absorbed most unemployed rural male youth. Sinhalese political

Table 5.7 Total employment in each sector from 2005 to 2009

Sector	2005	2006	2007	2008	2009
Total employment including Eastern Province (mn)	6,788	7,005	7,042	7,175	7,140
State workers share %	13.2	13.4	13.8	14.9	15.2
Private sector %	46.2	42.1	42.7	41.1	42.1
Employers %	2.8	3.1	2.8	3.0	2.7
Self-employed %	29.7	30.8	30.4	30.3	29.0
Unpaid family %	8.1	10.5	10.3	10.8	11.0
Unemployment %	7.2	6.5	6.0	5.2	5.7
Central government	850,321	887,674	937,494	990,410	1,047,041
Semi-government*	253,922	258,049	259,116	261,318	266,543
State workers	1,104,243	1,145,723	1,196,610	1,251,728	1,313,584
Net Increase	*9,329*	*41,480*	*50,887*	*55,118*	*61,856*
Taxes (LKR mn)	336,829	428,378	508,947	585,621	618,933
Salaries	138,603	175,031	214,160	239,078	271,229
Pensions	46,782	58,006	68,822	74,920	85,139
Total	*185,385*	*233,037*	*282,982*	*313,998*	*356,368*
As a share of Taxes %	55.0	54.4	55.6	53.6	57.6

Source: LBO (2010).

Note: * Semi-government establishments are partially owned by the state.

Table 5.8 Distribution of semi-government employees by major occupational group, 2007

Major Occupational Group	Total
Senior Officials and managers	15,212
Professionals	16,130
Technicians and associate professionals	26,768
Clerks and related workers	*65,576*
Services and sales workers	*22,671*
Craft and related Workers	*14,336*
Machine operators and related workers	*21,158*
Elementary Occupations	*53,590*

Source: Department of Census and Statistics (2007).

Table 5.9 Distribution of semi-government sector employees by institution, 2007

Institution	Total Number of Employees
Sri Lanka Transport Board	35,196
Sri Lanka Samurdhi Authority	25,566
Ceylon Electricity Board	14,300
Sri Lanka Ports Authority	13,665
National Water Supply and Drainage Board	8,768
Sri Lanka State Plantation Cooperation	6,579
Janatha Estate Development Board	6,473
Mahaweli Authority of Sri Lanka and Agencies	4,739
Ceylon Petroleum Storage Terminals Limited	3,402
Road Development Authority	3,305
Associated Newspapers of Ceylon Ltd.	3,196
Airport and Aviation services Ltd.	2,992
Ceylon Petroleum Cooperation	2,686
State timber cooperation	2,633
State Engineering Cooperation	2,555

Source: Department of Census and Statistics (2007).

Table 5.10 Public sector employment, 2007–2009

Category	2007	2008	2009
Executive and professionals	343,491	347,824	347,212
Non-executive	557,585	603,825	656,515
Minor employees	295,534	300,079	309,857

Source: Economic and Social Statistics of Sri Lanka (2010: 18).

Table 5.11 Unemployment, 2003–2008 (%)

Year	Male	Female
2003	6.0	13.2
2004	6.0	13.2
2005	5.6	1.07
2006	4.3	9.8
2007	4.3	9.0
2008	3.6	8.0

Source: Department of Labour, Selected Labour Statistics in Sri Lanka (various years).

Table 5.12 Registered unemployed female graduates, 1994–2001

Year	Total	% Female
1994	11,364	49.5
1995	10,460	58.1
1996	4,660	62.0
2001	25,515	63.1
2004	40,014	65.4

Source: Gunawardena (2003).

Note: These figures exclude the Northern Province.

elites certainly used expansion of the military amidst intensifying civil war to distribute patronage in the form of jobs for mostly male Sinhalese and mostly rural youth. The expansion of state-sector employment since the intensification of the civil war since the mid-2000s also corresponds with the political economy of war. In year 2005, the number of military personnel were estimated around 200,000 (World Bank 2020), but in 2008 alone, 53,164 were recruited newly (LBO 2010). In just one year, the budget for salaries in defence increased from Rs73.5 billion (in 2008) to LKR 88.8 billion (in 2009). The vertical mass clientelism offered to Sinhala-Buddhist rural youth was indeed largely in the defence sector, at the lower levels of the military hierarchy. Already in 1997, the military accounted for one in five of all government jobs. Overall, military employees ballooned from just 30,000 in 1982 to 250,000 by 2002 (Venugopal 2011: 71–73). In addition, at the highest military ranks, horizontal systems of patronage and corruption could be clearly observed in appointments and promotions (Rajasingham-Senanayake 2011b: 27).

Table 5.9 indicates a number of institutions in the semi-government sector where a high number of employees are concentrated. This suggests that these organisations, among them the Transport Board, the Samurdhi Authority, the Electricity Board, Ports Authority and National Water Supply and Drainage Board, have become enlisted in patronage politics and taken on large numbers of new staff. As some scholars point out, in all these semi-state institutions, the established trade unions are closely connected with political parties and controlled by local political patrons (Spencer 2008: 617). Politicising public and semi-public sector trade unions is just one of the ways that political elites have successfully diffused dissent and countered oppositional voices. In this way, political elites use the semi-public sector

Table 5.13 Ethnic composition of occupational categories of males 18–30 years of age

	Public (%)	Military (%)	Private (%)	Casual (%)	Business (%)	Farming (%)	Total Employment (%)
Sinhalese	63.2	97.1	61.2	60.5	63.9	75.5	65.5
SL Tamil	20.3	1.4	23.0	25.6	13.0	21.3	21.6
Indian Tamil	0.5	0.0	2.8	3.0	1.4	1.6	2.2
Muslim	15.6	1.4	12.4	10.1	18.5	2.1	9.9
Others	0.5	0.0	0.7	0.8	3.2	0.0	0.9
Total	100	100	100	100	100	100	100

Source: Adapted from Venugopal (2011: 73).

institutions to obtain consent and secure the loyalty of employees to UNP party rule, capturing the entire state apparatus and making it work to serve the dominant elites.

The statistics on various aspects of state sector employment and the linkage between patronage politics and state sector employment, including the gendered nature of patronage politics in the state sector, help to illuminate several other causal connections that are important for understanding the direction of overall state-building and the elites' hegemony-building project in the post-1977 period. As Table 5.13 shows, there is a higher percentage of the Sinhalese ethnic group in public and military occupations, which cannot be divorced from the nurturing of an ethnic-identity-based patronage system and the Sinhala-Buddhist ideological underpinning of the ruling elites' hegemonic political project. Another important aspect is the growing tendency of right-wing appeals to consolidate elite hegemony, which during the period of civil war was inspired by both a male-dominated, ideologically charged and an increasingly violent political culture.

HORIZONTAL PATRONAGE

The expansion of the public sector and political patronage system in the post-1977 period was enabled by the inventiveness of the ruling elites. One such invention was the introduction of 'mega cabinets', particularly notable since the inauguration of the fourteenth parliament of Sri Lanka in 1994. The number of cabinet and non-cabinet portfolios rose, corresponding to shifts in coalition politics and the patterns of patronage alliances. This expansion can be traced back to the system of PR that came fully into operation from 1989 (Nanayakkara 2006: 434). Overall, the PR system tended to produce more unstable coalitions and required broader political alliances (Nanayakkara 2006: 434) to increase the survival chances of smaller-sized political parties and enhance their relative worth in electoral politics. The PR system more or less rules out a single political party from forming a government. Since the larger political parties have to seek support from smaller political parties to form a government, the participation of smaller parties in coalition formation can come with a higher price tag, including government appointments.[13] Besides monetary and non-monetary inducements, offers of ministerial posts at cabinet and non-cabinet levels too became a bargaining tool between parties. Coalition formation can thus be linked to the increased size of cabinets during this period, in itself a costly venture (Samaratunga and Bennington 2002: 103). Next to their regular salaries, new ministers were often entitled to lucrative state pensions, even after serving just five years in a ministerial post, as well as housing allowances, petrol allowances, and tax-free vehicle permit(s). By contrast, private citizens had to pay 200 to 300 per cent in taxes to buy a car. These ministers from smaller political parties were also expected to be able to provide state employment for their most loyal party supporters. In 1994, when the SLFP led the People's Alliance government, the coalition it formed with smaller parties rested on offers of these kinds of patronage benefits to junior coalition partner, notably the JVP party leaders (Keethaponcalan 2008: 73). In exchange for their support, the JVP demanded lucrative ministerial portfolios related to aviation, eventually settling for a non-cabinet portfolio under the Ministry of Airport and Aviation. On assuming office, the JVP non-cabinet minister thus appointed started to recruit hundreds of party supporters into the ministry. Overall, Lanka Business Online (LBO) claimed that 'since 2004, JVP has absorbed tens of thousands of unemployed graduates into the state sector' (LBO 2010). LBO data shows that in just one year, 2006, 71,323 staff members were added to the state sector. New recruits to the state sector reached 107,505 in 2007 and 129,135 in 2008 (LBO 2010). Similarly, in 2009, thousands of excess employees swelled the staff of the most highly unionised state establishments, the Sri Lanka Transport Board and Sri Lanka Railways (LBO 2010). The best explanation for this trend of recruitment of large numbers of employees into state sector institutions is the political patronage associated with coalition-building under PR. This interpretation is shared by several respondents (R.2; R.3; R.6) and has also been reported on in local newspapers.

One of the main points of attraction of the People's Alliance election manifesto of 2000 was to reduce state expenditure and both cut the number of ministerial posts and reduce political appointees in the state sector. However, in practice, the new People's Alliance government added several more cabinet and non-cabinet ministerial posts, and absorbed many supporters of the political parties in the coalition, along with their relatives, as public sector employees. Some were recruited as the personal staff of ministers or as special management assistants to ministers. During President Kumaratunga's second term, she extended these benefits of state patronage when she was compelled to enter into a coalition pact with the JVP to save her government from collapse.

Generally, in the post-1977 period, the relations of subordination and political loyalty of political appointees to public institutions became notably more fluid, flexible and unstable, reflecting the nature of high politics during this period as well. This fluidity and instability was related to the mostly adaptive strategy adopted by political appointees, whose primary focus was to strategically manoeuvre their public political loyalties so as to secure work and the material benefits attached to state sector employment. Some others have noted that the flexible loyalties of political appointees in the face of short-lived governments were observable across all levels of employment in the public sector (De Alwis 2009: 100). The fear of losing one's job, of demotion or punitive transfers, or of losing benefits had a major part in shaping the behaviour of non-political as well as political appointees. One respondent, a high-ranking official in the Ministry of National Integration, lamented that public servants had learned to simulate political loyalty towards whichever political regime was in power as a strategy for avoiding any undesirable effects on their survival of repeated regime changes.

Outside the state sector, the ruling elites invented other ways to ensure mass incorporation, for example, through a system of rewards in the form of tax concessions and exemptions from established laws and regulations for favoured partners. Failure to pay taxes could be allowed to pass unpunished, and often for small scale and ad-hoc business ventures, this could secure their loyalty to the regime. According to one political observer, a harsh critic of the UNP,

> adopting an open economy [since 1977] did not result in creating a vibrant production economy in the country. Instead, the open economy

controlled by the UNP regime allowed a number of its supporters to engage in small-scale businesses buying and selling goods such as selling imported apples and oranges along the roadsides or selling clothing items on the pavement. (R.1)

The type of livelihood opportunities this created for small self-employed business people in the more open economic system that now characterised Sri Lanka enabled the UNP and successive political regimes to dispense patronage benefits systematically to one segment of the lower-middle class in Sri Lankan society. Those who benefited in turn became devoted party supporters and mobilisers at election times. Such measures allowed political elites in power to build patron–client relationships with large numbers of small businesses, mainly in urban areas. The dependency relationship created with political elites for this particular class of small business people ensure more lasting forms of political loyalty. These lower-middle class petty businessmen were instrumental in carrying out political work during election campaigns and through trade union activities (see McCourt 2007a: 17).

DEVOLUTION OF POWER AND PATRONAGE

It is widely accepted that devolution of authority and resources can support the settlement of ethnic conflicts and balance disparities in regional economic development (Gunatillake 2000). In Sri Lanka, in reality, various attempts to devolve power in order to resolve ethnically motivated tensions between the majority Sinhalese and minority Tamils, or find a regional mechanism to agree on resource distribution, have been disappointing. I suggest that political elites used various decentralisation measures to consolidate a state system that remained highly centralised. This section also shows how decentralisation of state institutions served to create a more decentralised patronage system, facilitating wider consent and the building of political alliance with masses in the peripheries.

In the post-1977 period, several important decentralisation schemes were introduced; the District Development Councils (DDCs) in 1981 and a system of Provincial Councils (PCs) in 1989. On paper, DDCs, introduced by the UNP government, were presented as a necessary next step for resolving ongoing ethnic conflicts in Sri Lanka. DDCs were supposed to approve annual development plans for the districts and supervise their implementation.

However, the DDC system was introduced without establishing any separate administrative machinery for its independent functioning. Therefore, DDCs depended on their leaders' ability to draw on contacts within the existing state bureaucracy of the central government to do their work (De Alwis 2009: 173). The DDCs' lack of an independent resource base, which meant their dependency on the central government, made this reform a 'dead letter' (De Alwis 2009: 175). Soon enough, DDC activities were subsumed into the wider existing networks of patronage.[14] This encroachment of patronage into the DDC system was especially visible in infrastructure development projects. The outcome proved a major disappointment to moderate Tamils who had enthusiastically supported the design and implementation of DDCs (Wijesinghe 1991: 46).[15] Like almost every other reform of state institutions, the DDCs mainly helped the Sinhalese political elites gain more influence over local-level bureaucrats on matters related to district administration. A new tier of the state could sustain the dominant party or parties' patronage networks (De Alwis 2009: 175).

The PC system was the next major decentralisation measure undertaken, and was facilitated by the Indo-Lanka Agreement of 1987, signed between the Governments of India and Sri Lanka. The aim was to reach a political settlement on the issue of the minority Tamil population's grievances against the Government of Sri Lanka. Under these new administrative units, the province was made an important unit of regional administration. PCs were vested with province-related administrative powers and functions, for example, making statutes for the province under the authorised subject matters, managing the finances of the province, raising revenue and incurring expenditures for meeting executive responsibilities, providing public services and public management via provisioning of public services – all that were previously under the authority of the central government (Bastianpillai 1995: 25). Under the 13th amendment to the second republican constitution, PCs were also given their own financial resources.[16] Unlike the DDCs, the PCs were not entirely subordinate entities in relation to the central government (Nanayakkara 2006: 432).

The members of the PCs were chosen through elections, and this involvement with electoral politics tended to undermine the neutrality of this new level of government rather than enhance its democratic qualities. Consequently, PC structures once again opened up new spaces for political party clientelism, and corruption flourished at the provincial level. Provincial governors were appointed by the executive president, who had overall responsibility for finance and personnel matters (Nanayakkara 2006: 432). Although legal provisions explicitly provided for a separate public service at the provincial level, senior positions in the provincial administration continued to be filled from the centre (Nanayakkara 2006: 432). The overall environment ensured that the PC system could not escape politicisation. Over time, overlapping functions and gaps in responsibility between the PC system, centralised state institutions and the government paved the way for new forms of corruption at the provincial level.[17] Some oversights in the Provincial Council Act related to sensitive issues of land use and soil conservation, perhaps reflecting the hasty drafting of the legislation (Nanayakkara 2006: 433). However, since state land was a major asset used to distribute material patronage, this 'technical error' may have been strategic.

A few respondents who are also keen observers of Sri Lankan politics, and including a past contestant in PC elections, pointed out that PC elections were used by the ruling regimes to cultivate new patronage networks, encouraging corrupt practices to finance those networks (R.2; R.3; R.9). These respondents shared a number of examples as evidence to their claims, especially in relation to election campaign financing. It was often the case that the PC campaign funding could be generated through pre-emptive corrupt transactions between candidates, political parties and members of the business community. If and when a candidate won an election, those who had funded him (it was mostly 'him') could expect the candidate to fulfil certain obligations promised in advance in return for political favouritism. Despite being widely documented in public discourse and the media, politicians and their alleged business partners normally deny that any such exchanges took place.[18] In politics, these kinds of practices have become so common that even the general public pays hardly any attention to reports of corrupt practices of these kinds. The repeated failure of PCs in public service delivery has been one outcome of the politicisation and corruption of the PC system (Samaratunga and Bennington 2002: 94). This decentralisation reform proved to be yet another 'white elephant' on the Sri Lankan scene. A white elephant is also a Buddhist symbol denoting prosperity. In this case, the only prosperity was for the ruling political elites and their supporters.[19] Despite the abundance of empirical evidence available to prove these illegal transactions, given the low level (absence) of intra-party democracy and complicity of all the political parties in these practices, it is in nobody's interest to probe these alleged incidents (FES 2008: 51).

The rural divisional councils (*pradeshiya sabha*) was another level of administrative unit that was used and manipulated to maintain the party- or regime-led patronage system. Similar to the PCs, the representatives of *pradeshiya sabha* were also chosen through elections. A member of the *pradeshiya sabha* received a low salary, estimated at around LKR 10,000. However, for the incumbents, this office brought a great deal of political capital their way, making it a very competitive post, since securing office at this level of state administration could build someone's career. One respondent, a keen observer of political corruption, explained it this way:

> In a developed *pradeshiaya sabha* close to Colombo, for instance, Kaduwela, the chairman is earning about LKR 1–2 million per month by engaging in corrupt practices. There are a few questions that need to be raised in this connection. First of all, other than contributing to … public good will, what is the real motivation of the candidates contesting for *pradeshiya sabha*s, especially for such a smaller salary? Let's say, out of goodwill a candidate wants to contest in the *pradeshiya sabha* elections; still the other question this situation raises is where does the money come from for the election campaigns and how the candidate is going to repay the money when he or she knows that he or she makes only LKR 10,000 a month? (R.2)

Another respondent, a leading political party member and a former contestant of the parliamentary general elections, pointed out to the fact that a candidate contesting for a *pradeshiya sabha* in the suburbs of Greater Colombo area needed to spend about LKR 3–4 million for one election campaign. Further, considering the number of elections conducted within the same electoral cycle at various levels of state administration, political parties were unable to provide funding and resources for all the candidates contesting from the party list. In Sri Lanka, the candidates who contested for *pradeshiya sabha*s were relatively poorer and often had no finances of their own for 'electioneering'. Given this situation, if the candidate was already a popular figure, fewer financial resources were needed from the party or from the candidate's personal funds. The often poor personal financial situation of the candidates was what tended to push them to forge obligations and corrupt relationships with well-to-do segments in the area, prior to being elected, to fund their election campaign.

In recent years, to overcome financial constraints on electioneering, political parties have started looking for new strategies. Sometimes celebrities and other 'popular' figures are enlisted as party candidates. Or they may be asked to endorse the party or candidates. Their popularity among voters in the electorates they compete in would be the key concern. As perhaps elsewhere in the world, it has become easier for a member of the national cricket team to contest national elections from a party list, than a seasoned MP. The cricketer's chances of winning the election for his political party may be better than for a regional beauty queen, for example, but both may be of interest to political parties.[20] Such new strategies – tied in with the rise of social media and popular TV programmes – enable political parties and individual candidates to capitalise on their previously established popularity, and lower the financial cost of electoral publicity. Instead of selecting candidates with a strong track record in public life or a seasoned political activist, parties are tending to select actors, sportsmen, actresses and beauty queens. For instance, in the 2010 Southern Provincial Council elections, several 'star candidates' contested and were elected. The same was observed during the Western Provincial Council elections in 2009, in which popular figures from cinema and sports contested and easily won seats for their respective political parties.

THE STATE SECTOR: IS IT UNREFORMABLE?

Since the early 1990s, with the advice and assistance of major international organisations, the United Nations Development Programme, the Asian Development Bank and the World Bank, three identifiable phases of state sector reforms were carried out. On each occasion, plans for reforms met with fierce resistance from state sector leaders and employees. The reforms arrived 'like waves on the ocean', receding faster than they arrived (McCourt 2007a: 7).

> Meanwhile the recommendations concerning the increase of salaries were embraced with glee.... More important recommendations were glossed over ... [and] when it came to biting the bullet, the political will evaporated. (Wijesinghe quoted in McCourt n.d.: 7)

What the phrase 'biting the bullet' in the above quote meant was committing to state reforms of a substantive nature. One rare exception to a generalised resistance to reform was during the short-lived government of the UNP in 2002–2003, when reforms as demanded by the International Monetary Fund were implemented in the public sector as part of a wider fiscal restructuring strategy (Venugopal 2008: 8). These public sector reforms froze new recruitments, encouraged voluntary retirement and removed many temporary and 'ghost' workers amidst protests by ministers of the ruling party (Venugopal 2008: 8). Not only public servants but also ministers and elected politicians are generally resistant to reforms. Sometimes the government is willing to implement reforms but may have to face resistance from their own party members and ministers. This situation speaks to a degree of vulnerability of the executive on the goodwill of the lower-level party members, especially those in the public sector, for their political survival and any chances of re-election.

Observing the outcomes of the New Public Management (NPM) process that attempted to reform state institutions, and reform relationships between state institutions and political elites, some scholars pointed out that the success of the proposed reform and restructuring of the state bureaucracy depended largely on the goodwill of politicians and bureaucrats, who would stand to lose the most from the reforms (Samaratunga and Bennington 2002: 90). However, in Sri Lanka, when it comes to state reforms, 'appearance of change' without jeopardising the agendas of politicians and bureaucrats was observed (Samaratunga and Bennington 2002: 90). Therefore, the ruling regimes tend to enact specific elements from a full reform package to protect their own interests and privileges as much as possible (Samaratunga and Bennington 2002: 90). This was the case with implementation of policies under NPM during the UNP government, where narrow and politically motivated practices won over principles of reducing governmental interference, something normally associated with the UNP's market philosophy (Samaratunga and Bennington 2002: 87). NPM's failure to implement the reforms pointed to the lack of broad consent within the ruling regime for such measures to be implemented (Box et al. 2001: 617).[21] However, the experiences of such reforms suggest that whether reforms are partial or are simply resisted, political elites are rarely the ones affected. According to the majority of the respondents, the 17th amendment to the constitution that was passed with a two-thirds parliamentary majority in 2001, and was one rare occasion of a bipartisan attempt to dismantle the patronage system in the state sector. Under Article 41B of the amendment, when appointing members to key positions in the state bureaucracy, the approval of the consultative committees was made mandatory.[22] These consultative bodies are constituted of the political party in power as well as the opposition political parties. The Election Commission, the Public Service Commission, the National Police Commission, the Human Rights Commission, the Permanent Commission to Investigate Allegations of Bribery or Corruption, the Finance Commission and the Delimitation Commission are a few important institutions that came under the scrutiny of the consultative committees. When making high-ranking appointments in these bodies, the approval powers vested with the opposition leader was especially considered as a significant improvement to the elite political culture. Contrary to the previous political practice of the president exercising the constitutional and executive powers to appoint judges to the Supreme Court, the Court of Appeal and high courts (Abeyratne and Shanthasiri 2009: 5), the 17th amendment also granted approval powers to a set of consultative committees. The appointing powers granted to the consultative committees, such as for the posts of the chief justice and judges of the Supreme Court, the president and judges of the Court of Appeal and members to the Judicial Service Commission, are crucial for retaining independence of these positions.

In addition, constitutional measures were established to separate all the high-level appointments from the electoral cycle. In theory, these measures should serve positively in rescuing the state institutions from politicisation. However, in practice, it turned out to be a different picture as there were some intentional gaps left in, or even built into, the amendment. For instance, the provisions of the 17th amendment are not applicable at the level of PCs. Therefore, political appointments at this level of state administration could continue.[23] Besides, the amendment was also silent on the issue of the limits on the number of provincial ministries and ministerial appointments. Similar to the national level, this loophole became an encouragement for creating jumbo cabinets at the provincial level too.

Many of the subsequent constitutional measures did not bear any positive fruit, as the newer constitutional amendments (R.18; R.19; R.20) were used to get rid of the positive aspects of a previous amendment. As of the time of writing, the executive president had claimed powers using the 20th amendment to the constitution enacted in October 2020. There were other more subtle moves to undermine the powers of these constitutional amendments targeting de-politicisation of the state bureaucracy. For example, in 2011 the executive president delayed appointing members to the Constitutional Council and taking swift steps to fill all the key positions in the highest authorities of the state apparatus in a unilateral and politically partisan manner. Also, in September 2010, the United People's Freedom Alliance (UPFA) regime introduced another amendment to the constitution, the 18th amendment. The new amendment overruled all the provisions of the 17th amendment. Interestingly, the 18th amendment was also passed with the approval of a two-thirds majority in the national legislature. This same two-thirds majority secured for contradictory amendments explains the nature of politics in the country. At one level, being able to get the approval of the same parliament for two contradictory amendments is a sign of strength of the solidarity of the political elites, regardless of their rhetorical differences on the public political stage. Further, it also demonstrates the power and the capacity of the political elites to collaborate when their grip over the state apparatuses is loosening. Also, as pointed out by a political observer, securing a two-thirds parliamentary majority for the 18th amendment was easier for the political elites, as the UPFA regime offered significant patronage benefits to minority political parties and to those who crossed over from other main political parties to the UNFA. Extending short-term clientelist concessions to the fellow political elites for buying out political loyalties indicates the disappearance of any meaningful opposition to the elites' rule from within.

In this politicised context of state reforms, instead of de-politicisation, there were new forms of politicisation. De Alwis who has systematically analysed the public sector reforms carried out from 1950 to 2005 finds that the case of Sri Lanka aptly demonstrates the inability of the state sector reforms to be successful without commensurate change in the overall political system (2009: 210). The hegemonic alliances forged between various forces in society and among the political elite groups, if not completely, at least to a larger degree, have closed the space and opportunity from societal forces for demanding any meaningful interventions for state restructuring and dismantling the patronage system that is being legitimised and institutionalised across the entire state apparatus. Therefore the state sector reforms often gave the ruling elites ample space and options to further solidify and sophisticate the patronage machinery to advance their hegemony-building attempts. This nature of the patronage political system was successful in bringing the lower-class masses ever closer to state power and to the ruling elites. However, there is no guarantee the hegemonic alliances the elites formed with them and the consent obtained to the elites' rule through the manipulation of the state system and the struggles of the masses will forever remain unchallenged in an environment where political alliance-building and bottom-up political mobilisation are dominated by short-term and synthetic loyalties towards the patron rather than political ideologies and principles. Hence, such a system is bound to favour one group over the other and develop into an extremely exclusive system that only benefits a small group of people.

APE (OUR) SYNDROME: FLUID IDENTITIES AND FLUID POLITICS

The state assuming the main role as the distributor and guarantor of resources under socialist and welfare policy could be an important juncture on post-colonial state transformation in its structural and ideological realms. Even today, the local syndrome of 'looking after, taking care of us' (expressed in Sinhala as *salakanawa, balaagannawa*) in everyday social and political exchanges is a sad legacy of this situation. This syndrome was seen throughout the post-independence period, especially during the period in which the official welfare state policy was implemented, and since 1977 has also come to be further manifested. In the latter period, the 'looking after us' syndrome appears to operate at a more personal-political level. Since independence, various degrees of this looking-after-us syndrome was projected onto the political elites and the state bureaucrats. Upon diffusing the power of the bureaucrats by successfully reforming the state bureaucracy and creating obstacles to bureaucratic hegemony, eventually the political elites who completely captured the state apparatuses assumed the role of the 'sole provider'. This transformation steadily created a structure and culture of inequality in the state, where the majority of the Sinhalese willingly subscribed to it. Thus, as one respondent of this study noted, the popular notion of *ape rajaya* (our regime) succinctly captures the underlying political dimension of it. As this respondent also shared, this notion of *ape* (our) is valid as long as the political elites, the regime or the government in power provides welfare and patronage benefits.[24] It seems that initially this *ape*-ness was formed on the basis of a wide range of social fault lines, beyond a specific class or ethnic group,[25] which underwent tremendous transformation and steadily targeted the Sinhalese ethnic group as their numerical strength in winning elections was far greater than all other minority groups combined and due to the dominance of the Sinhalese elites in politics.

Over time, especially in the post-1977 period, the *ape* sentiment did not follow a linear logical direction but certainly reduced any 'strong' political party affiliations and party-inspired loyalties as both patrons and clients frequently jockeyed between political parties by instrumentally using multiple identities to mobilise each other, as the prevailing political dynamics demanded.[26] Being aware of the short-lived nature of governments, the fluidity of coalition-building at the centre and the ability to access state resources when multiple social fault lines were enacted, the clients too were able to devise important adaptive strategies. This flexibility of the clients seems to have a reinforcement effect on the political behaviour of their patrons. In this regard, on the part of the patrons, entering into superstitious and fluid political alliances with fellow elites and nurturing a horizontal system of patronage have been observed. However, by entering into a system of patronage on the basis of flexible political loyalties, the clients in this relationship encouraged their political patrons to continually search for secure and credible avenues to reproduce their power, domination, authority and hegemony-building strategies. It is under these circumstances that the political elites (main patrons) are forced to look for permanent avenues for reproducing the patronage networks and keeping the already built political alliances intact by using, abusing and manipulating the state institutions and camouflaging any dubious reform attempt with a good dose of ethnic-nationalist ideology. As Gramsci described what politics is constituted of, one could observe, especially in the post-1977 period, how the ruling political elites manoeuvred the economic factors, the long and complex chain of mediation of moral norms and rules, the Sinhala-Buddhist ideological system and the general character of social relations to build a lasting patronage system in pursuit of hegemony. However, when patrons fail to deliver on their material promises, clients easily switch allegiances, which leads patrons over time to amplify their ideological rhetoric, often with a right-wing tone, as if to compensate for their inability to deliver the material needs of clients. The effects of such dynamics is to shift the overall symbolic-ideological political field to the right, the fewer are the material benefits of patronage. This has created a crisis of legitimacy for political elites that has come to be manifested in a worsening of inter-ethnic relations and social violence.

By way of conclusion, the politicisation of state institutions along with the institutionalisation of the patronage system throughout the state apparatuses by the ruling elites in post-independence Sri Lanka has gone through a number of different phases and transformations. Overall, it has been a deliberate strategy of political mobilisation and alliance-building, through which political elites sought out lower-class consent for their overall political domination and hegemony. In spite of the dire effects an extensive patronage system has had on efficient functioning of state institutions, such as the bureaucracy and public sector services, both under the 'socialist' state of the decades up to 1977 and under the more liberal and even right-wing ideology thereafter, a powerful patronage system has been used to harmonise the political struggles among factionalised elites seeking to dominate the centre. Elites are tied with the material, economic struggles of the masses in the periphery, mainly through patronage and electoral mobilisation. Socialist-inspired state welfare policy, which once played a vital part in consolidating elite hegemony, has declined and has been progressively replaced with right-wing rhetoric.

Although the ruling elites' political patronage system was able to deliver short-term benefits for both the patrons and the clients, the price of the short-term gains is in the loss of longer-term benefits that would have accrued from devising more equitable means of distributing state resources and mobilising for political participation on the basis of more democratic principles. However, the functioning of Sri Lanka's patronage system resembles a huge machine, and as Grindle cautiously reminds us, 'when and where appropriate the forces are not completely out of power to punish their provider' (2001: 351). Under the many structural constrains on the economy and on the state-accumulation processes, the continued dispensing of patronage benefits by the ruling elites has not always been possible. Under such conditions, elites may be punished by their clients, who might withdraw their electoral loyalty. This can produce intense competition among elites, and factionalising. Against this backdrop, whenever material resources are insufficient to retain clientelistic loyalties intact, competing elite factions will make appeal to ethno-religious ideological sentiments associated with the right-wing. When and where consent-building to elites' rule through material patronage benefits failed, the ruling elites' resorting to coercive measures to deal with the anti-hegemonic forces was guaranteed, hence nurturing the right-wing forces in the political centre.

Last but not least, elite patronage systems mainly gravitate around the majority Sinhalese, the main clientele. The serious benefits of representative democracy for the Sinhalese ruling elites are not replicated for the minority ethnic groups, who are continually sidelined in party politics, including through various coercive measures. It is in this overall context that the widespread social and political violence, manifested in the form of a three-decade-long brutal civil war, needs to be understood. This is the focus of the next chapter.

NOTES

1. In this chapter the term 'institutions' refers to as the official establishments that structure the state, that is, the bureaucracy, police, defence forces, public education entities and judicial system (DeVotta 2000: 57).
2. This aspect was discussed in detailed in the previous chapter
3. The task of establishing the commission was to lead the Salaries and Cadres Commission (known as the Wilmot Perera Commission, 1958–1961).
4. The unemployment rate in 1963 was 7.3 per cent, in 1969–1970 13.9 per cent, in 1971 18.7 per cent and in 1973 24 per cent (Central Bank reports quoted by Karunaratne 2007: 191).
5. According to Lakshman, during the first two regimes in post-independence Sri Lanka, there was an improving commodity terms of trade, an improved import capacity and favourable positions in external assets, which were used for the benefit of society (1987: 11–12).
6. According to De Alwis, there were 12 reforms implemented from 1977 to 2005.
7. For more on the elevation of the image of the state in terms of symbolism, read Spencer (2008) and Tennakoon (1988).
8. Youth uprisings in 1971 and 1989 are previous examples in this regard.
9. This respondent has a number of years of experience working at village and provincial levels to encourage female political candidacy in local government elections in the Central Province.
10. Sri Lanka often boasts producing the first world female prime minister (Mrs Sirimavo Bandaranaike in 1960). For a detailed survey and the number of women in the national legislature, provincial councils and local government, refer to Kodikara (2009).
11. One reason for the higher number of male workers in the private sector is because of the demand for jobs that required long working hours and night shifts, which are generally done by males.
12. For a detailed discussion on the gendered aspect of the labour force, see De Soysa (2000).

13. During Chandrika Kumaratunga's presidency, S. Thondaman of the Ceylon Workers' Congress (CWC) was given LKR 350,000 million for taking part in the coalition. In addition, he was also given the Chennai agency of Sri Lankan Airlines.
14. There are several reasons for the overall failure of DDCs, such as the lack of genuine participation in formulating development plans and the domination of village-level elites and ex-officio MPs (De Alwis 2009: 175).
15. It is known that money being allocated for the districts where Tamils are in the majority was not welcomed by some close followers of Jayewardene in the UNP.
16. For details, read Wickramasinghe (2008: 291–97).
17. The PCs undertake activities that had earlier been undertaken by central government ministries, departments, corporations and statutory authorities (The Provincial Councils Act No 42 of 1987, http://www.priu.gov.lk/ProvCouncils/ProvicialCouncils.html, accessed on 24 July 2012).
18. The donation money never appears in the official reports of these business groups. As suspected widely, such donations are often reported under different budget lines in the annual accounts.
19. In Buddhist *Jaataka* stories, a white elephant symbolises the impregnation of Princess Mahamaya (mother of Lord Buddha). In Buddhist culture, a white elephant is a symbol of greatness and prosperity.
20. For instance, in the Southern Provincial Council election in 2010, the national cricket star Sanath Jayasuriya represented the ruling UNF as a candidate for Matara district, his hometown. Jayasuriya secured 74,352 votes in absentia, as he was playing a game in the Indian Premier League during the elections. In the same election, TV show host, model and film star Anarkali Aakarsha also won a seat for the UNF. Other famous individuals in politics are former cricket captain Arjuna Ranatunga (national legislature), Rosie Senanayake in the Western Provincial Council (former Mrs World winner) and Susanthika Jayasinghe (Olympic silver medalist) who contested the general elections in 2009.
21. Among a number of other attributes, substantive democracy entails a process that rekindles a public discourse about the purpose of collective action, accepting role for citizens and public administrators in shaping the future (Box et al. 2001: 611; Bastian and Luckam 2003).
22. Please refer to http://www.priu.gov.lk/Cons/1978Constitution/Seventeenth Amendment.html (accessed on 28 January 2012) for more details.
23. See http://www.priu.gov.lk/Cons/1978Constitution/SeventeenthAmendment.html (accessed on 28 January 2012).

24. In Sri Lanka, in everyday usage, it is observed that the majority of the people think that state, government and regime are the same. Therefore the different political regimes that come to office are seen as the state as well as the government.
25. These could be based on ethnicity, caste and region as well.
26. Changes of governments in the post-1977 period were: 1977–1993 (UNP), 1994–2002 (SLFP-led coalition), 2002–2004 (UNP-led cabinet) and 2005–today (SLFP-led coalition).

6

WAR AND PEACE AS POLITICS BY OTHER MEANS

There is a considerable level of attention paid to analyse Sri Lanka's civil war. Especially since the early 1980s, the majority of the academically oriented studies seemed to have drawn inspiration from the works of Federick Barth on ethnicity (cited in Tambiah 1989)[1] and applied them generously to intra-state violent conflicts in this period. These studies have left a lasting and profound impact on the understanding of Sri Lanka's civil war as mainly an 'ethnic war' rooted in the antagonistic inter-ethnic relations between the majority Sinhalese and the minority Tamils. Their failure to take critical scholarship produced before the early 1990s on Sri Lanka's civil war into account evaded the opportunity for scrutinising the numerous global and local economic, political and social entanglements that contributed to the war (Jupp 1978; Jayawardena 1984, 1985b; Tambiah 1989; Hennayake 1993; Abeyratne 2004; Bandarage 2009). In spite of the gaps, the notions of inter-ethnic conflict and ethnic war became popular and were even promoted by the Sinhalese ruling political elites and their right-wing forces in the broader Sinhalese society, including some in the Sinhala-Buddhist intelligentsia.

By returning to the global and local literature that applied rich historical-sociological approaches to the study of war, in this chapter I hope to offer a broader interpretation of Sri Lanka's case of war and peace. In this regard, I find the seminal study by Charles Tilly quite helpful to frame Sri Lanka's case of war and peace as it devotes a considerable level of attention to several interlinked variables of war, politics, hegemony-building and state-building. Tilly's main thesis is that 'state makes war and war makes state and vice versa' (1985). He famously argued that banditry, piracy, gangland rivalry, policing and war making all belong to the same continuum and are intrinsically linked to the eventual laying out of the capitalist economic foundation of the modern state-building (Tilly 1985: 170). Notably, Tilly drew attention to the use and functions of war as coercive exploitation strategies that fulfilled a crucial role in the modern European state-making processes in the 16th century. As he observed, wars of that time resembled organised crimes that were used by the European state makers and entrepreneurs to consolidate power in the captured territories and to expand the resource-extraction and capital-accumulation process. As he further noted, the latter processes had laid the foundation for the birth of the modern state and one of the most important state apparatus, the fiscal administrative apparatus. Instead of using open strategies of banditry, gangland rivalry and piracy, one could observe the political elites in the 21st century employing similar coercive strategies by using organised militaries, militias, (extra-)legal measures and monopoly of violence endowed to the state to mobilise social forces and resources to wage wars within their national borders (sometimes spilling over these borders) to achieve certain political goals. Instead of the positive outcomes experienced in Europe in the forms of the birth of the modern state, the development of norms and rules governing civilian politics and the states' enhanced commitment and contribution to civilian welfare, the use of coercive strategies by the political elites in the post–Cold War period shows negative impacts on state-building. According to some scholars, contemporary civil wars as one important variant of coercive strategies that gained prominence in the developing countries show threatening effects on the state's capital accumulation, hence hampering modern state-building (Chowdry and Murshed n.d.: 1; Murshed 2010: 14).

In spite of the starkly varied conditions under which European state-making was unfolding since AD 990 onwards and more prominently in the 16th and 17th centuries, I find the applicability of Tilly's analogy that brought attention to the nexus of war-making and state-making helpful for understanding the ruling elite's overall hegemony-building by co-opting post-colonial state-building, where the use of the coercive instrument of civil war constituted an integral part of it. Further, in this chapter, I demonstrate how various Sinhalese ruling regimes in state power since the early 1990s were able to mobilise the much-needed alliances from the south to eventually wage an actual physical war in the north and the east of the country against the Liberation Tigers of Tamil Eelam (LTTE) by inventing several discourses on war and peace and by strategically placing these discourses within the prevailing dynamic alignment of local and global forces for and against war during this period. By assigning importance to the aspect of discursive construction of war (and peace), this chapter sheds light on the specific roles and functions these discourses had for the factionalised elites to overcome their personal-political struggles over political domination and hegemony. In this regard, I also rely on the reading of these discourses through the lens of the Clausewitzian classic dictum, 'war is politics by other means' (1976: 252). Inspired by the works of Tilly, Gramsci and Clausewitz, this chapter offers a systematic analysis of the state-in-society dynamics and the multiple struggles faced by the ruling elites in the centre for securing and consolidating their political power, and by the society in the periphery for upward social and economic mobility, where war and peace have been reproduced by the ruling elites at different scales and levels. Therefore, I undertake a rigorous analysis of the mainstream discourses from 1994 to 1999: the discourse of 'Peace by peaceful means' under President Chandrika Bandaranaike Kumaratunga (People's Alliance [PA]) 1999–2002; the discourse of coexistence of political peace and limited war during President Chandrika Bandaranaike Kumaratunga's second term (PA) 2002–2003; discourse of neoliberal peace under Prime Minister Ranil Wickremasinghe (United National Front [UNF]); and, last but not least, from 2006 to 2009, the cumulative discourse of war against terrorism, war for peace, total war and humanitarian war under President Mahinda Rajapaksa (United People's Freedom Alliance [UPFA]) to show the various linkages of war, peace, politics and hegemony-building.

KUMARATUNGA AND THE AGENDA OF PEACE BY PEACEFUL MEANS (1994–1999)

The presidential election in 1993 marked an important juncture in Sri Lanka's post-1977 political history. The Sri Lanka Freedom Party (SLFP)–led coalition government (PA) headed by Chandrika Bandaranaike Kumaratunga was able to defeat the United National Party (UNP) after 17 years of political domination. The PA's election manifesto entailed an attractive economic agenda (Venugopal 2008: 3), which received wide support from the local entrepreneurial class and from the rural poor as well. It promised the rural poor a number of subsidies important for the survival of rural agricultural communities (Samarasinghe 1994: 1022), a long-standing promise made by the UNP to these communities, which form a substantial segment of its voter base. It is not only the rural population that the PA made an impression on but also on the urban population, the latter through a clear pledge to improve good governance (Samarasinghe 1994: 1034). As pointed out by many political observers, the PA's agenda of governance became an important electoral consideration after the Bonaparte style of regime of President Premadasa (1989–1993), during which the country experienced widespread political violence in the southern parts that led to thousands of deaths of its youth, disappearances and open breach of law and order. Kumaratunga's election manifesto also promised to end the armed conflict in the north and the east with the LTTE and bring lasting peace. According to some political analysts, Kumaratunga's peace agenda was the most important point in her election manifesto (Keerawella and Samarajiva 1994: 153; Schaffer 1995: 416). However, peace was only one among many other promises made (bagged in the catchy slogan promising to get rid of the UNP-nurtured political culture of *duushana*–corruption, *bheeshana*–fear and *ghaathana*–killings),[2] hence the need to be cautious of interpreting Kumaratunga's election victory solely based on her peace agenda.

During the period of 1994–1999, in the social discourses, 'peace' had a number of different meanings to different sections of society. However, during Kumaratunga's election campaign, the term 'peace' was explicitly used in relation to the armed conflict with the LTTE. Moreover, 'peace' was always presented as an end state scenario as well as a precondition to reach a number of other social–economic and political goals especially in view of the troubled economic growth (Kelegama 2000: 1480).[3] Using multiple articulations of peace, Kumaratunga was able to build momentum towards peace by gaining support from a number of significant economic and political segments in society, from the north to the south of the country. In the run-up to the elections, the term 'peace' had had other meanings apart from interethnic peace, especially social peace. The latter was significant to many people who were regular witnesses to direct physical violence exerted during the Premadasa period against the country's youth who had supported the second anti-state movement spearheaded by the Janatha Vimukthi Peramuna (JVP) (Chandraprema 1991; Hoole and Thiranagama 2001: 246–55). Ending such violence was another key promise Kumaratunga made to the country's youth in particular. Her economic agenda also promised to end structural violence experienced by the debt-ridden rural peasantry, many of whom took their own lives after being unable to repay their debts (Samarasinghe 1994; Eddleston, Sheriff and Hawton 1998; Jayasuriya 2005: 26).

Initially, Kumaratunga was also regarded as a symbol of political unification as she was able to bring different elite political factions with socialist, liberal and capitalist inclinations together. Although her election campaign carried a socialist-leaning undertone, upon assuming office, she was compelled to follow the same neoliberal economic agenda as her predecessor, the UNP, due to domestic and international economic and political realities (Dunham and Jayasuriya 2001: 9–10). One of the landmark measures carried out under her leadership was the privatisation of national assets, which signified her early departure from the socialist economic agenda that she had promised during the elections. Given the state of the economy she inherited from the previous regime, pursuing this path was justified as essential to deal with the macroeconomic problems and to regain control of the state capital accumulation process. To deflect criticisms against privatisation of state assets, her government rebranded the process as 'privatization with a human face' or 'peoplelization' (Knight-John and Athukorala 2005: 419).

Kumaratunga's economic agenda was largely shaped by a group of liberal-minded elites and business elites (Venugopal 2008: i) and firmly tied to her political agenda, which contained political negotiations with the LTTE. Her peace agenda followed the slogan 'peace by peaceful means',[4] which found inspiration from the prevailing global trends following the UN Secretary-General's 'An Agenda for Peace' (Boutros-Ghali 1992). What is important to note of the global peace agenda of that time is its intricate link to the global economic agenda of aggressive promotion of market economy by the multilateral financial institutions and Western donors in developing countries during this time (Paris 2004: 5). Hence, Kumaratunga's peace strategy based on global peace by peaceful means mantra could not fully divorce itself from the international multilateral financial institutions' efforts to accelerate the global capital growth that made a case for the need to settle the numerous internal armed conflicts and civil wars in developing countries (Collier et al. 2003: v). The underlying theories posited that internal armed conflicts in developing countries are impeding the generation of a favourable environment for the expansion of local–global markets, free and orderly forms of resource flows and the local and global wealth production. It is in the background of favourable global context and the support and endorsement Kumaratunga received from local business circles that she sought assistance of the international community to embark on political negotiations with the LTTE, also with an invitation to the Norwegian government to serve as the facilitator to this process.

However, an in-depth understanding of the 'peace by peaceful means' agenda during her first term (1993–2004) requires an exploration of a few other national-level political dynamics of this period evident in a series of factional struggles among the ruling elites who outbid each other in attempts to restore their personal and group legitimacy and authority that had been seriously undermined during the Premadasa period. Premadasa's unapologetic use of the coercive apparatus to contain the second wave of anti-state armed insurrection of the JVP should be noted in this regard. Further, political elites losing on the monopoly of violence to new actors from the underworld and armed gangsters in the local political scene explains another root of the elites' struggle for legitimacy (Uyangoda 2008b: 73). The blurring of the boundaries between legitimate and illegitimate authority in politics also encouraged[5] fierce competition among the political elites at the micro and meso levels of politics. Given these multiple conflicts and their violent impacts on society, economy and politics, Kumaratunga's agenda of 'peace by peaceful means' had many different interpretations to different segments in society, including the political elites. More importantly, peace by peaceful means brought other personal-political benefits to Kumaratunga, who was embattled in a ferocious struggle to retain her legitimacy as the coalition leader of the PA and as the party leader of the SLFP. Given the lack of legitimacy of her leadership within her own party, pursuing peace by peaceful means became even more instrumental and integral for Kumaratunga to garner legitimacy to her leadership and the political programme from the general public, who were yearning for peace and order after the Bonaparte-style Premadasa regime. It is not only that; Kumaratunga might have seen the opportunity she had in embracing the 'peace by peaceful' slogan as it firmly resonated with powerful global forces, the liberal Western international audience and policy makers, who were instrumental in acting as a protective shield around her.

Next to the aforementioned forces that Kumaratunga managed to mobilise in support of her peace-political agenda, she certainly benefited from the legacy of her parents, both former prime ministers of Sri Lanka, and her father's legacy as the founder of the SLFP. Next to that, at the time of relaunching her political career under the SLFP flagship by securing the reputation of bringing youthful energy to the party, she edged out the old party stalwarts as well as impressed the same circles by featuring her previously established left-wing political credentials earned by working with her late famous-film-actor-turned-left-politician husband, Vijaya Kumaratunga, who formed an alternative left political party, the Sri Lanka Mahajana Peramuna (SLMP). During the initial years of the SLMP, Kumaratunga began political dialogue with Tamil political forces, including the LTTE, with the hope of enhancing mutual understanding and bringing about a political solution to the armed conflict between the state's armed forces and the LTTE. The principles the SLMP stood for in resolving the minority political grievances with a radical vision of ethnic harmony and socialist ideals made the SLMP a broad-based, popular and acceptable political party for the Tamil community and Tamil political forces. The party's popularity certainly irritated President Premadasa; hence, the daylight political murder of Vijay Kumaratunga in 1989 was blamed on President Premadasa and on the leftist JVP (Samarasinghe 1994: 1021). Some even attribute his assassination to an unknown mix of political–underworld circles (Hoole and Thiranagama 2001).

After her husband's death, Chandrika Kumaratunga was absent from the national political scene for two years and lived abroad with her two young children. Until her re-entrance into the political arena in 1991,[6] she lived a dormant political life, when her younger brother Anura Bandaranaike became more active as a member of the national legislature and in SLFP party politics. In 1991, when Kumaratunga returned to national politics and took over the deputy leadership of the SLFP, and in 1992, when she succeeded her feeble mother Sirimavo Bandaranaike (the world's first woman prime minister) as the party leader, it made some old party stalwarts in the SLFP and especially her brother Anura unhappy. The personal-family political tensions eventually ended up in a major rift between the two political siblings. This family-party political feud resulted in Kumaratunga taking full control of the party with her mother's blessings and her brother leaving the party to join the rival UNP (1994–2000). The back-and-forth mudslinging between the two siblings in the national political theatre was on the one hand entertaining to the public and, on the other, evidence of the political challenges Kumaratunga faced to establish her political authority within her own party and the imperative of mobilising forces beyond the party for obtaining a wide societal acceptance for her leadership.

In 1993, Kumaratunga secured her first election victory at the Western Provincial Council elections as the leading candidate of the coalition of People's Alliance (PA) led by the SLFP, where she secured 68.4 per cent of the votes to become the chief minister (www.slelections.gov.lk). This victory was followed by another victory at the 1994 general election which made her the prime minister. In 1995, she assumed office as the executive president (Samarasinghe 1994) and in 1999 got re-elected as the president. By securing these major electoral victories, Kumaratunga surprised her rivals and political sceptics within the SLFP and outside the party by proving her abilities to bring victory to the SLFP that was struggling to establish its political domination in national politics after 17 years of UNP rule. This rash of election victories also increased the public's trust on Kumaratunga to deliver on her election promises. In the eyes of many voters, both with and without strong political party affiliations, Kumaratunga was seen as the only hope for peace and prosperity. Many expected her to play a leading role in restoring the political-moral order of the country after Premadasa's Bonaparte style presidency. The high esteem in which Kumaratunga was held by all ethnic groups lent her agenda of 'peace by peaceful means' a major boost.

KUMARATUNGA CHALLENGED: CRISIS IN THE COALITION GOVERNMENT

The PA government was constituted with nine smaller political parties that were mostly left leaning, led by Kumaratunga's own party, the SLFP. Upon securing a decisive victory at the general election, the PA was able to form a parliamentary majority in the national legislature by securing seven seats from the Sri Lanka Muslim Congress (SLMC).[7] At this time, the SLMC was the only political party that was formed to address the issues concerning the country's minority Muslim population. Until 1993, the SLMC's influence was limited to peripheral regions and mostly to the Eastern Province, where the majority of the country's Muslims live side by side with an equal percentage of the Sinhalese and Tamil population. Kumaratunga managed to secure the SLMC's support by entering into a number of agreements with its leader, M. Ashraff. Kumaratunga's pursuit of the SLMC's support, as Keethaponcalan described, brought a significant change in coalition-building in Sri Lanka by making Ashraff the new 'king maker' in national politics. Earlier this title was held by S. Thondaman, the leader of the Ceylon Worker's Congress (CWC), who often secured collective concessions, patronage benefits to the Indian Tamils in the hill country and lucrative personal patronage benefits to himself by jockeying between the two main Sinhalese parties by enabling and disabling them to win elections (Keethaponcalan 2008: 3).

Apart from the SLMC, there were numerous other Tamil political parties that extended their conditional support to Kumaratunga's coalition and the government, which Kumaratunga reciprocated with communal patronage benefits to the constituencies of these parties. Meanwhile, Kumaratunga also extended personal patronage benefits using state resources to her close circle of friends, which drew heaving criticism from the general public (see Chapter 4 for more details). Kumaratunga was seen as not keeping to her promise of fair use of state resources that she had made to voters during her election campaigning. Despite being offered attractive ministerial posts to himself and some of his party members, Ashraff eyed more benefits for the Muslim community as well as for himself. Hence, keeping the SLMC leadership satisfied was a crucial issue for Kumaratunga if she were to keep her parliamentary majority and her coalition intact. Frequent rhetorical threats exerted by Ashraff to withdraw his support to the PA coalition government eventually led to tensions between the SLMC and other minority political parties within the PA coalition, which put Kumaratunga under enormous pressure (Keethaponcalan 2008: 4). The turbulent political context which Kumaratunga found herself in with her coalition partners seemed to have drawn her to pursue her peace agenda with the LTTE more vigorously as a way of securing her political image among the public. The culmination of the aforementioned personal and political circumstances could also explain Kumaratunga's decision to embark on political negotiations with the LTTE. This whirlpool of elite political conflicts at the centre during Kumaratunga's first term as president convinced her of the need for peace by peaceful agenda for Kumaratunga to overcome her own personal-political struggles to establish political authority and domination within her own party and the PA coalition government, and silence criticism from her political rivals.

NEGOTIATING WITH THE LTTE (1994-1997) AND INTERNAL POLITICAL PARTY DYNAMICS

As promised in her election campaign in 1992, Kumaratunga embarked on political negotiations with the LTTE. Albeit numerous motivations that might have led to negotiations, her efforts were widely regarded as courageous, especially in the background of alleged high-profile political assassination carried out by the LTTE (that is, President Premadasa in 1993, Democratic United National Front [DUNF] leader Gamini Dissanayake in 1993, and Indian prime minister Rajiv Gandhi in 1991).[8] According to some observers, in 1995 the LTTE embarked on negotiations with the PA government on an exploratory basis, mostly as a way of seeking to enhance their political status and to preserve the militarised quasi-state they were running in the north (Schaffer 1999: 138). Also, as some delegates who were in Kumaratunga's negotiation team shared with me, the PA government had other political–military–economic considerations to enter into negotiations with the LTTE, mostly resulting from the political and economic pressures that came Kumaratunga's way from her political rivals within and outside the SLFP.

As soon as the negotiation process started with the LTTE, the PA government became embroiled in increasing fights among the factionalised elites, which unfolded in parallel with the continuation of military activities by the LTTE during the negotiations. The LTTE's military operations pushed the country's economy to its rock bottom. These events challenged Kumaratunga personally to prove her credentials in the terrain of peace, not only for the sake of the survival of her government but also to save her personal political career. Some even argue her desperation to make peace with the LTTE was motivated by her rumoured ambition of securing the Nobel Peace Prize by settling the conflict in Sri Lanka through which she hoped to increase her political capital (De Silva n.d.). The combination of these circumstances meant that continuing negotiation with the hope of future delivery of peace and peace dividends were not options for Kumaratunga; rather, they were serious political imperatives and a gamble.

According to half of the respondents I interviewed, who regarded themselves as moderates in Sri Lankan politics, Kumaratunga's 'peace package' offered to the LTTE was the most advanced and progressive effort undertaken to date by any Sinhalese political leadership in the country to address the grievances of the Tamils and to end the civil war. One Tamil respondent, a leading lawyer, a scholar and an ex-commissioner of the National Human Rights Commission, shared, 'I should credit the efforts of Chandrika with reservations.... Chandrika was genuine in finding a solution. For example, she was even ready to accept the Post-Tsunami Joint Operational Management Structure (P-TOMS)' (R.19). Another high-ranked Tamil civil servant described, 'Chandrika was a democratic leader, and she did not go too far in the extremist end' (R.25). Analysing the shifting discourses and various mental frameworks supporting peace and war that were used interchangeably in electoral politics in the south, another Tamil scholar and political commentator also credited Kumaratunga as the only Sinhalese political leader who was able to liberate the majority Sinhalese people from the war mentality (R.19). According to the same respondent, in parallel to Kumaratunga's high political efforts, she also backed creating meso- and micro-level spaces for peace within the ordinary communities from all ethnic backgrounds, by providing state sponsorship to local peace movements and projects, such as the Saama Balakaaya (peace solidarity force), the Sudu Nelum Vyapaaraya (white lotus movement) and the Saama Thawalama (peace caravan). Her efforts also went as far as establishing the much-needed peace-focused state infrastructure facilities, such as the National Integration Programme Unit (NIPU) within the Ministry of Constitutional Affairs. In parallel to these measures, Kumaratunga also embarked on a process of constitutional reforms which is widely known as 'the political package'. This reform process produced a draft constitution that Kumaratunga updated and represented to the national legislature in 2000, during her second term in office. Given the highly militarised context in which many of the interviews for this study took place, there is room to believe how this condition might have had influenced the responses of my interviewees and their sense of nostalgic yearning for Kumaratunga's peace package amidst the preparations for a brutal final war. Although her overall efforts were seen positively, some of the respondents of Tamil and Muslim backgrounds expressed a reserved appreciation of Kumaratunga's efforts. Meanwhile, the majority of the Sinhalese respondents among those who showed no strong or declared political affiliations regarded Kumaratunga's peace initiatives as positive signs towards a permanent political solution at ending the war. According to the latter group of respondents, Kumaratunga's peace package was a positive breakthrough in southern Sinhalese politics towards constructing an ethical state.[9] As one female Sinhalese respondent recalled, 'even today, we can be happy about Chandrika's time; if not peace, at least the symbols of peace were there, and even the term federalism which was a dirty word in the Southern political discourse, became more accepted among the people' (R.11).

Quite contrary to the views of my interviewees and the general public of Kumaratunga's efforts, the LTTE leadership in the 2002 Hero's Day speech remarked, '... for the Tamils and the liberation tigers, Chandrika is no goddess of peace. We consider her a hardliner who bets on a military solution ... in our eyes Chandrika is a warmonger' (quoted in Hellman-Rajanayagam 2008: 93). Prabhakaran's views were fully in line with views shared with me by a few notable LTTE figures who served in the LTTE-run civilian administration in Jaffna district during the peace negotiations with the UNF government in 2005.

Further analyses of Kumaratunga's peace agenda and its effects on elite politics and in the Sinhalese south also suggests the positive impact that it had on making international mediation – a thorny issue in southern politics – acceptable to Sinhalese majority as well as to the LTTE. The LTTE's eventual acceptance of international mediation is striking especially given its continued rejection of any outside mediation after India's controversial role as a third party to Sri Lanka's conflict during the previous two UNP regimes of Jayawardene and Premadasa. During the Jayawardena regime, the JVP and other smaller Sinhalese nationalist political parties were also vocal in rejecting any foreign intervention.[10] Among all these parties, the JVP vehemently rejected any international engagement given their dark memories of state suppression during President Premadasa's regime for building a public movement against Premadasa's dealing with the Indian peacekeeping forces (IPKF) to deal with the war in the north. Apart from that, according to the JVP, Indian regional hegemony and the speculation of an Indian conspiracy to expand India's influence in Sri Lanka were other grounds for their island-wide protests and resistance (Wijeweera 1986: 156–158), which President Premadasa cracked down on brutally. It was not only for the JVP, but the IPKF's role in Sri Lanka was a bitter memory among the Tamil population in Jaffna as well, who suffered at the hands of the IPKF.

As Premadasa granted more powers to Sri Lankan police and security forces to clamp down on the JVP, the latter also reacted to these measures by killing members of the state security and armed forces and threatening those who served in the military and the police as well as their family members.[11] During this period, as many as 40,000 people were estimated to have died of violent incidents (Moore cited in Spencer 2000: 125). During these violent encounters, a huge number of lives were lost in the JVP's higher ranks, leaving behind painful memories among surviving members of the JVP, who continued to oppose any form of external intervention. Also using their usual anti-bourgeois lines, the JVP broadened its resistance by pointing to external interventions as a project of the global capitalist class and imperialist ideological forces. However, during Kumaratunga's second term from 1999 to 2005, by becoming a partner in her coalition government and upon being ordained as a fresh member of Sri Lanka's ruling elites, the JVP extended support for Kumaratunga's negotiation efforts. Until the JVP broke away from the PA coalition government, it largely stayed silent and showed a great deal of tolerance for the Norwegian government's facilitative role in Sri Lanka's conflict.

PA AND THE END OF PEACE BY PEACEFUL MEANS

The negotiation efforts launched in 1994–1995 can be considered as a political breakthrough for Kumaratunga. By temporary securing the LTTE's commitment to end hostilities, Kumaratunga was able to raise her stock of political capital to silence her critics. However, once the LTTE returned to violence, the positive public aura generated around peace negotiations evaporated as well. The initial positive backing Kumaratunga received from different segments in society and in high politics in favour of the negotiation process and her pro-federalist solution to address the Tamils' grievances began to wither away.

While Kumaratunga remained committed to her pro-peace political campaign, under the provocation of the LTTE, she simultaneously embarked on a decisive military campaign against it. Under her leadership, the government forces secured numerous 'politically valuable' military victories on the battlefield. By using the state and private media, the government managed to capitalise on these military victories by bringing these triumphant experiences closer to the majority Sinhalese who mostly live in the south, well outside the military battleground. Although Kumaratunga managed to keep the majority Sinhalese happy by regularly feeding the news of military victories in the battleground, the resurfacing of the long-standing UNP–SLFP political conflict affected the public momentum gathered in favour of Kumaratunga's political, military and pro-peace leadership. One of the overt manifestations of the UNP–SLFP political rivalry during this time was the frequent personal clashes between the UNP leader Ranil Wickremasinghe and Kumaratunga. To edge each other out, both parties wanted to secure the support of the LTTE to commit to the peace negotiations. The political rivalry between Wickramasinghe and Kumaratunga was so damaging to the entire peace process that they accepted an offer from the British parliamentarian Liam Fox to negotiate a political cohabitation pact between them. Moreover, they agreed to search for a bipartisan solution to the ethnic conflict as well. The main clauses of the Liam Fox pact targeted developing a cooperative political environment to address nationally important issues. Although the agreement appeared fine on paper, in reality it showed no advancement of cooperative relationship between Wickremasinghe and Kumaratunga. Despite all these efforts, in the end the Liam Fox pact did not add anything meaningful to overcome the personal-political rivalry between

Kumaratunga and Wickremasinghe (Bandarage 2009: 161). Continuation of hostilities became even more stark when the UNP leadership did not keep its promise of extending support to Kumaratunga's draft constitution presented to the national legislature in 2000. Kumaratunga was furious with the UNP leadership although Kumaratunga had given her best to incorporate all the constitutional changes proposed by the Parliamentary Select Committee that was appointed to oversee the constitutional reform process to which the UNP was a member (Edrisinha 1999: 170). The UNP's betrayal of Kumaratunga came at a time when the LTTE leadership also began to stymie her efforts. Overall, these various scenarios on the military battleground in the north and the political battleground of the Sinhalese political elites were hurting Kumaratunga's previously popular political-peace plan. The initial glimpses of success gained at the negotiation table with the LTTE which received approval from the Sinhalese began to fade quickly as well. Further adding fuel to the political fire in the south, the LTTE leadership also intensified its military actions, delivering the biggest blow to Kumaratunga's hard-won moral bloc for 'peace by peaceful means' in the south. The LTTE's declaration of Eelam War 3, launching of heavy military attacks in the north and sinking of valuable naval crafts of the Sri Lankan Navy left almost no hope for peace anymore. Hence Kumaratunga decided to strike back by ordering a major offensive against the LTTE. Kumaratunga justified her intensified military offense based on *jus in bello*,[12] which she nailed by driving the LTTE away completely from the areas that they controlled in the Jaffna peninsula. Initially, this turnaround of events on the battleground brought the much-needed political benefits to Kumaratunga and to her ailing coalition government. However, as these military victories came to be celebrated in the south with invigorated spirit and feelings of patriotism, at the same time they also turned the tide against the previous public moral stance of 'peace by peaceful means'.

Despite these mentioned initial victories secured by the government forces, at the end of Eelam War 3 the overall balance sheet of military victories between the state forces and the LTTE did not look good for the government. For example, although the government forces recaptured the previously LTTE controlled territories in the Jaffna peninsula, soon these areas came under siege as the LTTE launched a series of military offenses under the banner of 'Oyada Alaigal', or Unceasing Waves (Keethaponcalan 2008: 17). As the LTTE became more and more successful on the military front, it entered into an aggressive path of attacks by extending its targets to the south, including economic targets. The bomb blast it carried out on the Central Bank of Sri Lanka (1996) that killed about 100 persons and the attack on the country's only international airport (1997) were already hurting the national economy. Apart from the economically important targets, in 1998 the LTTE also carried out a massive bomb attack on the country's most sacred Buddhist site, the 'Temple of the Tooth' in Kandy, where the tooth relic of Lord Buddha is housed. Especially the latter attack caused outrage among the majority Sinhalese Buddhists, who began to have serious doubts about Kumaratunga's peace plans with the LTTE.

Under these pressures coming from the southern polity and from the battle front, Kumaratunga was compelled to change her previous stance of 'peace by peaceful means' to 'peace by limited war'. Her latter stance required sacrificing enormous amount of valuable state resources even though she received no assurance of winning from her own military advisors. By going to a limited war with the LTTE, Kumaratunga was ready to sacrifice not only state resources but also her hard-earned moral bloc for peace. As the military confrontations escalated, Kumaratunga ordered extra nation-wide measures to increase the number of surveillance operations and checkpoints, which made the PA government even more unpopular among ordinary Tamils who suffered the most under these measures restricting their physical movement. The military confrontation on the battleground became personalised between the LTTE and Kumaratunga after the LTTE carried out an attack on Kumaratunga in 1999 which she survived by sustaining serious injuries that blinded her in one eye. Although the LTTE's attempted assassination of Kumaratunga won her some personal sympathy from the majority in the south, these sympathies soon dissipated when the LTTE captured the government's main military base in Elephant Pass in the Jaffna peninsula in 2000 (Sambandan 2000). These events made selling of Kumaratunga's constitutional package aimed at a political settlement with the LTTE even harder to the general public. Personally, this turnaround of events made Kumaratunga more vulnerable to criticism from her political opponents who were waiting for an opportunity to undermine her leadership and her political credibility.

KUMARATUNGA'S SECOND TERM AND MAJORITY-MINORITY POLITICS

During her second term as the president (1999–2005), Kumaratunga experienced another series of decisive challenges from her political rivals.

This time, many challenges she faced came from her own party, the SLFP, and from the coalition partners in PA. One significant challenge she faced was from the SLMC leader M. H. M. Ashraff (Keethaponcalan 2008: 4), who believed that the issues compelling minority Muslim community should deserve the same level of attention as the issues faced by the minority Tamils. Although this specific threat became neutralised with the sudden demise of Ashraff, it later resurfaced as the political struggle for the leadership of the SLMC among different factions intensified. Meanwhile, by capitalising on these intra-party squabbles within the SLMC, Kumaratunga secured a working majority in the parliament by personally pursuing Ashraff's widowed wife, Ferial Ashraff, to accept the co-leadership of the SLMC. Although she was a complete novice to politics, Ferial Ashraff managed to influence SLMC party members to continue to support the PA government and helped prevent the collapse of the PA government. However, within the SLMC, a new faction led by Rauf Hakeem, the deputy leader of the SLMC, challenged Ferial Ashraff's party leadership, again raising concerns for Kumaratunga's coalition government. Although initially both factions extended their support to the PA coalition, later by crossing over to the opposition, the SLMC faction led by Hakeem (known as the National Unity Alliance, or NUA) reduced the PA government to parliamentary minority. These developments were followed by more ministers and other members in the PA government (altogether nine members including the general secretary of the PA) crossing over to the opposition led by the UNP. Empowered by its newly gained parliamentary majority, the UNP wasted no time in planning to bring a no-confidence motion against the PA government (Keethaponcalan 2008: 79).[13] The UNP-led no-confidence motion was supported by the CWC, another minority Tamil party that had crossed over to the opposition. These changing loyalties among the PA coalition partners assured the imminent defeat of the PA during the planned no-confidence motion voting. During these chaotic times, the only silver lining for Kumaratunga was her brother Anura crossing back to the SLFP from the UNP.

Capitalising on all these opportunities, on 3 August 2000, the UNP unleashed its final move against the PA government by opposing the Constitutional Bill of 2000 presented by Kumaratunga to the national legislature by signalling the negative impact of the bill on the unitary status of Sri Lanka (also discussed in the previous section). As shared by a few respondents interviewed by me, the UNP's claim of the potential damage to the unitary status of the state by the Constitution Bill was more 'a tune played to the gallery'. As these respondent shared, the real motivation for the UNP's claims were nothing other than grabbing power from the ailing rival PA government, which Kumaratunga also expressed in a morally charged speech during the parliamentary debates over the new Constitution Bill of 2000. In her words:

> Today is indeed historic. It is a special day in the history of a great people, with a history of over thousands of years. This Constitution is designed to end the ethnic war, which totally destroyed the lives of the people of this country, a war which has been a curse impeding the forward march of this country. I ask whether the UNP, which deepened the ethnic crisis and caused it, at least now, on behalf of the country, can they not act in mature manner, when our Government has taken the responsibility, at the risk of our lives, to establish a permanent peace, thereby putting an end to this war, which was started under the patronage of the UNP Government, by killing, and burning the Tamil people and destroying their property, on five occasions between 1977–1983? If the UNP members here today, like a pack of jackals, it is a major concern for me as to how can they form a responsible government in this country? (Somasundaram 2000: 181)

The only way to avoid facing the no-confidence motion was to suspend the parliament and call a general election, which Kumaratunga was compelled to do in 2001 as she lost the parliamentary majority.

Upon re-reading these intense political events towards the end of Kumaratunga's first term, it can be safely argued that winning either peace or war was desirable but contingent on a number of factors beyond the military battleground, especially the conditions on the elite political battleground. Hence Kumaratunga's pursuit of peace and war should be understood taking the dynamic shifts occurring in the broader political context into account. However, all the approaches to peace and war that were explored during Kumaratunga's presidency pointed at reaching negative peace – the most desired outcome, morally and politically. However, the pursuit of this particular end result was also tied to the President's political agenda of holding onto state power, increasing political legitimacy to her rule and gaining an edge in the elites' struggle for hegemony-building. As one respondent, a well-respected high-profile public intellectual closely linked to the UNP leadership, shared as to why the UNP opposed the 2000 Constitutional Bill at the last minute:

> For political parties, it's a matter of staying in power. I think reality changes when you are in power. You get isolated. When you are a leader, you automatically become a political celebrity. How you think changes with power in your hand. For example, for Chandrika, it was all about staying in power. (R.18)

Below is an excerpt from the rejoinder made by the opposition leader Ranil Wickremasinghe in parliament to the scathing speech previously delivered by President Kumaratunga, which stands testimony to the 'real politik' underlining the ruling elites' gamble for war and peace, politics by other means:

> On the 20th July, we were informed by the Government of the matters raised by the Tamil parties. A joint meeting of the UNP Parliamentary group and the UNP Working Committee was held on the 27th July to consider the transitional provisions to retain the executive presidency for a period of six years. At this meeting, it was decided that the UNP could not agree to this provision since the government and the UNP had already agreed to the abolition of the executive presidency in accordance with the government's Constitutional draft in 1997. This was conveyed to the Government by the UNP delegation. Thereafter, the government unilaterally decided to present this bill to parliament, to repeal and replace the existing Constitution. This bill retains only part of the agreements reached between the government and the UNP. Some of the important areas of consensus have been changed unilaterally. Furthermore, several issues, which have not been discussed during these meetings, have been included in the Bill.... (Somasundaram 2000: 283)

An analysis of the two speeches delivered by Kumaratunga and Wickremasinghe alone explains how the elites' factionalised conflicts and their desire for hegemonic power and domination can be translated into short-sighted state policies on matters of war and peace, which is capable of leaving serious moral implications on the whole of society.

POLITICAL TURMOIL IN THE SOUTH AND THE CONTEXT OF THE GENERAL ELECTION IN 2001

The general election in 2001 was held just after two years of the previous general election. Based on the popularity of the PA regime during the 1994 election, many political commentators doubted the UNP having any chance of coming back to power in the near future (see Table 6.1 for a comparative analysis of the percentage of votes received by the UNP, the SLFP, and the SLFP with its allies in four general elections between 1994 and 2004). However, the public's dissatisfaction with the PA government has been mounting steadily because of its failure to deliver on the promises made during the previous elections. Among others, not fulfilling the promises made on economic development and peace dividends were the most concerning for the voters. As Table 6.1 depicts, in the 2001 general election the SLFP's share of total votes, including the votes of its allies who contested under the PA banner, was as low as 37.19 per cent. These numbers explain the pressures faced by the ruling political elites to deliver on their election promises. As some suggest, the PA's defeat in this election was also well linked to its mismanagement of the economy that resulted in high inflation rates (Uyangoda, quoted in Jayasuriya 2005: 65) and backtracking on its visionary idealism and the promise of harmonious ethnic relations (Uyangoda, quoted in Jayasuriya 2005: 65).

As this study finds, voters' increasing dissatisfaction with the PA and Kumaratunga grew even bigger as the economy suffered due to the coalition government's engagement in a costly unwinnable war. The same led to low confidence in the private sector, which initially had supported the PA and Kumaratunga, as the war stalled investments. As the state coffers became empty, Kumaratunga had to look for new ways of generating resources to stay in the war path with the LTTE. The PA government addressed this gap

Table 6.1 Votes (percentage) secured by the UNP and the SLFP in general elections, 1994–2004

Year	UNP % Votes	SLFP % Votes	SLFP and Allies % Votes
1994	44.04	48.94	50.74
2000	40.22	NA	45.11
2001	46.86	NA	37.19
2004	37.83	NA	45.60

Source: Adapted from Jayasuriya (2005: 138).

Table 6.2 Colombo Consumer Price Index and Greater Colombo Consumer Price Index

Year	All Items	Rate of Inflation	Food	GDP Deflator, 1996 = 100
1991	1,131.5	12.19	1,220.3	62.50
1992	1,260.4	11.39	1,366.0	68.76
1993	1,408.4	11.74	1,519.4	75.28
1994	1,527.4	8.45	1,654.1	82.29
1995	1,644.6	7.67	1,768.1	89.20
1996	1,906.7	15.94	2,107.6	100.00
1997	2,089.1	9.57	2,336.9	108.67
1998	2,284.9	9.37	2,592.1	117.83
1999	2,392.1	4.69	2,695.4	122.98
2000	2,539.8	6.17	2,815.8	131.18
2001	2,899.4	14.16	3,244.7	147.3

Source: Price Indicator of Sri Lanka (http://www.ices.lk/sl_database/price_indices/ccpi.shtml, accessed on 8 March 2011) (adapted by the author).

Note: The table shows a combined version of the two indices – the Colombo Consumers' Price Index (CCPI), the official index of consumer price inflation, computed and published by the Department of Census and Statistics (DCS), and covering low-income households in the Colombo municipal area, and the Greater Colombo Consumer Price Index (GCPI), an alternative measurement of the aggregate price level with a broader geographical coverage than the CCPI.

Although the rate of inflation shows an improvement during the Kumaratunga period, the skyrocketing trend of food prices shows a worrisome picture.

by imposing new taxes, such as a defence levy on private business in addition to the already existing goods and services tax (GST). Although it was the private businesses that immediately faced these new taxes, they strategically passed on additional taxes to the consumers (Table 6.2).

Despite the positive steps taken by the PA government to extend state patronage to the private sector, the entrepreneur class that supported Kumaratunga's government remained sceptical of her new militarised economic agenda. Theoretically, in the PA agenda, the private sector remained the engine of growth, but in practice the government's entanglement in a war made it difficult to get them to support her economic agenda (Venugopal 2008: 4). The burden on the PA's overall economic performance was further aggregated by the old-fashioned socialist-oriented state bureaucrats appointed by the PA to economically important positions who were reluctant to implement a fully fledged liberal economic plan where a prominent role for the private sector in the country's economic development was assigned. Given these circumstances, during the 2001 election campaign, the entrepreneur class switched their support to the more liberal-leaning UNP.

SAVING KUMARATUNGA: PA–JVP MEMORANDUM OF (MIS)UNDERSTANDING

In order to cling to power, the PA coalition had to convince the self-proclaimed nationalist JVP into another political cohabitation pact with them. Upon keenly observing the patronage benefits extended to other ethnic minority parties, namely the SLMC and the Eelam People's Democratic Party (EPDP), during the PA's first coalition government, the JVP saw the opportunity to build their party further with potential state patronage by becoming a coalition partner for the PA. Moreover, the JVP must have had calculated its potential influence in national politics by becoming a member of the ruling coalition and to counter the rising influence of other minority parties, especially that of the SLMC in Sinhalese elite politics. Therefore, by temporarily suspending its traditional anti-bourgeoisie criticism of the SLFP, the JVP joined the PA as a coalition member.

The memorandum of agreement (MOU) that was signed between the SLFP and the JVP was effective for one year, running from September 2001 to 2002. There were a number of clauses included in the MOU on issues pertaining to democratisation, growth of the capitalist economy, continuation of the privatisation of state assets by the PA and reduction of government expenditure, all reflecting the main concerns of the JVP. All of the clauses in the MOU, as Keethaponcalan notes, were similar to the clauses of the JVP's own election manifesto (2008: 76). In addition, there were two other side agreements signed by the SLFP and the JVP with the aim of preventing the JVP from launching any action to destabilise the PA government and assuring the JVP's commitment to support the PA government to gain stability in parliament. However, under the pressure of the JVP, the SLFP was compelled to sign a few additional side agreements preventing it from sharing political power with the ethnic minority political parties. In the views of the rival UNP, members of the business community and the minority political parties, the JVP–PA MOU and the other related agreements that they signed did more harm to the country than good, particularly due to the JVP-imposed clauses in these agreements preventing the PA from devolving power and forcing it to take an anti-LTTE negotiation stance. Therefore, the JVP–PA agreements became quite unpopular among those who wished to see an end to the war through a political settlement. However, just after four months of signing this MOU and other agreements, both parties realised that they are unable to manage a fruitful and mutually beneficial partnership, leading the JVP to pull out of all agreements. The end of this brief cooperation between the PA and the JVP triggered another general election in 2001. As soon as the pact of political cohabitation fell apart, the JVP began to mobilise public sentiments against political negotiations with the LTTE and the Norwegian intervention in the conflict. According to a number of those interviewed for this study, the JVP's fallout with the PA in 2001 had little to do with their dissatisfaction with the PA's political stance on matters of economy or peace, but were largely due to the unreasonable demands they put forward for the PA in exchange for their support to the government. As one veteran left-wing political party leader observed, during this time, the nature of the JVP became even more apparent:

> JVP is not left; it is a 'peculiar animal', fanciful in its demands, 'ultimatist' and with no transitional approach to politics. Their vision is guided by proposing what cannot be done, resist any reforms, play flesh and fowl. They are left in appearance, but they are chauvinists, repressive, undemocratic and violent. (R.13)

According to another political party member interviewed for this study, the JVP's initial cooperation extended to the PA government and its subsequent total opposition to external intervention to find a political solution to the conflict with the LTTE can be only understood within the logic of political survival (R.16). Even though small in size, the JVP was still highly effective as a grassroots-oriented political party with a sophisticated propaganda machine and a substantial constituency in the rural areas. They also had some following among certain segments in the urban lower-middle class. Hence, albeit short, the JVP's identification with the bourgeois-oriented PA and the support extended to the PA's peace and economic development agendas left a mixed feeling among the public who were puzzled by the JVP's self-claimed core identity as a Marxist-nationalist political party but which supported the bourgeois ruling class whom the JVP always accused of being pawns of the globally oriented hegemonic project of the 'New Right'. Therefore, the advantages gained being a partner to the PA coalition government overweighed the JVP's long-term, ultimate goal of capturing state power as a single political party. The damage caused by the JVP's political propaganda against the PA and its political stance on key nationally significant issues led to it losing public support from several constituencies in the south. This coincided with the PA's growing unpopularity among the Tamil community in the north, most of whom suffered under the government's economic embargo and the restriction of movement imposed on the northern part of the country.

THE 2001 GENERAL ELECTION: PEOPLE'S VERDICT DISMISSED!

Until the parliamentary general election that was held on 5 December 2001, President Kumaratunga repeatedly appealed to the public to give her and her political coalition, the PA, a clear mandate to solve many national issues of concern. She stressed the importance of winning a clear majority in the elections for the effective functioning of the government. Her appeals to the public became further amplified as the UNP–SLFP and the personal-political rivalries between Wickremasinghe and Kumaratunga made headlines. Applying a Freudian psycho-analytic approach to the Kumaratunga–Wickremasinghe feud, Uyangoda, a veteran political scientist who also served as a member of Kumaratunga's negotiating team with the LTTE during her first term, opined that the difference of the two leaders can only be explained by applying Freud's 'narcissism of minor differences'[14] (Uyangoda 2002). As these personal tensions with Wickremasinghe intensified, Kumaratunga needed a landslide win to avoid a situation where the UNP secured parliamentary majority and Wickremasinghe become the prime minister while Kumaratunga continued as the executive president.

However, the election results were beyond Kumaratunga's worst nightmare, as the rival United National Front (UNF) coalition led by the UNP under the leadership of Wickremasinghe secured a majority of the parliamentary seats. As the executive president, Kumaratunga was forced to work with the UNF-led cabinet, constituted of the UNP, the SLMC, the CWC and other dissident members of the PA. According to many political analysts, the situation at the political centre was one of the rarest occasions in Sri Lanka's national political history where voters had given a clear verdict to the factionalised Sinhalese political elites to develop a common vision and a bi-partisan approach to deal with compelling issues. The victory of the UNF in this crucial election can also be interpreted as an approval of the UNP a leadership under Wickremasinghe and the party's liberal peace agenda, which was intrinsically linked to peace dividends. However, delivering the promised peace dividends by the UNF was not easy as the elite factional conflicts during the time did not inspire much confidence among local and foreign investors.

UNF EXPERIMENTING (NEO)LIBERAL PEACE

In 2001, the leader of the UNF, Ranil Wickremasinghe, who secured the support of a few minority political parties, claimed general election victory on another peace–economic development platform. The UNF received support from the Tamil National Alliance (TNA) that was composed of four Tamil political parties. Their support was contingent on the UNF's willingness to commence political negotiations with the LTTE, to which the UNF had to agree. Despite the pressure Wickremasinghe faced from his UNF coalition members, as two UNP members interviewed for this study claimed (R.3; R.18), the UNF's approach was consistent with its historical general belief in a political power-sharing arrangement with the Tamils. Meanwhile, the UNF's motivation to engage in negotiations with the LTTE also found resonance with its usual liberal global–local economic perspectives and policies.

To neutralise the undesirable attention from its political competitors and rivals, first the UNF leadership framed the conflict in Sri Lanka as a 'North-East war' and emphasised the urgent need for settling the conflict for economic reasons. Apparently, Wickremasinghe faced significant pressures from the international community to choose this new framing of the conflict and a matching economic strategy based on global 'liberal peace' agenda dominated by the global New Right (Uyangoda and Perera 2003: 4; Stokke and Uyangoda 2010: 1). As the liberal peace agenda came to be solidified in the global aftermath of the 9/11 attacks, supported by the West's global campaign of 'war on terrorism', the UNF and the LTTE entering into political negotiations can be seen as an attempt by both parties to capitalise on the looming mutually hurting stalemate (Zaartman 2001: 8).[15] Wickremasinghe's political negotiation initiative was built on the foundation laid by the PA government, hence he extended the role of Norway as the facilitator.[16] Although this new phase of negotiations under the UNF government managed to attract an enormous level of attention from Western countries, the UNF's local political rivals did not welcome this initiative. Even before the UNF's signing of the ceasefire agreement with the LTTE in 2002, its rival political forces (mainly sitting president Kumaratunga's PA political coalition, the JVP and the EPDP) mobilised public opinion against the agreement. Meanwhile the growing factional conflicts among the Tamil political forces at this time, including conflicts between the EPDP and its arch political rival, the TNA (known as the LTTE's proxy), had doubts about whether to support the UNF initiative or not.

The uncertainties among the Tamil political parties were met with the southern opposition to a ceasefire, which based on the ill-supported assumption of a ceasefire leading to the establishment of a separate state in the north under the LTTE's rule. In the 2002–2003 run-up to the signing of the ceasefire agreement, with the covert blessings of the PA, the JVP launched massive public demonstrations against the ceasefire agreement. The propaganda carried out by the JVP and Wickremasinghe's other political rivals managed to shift the previous pro-negotiation stance that Wickremasinghe had managed to build during the election campaign into an anti-negotiation stand. What was interesting to observe during this period was the actions of President Kumaratunga, who had successfully mobilised the southern polity in favour of a negotiated political settlement during her previous term, now mobilising the same forces against a political settlement under the UNF leadership.

Those who publicly criticised the MOU that was eventually signed between Wickremasinghe and the LTTE leadership further encouraged a factional political environment that was hostile for the survival of the MOU. They particularly attacked Article 1 of the MOU, which deals with the suspension of state military actions against the LTTE (see CJPD 2006: 428–429 for a copy of the MOU). The JVP, the SLFP and the other opposition political parties criticised this specific clause by claiming that the MOU was aiding the LTTE to rearm freely. This specific argument gathered quite some support from the Sinhalese south, who recalled similar instances during the previous failed peace negotiation and the scale of violence that the LTTE unleashed after the collapse of the negotiation process. In addition to the aforementioned groups, the MOU also came under criticism from liberal human rights groups, loosely organised as 'apolitical technical oppositions' in the south and in the north, who grounded their arguments on the constitutionality and the legality of the MOU (Uyangoda and Perera 2003).

According to them, the MOU violated two major fundamental provisions: First, the prime minister does not hold the constitutional authority to enter into any agreement pertaining to war as such powers are constitutionally vested in the hands of the executive president. Second, they pointed to the fact that the signing of an MOU with an armed group banned under the Prevention of Terrorism Act (PTA) of 1972 in Sri Lanka was a violation of the PTA. Albeit these shortcomings as pointed out by different groups, Wickremasinghe managed to reach out to the LTTE using Norwegian communication channels to get them to agree to attend the negotiations. The UNF government even promised the LTTE to lift the internal ban on the group that was imposed under the PTA at least 10 days before the negotiations started.

This MOU also faced criticism from a number of other interest groups that claimed to have no political affiliations in Colombo or in the north and the northeast. For instance, Colombo-based human rights organisations pointed out that by entering into the MOU, the Sri Lankan government legalised and legitimised the LTTE's self-proclaimed position as the 'sole representative' of Sri Lanka's indigenous Tamils. They also argued that the MOU automatically disrespected the claims of other Tamil groups, especially that of the moderate Tamils who also claimed to represent the same Tamil constituency through democratic political engagement. By taking a moral high ground, these groups accused the UNF of trying to deliberately eliminate alternative, moderate, democratic and liberal Tamil groups from the Tamil political field, who often suffered at the hands of the LTTE's brutal fascist, de-facto state in the north. Further, they predicted that the MOU between the UNF and the LTTE will serve as an encouragement for the LTTE to impose totalitarian rule in the north and the east. For them, the MOU also signified the government's deliberate acceptance of the LTTE's violation of the regional minorities' human rights and the discarding of democratic-pluralist politics. Last but not least, these oppositional groups accused the government of paving the way for 'totalitarian peace' and further nurturing the LTTE as a fascist organisation (Uyangoda and Perera 2003: 21).

With the public momentum against commencing political negotiations with the LTTE steadily rising from the north to the south of the country, the LTTE also refused to begin the proposed negotiations until the proscription imposed on them during the previous PA regime was lifted (this was imposed after the attack on the sacred Buddhist site of the Temple of the Tooth in 1998). The LTTE also pointed out to the fact that their status as a banned organisation was unacceptable as such status undermined their self-proclaimed position as the sole representative of the Tamil people. These arguments of the LTTE received a number of reactions from many quarters in the field of conflict resolution, who were quick to point out the LTTE's concerns as a classic theoretical dilemma in negotiations. Citing internationally used jargons such as 'parity of status', they pointed out to the immediate need for lifting the ban on the LTTE to lay out a solid political foundation for a successful negotiation process (Uyangoda 2007c). The SLFP-led PA coalition that had previously, when in government, worked tirelessly to secure the ban domestically (which eventually led to an international ban in 2006 when the LTTE was listed as an international terrorist organisation in Europe, the United States and in a number of other Western countries) was now vehemently opposed to the lifting of the ban.

Meanwhile, on 10 April 2002, making a rare televised appearance, the LTTE leader Prabhakaran suggested a way out of the war. To the surprise of many political opponents of the UNF, Prabhakaran expressed his willingness to seek a political solution to end the war within a political framework based on the principles of autonomy and internal-self-determination. This new move of the LTTE leadership stood in contradiction to its past tradition of hard bargaining based on the controversial Thimpu Principles.[17] It was the first time in the history of the conflict that the LTTE leadership publicly declared its readiness to accept a settlement that was meeting only the first four Thimpu Principles (recognition of Tamils as a separate and distinct nation, recognition of a Tamil homeland and guarantee of its territorial integrity and the right of Tamils to self-determination (Uyangoda and Perera 2003: 31). Hence the LTTE's willingness to shift its political position from conditional negotiation to principled unconditional negotiations provided the UNF government a new lease of life. However, the LTTE's move was not enough to swing the opinion of the majority Sinhalese who had already been mobilised by the JVP and PA political propaganda against the UNF's negotiation efforts.

WORKING AROUND POLITICS OF PEACE: RE-SHIFTING THE DISCOURSE

In spite of all the political drama in the run-up to the negotiations, the LTTE and the UNF government entered into political negotiations with a mutually accommodative understanding of peace. They were careful to define the conflict in non-controversial ways. From the LTTE's perspective, the conflict was presented as a national question and a problem between the Sinhalese and the Tamil nations. From the UNF government's point of view, it was a 'war in the North and the East'. These seemingly politically neutral, non-comprehensive definitions agitated the nationalist critics. According to these critics, the UNF's definition of the war meant limiting the phenomenon to a smaller geographical area, diluting or even hiding the deep-rooted causes of the conflict. Hence, the UNF's conceptualisation of the conflict was seen as a threat to certain political forces whose political survival largely relied on a different reality of the war. In particular, this specific re-conceptualisation by UNF was problematic for the nationalist political parties such as the JVP as its main political programme, propaganda machinery and political survival were deeply linked to right-wing chauvinist ethno-nationalist overtones.

Meanwhile the UNF and the LTTE also presented their shared vision of peace that was pragmatic and limited. As Uyangoda observed, their joint notion of peace entailed a political engagement to achieve 'what is possible' (Uyangoda and Perera 2003: 26). Hence, they entered into political negotiations by leaving the most contentious issues, such as constitutional reforms, power-sharing arrangements, and so on, aside. From the UNF government's point of view, the primary focus was to secure a limited peace agenda by deliberately limiting the emergence of unfavourable trajectories by de-linking the ethnic conflict from war and violence. Therefore, the UNF selected only a few consequences of the armed conflict to focus on during the initial phase of negotiations, which they hoped to develop into a step-by-step approach to manage it through a number of interim phases. According to technical experts on conflict negotiations, the UNF's approach only allowed the negotiating parties to address one issue at a time and secure incremental progress, which was pragmatic and not aimed at arriving at a final and permanent solution (Uyangoda 2003: 4). With this specific negotiation strategy the UNF hoped to gradually open the space for the institutionalisation of a political process in which other relevant parties could also participate to design joint alternatives to main and peripheral issues.

As one veteran political analyst observed, the UNF's preferred negotiation framework could only lead to a 'peace deal' (Uyangoda 2003: 4) to manage the conflict within a limited and pragmatic framework acceptable to the international custodians of the peace process. Unfortunately, the UNF's specific negotiation framework ignored building society-wide political conditions conducive to the success of the negotiations (Uyangoda 2007a: 46).

However, as the interviewees of this study shared, there was little chance of creating a wider societal consensus at that time with an extremely polarised Sinhalese polity and with the UNF's rival political elites having developed a political habitus of opposing each other's endeavours (R.5; R.16; R.18).

INTERNATIONAL ACTORS AND A RENEWED SENSE OF NATIONALISM

In spite of all the political drama in Colombo, the external international actors involved in Sri Lanka's 2002 negotiation process secured space for negotiation between the UNF and the LTTE. Initially these external actors were warmly welcomed by the UNF government despite the historical memories of negative experiences of external involvement in Sri Lanka's conflict under the earlier UNP government.[18] The UNF's warm welcome to the external actors to serve in various capacities to facilitate the peace negotiations soon led to their overwhelming involvement in the process (Goodhand 2006: 215–219). In addition to Norway, which was assigned the most direct role as the main facilitator, communicator and mediator, this phase of peace negotiations were also joined by the United States of America, the United Kingdom, Canada and Japan as the main international custodians of the 2002–2003 negotiations.[19] Their role as custodians was consolidated by them sending individual country representatives to Colombo to assess the progress of the peace process. In addition, a few notable international multilateral organisations, such as the International Monetary Fund, the ADB and the World Bank, also began to work closely with all the parties involved in the negotiations. Further, the United Nations and its agencies that already had a presence in the country were closely engaged in the negotiation process. The United Nations Development Programme (UNDP) showed its commitment to the peace process by adjusting their on-going development project activities in line with the needs and concerns emerging from the post-ceasefire context. For the UNF, although it was overwhelming, the scale of international involvement was essential to garner legitimacy to the process as well as to secure financial commitments necessary for delivering the promised peace dividends. The latter was evident from the roles assigned to the international custodians in the post-conflict economic recovery plans for the war-ravaged areas (Goodhand 2006: 218–21). However, this massive involvement of the international actors came under heavy criticism of the UNF's rival political parties and a few vocal members of the local academic community (Bastian

2003a: 149–50; Rajasingham-Senanayake 2003: 129–30). They argued that the international actors had hijacked Sri Lanka's negotiation process. The JVP was instrumental in campaigning against the international involvement by framing it as part of a global experiment of '(neo)liberal peace'; the JVP's criticism was also complemented by the academic critique of the role of the multilateral financial institutions in aiding neoliberal peace templates (Rajasingham-Senanayake 2003: 112).

In spite of all these challenges, the UNF government was motivated to include the international actors in order to benefit from their technical skills, their supposedly neutral communication channels and their valuable financial resources to reach a settlement with the LTTE. Perhaps it also foresaw the strategic advantage of these actors in mobilising 'carrots and sticks' to encourage the LTTE to stay in the the negotiation process. Meanwhile the UNF's lack of regard for the critical local voices alleging the West's stake in the design and ownership of the peace process, their attempts to disregard local knowledge, local political forces and local power politics, isolated the UNF from local circles. As the majority of the respondents of this research opined, the UNF and Wickremasinghe became increasingly ignorant and insensitive to local political realities, thus clumsily providing more opportunities for the eager spoiler to destabilise the negotiation process. This end result of the UNF's own behaviour was that the entire political negotiation process grew increasingly isolated from the rest of the local societal forces and politics. Additionally, the alleged neoliberal peace approach of the UNF government and its technocratic blueprint provided grounds for the resurgence of Sinhala-Buddhist nationalism with a right-wing political spin. According to these right-wing nationalist forces, the UNF's complicity in the external actors' neo-imperial economic and political project was completely unacceptable. Undoubtedly, these views caught the attention of the majority in the Sinhalese polity by reigniting their long-standing anti-Western nationalism, which in turn helped in justifying their Sinhala-Buddhist hegemonic political project and the UNP leadership's continued class and ideological biases that went way back to British colonial period.

These local critics were also inspired by the global scholarly literature condemning the neoliberal peace frameworks as endorsed by the UNF government. They were swift to point out the limitations of these frameworks in addressing the deep-rooted structural issues of the conflict. They argued that supporting the new set of institutional arrangements proposed by international multilateral institutions to settle Sri Lanka's conflict was harmful and would undermine the state's sovereignty (Bastian 2003a: 149–50; Rajasingham-Senanayake 2003: 129–30). These scholarly critiques provided more ammunition to the local nationalists to justify their pursuit of Sinhala-Buddhist nationalism, post-colonial national self-determination and neo-colonial resistance. As shared by one respondent who was an active member of the SLFP at the time of interviewing, Wickremasinghe's economic development proposal within the overall peace plan called 'Regaining Sri Lanka' was developed strictly based on a neoliberal peace framework aligned with the political and economic project of the international multilateral institutions (or the so-called Washington Consensus) that was clearly insensitive to the needs and aspirations of the local communities (R.23). As another respondent, who is a Western-educated theoretician of a nationalist-oriented political party, shared,

> Ranil and his cultural, social and economic background are not local; he (and also Chandrika, during 1994–2004) did not allow Sinhala-Buddhist nationalism to exist; instead, they told the people to be Sri Lankan. (R.20)

Also as shared by a reputable economist I interviewed, the UNF's 2002–2003 negotiation process mainly focused on seeking technocratic solutions by disregarding local knowledge and participation (R.10).

Amidst all the mounting pressures against the negotiations, the UNF and the LTTE were able to hold only six rounds of talks from the proposed nine rounds planned in the first phase of negotiations. Unfortunately, the last three rounds of negotiations in the first phase were overshadowed by tensions between the negotiating parties around several issues, namely security concerns, progress of rehabilitation work in the north and the east and the question of parity of status between the parties. From the fourth round of the negotiations, the initial warm and cordial relations between the negotiating parties were already withering away. These tensions escalated as the parties commenced their discussions on Muslim–Tamil relations in the east[20] and the LTTE demanded the removal of high security zones in the north. Cordiality was also disrupted by various naval confrontations instigated by the LTTE to provoke the Sri Lanka Navy to react under the orders of Executive President Kumaratunga, who was constitutionally responsible to give orders as the head of the armed forces. Eventually, in March 2003, the LTTE withdrew from the negotiations citing its disappointment at not receiving an invitation to the international pre-donor conference organised in Washington DC related to the peace process. Later, it boycotted the donor conference organised in Tokyo, during which the agendas of reconstruction and development of the north and the east were discussed. The LTTE's engagement was of paramount importance for Wickremasinghe, not only to face his political opponents but also to access the USD 40 million aid pledged during the Tokyo conference that was strictly tied to the progress of the negotiation process.

These negative political developments around the main negotiating table were further exacerbated by the LTTE's numerous violations of the ceasefire agreement as highlighted by the international monitoring mission in Sri Lanka (the Sri Lanka Monitoring Mission, or SLMM).[21] According to the SLMM, during this period, the LTTE carried out 119 assassinations, abducted 253 children and 579 adults, and recruited 1,743 child soldiers.[22] Their reports mentioned specific instances of ceasefire violations, mostly in the Eastern Province, that became grave as the LTTE began to kill Muslims living in this province and increased its extortion activities. The LTTE's behaviour brought enormous pressure on the UNF government and Wickremasinghe.

Having undertaken a detailed analysis of the ways in which political forces supported and opposed the UNF's negotiation initiative with the LTTE in 2002–2003, the ultimate failure of this particular phase of negotiations boiled down to the nature of elite politics in the country. Thus, against this background of long-standing and immediate dynamics surrounding the political negotiations of 2002–2003, it is reasonable to suggest that the pro- and anti-negotiation stances taken by different factions within the ruling elites were nothing more than a continuation of their usual politics.

KUMARATUNGA STRIKES BACK: FROM LIBERAL PEACE TO LIMITED WAR

Concurrent with the setbacks in the 2002–2003 negotiations, the tensions between President Kumaratunga and Premier Wickremasinghe also increased dramatically, specially surrounding some items in the internal power sharing arrangements signed between the president (PA) and the prime minister (UNF) after the 2001 general election. After a few rounds of open conflict with Wickramasinghe, in February 2002 President Kumaratunga let go of the control of a few important ministries, namely finance, defence and media, which Wickremasinghe considered important for resolving the war. The

UNF's control over these ministries allowed it to have access to the financial resources necessary to conduct negotiations with the LTTE, which naturally undermined Kumaratunga's powers as the executive president.

Meanwhile, citing the urgent need to resettle Tamil civilians and to speed up the processes towards normalising life, the LTTE continued to demand the withdrawal of government forces from the high security zones, to which the UNF government did not respond favourably. The UNF's decision not to withdraw forces from these areas was based on concerns expressed by the UNF's anti-LTTE allies, such as the EPDP, who warned against the withdrawal of state armed troops from Jaffna. According to the EPDP's assessment, withdrawing troops from Jaffna could lead to the state armed forces losing control over Jaffna peninsula as well as paving the way for the LTTE to gain full control over the entire region by force. The assessment was also endorsed by the army commander, General Sarath Fonseka, citing the dangerous consequences of taking such a step while the LTTE remained mobilised and armed.[23] Meanwhile, although the premier oversaw the activities of the Ministry of Defence, on three separate occasions the government naval forces conducted massive defensive attacks on the LTTE's naval vessels and boats under the direct orders of President Kumaratunga. The president's orders were backed by the hardliners in the navy, especially the naval chief, Admiral Daya Sandagiri. These naval confrontations further undermined the UNF's negotiation efforts (Dias 2003). The animosities between all parties escalated further as the LTTE unveiled a unilateral proposal for an Interim Self Governing Administration (ISGA) for the Northern Province that was in complete contradiction to the government's proposed version of ISGA.[24] Many in the south and anti-LTTE Tamil political groups alleged that the LTTE's version of ISGA was nothing short of laying the first stepping-stone towards establishing a separate state. Using the new dynamics sparked by the establishing of the ISGA, in November 2003 President Kumaratunga declared a state of emergency and took back control of the three vital ministries – the ministries of Defence, Interior Affairs and Mass Communications – from the prime minister.[25] She justified her actions by pointing to the UNF's dangerous appeasement of the LTTE and the implication of Wickremasinghe's actions on national security. At this point, the Norwegian government and the international co-chairs of the negotiation process suspended negotiations with the UNF and the LTTE and left Kumaratunga and Wickremasinghe to solve the power crisis between the two. The withdrawal of the international facilitators left Wickremasinghe completely handicapped to deal with the LTTE. The LTTE was quick to capitalise on this newest development by expressing its own disappointment at the UNF's inability to make any credible commitment. Reflecting on this peculiar political crisis, in 2005 Wickremasinghe recalled, 'The President took over the Ministry of Defence and dissolved Parliament, making it impossible for my government to effectively manage the peace process any further' (Wickramasinghe 2006: 9).

Following this turnaround of events, even with the bitter memories of the PA and the JVP's failed cohabitation, in January 2004 the SLFP entered into a new agreement with the JVP and formed the UPFA coalition to contest in the upcoming general election. However, this new partnership did nothing to temper the JVP's anti-peace rhetoric during the election campaign, which was clear in a firebrand speech delivered by the JVP's propaganda secretary, Wimal Weerawansa, who even went as far as to hint at the possibility of a future total war. Such hard-line JVP opinions were tolerated by the SLFP, as the political advantages of such propaganda could also work in its favour. During the election campaign, the JVP came out strongly against any future negotiations with the LTTE, which also sparked a stern reaction from the LTTE, the latter in turn rejecting any form of negotiations with the UPFA coalition of which the JVP was a member.

Despite all the efforts made by the UPFA, it was unable to secure enough number of seats to form a parliamentary majority to form a government, thus leading to a hung parliament. Following the same fate of the previous alliance between the SLFP-led PA and JVP alliance, this time the UPFA alliance fell apart in a matter of a few months as Kumaratunga was unwilling to fulfil the JVP's demands in return for their support to the coalition.[26]

COMPLEXITIES, THREATS AND OPPORTUNITIES: TSUNAMI POLITICS

In December 2004, giant tsunami waves struck Sri Lanka. This affected the coastal belts in the east and the south and hit the north of the country the hardest, taking more than 30,000 lives (Goodhand and Klem 2005: 22) and causing immense financial and infrastructural damage.[27] To address the immediate and long-term needs of the affected population, the international community convinced President Kumaratunga, opposition UNP and the LTTE leadership to work jointly. This catastrophic environment pushed the Sri Lankan state and the international actors to search for a suitable mechanism to address the suffering of the affected people in the southern and northern coastal belts. Their efforts eventually materialised in the setting up of a Post-Tsunami Operational Management Structure (P-TOMS), signed on 23 June 2005 with the main objective of smoothening the flow of international aid to these areas.

However, Kumaratunga efforts to reach out to the north and the east to bring relief to the people were not welcomed by some vocal voices in southern politics, especially due to their concerns over the LTTE's involvement in it. Therefore, their propaganda against the P-TOMS undermined Kumaratunga's effort towards implementing the agreement. As a mark of protest against its implementation, the JVP withdrew its support to Kumaratunga's UPFA coalition government. Their withdrawal of support was followed by two consecutive weeks of public rallies attracting a massive number of protesters against the P-TOMS. Not only that; the JVP went as far as filling a legal case in the Supreme Court against the implementation of the P-TOMS. To the disappointment of Kumaratunga, the Supreme Court declared the proposed structure unconstitutional and suspended most of its clauses. This Supreme Court's decision was a huge political boost for the JVP, which coincided with Kumaratunga announcing of the next presidential election in November 2005. Capitalising on Tsunami politics, the SLFP-led UPFA government this time under the leadership of Mahinda Rajapaksa came to power.

COMPLEXITIES, THREATS AND OPPORTUNITIES: SPLIT IN THE LTTE

A nation has no permanent enemies and no permanent friends, only permanent interests.

—Lord Palmertson

While the crisis in southern politics was marked by a number of incidents that further polarised the southern polity and the factionalised ruling class, an unexpected development took place in the Tamil military–political balance in the north. In March 2004, the LTTE split into two factions, dividing along the northern and the eastern commands. Media reports attributed this split to many different factors (Fernando 2011). One that gained the most currency was the mistreatment and discrimination of the eastern command

and its cadres by the northern command. These media reports also revealed that the eastern commander's expressed unhappiness with the northern leadership over the latter's unfair division of funds raised from abroad between the east and the north commands and also for taking a soft-line approach towards the SLMC during 2002–2003 political negotiations. The LTTE's eastern commander complained that the northern commander's soft approach had led to a destabilisation of the authority of the eastern command. Also, according to one of the US diplomatic cables released by WikiLeaks, the defection of the eastern command under Colonel Karuna was allegedly linked to Wickremasinghe and the encouragement he gave Karuna during the peace process under the UNF government (quoted by Fernando, cable dated 15 March 2004 in www.asiatribune.com). Undoubtedly, for the majority in the south and for the Sinhalese ruling political elites, Karuna's defection was a welcome sign as this move greatly undermined the LTTE's self-claimed status of being the sole representative of the Sri Lankan Tamil community. Quickly capitalising on this new situation, the UPFA government arranged a political passage for Colonel Karuna to enter into the national political scene. He was first appointed as a provincial councillor, then as a member of parliament in the newly elected UPFA government under Mahinda Rajapaksa in 2005. Karuna's support was crucial for the UPFA to win votes in the Eastern Province, which Rajapaksa rewarded by granting complete political immunity from prosecution for the various atrocities Karuna and his soldiers had committed in the past. As highlighted in numerous newspaper reports, securing Karuna's support played a major role in the UPFA government's eventual decision to embark on a full military offensive on the LTTE in 2008. Reminiscent of the proverb 'the enemy of my enemy is my friend', Karuna became an important political ally of Rajapaksa by undermining the influence of other 'king makers' in national politics. However, Karuna's entry into the national political scene increased polarisation and fractionalisation among the Tamil political forces as well as among of the Sinhalese political elites, as Rajapaksa later cleared the way to appoint Karuna as the deputy president of the SLFP in 2009.

THE RISE OF RAJAPAKSA: VICTOR'S PEACE TO DYNASTIC POLITICS

Towards the end of Kumaratunga's tenure as the president, her position as the party leader within the SLFP was challenged. Although some predicted that her brother Anura Bandaranaike would receive the party nomination to be the next presidential candidate to contest in the 2005 presidential election, the Rajapaksa family, who were long-serving party members, were also eyeing this crucial nomination. As the tensions arose between the two families (Bandaranaike and Rajapaksa) for securing party leadership, Kumaratunga attempted to prolong her tenure as the president by manipulating the dates of her second swearing-in as the president.

This internal party crisis ended up with the SLFP splitting into two factions, one led by the aristocratic Bandaranaike and the other led by Mahinda Rajapaksa hailing from low country and the Goyigama caste. Rajapaksa vigorously campaigned for a non-Bandaranaike leadership. These internal SLFP factional conflicts brought the Sinhalese political elites' long-standing underlying class, regional and family fights back in the national political spotlight. To buy support from party members, both factions sought new alliances by extending extensive patronage benefits to SLFP members and to other political parties from minority ethnic groups and Sinhala-Buddhist nationalist parties such as the JVP and the Jathika Hela Urumaya (JHU). Much to Kumaratunga's and her allies' dissatisfaction, Rajapaksa managed to secure greater support and establish himself as the new party leader. His rise to the party leadership also earned him the party's nomination for the upcoming presidential election. However, Kumaratunga's continued presence in the party led to Rajapaksa's isolation within his own party. Hence Rajapaksa's choice to rely on his own family members for support and legitimacy within the party was not surprising.

Rajapaksa's 2005 presidential election manifesto titled *Mahinda Chinthana* laid down a framework for addressing numerous local issues. As shared by one respondent, even *Mahinda Chinthana* was drafted with the help of the JVP and the JHU as Rajapaksa's own party members from the SLFP did not extend their support (R.20). As this same respondent recalled, 'at that time, there was no party to help Mahinda even to draft his election manifesto, there was no money to run for elections, only the JVP and JHU helped him' (R.20). The influence of the JVP and the JHU was manifested in the *Mahinda Chinthana* that was firmly anchored in Sinhala-Buddhist nationalism and hegemony. According to the majority of respondents, the influence of the small nationalist parties was also pronounced through Rajapaksa's anti-negotiation posture towards the LTTE and his explicit denial of the LTTE's claim to an exclusive Tamil homeland, rejection of the P-TOMS and scrapping of the ceasefire agreement signed by his predecessor.

Meanwhile, blessed with the various factionalised elites' conflicts, Rajapaksa assumed a patriotic image on the national political scene. Frequent over-emphasis paid to his personal and political roots in his remote rural electorate of Hambantota district in the extreme southern coastal tip of Sri Lanka, especially by the JVP and the JHU, helped Rajapaksa to effectively harmonise the struggles he faced in the centre of national politics and those in the peripheries. Their strategy was successful in bringing back the rural masses into the national political discourse again. These strategic moves made by smaller nationalist political parties supporting Rajapaksa also inspired new forms of sub-regional, southern nationalism in the country. Rajapaksa's election campaign based on this rural, southern platform therefore strengthened his voter base as the main content of the election campaign aroused their long-suppressed regional identity sentiments and the historical rivalry between the rural south and the urban-capitalist Colombo and its suburbs. Rajapaksa's rival, the UNP's Wickremasinghe, with his image as the godchild of capitalist, urban elites, was nowhere near matching Rajapaksa's rural persona that appealed to a vast number of voters in the Sinhalese deep south. Without wasting the opportunity in hand, both the JVP and the JHU also unleashed a series of scathing criticisms against the aristocratic and urbanised, Western bourgeoisie domination of national politics to which the UNP leaders Wickremasinghe and the SLFP's Bandaranaike fit in as the perfect poster children. This rebranding exercise of Rajapaksa launched by the JVP and the JHU during the election campaign and after rekindled Rajapaksa's image as the reincarnation of the ancient Sinhalese king Dutugemunu who defeated the Tamil king Elara according to an ancient chronicle of the island called *Mahawamsa*. Next to his impersonation of Dutugemunu, Rajapaksa was also given the fitting tile of 'Dakune ape kena' (Our Southern Man), adjusted to the contemporary political conditions. The latter was also immensely strategic in arousing subconscious identity intrinsically linked to the political economy of southern nationalism and its class bias that was resurfacing since the UNF regime (Jayasuriya 2005: 87). The sense of *dakune ape kena* soon became inseparable from the expectations of the lower classes living in the margins of the traditional southern society for Rajapaksa to fulfil southern-based identity needs in national politics. The political economy of sub-nationalism had no place or recognition during the UNF government and in its neoliberal policies. Being acutely aware of such sentiments, Rajapaksa's election manifesto reassured the identity of the ordinary men and women by unveiling new indigenised moral values as well. For example, the preamble of the manifesto and various subsections of *Mahinda Chinthana* appealed to the village-centric virtuous society and to a virtuous state. Although many credited Rajapaksa's eventual narrow electoral victory at the presidential election to the south-based nationalist sentiments and forces, a respondent who was a political ally and a senior member of the national legislature opined that Rajapaksa's 2005 election was also helped by the LTTE leadership (R.13).[28] Even with the massive support gathered from the north to the east and the south Rajapaksa managed to secure only 50.29 per cent votes against his rival Wickremasinghe, who received 48.43 per cent of votes. (www.slelections.gov.lk). Rajapaksa's narrow victory showed the difficulty of ignoring the strength of Wickremasinghe and his allies in national politics (who despite losing elections for nine consecutive years were worthy opponents in national politics). By looking at the broader picture of the 2005 election results, another respondent of this study was of the opinion that the election outcomes were not determined on the basis of stable constituencies of the main political parties, but rather on the successful mobilisation of around 20 per cent of floating votes (R.10). Complementing this view, another respondent suggested it was time to debunk the myth about 'majority politics' (R.9). As he was convinced, politics in Sri Lanka is an affair of (various) minority political brokers who get to decide who wins.

Acutely aware of the prevailing electoral political dynamics, Rajapaksa made no mistake in putting together a winning coalition. Whether he liked it or not, the same coalition was hugely influential in him choosing to go to war with the LTTE to bring peace. According to the results of a Gallup survey conducted in 2006, 88 per cent of the respondents expressed their confidence in Rajapaksa's handling of a peace process to end the war and the conflict (Srinivas and Crabtree 2006). His decision was favourably received by those who were getting weary of endlessly waiting for the promised peace dividends under both Wickremasinghe and Kumaratunga to arrive. The overall local political sentiments among the majority Sinhalese and their psychology of winning (R.18) were complemented by the prevailing international sentiments in the background of 'war against terrorism'.[29] Despite the widely alleged support Rajapaksa received from the LTTE to win the presidential election, the latter soon realised its grave misjudgement of Rajapaksa's ability to follow a total war agenda. Perhaps the LTTE extended support to Rajapaksa just like they did for Premadasa in the hope of buying time to rearm. However, in the end, the shrewd political strategy of the Sinhalese political elites triumphed over the LTTE's military strategy.

RAJAPAKSA AND THE ALL PARTY REPRESENTATIVES COMMITTEE (APRC)

In mid-2006, Rajapaksa established the All Party Representatives Committee (APRC) to find a political settlement to address the rights of the Tamil minority. The establishment of the APRC was a contradiction to Rajapaksa and his allies' election-time rhetoric opposing a political settlement with the LTTE. On paper, the primary aim of the APRC was to forge a consensus among all the national political parties to bring peace. At the beginning, the APRC was attended by many political parties. Later the UNP decided to withdraw from the process to protest the president's decision to include ex-LTTE commander Karuna in this political platform.[30] The UNP's withdrawal also triggered the JVP to walk out of the APRC as well. On its way out, the JVP also demanded the dissolution of the APRC process fully. Amidst these setbacks, the APRC continued its work for another brief period mostly to satisfy the demands of the international community for the continuation of political negotiations. As one high-ranked UNP member interviewed for this study recalled, 'APRC is a hoax' (R.3), while a few others saw the APRC as Rajapaksa's puppet (R.22; R.25).

As these respondents further shared, the outcome of the APRC process was already predetermined by Rajapaksa. As they pointed out as an example, when the long overdue interim report of the committee's work was presented in 2007, unsurprisingly to many observers of the process, the solutions mentioned in the report only went as far as recommending full implementation of the 13th Amendment of the Constitution.[31] Even though this outcome was expected, again the JVP, the LTTE and the UNP condemned this particular solution for different reasons. Some respondents who were in the inner circles of the chairman of the APRC, Professor Tissa Vitharana, shared that the 2007 public interim report released by the committee was without the original far-reaching conclusions arrived at by the committee. They alleged that the report's recommendation to implement the 13th Amendment fully was the president's pre-decided solution. These underhand moves of President Rajapaksa showed his deliberate intentions, on the one hand, to undermine the credibility of his own initiative and, on the other hand, to use the APRC process to buy time to prepare for war and build necessary alliances. Also behind the cover of the political drama of the APRC, Rajapaksa wasted no time to introduce crucial institutional changes to secure his political domination as well. Rajapaksa's ulterior motives were captured by the leader of the Muslim Congress Rauf Hakeem during a newspaper interview in 2009:

> ... for certain, this (APRC) was only a mirage and nothing tangible would happen even after the next Presidential election.... Frankly, I do not expect President Mahinda Rajapaksa to publicly take a position, until and unless he gets a fresh mandate in an island-wide Presidential or Parliamentary election. (*Sunday Leader* 2009)

Hakeem was not alone in his opinion as a few other vocal political personalities interviewed for this study also shared similar opinions. Some among the latter thought seeking a political solution agreeable to all the political parties was anyway a waste of time, unnecessary and futile. These respondents rather preferred the government undertaking reforms for the democratisation of the state and the restoration of democratic principles and values.

TOTAL WAR AND MILITARY DEFEAT OF THE LTTE: TRIUMPH OF THE DISCOURSE OF SINHALESE HEGEMONY

Despite the public anti-LTTE and anti-negotiation stand that Rajapaksa initially took, he still sent a government delegation to meet the LTTE in Geneva with the assistance of Norwegian facilitators. The most important immediate reason for going to Geneva was the LTTE's continued violations of the ceasefire that they were still theoretically committed to as part of the ceasefire agreement in 2002 (Rupasinghe 2006: 45). As already predicted by a number of political observers, the initial round of talks in Geneva aimed at cessation of hostilities ended rather quickly as nether party was not in the mood for negotiations.

Meanwhile, inspired by the European Union's decision announced on 30 May 2006 to enlist the LTTE as a terrorist organisation with the intention of obtaining its commitment to reach a negotiated political settlement (Nesan 2006),[32] nationalist parties in Rajapaksa's coalition government began to mount pressure on him to eradicate 'Tiger terrorism'. By using the global context of war against terrorism, the JVP and the JHU organised massive propaganda campaigns linking global and local terrorism and pushed Rajapaksa to go to war against the LTTE. Given Rajapaksa's dependency on the JVP's 30 parliamentary seats in the national legislature to keep his parliamentary majority, at this point it was unthinkable for Rajapaksa to go against the JVP's demands, which already had gathered impressive public support.[33] Meanwhile, the idea of waging a full military offensive against the LTTE was supported by a new patriotic, politico-moral bloc formed of key figures in the Sinhala-Buddhist intelligentsia (R.5; R.6; R.11; R.15). As some of these respondents opined, this group went as far as manufacturing Buddhist doctrinal principles to justify and legitimise the imminent 'just war' (R.5).[34] In order to bring their ideology and moral values closer to the lay Sinhala-Buddhist segments, these mentioned key figures, especially those who had ties with the JHU, and frequently performed various Buddhist religious rituals such as Bodhi Pooja (sacred offerings and prayers to Buddha) asking for special blessings to the president while cursing his enemies. This new politico-moral-religious alliance even justified carrying out a major military offensive in the north as a 'humanitarian operation' to save the Tamils from the LTTE's brutality. Many of my respondent believed that, at the beginning, President Rajapaksa was not ready to go for a costly all-out war and his preference was only to engage in a low-intensity military campaign against the LTTE. His military strategy was limited to increasing his political capital by securing a few occasional military successes on the battlefield. Perhaps this strategy was also intended to brush aside his alleged relationship with the LTTE that helped him to win the 2005 election.

The political dynamics surrounding war and peace and elite's choice of strategy for pursuing war or peace by frequently blurring the physical, mental and moral boundaries between war, conflict and peace reveal the extent to which the ruling elites in Sri Lanka were willing to manipulate the public to pursue their own narrow political goals and political survival. Among all these political games and strategies, the political work undertaken by right-wing Sinhalese nationalist parties like the JVP and the JHU was the most vociferous in shifting public opinion in favour of war since 2005. The drastic pendulum shifts noted in elite strategies and public opinion since 1994, starting with President Kumaratunga's peace by peaceful agenda to the humanitarian war under President Rajapaksa, should not be mistaken as spontaneous decisions but as part of the factionalised ruling elites' strategies for political domination and hegemony-building. But at the same time, as revealed by the result of a Gallup poll conducted around the time when President Rajapaksa was contemplating his final war against the LTTE (Naurath 2007), poll participants expressed overwhelming confidence in the military over politicians, with figures as high as 92 per cent in favour of the former. The trust extended towards the military could be explained as a sign of people's weariness with the political elites' continued horse-trading and betting on war and peace contributing to the latter's personal and political enrichment at the expense of the former's everyday basic needs.

A breaking out of a full-scale war in Sri Lanka would also make the previously highly involved international community take a back seat and become mere spectators of the war. At this point the international community had also realised the seriousness of the political conflicts in Colombo and lost faith in the LTTE after the Geneva talks in 2006 during which they realised that the LTTE was an impediment to any kind of political solution. Making use of all these shifting of conditions, sentiments and opinions, and the developing impulsive psychological momentum of winning among the majority Sinhalese, Rajapaksa launched a full-scale military assault against the LTTE. After several months, in May 2009 the government armed forces emerged as the victor.[35] Just prior to the armed forces' imminent victory, various media reports, both local and international, vividly described the battlefield events, bringing the northern battlefield closer to the southern public, as follows:

> The war is not far off. The strip of sand where the Tamil Tiger rebels are holed up with thousands of civilians is an hour up the coastline, but this is as close as reporters can get without government approval. We have no such permission, and are forced to turn back. This has been called a war without witnesses. (Stewart Bell, 7 May 2009, *National Post*)

According to other reports,

> The current military hold up in the North now with a mere four square kilometres to be cleared is due to some difficulties in terrain coupled with harsh weather conditions but that would in no way daunt the prospect of reaching the anticipated photo finish, top government officials believe. The government is of the view that end of May would see an end to the island's civil strife. According to Military Spokesperson, Brigadier Udaya Nanayakkara there are no new challenges but the troops are moving ahead with extreme caution in a bid to prevent civilians from being harmed. In warfare, it is pointless to give deadlines. There are diversions, tactical withdrawals, wins and

defeats. All these factors are common to all parties to a conflict. The war will soon end, insists Nanayakkara. (Dilrukshi Handunnetti, 10 May 2009, *Sunday Leader*)

No time for ceasefire: time yet for surrender – President. We have at no time gone for a ceasefire. We will not do so now. There is no time for that now. In the five or six days remaining we are given the opportunity for the LTTE to lay down their arms and surrender to the Armed Forces and, even in the name of God, free the civilians held by them. (Ministry of Defence, 30 April 2009, retrieved from https://m.reliefweb.int/report/306685?lang=ru, accessed on 30 August 2009)

'... Rajapaksa may be keen to broaden his Sinhala support base rather than providing a constitutional solution,' says V Suryanarayan, South Asia expert.... Sri Lanka's State television station announced on Monday that Tamil Tiger rebel Chief Velupillai Prabhakaran has been killed, and the army commander said the last pockets of rebel resistance have been cleared from the North. (V. Venketaraman 20 May 2009, *Times of India*)

Also as reported, the LTTE International head K. P. Pathmanathan issued a statement of surrender on May 17 that stated,

We have decided to silence our guns. However as the LTTE received no confirmation regarding the final surrender arrangements from the military desperate cadres mounted a last ditch attempt to break out of the no-fire zone on May 17 by crossing the Nanthikadal lagoon at which point a majority of them were killed and the LTTE came to a final end. However the report states that several senior LTTE leaders were massacred by the Army in subsequent mopping-up operations and that LTTE political wing leaders B. Nadesan and S. Pulidevan and their wives were gunned down by troops while holding white flags and attempting to surrender on May 18. The report offers no conclusions on the final fate of Pirapaharan's wife and his daughter Dwarka. It however highlights inconsistencies in reports from the government regarding developments in the final days and hours of the war and offers its version as the clearest and most accurate account of events. (Reported after the defeat of the LTTE on 14 June 2009, *Sunday Leader*)

According to a political observer, the LTTE was waiting for the government to launch a major offensive to draw the attention of the international community to the catastrophic human cost of the war (Uyangoda 2007b: 4). The 'logic of circumstance'[36] that the LTTE expected was a sure way of creating a favourable environment to embark on a full-scale war. As stated by one respondent, the LTTE misjudged the government and did not expect the latter to sacrifice all its resources to waging a full-scale war, that too by disregarding the concerns expressed by the international community about the potential catastrophic consequences of such an offence.[37] As one Tamil respondent shared, Rajapaksa going to war with the LTTE cannot be divorced from the realities of politics in Sri Lanka and the potential that military victories have in generating an enormous amount of political capital for the elites to stay in power (R.5). To the latter effect, the case of war in Sri Lanka supersedes Tilly's thesis that war makes the state and vice versa, extending it further to incorporate war-making, state-making and hegemony-making. It was not only the key figures in the centre of national politics who were keen to capitalise on the victories in the northern battlefields, but even the emerging local political groups in the deeper peripheries of national politics with bigger future political ambitions. According to a respondent from Kandy district,

> These days there is a 'Ranaviru business'[38] going on. We are even witnessing poor villagers in Doluwa in the Central province being forced to contribute with Marmite for the soldiers fighting in the war. This order was given by the provincial Chief Minister. They are manipulating people to think, not donating Marmite is an anti–Sri Lanka and anti-patriotic behaviour. Also, these poor people were told if the war was not won this time, they all will have to jump into the ocean. (R.11)[39]

The irony of this particular case is that neither the military battlefield nor the ocean is anywhere near where this specific rural community lives. However, what this story reveals is the elite's ability to strategically manipulate people's sentiments, especially those who were physically and geographically separated from the actual war zone in the north and the east, by making the 'distanced' war a reality in their everyday life through certain narratives with particular emphases and exclusions.

As tensions in society arose among different political groups in parallel with the tensions on the military battleground at the time of interviews, one respondent who was known in the Sri Lankan high political circles as an ultra-nationalist openly supported the war efforts of the Rajapaksa regime, while not forgetting to completely discredit and ridicule the anti-war circles in academia and in the Colombo civil society. This respondent angrily remarked,

> The so-called peace discussions held in Colombo by ICES, CPA, SSA and NPC left us out. The idiots like Keerawella, Sara, and Uyan were bribed by NIPU. Also the Berghof initiative called ONE TEXT even excluded JHU, while having LTTE representation in it.... There is a manifest antipathy towards Sinhala-Buddhist nationalism. Flawed articles were taken as articles of faith. Rhetoric was changed later by CPA. Earlier these people said the government cannot defeat the LTTE. Now they are silent. All these are Catholics; they have a hidden agenda.[40] (R.20)

This interview ended with him assuring that the timing of the war was ripe, which he found auspicious for the occasion. In his words, 'I believe in auspicious time, the earlier efforts we made were not done at the right time. We know "samsara" not heaven and hell' (R.20).[41] Similar attitudes were shared by several other interviewees who are members of the JVP and the JHU, testifying further to the increasing polarisation and fragmentation of the Sinhalese political elites. The war unfolding in the northern battleground was used by them to overcome their feeling of exclusion (even perhaps self-imposed exclusion) in national politics that was being long dominated by the bourgeois elites. Their views stand testimony to the continuation of deep-seated class conflicts in Sri Lanka's politics. The resurgence of old political conflicts based on class fault lines demonstrates their potential future use to further polarise society in the post-war period. As one interviewee with JVP background reminded, this could be around who could legitimately claim the credit for the military victory. As he shared one of John F. Kennedy's statement, 'ada jayagrahanayata piyavaru gananawak innawa, parajaya hariyata anatha daruwek wagei' (victory has a thousand fathers, but defeat is an orphan) (R.21).

Altogether, since the early 1990s, the dominant ruling elites in national politics in Sri Lanka have been able to invent a series of effective discourses and a supporting set of high-level political agendas on war and peace by strategically combining their own personal-political struggles for power and domination with the compelling socio-economic struggles of the masses in the periphery. I claim that these numerous elite discourses on war and peace and the related agendas of this period had been an integral part of the elites' overall hegemony-building project that closely resembled the Clauzewitzean dictum of 'war is politics by other means', which I extended to the case of peace-making in Sri Lanka. In addition to the concerning military activities of the LTTE in the northern battlefield and the periodic attacks they carried out in the south, the aforementioned elites' political discourses became important mass political mobilisation tools targeting the public. This particular mobilisation strategy complements the already established mutually interdependent relations between the political elites and the subalterns at the margins of society, thanks to the patronage politics of the past, which became even more accentuated since the early 1990s due to the aggressive dismantling of the social welfare state policies following the ruling political elites' adoption of global neoliberal development agendas (Kelegama 2000: 480; Dunham n.d.: 3). In spite of all the shortcomings of the neoliberal economic strategy in addressing the material struggles of the majority living in the rural areas, as Foucault reminds us in his work on power, truth and knowledge (Foucault 1972 cited in Jorgensen and Philips 2002), the elites' political discourses and agendas on war and peace of this period played a crucial role in cementing a social world and a manifested truth of a pacified war based on Sinhala-Buddhist ideology.

By applying Tilly's analogy of European 16th-century war-making and state-making and Gramsci's theorising on hegemony-building, this chapter was able to show that the various seemingly contradictory discourses and agendas of war and peace had been the most powerful and damaging hegemony-building strategy pursued so far, given its open right-wing tendencies. On one hand, findings of this chapter support the claim that the eventual triumph of the discourses of total war for peace and humanitarian war under President Rajapaksa has left the most damaging legacy for democratic politics and state-building in Sri Lanka. On the other hand, in the post-war period, the same discourses have been instrumentally used by the right-wing populist political forces to justify a regressive new moral and ethical order for society. Meanwhile, the global and local political-economic dynamics in the post-war were not optimal for the elites to deliver on their war-time rhetorical promises, especially the peace dividends to the most marginalised in society. The societal unrest these unfulfilled promises led to in the post-war period, however, helps in understanding the ruling elites' resort to military-authoritarian style of governance and making it a key pillar in the post-war state-building and hegemony-building plans (for more see next chapter). Based on the observations made so far on post-war Sri Lanka, it is too early to predict how the elites' coercive strategies towards the anti-hegemonic and dissenting voices for democratic rule will fare. Most importantly, only time will tell how far the ruling elites' consent-building strategies for political mobilisation and hegemony-building on the platform of right-wing Sinhala-Buddhist ideology and the majority in the Sinhalese community's nostalgia of war victories could shape the future trajectories of politics of post-war state-building.

NOTES

1. The literature on war deals with both inter-state and intra-state wars (Gurr 1993; Collier et al. 2003; Fearson and Laitin 2003; Sambanis 2004; Ramsbotham, Woodhouse and Miall 2009: 119–20; Murshed 2010). In particular, the literature on intra-state wars, also known as civil wars, constitute the bulk of the literature since the fall of the Soviet Union in 1989 (Herbst 1990; Sorensen 2001; Theis 2005; Nieman 2007; Taylor 2008; Helling 2010).
2. These include scrapping the executive presidential system, eradicating bribery, corruption and waste, getting rid of the UNP's 'crony capitalism' and replacing it with capitalism with a human face (Schaffer 1995).
3. In the years 1987, 1988, 1989, 1991 and 1992 Sri Lanka's economy grew at the rates of 1.5, 2.7, 2.3, 4.6 and 4.3 per cent respectively (Central Bank of Sri Lanka cited by Kelegama 2000).
4. Premadasa also carried out talks with the LTTE; however, they were a less public affair.
5. Details of this situation are explained in Chapter 3 of this book in relation to the patronage politics of this period.
6. She started a short-lived new political party called the Bahujana Nidahas Peramua.
7. Others who extended support to the PA were a Tamil member of parliament of the Up-Country People's Front and three Tamil parties representing the North Eastern Province.
8. In 2005, the LTTE assassinated the foreign minister of the PA government, Mr Kadiragamar.

9. Gramsci defines 'ethical state' as one that tends to put an end to the internal divisions of the ruled and create a technically and morally unitary social organism.
10. The JVP's political position on the framing of the conflict was shaped by Rohana Wijeweera, the leader of the JVP in the 1960s. According to Wijeweera, the problem in Sri Lanka is rooted in the class issue rather than in the issue of ethnic identity. According to the JVP, when class emancipation is achieved, the problems of self-determination of Sri Lankans will be solved naturally. Therefore, in the JVP's thinking, there is no special attention or process needed to address the so-called ethnic conflict. Following this logic, even contemporary members of the JVP were quick to blame the Tamil nationalist project and the armed struggle of the LTTE for distracting the struggle of entire Sri Lankan nation in achieving self-determination in its post- colonial phase of state-building.
11. Due to these reasons, during this time period Sri Lanka recorded the highest incidence of violence and killings. However, it is also known that it was not only those who took part in these anti-state activities that got killed, but also thousands of innocent civilians who had no connection to these events. Under the umbrella of the state of emergency, many other political scores were believed to have been settled by various groups.
12. 'Jus in bello' serves as a criteria in international humanitarian law for regulating the conduct of parties engaged in an armed conflict.
13. Instead of a widely speculated impeachment motion against the executive president, the UNP brought a no-confidence motion against the chief justice, who was a political appointee of the president.
14. In *Civilization and Its Discontent*, Sigmund Freud refers to the ways in which insignificant differences among people, who are otherwise alike, form the basis of feelings of strangeness and hostility between them. According to Uyangoda's analysis, the two leaders of the UNP and the SLFP (PA) also faced this paradox in politics, where the real differences between them had begun to diminish, while symbolic and personal differences had become belligerently salient.
15. According to Zaartman, 'mutual stalemate' refers to a situation when a party will pick the alternative that it prefers, and that a decision to change is induced by the increasing pain associated with the present (conflictual) course (2001: 8).
16. The advent of Norway in the context of Sri Lanka was largely the result of of a personal invitation by the Sri Lankan foreign minister to the Norwegian ambassador to Sri Lanka in 1997.

17. For an analysis of the Thimpu Principles, see http://www.sangam.org/ANALYSIS_ARCHIVES/ Edirisinghe.htm (accessed on 2 June 2011).
18. The role played by India as the mediator of the 1987 peace process and the bitter memories it created in the aftermath of the failed peace talks facilitated by Norway in 1997 are significant.
19. Norway's support for peace processes in the Middle East, Guatemala, Colombia and elsewhere, Norwegian participation in a number of international peacekeeping operations, as well as the fact that the Nobel Peace Prize is awarded in Oslo – all have contributed to Norway's reputation as a country of peace.
20. The SLMC leader was later included in the talks and he signed a bilateral agreement with the LTTE leadership to resolve the issues.
21. According to the Sri Lanka Monitoring Mission (SLMM), during the period from 2002 to 2007, the LTTE had committed 3,830 ceasefire offences and the government forces had committed 351 offences(www.peaceinsrilanka.org/ negotiations/slmm-statistics, accessed on 9 January 2011).
22. See www.peaceinsrilanka.org/ negotiations/slmm-statistics (accessed on 9 January 2011).
23. More details of the report can be read at http://www.southasiaanalysis.org/%5Cnotes2%5Cnote174.html (accessed on 18 June 2011).
24. The ISGA proposal of the LTTE can be read at http://www.idpsrilanka.lk/Doc/Related%20Articles/ISGA.pdf (accessed on 18 June 2011).
25. Later Kumaratunga also took over a few other important state bodies that generate large sums of revenue for the government, like the National Lotteries Board. As reported, during 2002, under the UNF the Lotteries Board had generated Rs 940 million but only Rs 470 million was put in the President's Fund (Dias 2003).
26. The JVP was demanding the portfolio of the Ministry of Mahaweli Development. The work of this ministry is closely tied to the agricultural and rural areas of the country, both of which constitute the JVP's main voter base.
27. Estimated at USD 1.5 billion (Goodhand and Klem 2005: 22).
28. In 2007 there were numerous newspaper reports published by Rajapaksa's ex-confidants Sripathi Suriyaarachchi and Tiran Alles about the LTTE being provided LKR 15 billion to prevent Tamils in the north from casting their votes. The electoral results from the north of the country provides clear evidence that people under the LTTE's control did not cast their votes. During this time period, many predicted Wickremasinghe would

win the elections provided that the Tamils voted, as they were suspected to be politically inclined towards the UNP and Wickremasinghe rather than Rajapaksa, who contested elections in alliance with the JVP and the JHU, the nationalist political parties.

29. Murshed refers to 'windfall' as an unexpected source of income that can arise either because of a surge in external assistance or a sudden increase in the process of existing natural resources (2010: 178). Like both Kumaratunga and Wickremasinghe, who bet on the surge of reconstruction funds after securing a peace agreement, Rajapaksa seemed to have expected a surge of reconstruction funds by ending the war through military means despite the catastrophic humanitarian situation a large-scale military action would lead to. For an economic explanation of the political economy of reconstruction with a focus on re-distributional issues and inequality, refer to Murshed (2010: 81–83).

30. Rajapaksa secured the support of 17 parliamentary members of the UNP, including its deputy party leader, Karu Jayasuriya. All these members received important cabinet ministerial portfolios in the Rajapaksa government.

31. The 13th amendment to the constitution established the Provincial Council system in Sri Lanka in 1987 as a part of the Indo-Lanka Agreement.

32. Following the ban, the European Union member states froze the LTTE's financial assets and prohibited the provision of fundraising directly or indirectly to the LTTE, and enforced a travel ban on LTTE officials (Nesan 2006).

33. As a number of respondents pointed out, in general, at the time of fieldwork, a large number of Sinhalese people still seemed to be 'okay' with finding a political settlement and waging a total war with the LTTE. According to an opinion survey conducted in the whole island (excluding the Northern Province) in 2008, the violence of war was cited as the top priority to be addressed in Sri Lanka (Irwin 2008: 3). According to 60 per cent of the Sinhalese interviewed for this survey, a continuation of violence of the LTTE was mentioned as a very significant problem faced by the country, whereas 73 per cent of Tamils recognised the ongoing war as the main problem faced by them (Irwin 2008: 5). According to the opinions expressed by the Tamil respondents of the same survey, escalating violence during 2006 and 2007 was a major concern for them as an ethnic group (Irwin 2008: 5). Also see www.gallup.com/poll for more opinion surveys conducted in Sri Lanka between 2006 and 2010 on the issue of conflict, war and peace.

34. This respondent also pointed out to the fact that the developments in Sri Lanka are totally comparable to India where the Bharatiya Janata Party's political agenda is shaped by the right-wing Hindu nationalist Rashtriya Swayamsevak Sangh (RSS).
35. In local propaganda Rajapaksa was compared to King Dutugemunu. According to an epic story in *Sinhala Vamsa*, King Dutugemunu defeated the Tamil king Elara in a final battle and unified Sri Lanka.
36. Term borrowed from Uyangoda (2007).
37. During the last phase of war, the United Kingdom (UK) alone is reported to have supplied new military equipment to the government. In 2009 the UK government issued eight arms licenses to Sri Lanka (www.caat.org.uk).
38. 'Ranaviru' is the Sinhala term for war hero.
39. Doluwa is a small village in the hinterland of the hill country, far away from the conflict and the coastal zones of Sri Lanka.
40. The abbreviations refer to government and civil society organisations with mandates to work for promoting peace in Sri Lanka. The individual names mentioned in this statement are those of a few academics who are known as pro-peace allies of previous governments (Rayner, Scarborough and Allender 2006).
41. In Buddhism, *samsara* is referred to as the cycle of death and rebirth to which life in the material world is bound.

7

WHAT CAME AFTER WAR?

In the previous chapter, I argued that the Sinhalese ruling political elites' pursuit of war and peace was politics by other means and the numerous elite-invented discourses of war and peace served as an important hegemony-building strategy with the Sinhalese masses. One Marxist parliamentarian I interviewed on the verge of the announcement of the military defeat of the Liberation Tigers of Tamil Eelam (LTTE) observed that at that time 'in general the Sinhalese are happy about the LTTE defeat' (R.13). However, another respondent with no open political party association noted at the time of the interview during the last days of war in May 2009 that 'today, people like war, they focus on a set of selected events' (R.11). In the words of an academic with United National Party (UNP) affiliation, 'in 2003, there was a muted sense of security, under that context people supported peace. But today in the context of heightened security the same people support war' (R.18). Contrary to popular belief, immediate political developments in post-war Sri Lanka suggest that military defeat of the LTTE was not enough to complete the elites' hegemony-building project. One foreign journalist noted,

> A number of factors helped sweep him [Rajapakse] to re-election victory on Tuesday: his fiery rhetoric and sure popular touch; his emphasis on his role in last year's war victory; and ordinary people's sense that their streets are simply safer than they have been for the past 30 years because of the defeat of the Tamil Tigers. (Charles Haviland, BBC News, 29 January 2010)

Various dynamics in post-war high politics and state-in-society relations meant that ruling elites holding on to state power needed to invent new alliance-building and hegemony-building strategies, beyond manipulative tactics associated with Sinhala-Buddhist nationalist rhetoric. This was mainly due to their limited capacity to offer most Sri Lankans the hope of overcoming material economic struggles given the serious structural problems in the economy (IPS 2011: 15). The entrenched war economy remained one of the few sectors still growing after the end of the war (Jayasundara-Smits 2018: 4). The removal of the LTTE as an anti-hegemonic political force, the arch-rival of Sinhala-Buddhist hegemony, meant that they could no longer be blamed for the country's deepening economic woes. There was no other 'Other' that the ruling elites and regimes could blame for the increasing economic hardships felt by most Sri Lankans in the 10 or more years since the end of the war. State coffers remained largely empty, raided to fight the war, and valuable investment opportunities squandered in political corruption.[1] Instead of reaping the expected 'peace dividend', ruling regimes since 2009 have found it harder than ever to dispense material benefits to the economically hard-hit masses. Those at the bottom of the social and economic pyramid, the lower classes, continue to bear the brunt of the lingering effects of high wartime expenditures and accumulated national debt. This makes it harder than ever to sustain the mobilisation of the Sinhalese 'masses' for the purposes of the elites' political alliance-building. However, these seemingly distinctly national developments are not without connections to the global-level developments observed around this time, where the failure of neoliberal globalisation was manifesting in increased socio-economic exclusion of the peripheral states and their citizens and effectively preventing them from accessing the leftover benefits of the liberal international order. The government's fallout with the liberal Western international community that accused Sri Lanka of committing war crimes further added fuel to the brewing local rage against the West, further pushing the Sinhalese masses to embrace the right-wing populist propaganda of the regime.

Soon after the war, the elites' long-term project of political hegemony faltered, especially as the material base needed for consent-oriented hegemony-building projects took a new tumble. Also, President Rajapaksa's pursuit of oligarchic aspirations (Kadiragamar 2010: 22) in the guise of post-war state- and nation-building faced severe challenges from within the same societal forces that had once supported the concerted war effort. Ending the war by defeating the LTTE was a massive but passing achievement for the Rajapakse regime, as well as a major relief to many in society. Post-war political dynamics were not restructured, however, and instead there was the continuation of 'politics as usual', as ruling elites competed to dominate and capture state power at the expense of any genuine investment in state- or nation-building without any major economic or political transformations. Post-war governance under Mahinda Rajapaksa (2010–2015) showed an increasing turn towards openly right-wing populist discourses and strategies and the more frequent use of the state's coercive apparatus against any dissenting voices (Spencer 2016: 104). President Rajapaksa managed to hold on to the votes of the majority Sinhalese by keeping them on a Sinhala-Buddhist ideological leash. Yet soon after war ended, political[2] and societal forces within the majority Sinhalese community disintegrated, as decisions had to be made about the future direction of state-building and reconstruction, known as 'peace-building'. There was fierce contestation around specific post-war strategies, between continued militarisation of the state, society and economy, an increasingly authoritarian style of governance and different ways of (not) dealing with a violent past. The statements below reveal some of these new divergences:

> We have removed the word minorities from our vocabulary three years ago. No longer are the Tamils, Muslims, Burghers, Malays and any others minorities. There are only two peoples in this country. One is the people that love this country. The other comprises the small groups that have no love for the land of their birth. Those who do not love the country are now a lesser group. (Victory speech of President Rajapakse, Government of Sri Lanka, 2010)

> Now the war is over, Tamil people must be given freedom to live. We should not contribute towards creating a situation that can give birth to another Prabhakaran. We should not allow the country to go on the wrong path. If this happens, I am ready to correct the path, leaving behind my uniform. (Extract from speech by former Army Commander General Sarath Fonseka, Washington, reported 27 October 2009, *Sri Lanka Guardian*)

> While regrettable, the lack of attention to accountability is not surprising. There are no examples we know of a regime undertaking wholesale investigations of its own troops or senior officials for war crimes while that regime or government remained in power.... In Sri

Lanka this is further complicated by the fact that responsibility for many of the alleged crimes rests with the country's senior civilian and military leadership, including President Rajapaksa and his brothers and opposition candidate General Fonseka. (Bryson Hull quoting US diplomatic cables sent by the US Ambassador in Colombo, H.E.Butenis, Reuters 2 December 2010)

These observations on Sri Lanka's post-war dynamics pointed to further factionalising of the Sinhalese ruling class and dents to their political domination, following their period of temporary and pragmatic solidarity during the last phases of the war. And the same issues causing contention among the ruling elites were being manifested in the wider society, especially in their everyday politics. This resulted in new and re-emerging forms of polarisation within the Sinhalese community, mainly along class and regional lines (Kadirgamar 2020: 53). In the post-war context, such societal-level dynamics became more pronounced, renewing the pressure of sub-regional identities that had intensified during the last phase of the 'war for peace' under Rajapaksa's leadership (Venugopal 2018). These sub-regional identities were observed in the deeper rural hinterlands of southern Sri Lanka, where Rajapaksa originated from. As mentioned in the previous chapter, a strong sense of what is *ape* (ours) and who is considered to be *ape* in the popular imaginaries was closely aligned with the political and economic aspiration of the rural-agricultural population. They yearned for a morally righteous state, more in line with the Sinhala-Buddhist ideology to which President Rajapaksa claimed to subscribe.

MILITARISATION

With his confidence high following defeat of the LTTE in May 2009, the following year, President Rajapaksa called for early presidential election. His ambition was to secure another presidential term, but this goal was overshadowed by his former army general's announcement that he would present himself as the common presidential candidate backed by the opposition parties. Fonseka's announcement marked a turning point in political dissent in Sri Lanka (Kadiragamar 2010: 22), exposing cracks in the usually holy trinity of Sri Lankan politics – the political elites, the Buddhist clergy and the military elites. Fonseka's presidential ambitions ignited fears among the ruling political elites of a possible military coup. Two attempted military coups took place in 1962 and 1966, the first during the ruling Sri Lanka Freedom Party (SLFP) regime, the second under the UNP government, and were reminders that this was a real risk in a situation where political and military elites came into conflict (De Silva 2001: 4). Memories of these past events help explain extra measures President Rajapaksa put in place to keep the military busy in the immediate post-war period through continued militarisation and politicisation of the economy (Kadirgamar 2010). This was also a way to prevent any social forces, especially rural Sinhala-Buddhists, gathering around the military as a potential third force in politics (Kadirgamar 2010: 22). Fallingout with the military was not at option for Rajapaksa, who was compelled to build strategic alliances with military elites to undermine Fonseka's candidacy.

Renewing alliances with fellow ruling-class elites and reconnecting with the Sinhala masses was imperative for Rajapaksa, who did this by distributing various lucrative political positions as forms of patronage. State patronage offered by Rajapaksa in the run-up to the election was not targeted at ethnic minority groups or the economically marginalised Sinhalese majority, but at fellow Sinhalese elites (Kadirgamar 2010: 21). As competition for state power intensified around the 2010 presidential election campaign, Rajapaksa was compelled to neutralise the unexpected challenge from General Fonseka in order to secure a second term and save face with rival members of the ruling elites, who had started to gather around Fonseka in his new political party, the New Democratic Front (NDF). Despite having waged war, Fonseka was even popular among minority ethnic groups, who were willing to trust a former military commander to address their post-war needs rather than the usual corrupt, horse-trading Sinhalese political leadership (Kadirgamar 2010: 22).

The aborted military coups of the 1960s were largely forgotten. However, Fonseka's election campaign targeting the corruption of political elites and their right-wing populist politics resonated with justifications provided back in the 1960s by an earlier generation of military generals seeking to 'clean up' Sri Lankan politics (De Silva 2001: 8). For Fonseka, giving a militarised spin to his usual brand of Sinhala-Buddhist nationalism would not be enough. The new political narrative targeted Rajapaksa's nepotistic family politics and their corrupt governance practices. It was believed by the NDF that this anti-Rajapaksa and anti-corruption line would appeal to economically hard-hit masses across the entire country, from north to south. It was believed those who were tired of ever seeing the promised peace dividend would support Fonseka.

What Fonseka's campaign revealed was the fragility of inter-elite alliances, and the fragmentation and polarisation of the country's ruling class. The end of war presented new opportunities for the elites to establish political domination and pursue their hegemony-building project, through nostalgic platforms glorifying victory in the war and a strident Sinhala-Buddhist form of nationalism (Kadirgamar 2010: 23). However, the political climate in post-war Sri Lanka suggested the deepening of older struggles for domination and hegemony among a highly factionalised ruling class. In this context Sinhala-Buddhist nationalism was elevated to a Sinhala-Buddhist supremacist project, with open authoritarianism and use of violence against the political opposition at a new level. Rajapaksa justified these new strategies, claiming there was a need to consolidate military victory by introducing a high level of national security. Yet it was also obvious that the president's growing tendency to resort to violence had other motivations. These were tied to the grim realities of Sri Lanka's post-war economic situation, which showed little prospect of improving (Spencer 2016: 105). Unable to deliver on wartime promises of a future economic peace dividend, and with economic growth as low as 2.5 per cent as forecast by the Central Bank in year 2008 contrary to the government's projection of 6 per cent (Uyangoda 2009: 110), the situation was not promising for Rajapaksa. However, during the war and early post-war years, the government claimed that the country reached an impressive 8.1 per cent economic growth rate in 2011 (Goodhand 2012: 121). While on the one hand, the regime boasted about the rosy economic figures with regard to declining unemployment and inflation, increase in per capital income, and achieving the fastest growth in post-independence history, on the other hand, economists rolled their eyes at these figures by pointing to the 'creative accounting practices' (Athukorala and Jayasuriya 2015: 15). Economic data for the post-war period showed rising cost of living due to high inflation rates recorded at 6.22 per cent in 2010, 6.74 per cent in 2011, 7.53 per cent in 2012 and 6.94 per cent in 2013, which only showed a decreasing tendency since 2015 (Goodhand 2012: 133). These high inflation rates were somewhat obvious given the government's continued spending on the post-war military establishment (Nanayakkara 2016). Next to that, the widespread accusations of nepotism and open corruption paint the rest of the picture. The only significant economic boom that was observed was in the north and the east as a result of massive investments made to improve the infrastructure and agricultural productivity. The many road construction projects undertaken by the regime came under public scrutiny not only for the reason that some of these roads were leading to nowhere, but mostly due to the rampant corruption associated with these projects (Athukorala and Jayasuriya 2015: 14). The re-distributional effects of these investments were quite marginal since this infrastructure and new agricultural expenditure were mainly tied to the regime's strategy of continued militarisation and ensuring the 'security' of land and population in post-war zones (Goodhand 2012: 133). As Sarvanathan (2016) has noted, levels of household poverty in the former directly war-affected areas continued to be high, albeit the massive government infrastructure investments directed to these areas. In this sense, the patriotic branding of the government's celebrated mega infrastructure investments, such as Uthuru Wasanthaya (Northern Spring) and Neganahira Udaanaya (Eastern Awakening), can be seen as attempts at seducing the southern Sinhalese constituencies ideologically, rather than meeting the everyday needs of the people in the north and the east. Despite the mounting criticisms against the government's post-war economic activities, the repressive apparatus of the state was being used to enable Rajapaksa to stay in power and control his critics, especially Fonseka and the NDF.

In the immediate post-war period, state resources were dedicated to maintaining an army of 450,000 soldiers. Soldiers to civilians numbered close to 1:5 among the adult population. In the absence of any active armed conflict or a threat of such, maintaining an army of this size was questionable (Jayasundara-Smits 2018: 89). The opportunity cost of these state resources spent on maintaining a massive military force could instead have provided much-needed livelihood opportunities ans social services for war-battered communities. Instead, the Rajapaksa brand of post-war development strategy pertaining to the north and the east mainly relied on assigning the military a key role in state-sponsored economic activities in the post-war years. Heavy military involvement was reported in large-scale property development ventures and state-sponsored mega-infrastructure development projects, such as building roads, bridges, houses and sports stadiums. For example, in 2012 the Defence Ministry annexed the Urban Development Authority and accessed an additional sum of LKR 229.9 billion in the national budget (Goodhand 2012: 70). The government justified its development strategy by citing the need to station the military in former war zones to consolidate the 'peace' and ensure security as well as to maintain the officially high but contested economic growth level of 4.8 per cent achieved during the war

(Wijeweera and Webb 2009: 506). The opening up of opportunities for patronage to the military after the war was nothing more than a part of the hegemony-building strategy for regime domination, given the volatile post-war political and economic situation. Rajapaksa's post-war security model of governance allowed the ruling regime to deploy the state's coercive apparatus to crush and even pre-empt emerging dissident and anti-hegemonic voices. Keeping the military actively engaged in post-war economic development and reconstruction could be viewed as prudent, given that this powerful and well-respected (and of course well-armed) segment of society was constituted of 98 per cent Sinhalese (DeVotta 2017: 75). Rajapaksa was ultimately able to sustain the consent of the majority in the Sinhala-Buddhist constituency to the military-Sinhala-Buddhist supremacist ideology through a time of economic and political distress. Rajapaksa and his regime needed to obtain this consent from the military in order to legitimise their rule more widely among the Sinhalese electorate. Yet there was a price to be paid, since this strategic manoeuvring was counter-productive in its effects on socio-economic groups located at the margins of Sri Lankan society who were not enjoying the material benefits that had been promised during the long, hard years of war. Rajapaksa only means to keep poorer civilian groups politically mobilised in his support was through ever more voracious expressions of Sinhala-Buddhist ideology. The threat that the military would become more popular than civilian politicians remained a real possibility, however. New tactics were needed to prevent the military from becoming a political force and, at the same time, capitalise on the military's popular image as the true guardian of the nation.

The political fortunes of Fonseka were sharply reversed when Rajapaksa sent him to prison for three years following Fonseka's defeat in the 2010 elections.[3] He was subsequently charged with treason, misappropriation of funds and engaging in politics while in uniform. The new challenge faced by the ruling political elites to their overall political dominance and personal hegemony-building projects started with Fonseka's entry into national politics. This had not been expected by the ruling political elites, whose long-held belief was that winning the war would prove a ticket to staying in power for years to come and virtually unchallenged. Shifting public opinion favouring military elites was captured in the social indicator project statistics where the trust placed by the majority Sinhalese in the military in the post-war period from 2011 to 2018 remained as high as 91.4 per cent compared to the 16.7 per cent in the political parties (Pieris, Moinudeen and

Krishmamoorthy 2020). Therefore, in many ways, these specific post-war civil–military relations related developments point to the potential rise of new anti-hegemonic forces within the conventional ruling class composed of dominant Sinhala-Buddhist political–Sangha–military elites and the dents any one of these forces alone could make on each other's projects.

In the post-war period the fragmentation of the ruling class and their hegemonic project became more marked than it had ever been since independence. And the challenge to the ruling political elites came not from the marginalised or from ethnic or religious minorities, but from what was arguably the most powerful institution of the war and the post-war period, the military. This challenge can help explain why the Rajapaksa regime continued to extend the militarisation of the state and society during the post-war period. This post-war militarisation and the resulting politicisation of the military extended state patronage by including potentially leading military officers – and former military officers – in various high-profile civilian positions, especially in former war zones, where they served as governors and secretaries to ministries. Such a move went well beyond what would have been needed to consolidate state control over these territories (Åkebo and Bastian 2021). Continued militarisation of the state and society and populist-authoritarian governance, two hallmarks of two post-war political regimes under two Rajapaksa brothers (2010–2015 and 2019 to date), are indicative of the rapidly changing nature of elite power struggles and the future direction of state transformation. In Rajapaksa's grand scheme of political mobilisation, military elites are manipulated by extending state and regime patronage to obtain their consent to the continuation of the dominant political elites' rule. To a certain degree the same strategy was applied to the lower rungs of the military, mainly comprised of rural Sinhalese youth, by enabling them opportunities to engage in economic activities in the former war zones with state patronage (Venugopal 2018: 113). Their continued mobilisation in the post-war period by assigning them roles in the infrastructure and economic activities often painted in patriotic terms was useful for Rajapaksa for two reasons. Their continued mobilisation was imperative, on the one hand, to prevent them from gathering around Fonseka to become a third force in politics[4] and, on the other hand, to keep the rural constituencies mobilised in favour of the ruling regime with the help of the lower-rung military cadres, the majority who come from the rural areas.

From 2007 up to 2015, the Rajapaksa regime spent massive sums of money borrowed from Chinese banks at a commercial rate on infrastructure and development projects, with few of these large-scale investments ever benefiting the average citizen (Wickramasinghe 2014). Meanwhile the regime's military expenditure continued to rise (Selvanathan and Selvanathan 2014: 70), siphoning out state resources that would otherwise have been allocated to paying for essential social services, health and education that the poorer segments of society could directly benefit from. This also happened in the backdrop of an already deepening debt crisis, for which some researchers put the responsibility not on China but on Colombo's political elites and on the Western-dominated international financial markets (Jones and Hameiri 2020: 15). Rajapaksa capitalised on Sri Lanka's geostrategic importance in the Indian Ocean region, exploiting rivalries between the United States, India and China and the faltering liberal international order (Jayasundara-Smits 2020: 14). Rajapaksa leaned more towards China in his foreign and economic policies, a relationship that proved personally and politically lucrative. The Chinese funded some massive infrastructure projects that benefited the president, his family and close allies. On the other hand, the close relationship with China provided a degree of protection against demands from Western countries and international organisations that the government address human rights violations and bring perpetrators of war crimes to justice (DeVotta 2017: 76). The post war regime lacked commitment, indeed was unwilling to address such crimes and violations, a concern frequently raised by EU member states, who in in 2010 withdrew Sri Lanka's Generalised Scheme of Preferences Plus (GSP+). This ended the preferential trading arrangement under which Sri Lanka had tariff-free access to EU markets in exchange for compliance with international human rights norms and conventions (HRW 2020). Rajapaksa's post-war economic strategy was tied to his political strategy for dynastic domination and personal hegemony. In co-opting democratic forces to these ends, and ensuring higher military spending than even during the war, the GSP+ scheme was sacrificed to domestic parochial personal-political goals. Combined with natural disasters such as droughts and the tsunami in the years that followed, an economic crisis loomed large.

The negative effects of this brewing crisis were already evident as unemployment grew from 4.4 per cent in 2014 to 4.7 per cent in 2015, and levels were significantly higher than this average in many rural areas (Department of Census and Statistics 2018: 24). In the early post-war period, youth unemployment was estimated to be as high as 14 per cent in areas most hit by the war, both directly and indirectly (Bowden and Binns 2016: 204). Southern districts like Matara and Kegalle were only slightly less affected by youth unemployment than the directly war-affected Jaffna, Killinochchi and Ampara (Ministry of National Policies and Economic Affairs 2016). Tragically, post-war economic woes as experienced by the youth were manifested in rising youth suicides, depression and post-traumatic stress disorder (PTSD) and increased levels of petty crime (Jayasundara-Smits 2018: 10). The loss of lives among the youth in former war zones was blamed by analysts more on financial hardships and the loss of livelihoods they endured and the penetration of liberal economic policies than on direct mortality related to injury or harm during the war (Kadirgamar 2017: 122, 126).

CONTESTATIONS AROUND THE POST-WAR TRANSITIONAL JUSTICE AGENDA

Delivering justice to war victims remained an empty promise, giving rise to social and political contestation and polarised views on how best the injustices that took place during the last phase of war could be addressed (Jayasundara-Smits 2018). In the immediate post-war context, two transitional justice agendas were promoted, one more by local and the other more by international actors. For President Rajapaksa however, none of this was necessary, since, in his own consistent framing, the last phase of civil war was described as a 'humanitarian war' and a 'war against terrorism'. The aim was to secure unilateral military victory for the government armed forces. This left little room for initiatives that sought to establish a collective national political agenda for accountability and justice that would appear fair to all sides. By framing the war in Sri Lanka in this way, using the international trope of a 'war against terrorism', President Rajapaksa hoped that special accountability mechanisms and justice agendas could be avoided. As the majority Sinhalese took to the streets to celebrate the end of war and 'defeat of terrorism', a more 'top-down' and punitive international transitional justice agenda, advocated by a number of liberal Western states, made swift inroads into the post-war political discourses (Jayasundara-Smits 2018). Much of the post-war political debate has been shaped by the fierce competition between rival political and civil society groups who both oppose and support different international and regime-inspired transitional justice agendas. As many analysts and scholars have noted (Uyangoda 2016; Xavier 2015; Bala 2015; Höglund and Orjuela 2013), these clashing agendas have blatantly exposed their instrumental use by the factionalised political elites for achieving their own narrow political interests. A report titled 'Flipflopping on Accountability', which compiled the public statements made by the political elites from 2015 to 2017, by the Centre for Policy Analysis (CPA captured the contradictory and confusing views expressed by the post-war ruling regimes and elite factions supporting and opposing the visions, shapes and forms of post-war transitional justice agendas (Wickramatunge 2018). According to this report, in January 2015, the government spokesman Rajitha Senaratne declared 'no international inquiry'; in February 2015, according to the Foreign Minister Mangala Samaraweera, 'we hope to have technical assistance from UN, judges from commonwealth'; in September 2015, the chief minister of the Northern Provincial Council, C. V. Wiganeswaran, declared 'no local judges, prosecutors for war crimes cases'; again in end-September 2015, the Tamil National Alliance member of parliament (MP) R. Sampanthan emphasised, 'international involvement gives credibility'; and in October 2015 and February 2016, the United People's Freedom Alliance MP Vasudeva Nanayakkara even rejected a recommendation made by the Maxwell Paranagama Commission that was mandated to investigate the complaints of abductions and disappearances committed during the last phase of the Vanni offensive, stating that the local Paranagama Commission had no mandate to make such a recommendation. In February 2016, during a visit to India, Prime Minister Wickramasinghe (of the Sirisena government) stated, 'We may not have the full expertise to identify the exact factors that led to those casualties. So international participation is welcome for determining such causes,' and in March 2017, President Sirisena declared in an executive meeting of his party, the SLFP, that he 'had guts to dismiss UN demands'; meanwhile, former president Mahinda Rajapaksa released a statement saying that the constitutional and legal reforms initiated by Sirisena's government are aimed at punishing the armed forces for winning the war. Last but not least, it is also worthwhile to cite the former-army-commander-turned-politician Sarath Fonseka, who at the time of issuing this statement was also the Provincial Development Minister and Field Marshal. He said in September 2017, 'It is unjust to protect wrongdoers because they are war heroes and it is unjust to protect wrongdoers for the sake of being war heroes clad in military attire and that every politician and every leader of the government should understand that fact' (Wickramatunge 2017). These contrasting visions of how to go about ensuring justice or even whether to deliver or not deliver justice at all to the victims are becoming increasingly problematic under the current Gotabaya Rajapaksa government as both Rajapaksa brothers have been accused of committing war crimes during the last phase of war, which they consistently deny in addition to any charges of criminal accountability on the part of the state or its armed forces (*The Hindu*, 17 November 2019). However, these mentioned tensions ignited around the international transitional justice agenda have been instrumental in allowing both Rajapaksa regimes to sustain their authoritarian politics in the guise of anti-Western and patriotic rhetoric.

For the post-war Rajapaksa regime, from 2010 to 2015, tensions arose around the international transitional justice agenda, which was to be carried out in a highly volatile political and economic environment. In the absence of the LTTE that was always dressed as the long-identified sworn enemy of the Sinhala-Buddhist hegemonic state, the new confrontations surrounding the proposed mechanisms and the liberal Western states that supported some radical Tamil diaspora circles were presented as the nation's primary enemy, which has become a cover for both the post-war Rajapaksa regime and its right-wing supporters to pursue their own hegemonic ambitions. Since the war ended, both Rajapaksa brothers and their respective regimes continued to capitalise on the war victory platform. They also have wasted no time in appropriating the international transitional justice agenda as their main point of electioneering and mobilising the masses towards their political camp. Mahinda Rajapaksa continued to justify the war as a necessary measure, even a humanitarian one. The duty of the state to exercise its sovereignty in a responsible way – to protect the legitimate rights of its citizens and innocent Tamils fleeing LTTE terrorism – did not figure. (Höglund and Orjuela, 2013). The specific ways of framing the war in the post-war period, especially in relation to war crimes and transitional justice, enabled the Rajapaksa regimes to exploit long-standing tensions within the international community, further fuelling an on-going fight between 'sovereigntists' and 'cosmopolitans' (Höglund and Orjuela 2013).

The unexpected defeat of Rajapaksa in the mid-term presidential elections in 2015 further exacerbated the domestic political divisions related to the international justice agenda. Some regime-friendly forces in the southern Sinhalese constituencies continue to frame Rajapaksa's electoral defeat as a plot by Western governments, who were aided by Colombo-based Westernised civil society groups and the liberal intelligentsia that are plotting to tarnish the image of the nation's war heroes. On this basis, they continue to disregard the international demands for conducting an impartial investigation into the crimes committed, especially in the final stage of the war. Given the doubts about delivering justice to the war victims through a purely local mechanism, namely the Lessons Learnt and Reconciliation Commission (LLRC) appointed by the president in 2010, to date the UN and other Western governments have adopted several resolutions sponsored by the United Nations High Commissioner for Refugees (UNHCR) demanding the Sri Lankan state to probe the alleged war crimes committed by all parties concerned (that is, the UN resolutions 11/1 in 2009, 19/2 in 2012, 22/1 in 2013 and 25/1 in 2014). These resolutions were supported by a series of high-level recommendations based on several other UNHRC reports that investigated Sri Lanka. The only exception to the international efforts was the UNHCR resolution 30/1, which was co-sponsored in 2015 by the Sirisena government that had come to power in between the two regimes of the Rajapaksa brothers (Verite Research 2019: 5–7). The national-level institutional mechanisms adopted by the Sirisena government as a follow-up to the 2015 joint UNHCR resolution offered a slight glimmer of hope of justice for the war victims. Sadly, once Gotabaya Rajapaksa was sworn into office in November 2019, this particular joint resolution and two other related resolutions were withdrawn (HRW 2020). President Sirisena's coalition government that held power from 2015 to 2019 in between the two Rajapaksa regimes was also careful not to succumb to external pressures promoting retributive justice measures against the state armed forces (Walton 2015: 18). Considering the challenges faced by his short-lived fragile coalition government and the uncertainties around political alliance-building, Sirisena was careful not to implicate his predecessor in any war crime as such a move could have negative repercussions for Sirisena's political career and elite political dynamics. Most of all, the damage to his own personal-political career was looming large if such an investigation took place, given Sirisena's own role during the war under the Rajapaksa government as the acting defence minister on several occasions (DeVotta 2017: 76). By all accounts, as Walton sums up, 'Sirisena's election victory also revealed the wider constraints facing Sri Lanka's Southern elite in their efforts to build peace' (2015: 18). Given the far-reaching measures that Gotabaya Rajapaksa has already undertaken since coming to office in November 2019 to assign the military a substantial role in his administration by appointing an entourage of former military personnel, especially to the intelligence services, many of whom were implicated by the UN as responsible for alleged war crimes, it is unlikely that any transitional justice agenda in the near future will be realised.

The political and societal polarisations witnessed since the end of the war, especially on the transitional agenda, have been a tug of war between different political factions that is further eclipsing the long-term critical goals of democratisation and democratic state-building. Under these conditions, as Goodhand correctly pointed out on transitions from war to peace, Sri Lanka's transition from war to peace only resembles an uncertain peaceful stalemate (Goodhand 2005). Undoubtedly, this nature of stalemate keeps the door open for dangerous possibilities of prolonged military and authoritarian rule under Rajapaksa and the capture of political space by right-wing forces supporting the regime. Their manipulation of the ideological sentiments of the majority Sinhalese-Buddhists by elevating the Sinhala-Buddhist hegemonic project to a Sinhala-Buddhist supremacist project infused with strategic 'temple politics' proved to be a winning formula for both Rajapaksa brothers in 2005, 2010 and 2019 during the presidential elections (Riaz 2021: 24). Although the latest election victory of Gotabaya Rajapakse was popularly attributed to the 2019 Easter bomb attacks that were carried out by radical homegrown groups, which also questioned the Sirisena–Wickramasinghe government's handling of the post-war national security, Gotabaya's election win confirms the failure of the post-war ruling regimes to bring about reconciliation to the divided communities (DeVotta 2017: 76). Especially upon observing the post-war anti-Muslim propaganda and violent attacks against the Muslim community that took place with the encouragement of the Rajapaksa regime and the ultra-right-wing forces such as the Bodu Bala Sena (BBS), which are closely associated with the ruling Rajapaksa regime, neither the Easter attacks nor the ruling elites' bloody and coercive paths to winning elections should come as a surprise to any long-term observer of Sri Lanka's political dynamics. The plight of the Muslim community in Sri Lanka is yet to fully unfold as President Gotabaya Rajapaksa continues to incite anti-Muslim sentiments and propaganda (DeVotta 2019a).

AUTHORITARIAN POPULISM

It is evident that so far the new ruling class in post-war Sri Lanka has continued to gravitate around and under the firm grip of the Rajapaksa dynasty. It shows a new brand of elite politics where kith, kinship and 'Bonaparte politics' as its main characteristics. The post-war political developments suggest how this new brand of politics is dangerously constituted of military and populist-authoritarianist politics. After the defeat of the LTTE, new political-moral alliances secured by the ruling political elites with the support of

Sinhala-Buddhist right-wing forces effectively silenced the opposition. At the same time, rising tensions have emerged as the consent-building strategies of the dominant political elites have dwindled. The result has been an increasing resort to coercive and 'lawfare' instruments of state power to suppress dissent and criticism (HRW 2018). Under President Gotabaya Rajapaksa, the military is becoming the third pillar in the triumvirate or 'new holy trinity' of Sinhala-Buddhist elite hegemonic politics, gradually outweighing the second leg of this construction, the Buddhist clergy. Post-war election results demonstrate the capacity of these three allied institutions to garner votes for these dynastic, authoritarian rulers.

To avoid future uncertainty and a shift in the fragile political alliances between these factions of the elites and the masses, it is paramount that the current regime introduces structural changes to the economy to prevent a societal backlash along the way as they go about establishing their own political domination and overall hegemony. Under these conditions, post-war ruling regimes have tried to introduce a few decisive changes to state institutions, with a few controversial constitutional amendments. However, instead of introducing deeper economic and social reform, the aim of such amendments was limited to further centralising authority and strengthening the executive powers of the president. Three constitutional amendments in just over a decade since the war ended included two measures under President Mahinda Rajapakse and his brother Gotabaya. The 18th amendment was passed in 2010 and the 20th amendment in 2020. Their damaging effects on the degree of democratic 'checks and balances' in politics are considered to be far-reaching. Both amendments allowed a 'power grab' by the president, with an end to the fixed term of the presidential office under the 18th amendment and removing all but a ceremonial role from the prime minister under the 20th amendment.[5]

Both Rajapaksa brothers framed such amendments as justified by the need for more rapid economic recovery and development in the country, seeking to match popular expectations in a war-battered economy (ICJ 2020). Yet the latest 20th amendment to the constitution consolidates the levers of power more in the hands of the president, and in this sense can be seen as a seriously regressive and authoritarian move. The 20th amendment is in stark contrast to the progressive provisions of the 19th amendment, especially with regard to maintaining checks and balances in a democratic system by curtailing executive presidential powers and re-establishing the independence of key state offices and de-politicising public institutions, introduced during President Sirisena's term in 2015. In general, the 19th amendment is viewed by all favourably; some of its clauses are reflective of the political tug of war in Colombo between the Rajapaksa and anti-Rajapaksa forces. According to DeVotta (2021), albeit the democratic credential of the 19th amendment, it ignited the rifts between those who were eager to see a Rajapaksa comeback. As he further noted, the two-term limit imposed by the 19th amendment was a targeted measure to make sure that Mahinda Rajapaksa could not run for president's office, and the clause disqualifying dual citizens from contesting was a similar move to keep Mahinda Rajapaksa's two brothers, both of whom hold dual US and Sri Lanka citizenship, from seeking office.[6] Last but not least, introducing 35 years as the new age requirement to run for president was aimed at preventing Mahinda Rajapksa's older son, Namal Rajapaksa, running for office until 2021 (DeVotta 2021: 99). As the International Committee of Jurists also noted, new provisions under the 20th amendment have damaged the state of 'law and order' in Sri Lanka, by giving the president the power to make important judicial and public appointments, including judges to the Supreme Court. In this way, the 20th amendment undermines principles of justice and accepted international standards by openly politicising such appointments (ICJ 2020). These constitutional moves introduced under the 20th amendment are even more worrisome as state security forces and intelligence services are put under the leadership of the defence ministry or of military personnel also appointed by the executive president (HRW 2020). By using the 18th amendment, President Mahinda Rajapaksa attempted to cling to power in 2010, but in 2015 the voters' verdict in the elections ousted his regime from office. Succeeding President Sirisena, President Gotabaya Rajapaksa then repealed the 19th amendment and replaced it with the 20th amendment. This was in spite of his brother Mahinda Rajapaksa having endorsed the 19th amendment in 2015 from the opposition benches of the legislature (*The Hindu* 2020). With the 20th amendment to the constitution in place, Rajapaksa's right-wing populist brand of politics co-opted democratic politics, or in Mouffean terms the 'antagonism' that is essential for vibrant democratic politics (Mouffe 2005). So far my observations on post-war elite political dynamics suggest that the plan may be to rule by force and stay in power as long as possible. Meanwhile, the regime in power, and indeed the entire ruling class, fails to lay any solid socio-economic-political foundation for genuine 'rule by consent'. The governments of the Rajapaksa brothers have struggled to secure their own legitimacy, even in a modest liberal-Lockean sense of governance, from those being ruled over.[7] In the absence of a clear enemy since the demise of the

LTTE, there is a real possibility that the older fault lines may widen between the so-called corrupt (neo-) colonial-bourgeois and the supposedly authentic and morally righteous Sinhala-Buddhist traditional bourgeois faction of the ruling class. The latter is claimed and performed by the Rajapaksa family. In other words, the overall picture of the post-war period so far indicates the difficulty of germinating a new historical bloc.

As the political destinies of Rajapaksa's predecessors showed, even winning a war may not be sufficient to survive in the contest for political power and achieving hegemony, especially if it is not accompanied by addressing the economic needs of the vast majority of the poor population. As proven historically, when economic struggles in the peripheries deepen, the fragile alliances of historical social forces gathered under specific historical material-discursive conditions can lose their relevance to elites struggling to hold onto political power. With Sri Lanka's authoritarian turn in post-war politics, a majority of the respondents cast doubt on the Rajapaksa brothers' capacity to wage a follow-on 'war on development and economic prosperity' with the same conviction and support they gained by mobilising to win the physical war. Commentators also question President Gotabaya Rajapaksa's ability to rule by consent and to retain sufficient legitimacy from all the various communities, given his controversial handling of major post-war challenges, including most recently the COVID-19 pandemic (DeVotta 2021: 110). Rajapaksa's handling of the COVID-19 crisis has come under enormous public criticism, while the economy has taken a deep tumble as the country's tourism industry has been hard hit by the crisis. Rajapaksa's past reputation of winning the war by ruthlessly 'taking lives' does not seem good enough anymore if he is unable to 'save lives' from the virus this time. Already his performance and image have been downgraded by critical onlookers, which is reflected in their everyday practices of even addressing him by his first name, Nandasena, instead of his more regal second name, Gotabaya, the latter associated with his war-time heroic figure and performance. Agitated by his new reputation of being incompetent and 'so ordinary', the president has wowed to show his 'true colours', which is captured in the following statement delivered at a political meeting:

> Remember when Prabhakaran started his tricks and attacked me at the Pittala Junction? I finished that job by killing him and sprawling him out like a dog and bringing him across the Nandikadal Lagoon – I can be that person too. (*Colombo Telegraph*, 10 January 2021)

He cannot simply lead his followers, as if they were his military troops, to support his brother's government. In the current political and economic dynamics in Sri Lanka, I am reminded of a warning from a young Jathika Hela Urumaya member whom I interviewed in the last days of the war in May 2009: 'Things can go either way. Due to the economic hardships faced by the country and people, sometimes, even Ranil can get elected. Ranil is the image of the liberal consumerist society' (R.21). Perhaps time will tell whether the ruling Sinhalese elites' hegemonic politics in the post-war period will be able to walk a finer balance between the material and the ideological that is required for a winning hegemony-building strategy by the dominant class now led by the Rajapaksa brothers. With regard to the robustness of the Sinhala-Buddhist nationalism and supremacy as a hegemony-building strategy, yet again only time will tell, whether, as Marx (1981) noted, 'it is not the consciousness of men that determines their being, but, on the contrary, their social being that determines their consciousness' holds true in post-war Sri Lankan politics, which was also implied by my interviewee back then (R.21).

There remains the overriding importance of addressing the material needs of those Sri Lankans living in the margins, and in poverty, regardless of what ideological project appeals to them. The prevailing global economic and political conditions do not paint a promising picture either on how to deliver to the stomach (Babic 2020). Unless Sinhala-Buddhist nationalism alone in politics can also 'fill stomachs', ensure livelihoods and fulfil the needs of the working and peasant class, Sinhala-Buddhist ruling elites will remain factionalised, internally riven with conflicts. If the overall goal is to achieve hegemony, understood as domination and moral and intellectual leadership, as Gramsci warned from his prison cell in fascist Italy, there needs to be a balance of different strategies, beyond an appeal to 'hearts and minds'. Any strategy capable of succeeding should take into account the complex matrix of structure and superstructure, coercion and consensus, materialism and idealism that are needed to appeal to a wider public (Mouffe 2005; Gramsci 1971: 180–83). As Gramsci wrote on hegemony capturing this aspect of the balance of various forces, which is beyond a simple political alliance but as a historical bloc (dialectical unity of the social whole, the relation between material tendencies and ideological representations) that entails the following characteristic:

> The complete fusion of economic, political, intellectual and moral objectives which will be brought about by one fundamental group

and groups allied to it through the intermediary of ideology when an ideology manages to spread throughout the whole of society determining not only united economic and political objectives but also intellectual and moral unity. (Mouffe 2013: 25)

Perhaps the best one can hope for is that the dominant Sinhalese Buddhist elites and their Sinhalese subaltern support base will be willing to embark on a politics of consent by shunning strategies of violence in the post-war period.

FINAL THOUGHTS

This book attempted to re-problematise the case of politics and the politics of state-building through the lens of hegemony-building in Sri Lanka by using Gramscian notions of hegemony and politics. In particular, the concept of hegemony was applied to unveil the true nature of politics and its role in social formation (Mouffe 2013: 42) and the influences these have on Sri Lanka's state-building. As rightly pointed out by Åkebo and Bastian (2021) recently, I also realised the importance of reading the past and present events concerning Sri Lanka within a broader historical framework which I captured using hegemony and state-in-society approach. These two specific approaches allowed me to work through the legacies of the past and identify key turning points and continuities in Sri Lanka's post-independence political developments. A historical perspective underpins the conclusion that the politics and policies of particular regimes are inevitably embedded in longer-term patterns and dynamics of politics and state-building (Akebo and Bastian 2020: 2). This historical perspective should be anchored within the global historical context as well, in which the national context is firmly embedded in, and in which the dominant class continue their struggle to mobilise masses to establish their dominance and hegemony in every aspect of politics, economy, state and society. Paying attention to the global seems becoming ever more important to understand what hegemony-building strategies are going to be invented by the elites, as post-war Sri Lanka is being caught up in an interregnum in the global political order, in which the elites are forced to look for new strategies as some of the advantages they had in the previously dominant liberal international order have come under challenge from new actors.

As this book tried to also show, hegemony-building was not a linear, easy or a quick process in the past and will not likely be so in the future, and that it will not go unchallenged by anti-hegemonic social forces as has been the case always. It requires constant strategic adjustment in the dominant groups' political strategy to build new historical blocs under any given national and global economic and political conditions. Hence, hegemony-building requires continued strategic adjustments of programmes and tactics and masterful navigation of various economic, political, social and cultural conditions in the long, medium and short terms. As Gramsci contended, hegemony requires achieving the dialectical unity of structure and superstructures, which does not come about easily, as the case of Sri Lanka testifies to. It requires multiple political strategies, creating new historical blocs to capture the prevailing opportunities in economy, politics, culture and society, and devising political programmes to capture the collective struggles of the masses, and the ingenuity of and experimentation by the subaltern classes with new organisational forms, new political practices and new political intellectualities (Sotiris 2018). I demonstrate this uneasy path to hegemony-building in Sri Lanka by delving into several of the notable trajectories over time in elite–subaltern politics, state-in-society relations and state-building processes in postcolonial Sri Lanka. I did this by examining four key forms of elite hegemony-building – Sinhala-Buddhist nationalism (Chapter 3), patronage politics (Chapter 4), patronage in state reforms (Chapter 5) and war-making and peace-making (Chapter 6) – which allowed for a better understanding of the trajectories and transformations of Sri Lanka's state, society, elites and subaltern politics. Ultimately, the roots of the present political arrangements are located in the dynamics of constantly transforming class relations that can be traced back to at least the 18th century. Class has thus been brought back from the cold as a key analytical category that moves us beyond the dominant focus on inter-ethnic relations and conflicts in Sri Lanka. I mainly applied class in the Gramscian notion of the term in his work on hegemony, where class is understood not strictly along reductionist economic terms (structure), but also along social relations of production and social relations of power, where ideology (superstructure) and structure find convergence and (re)produce each other. This dynamic view of class allowed me to understand the formation of political subjects more broadly (as sometimes Gramsci has done by using the term 'social groups'). Ethnic explanations of violence and war were favoured by most centrist and liberal-leaning academic studies since at least the 1980s, following the start of the civil war in the early 1980s. In contrast to such work, taking class as a key point of departure for analysis, the approach in this book sought to bring into greater focus both the material and the discursive aspects of politics affected and enacted by members of the subaltern groups into the overall framework. Using class as a point of departure and a central analytical category that is captured, instead of the more usual categories of ethnic identities and inter-ethnic conflict, the aim has been to shed greater light on the role of the economy and of material as well as ontological conditions and how they mater in shaping political subjects. Changing class dynamics were also linked to local, national and global conditions, which helped to shape elite and subaltern political life. A second purpose of reinforcing the focus on class is that it might help not only to overcome the weaknesses of the dominant yet narrowly liberal analysis of Sri Lankan politics, inspiring renewed debate on how to achieve a more equitable society and longer-term goals around social justice. For locating the struggles that should be focused on in future, and for the sake of a more egalitarian future, class as a broader social identity category should be associated with deep democracy and overcoming the fractious effects of focussing narrowly on divisive ethnic, language and religious boundaries.

The salience of class-based and material struggles was especially evident when it came to tracing the historical evolution of Sri Lankan Sinhala-Buddhist nationalist ideology, especially in the rural hinterlands, where most of the majority Sinhalese still live. By applying the Gramscian notion of class in the examination of the nexus of hegemony and ideology (as opposed to Marxian reductionist economistic view of class), I was interested in showing how the political struggles are about political subjects with collective wills comprising an ensemble of social groups fused around a fundamental class whose emergence can be traced all the way back to the capitalist transformation that Sri Lanka underwent during the British colonial period. Tracing the structural-economic roots was helpful in understanding the material-historical base of the dominant class – in this case the elite Sinhalese faction of the ruling class, who try to win over the other subaltern social and economic groups by inventing various strategies (the four hegemony-building processes described in this book); even though the latter have no clear class belonging or do not ideologically represent the interests existing at the economic level, yet they are subjected to and mobilised around the ideological practices of the dominant class which is in the pursuit of hegemony. As Gramsci wrote, these 'other groups' (subaltern groups) are as important as the dominant class since they are fundamental in providing the historical base of the dominant class, the formation of historical blocs and the struggle for hegemony in which the dominant class tries to win over these other social groups through various strategies (Mouffe 2013: 39).

By bringing class formation and class as the main point of departure in the political analysis, I hoped to situate the emergence of Sinhala-Buddhist nationalist ideology in the late 19th century by connecting it with the material underpinnings in the extraverted capitalist economic path under British colonial rule and its role in the past and present dynamic configuration of social forces. Investigating the historical context pertaining to the genesis of Sinhala-Buddhist nationalist ideology by locating its material foundations also enabled me to re-establish the usefulness of class as an analytical category for the study of state-building and hegemony-building in postcolonial Sri Lanka. By 'bringing class back in', and making it central to political analysis, the intention was to mark a break with many other analyses of politics and state-building in Sri Lanka, which tend to focus on explanations of political life grounded in inter-ethnic competition and conflict. By focusing instead on the dynamic transformations over time of intra-Sinhalese class relations, the aim is to better identity manifestations of some of the deeper historical roots of contemporary political trajectories, hegemony-building and state-building. It is within this intra-ethnic framework of analysis that the place of minority ethnic groups and their political relations with the dominant majority Sinhalese, especially that of the Sri Lankan Tamils, is being dealt with.

The four key hegemony-building processes of Sinhala-Buddhist nationalism; patronage politics at political party level; patronage politics at state level; and the events and discourses on conflict, war and peace were discussed separately in the chapters of this volume. Yet together they form a complementary whole, constituting a grand overall strategy for political hegemony-building by competing, factionalised Sinhalese elites. Along David Waldner's seminal work on state-building (1999), as discussed in the previous chapters of this book, the elites' invention and continued use of patronage politics as a mobilisation and hegemony-building tool was observed in Sri Lanka. It has mainly been through patronage that dominant Sinhalese elites have sought to incorporate the lower-class Sinhalese masses, especially those in the rural hinterlands. On the other hand, the spaces open to egalitarian politics and a genuine social justice agenda for these subaltern supporters have been very restricted, given the nurturing of a markedly right-wing

Sinhalese nationalist agenda and the series of weaker class compromises they have made since early on. State resources have been geared almost entirely to reproducing this patronage system at various different levels. Sri Lankan ruling elites, by diverting state revenues and private funds into patronage, failed to lay a solid foundation for long-term economic development, capital accumulation and state budgets. One result has been the widening social and economic inequalities and the growing tendency to resort to violent measures to curb demands for social and economic justice.

As far as the main outcomes of the use of the four hegemony-building processes, and its impact on co-opting state-building is concerned, this book shows that there a limiting space in realising egalitarian politics or democratic state-building, especially in the post-war period. This is because the elite hegemony-building processes have long been encouraging passive and instrumental forms of political mobilisation and participation of the majority Sinhalese and they have already curtailed their moral-political capacity to challenge or redirect the state-building project away from the elites' hegemony-building project towards an inclusive, egalitarian and a democratic direction. Only such an inclusive approach could serve better to overcome their long-standing and deep-seated grievances and struggles for upward socio-economic mobility. In the post-war period, the direction of the elites' hegemony-building is yet to be fully consolidated as they struggle to gain legitimacy for their rule from those who are being ruled, which is deepening in the backdrop of increasing socio-economic challenges faced by the subalterns. This developing scenario is what Gramsci described as 'morbid symptoms'[8] when he alluded to a crisis of authority in a background where the old is dying and the new cannot be born. Perhaps the overt post-war coercive strategies embarked upon by the Rajapaksa-led ruling coalition speak of such morbid symptoms that are demonstrated through post-war militarisation, open political violence, acceptance of extreme political positions, right-wing populism, and shifts in foreign policy more towards an Eastphalian-led global order.[9] Only a very close observation of these developments within the global interregnum of politics can be helpful in identifying the sources of such morbidities, by tracing their different locations in discursive, political and economic factors.

Furthermore, as shown in this book, as much as the study of major political events in high politics and elite politics, a detailed understanding of Sri Lanka's trajectories of state-building, hegemony-building and political dynamics requires grasping subaltern politics, their visions, aspirations, motivations and the surrounding material-ontological conditions enabling and facilitating their voluntary and induced forms of political mobilisation, integration and participation. By highlighting their role, regardless of being passive or active, this book also assigned importance and responsibility to these groups in charting Sri Lanka's future political trajectories. Hence, the various subaltern groups among the majority Sinhalese belonging to various classes are not considered as mere passive spectators and victims of elite politics, but as an active agency and an enabling force of the elites' hegemony-building project and their right-wing populist politics. This way the book points to the future opportunities and the agency latent with the subaltern groups to change the current course of politics.

Last but not least, this book also has a message to the global policymakers who are playing a dominant role in the post-9/11 era in state-building in war-torn societies. The analysis undertaken in this book shows the importance of prioritising politics, both high and mundane levels, and addressing the long-due questions 'on the political' over the technical approaches to state-building as part of reproducing the liberal international order by paying equal attention to the material–ideological, historical–contemporary and local–global entanglements. Especially for anyone interested in understanding the resurgence of populist and ultra-right wing politics in the national and global scenes, this book can be of some help in finding several of the missing pieces in the mainstream political analyses.

NOTES

1. According to Transparency International's Global Corruption Perception Index 2019 report, Sri Lanka is currently ranked 98th out of 198 countries. In 2019, Sri Lanka's overall ranking dropped by four places from the 2018 rank. See https://www.transparency.org/en/cpi/2019/results/lka#details (accessed on 20 March 2021).
2. The highest manifestation of the disintegration of the political class was noted during the constitutional coup attempted by President Sirisena, who removed the prime minister (UNFPA) of his coalition government and appointed Mahinda Rajapaksa as the new prime minister, which led to a situation of two concurrent prime ministers (Groundviews 2018, https://groundviews.org/2018/11/02/the-constitutional-crisis-a-round-up/, accessed on 18 March 2020).

3. Rajapaksa, who contested from United People's Freedom Front, won the elections by 57.88 per cent of the votes, whereas Sarath Fonseka, contesting from the New Democratic Front, secured 40.15 per cent of the total votes.
4. According to one local newspaper report, the regime was alleged to have even targeted disabled former army veterans who were helping Fonseka's election campaign. See http://www.srilankaguardian.org/2010/02/disabled-soldier-abducted-and-told-to.html (accessed on 16 June 2011).
5. According to the Ministry of Foreign Affairs of Sri Lanka, the 19th amendment was an improved version of the 17th amendment, and it aimed at doing away with the arbitrary nature of the 18th amendment by which the powers of the executive president were made centralised and dictatorial in nature. For a brief guide to the 19th amendment, visit https://www.cpalanka.org/wp-content/uploads/2015/05/A-Brief-Guide-to-the-Nineteenth-Amendment.pdf (accessed on 7 March 2019).
6. The validity of Rajapaksa's Sri Lankan citizenship, which was obtained in 2005, was challenged in court by two prominent members of Sri Lankan civil society. In the same year, Gotabaya Rajapaksa renounced his US citizenship which he was holding since 2003. However, this legal case against Rajapaksa was unanimously dismissed by the three-judge panel of the Appeal Court.
7. According to John Locke (1632–1704), political legitimacy is derived from popular explicit and implicit consent of the governed.
8. Those symptoms are defined as morbid because the underlying problems are existential; they cannot be solved within the existing order and there is no clear sight of a new hegemonic stable order in the horizon.
9. Eastphalia refers to an alternative world order led by a powerful group of states in the non-West, led by China. The Eastphalian order also signifies the end of the domination of the Anglo-European states since the signing of the Westphalia peace treaty in 1648.

AFTERWORD*

As this book is being readied for publication in a few weeks' time, Sri Lanka is being swept by a serious economic and political crisis. The unfolding of the crisis in the coming weeks and months and the strategies the ruling regime will resort to will play a very important role in shaping the future trajectories of state-building, the elites' hegemony-building project and addressing the broader issues pertaining to social justice.

Since the beginning of 2022, the country has slid into a deep economic and political crisis. This is a major setback for Gotabaya Rajapaksa's presidency, who came to power in 2019 promising a brighter future. Since early April 2022, people have been increasingly taking to the streets and chanting 'go home', the latter directed at the president. The majority of the protesters are drawn from urban, lower and upper middle class Sinhala-Buddhists, the same constituency who voted the Rajapaksas in. As the economic crisis is worsening by the day, the political crisis in Colombo is heating up too. At the time of writing of this afterword, the government has lost its simple parliamentary majority; its cabinet of ministers have resigned and parliamentarians from the ruling party have declared independent status. Despite protesters' calls for resignation of the Rajapaksa brothers, they are making every move possible to cling on to power.

---

* This afterword is a modified version of the author's published short invited analytical piece that appeared in January 2022 in the East Asia Forum special feature series on '2021 in Review and the Year Ahead'. The original article is titled 'Rajapaksa Family's Tightening Grip on Sri Lanka', East Asia Forum, Special Feature Series, available at https://www.eastasiaforum.org/2022/01/29/the-rajapaksa-familys-tightening-grip-on-sri-lanka/ (accessed on 8 April 2022).

The looming economic and political crisis was already evident shortly before the year 2021 ended as the hold of the Rajapaksa family on the Sri Lankan state tightened. Some aspects of the economic crisis could have been better handled just six months ago if the ruling regime had listened to independent economic analysts and sought early financial assistance from the International Monetary Fund (IMF) to address its growing sovereign debt crisis. The Rajapaksa regime's economic mismanagement of state resources through continued rewards to capitalist cronies and family members further reinforced Colombo's economic decline. Even on the edge of the worst economic crisis since independence, the rapid passage of the Port City Bill raised concerns of some citizens and the media, who noted that the bill mainly benefited close friends and relatives of the Rajapaksas, while reinforcing close ties with Chinese state companies. Further militarisation of the state as part of Gotabaya Rajapaksa's governance formula was carried out with the appointment of more military personnel to civil posts. Partisans, military elites and Buddhist monks were richly rewarded for supporting the regime, while Rajapaksa ensured an intensified 'Buddhisation' of state institutions. The Bodu Bala Sena (Buddhist Task Force) leader Galagoda Aththe Gnanasara – who has incited violence against the minority Muslim community – was appointed by the president to lead a new pet political project, 'One Country, One Law'.

The credit agency Fitch Ratings predicted impending economic crisis after downgrading Sri Lanka's economy to CC status in December 2021. In the last quarter of 2021, Sri Lanka's economy contracted by 1.5 per cent and foreign currency reserves shrank from USD 7 billion in 2019 to USD 1.5 billion in December 2021. Subsequently, the government's import restrictions led to widespread food and fertiliser shortages. Further misery was added to households battling soaring inflation by a series of gas cylinder explosions due to poor quality gas imports. Colombo also fell out of grace with the IMF, which offered COVID-19 relief packages to most countries other than Sri Lanka, citing the government's unwillingness to restructure its ailing economy.

While Fitch downgraded Sri Lanka's economy to CC, disheartened citizens downgraded the president's status from the 'Terminator' to 'Nandasena', his first name. This symbolic political move was an attempt to distinguish between the decorated war-winning defence secretary – often identified by his second name, Gotabaya, or pet name 'Terminator' – from the president entrusted with the responsibility of looking after the welfare of all.

Although the president initially tried to blame the economic crisis on the pandemic, followed by some of his loyalists blaming the on-going Ukraine–Russia war, using the pandemic and the external factors as covers for the regressive turn in Sri Lankan politics and gross economic mismanagement since Gotabaya Rajapakse assumed the presidency did not have the expected appeal. The regime's clamp down on dissident voices, curtailment of freedom of expression, arrest of journalists and application of overtly securitized measures to handle the pandemic did not go unnoticed in local and international fora. Some policy changes that were introduced in the past year were mainly aimed at averting harsh criticism at the March 2021 deliberations of the UN Human Rights Council (UNHCR) in Geneva, when a country-specific resolution on Sri Lanka was delivered.

Strong words at the UNHCR in March and in the High Commissioner's September 2021 oral report on Sri Lanka added pressure on the government to address past injustices with seriousness and urgency. Strong objections were raised about Sri Lanka's poor human rights record during debates related to extending the European Union's Generalised Scheme of Preferences Plus (GSP+) tariff scheme in the European Parliament in June 2021. Sri Lanka's foreign minister in Geneva and permanent representative to the United Nations in New York both claimed an international conspiracy in response.

Broader observation of Sri Lanka's current economic and political crisis suggest the ruling elites' right-wing populist political slogans are not enough to get through with bare material necessities of daily life. Perhaps, in Gramsci's words, current conditions in Sri Lanka testify to 'the old is dying, and the new cannot be born; in this interregnum, a great variety of morbid symptoms appear'. The crisis can be grabbed by those who took to the streets as an opportunity to reclaim their political agency and contribute to changing the course of Sri Lanka's politics and the future direction of state-building, by forming an inclusive social and political movement and even a new historical bloc.

APPENDIX 1

MAP OF SRI LANKA

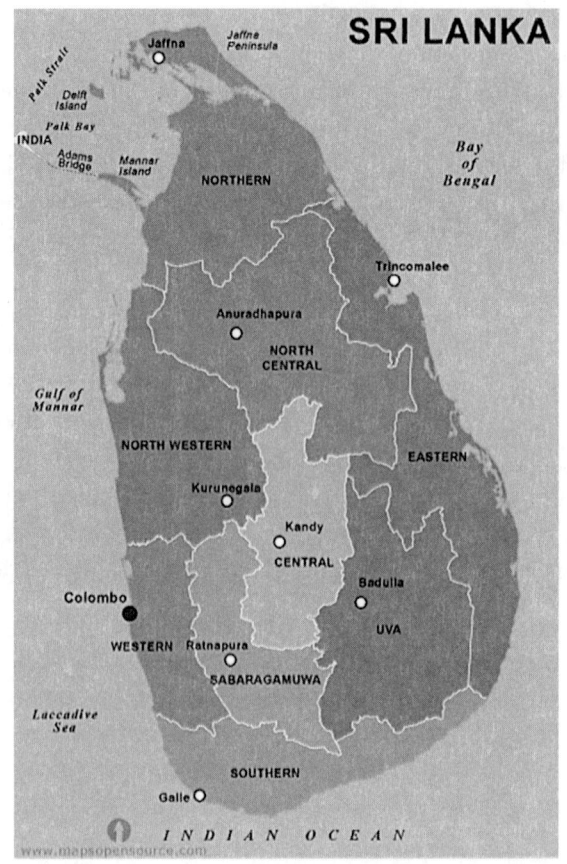

Source: www.mapsopensource.com (reproduced in this book under the Creative Commons Attribution 3.0 Unported Licence).

APPENDIX 2

INDICATION OF BACKGROUND OF KEY INTERVIEWEES (FROM JANUARY TO MAY 2009)

Respondent No.	Academic/ Researcher	Politician or a High-ranked Member of a Political Party	Journalist	Active Member of Civil Society	Govt. Official (Current/ Former)
R.1	X	X			X
R.2			X	X	
R.3		X		X	
R.4					X
R.5	X			X	
R.6	X			X	
R.7	X			X	X
R.8	X			X	
R.9		X		X	X
R.10	X				
R.11	X			X	
R.12	X	X		X	
R.13		X			X
R.14	X			X	X
R.15	X			X	
R.16	X				
R.17	X			X	
R.18	X				
R.19	X			X	X
R.20		X	X		X
R.21	X	X	X		
R.22	X	X	X		X
R.23		X	X		X
R.24				X	
R.25					X
R.26				X	

BIBLIOGRAPHY

Abeyratne, S. (2000). 'Policy and Political Issues in Economic Growth in Sri Lanka'. In S. T. Hettige and M. Mayer (eds.), *Sri Lanka at Crossroads: Dilemmas and Prospects after 50 Years of Independence*, 19–50. New Delhi: Macmillan.
——— (2004). 'Economic Roots of Political Violence, the Case of Sri Lanka'. *World Economy* 27(8): 1295–314.
——— (2008). 'Economic Development and Political Conflict: Comparative Study of Sri Lanka and Malaysia'. *South Asia Economic Journal* 9(2): 393–417.
Abeyrathne, G. D. R. U. U. and Shantasiri Abeywarna. (2009). 'Political Crises and the Role of Judiciary in Sri Lanka'. *Asia Pacific Journal of Social Sciences* 1(2): 1–20.
Abeysekara, A. (2002). *Colors of the Robe: Religion, Identity, and Difference*. Columbia: University of South Carolina Press.
Adams, I. (1993). *Political Ideology Today*. Manchester and New York: Manchester University Press.
Adamson, Walter L. (1980). 'Gramsci's Interpretation of Fascism'. *Journal of the History of Ideas* 41(4): 615–33.
Åkebo, M. and Sunil Bastian (2021). 'Beyond Liberal Peace in Sri Lanka: Victory, Politics, and State Formation'. *Journal of Peacebuilding and Development* 16(1): 70–84. https://doi.org/10.1177/1542316620976121.
Ali, A. (2001). *Plural Identities and Political Choices of the Muslim Community*. Colombo: Marga Institute, Sri Lanka.
Almond, G. A. (1956). 'Comparative Political System'. *Journal of Politics* 18(3): 391–409.

―――― (eds.) (1960). *The Politics of the Developing Areas*. Princeton, NJ: Princeton University Press.

―――― (1965). 'A Developmental Approach to Political System'. *World Politics* 17(2): 183–214.

―――― (1988). 'The Return to the State'. *American Political Science Review* 82(3): 853–74.

Almond, G. A. and G. B. Powell, Jr. (1966). *Comparative Politics: A Developmental Approach*. Boston: Little Brown and Company.

―――― (2004). *Comparative Politics: A Theoretical Framework*, 4th edn. New York: Pearson Longman.

Almond, G. A. and J. S. Coleman (1960). *The Politics of the Developing Areas*. Princeton, NJ: Princeton University Press.

Almond, G. A. and V. Sidney (2007). *The Civic Culture: Political Attitude and Democracy in Five Nations*. Newbury Park: Sage Publication.

Almond, G., G. B. Powell, Jr., R. J. Dalton and Kaare Strom (2004). *Comparative Politics Today: A World View*, 8th edn. New York, NY: Pearson Longman.

―――― (2010). *Comparative Politics Today: A World View*, 9th edn. New York: Pearson Longman.

Althusser, Louis. (1970). 'Ideology and Ideological State Apparatuses (Notes towards an Investigation)'. In *Lenin and Philosophy and Other Essays*, Monthly Review Press. Available at: http://www.marxists.org/reference/archive/althusser/1970/ideology.htm (accessed on 27 April 2013).

Amaratunga, C. (ed.) (1989). 'Ideas for Liberal Democracy'. Proceedings of a series of seven seminars on the constitution of Sri Lanka, Council of Liberal Democracy and the Friedrich Nauman Stiftung, Colombo.

Arasaratnam, S. (1967). 'Nationalism, Communalism and the National Unity in Ceylon'. *Pravada* 5(10 and 11): 260–78. Republication from P. Mason (ed.), *India and Ceylon: Unity and Diversity* (Oxford: Oxford University Press, 1967).

Archer, R. P. (1990). 'The Transition from Traditional to Broker Clientelism in Colombia: Political Stability and Social Unrest'. Working paper No.140, Kellogg Institute for International Studies, Notre Dame, IN.

Athukorala, P. and Sisira Jayasuriya (1994). *Macroeconomic Policies, Crises, and Growth in Sri Lanka, 1969–90*. Washington, DC: World Bank.

―――― (2015). 'Victory in War and Defeat in Peace: Politics and Economics of Post-Conflict Sri Lanka'. *Asian Economic Papers* 14(3): 22–54.

Avineri, S. (1991). 'Marxism and Nationalism'. *Journal of Contemporary History* 26(3/4): 637–57.

Babic, Milan (2020). 'Let's Talk about the Interregnum: Gramsci and the Crisis of the Liberal World Order'. *International Affairs* 96(3): 767–86. https://doi.org/10.1093/ia/iiz254.

Badescu, G. and P. E. Sum (2005). 'The Important of Left–Right Orientation in the New Democracies'. Paper presented at the International Conference on Electoral and Democratic Governance, Taipei, 10–11 April.

Bala, Mytili (2015). 'Transitional Justice in Sri Lanka: Rethinking Post-War Diaspora Advocacy for Accountability'. *International Human Rights Law Journal* 1(1): 1–47.

Balakrishnan, N. (1973). 'The Five Year Plan and Development Policy in Sri Lanka: Socio-Political Perspectives and the Plan'. *Asian Survey*, 13(12): 1155–68.

Balasooriya, A. F., Q. Alam and K. Coghill (2008). 'Market-based Reforms and Privatization in Sri Lanka'. *International Journal of Public Sector Management* 21(1): 58–73.

Bandarage, A. (2009). *The Separatist Conflict in Sri Lanka: Terrorism, Ethnicity, Political Economy*. London and New York: Routledge.

——— (1950). *Colonialism in Sri Lanka, The Political Economy of the Kandyan Highlands 1833–1886*. Berlin: Walter de Gruyter & Co.

Barad, Karen (2007). *Meeting the Universe Halfway: Quantum Physics and the Entanglement of Matter and Meaning*. Durham and London: Duke University Press.

Bass, D. (2001). *Lanscape of Malaiyaha Tamil Identity*. Colombo: Marga Institute.

Bastian, R. (2001). *Globalization and Conflict*. Colombo: Marga Institute.

Bastian, S. (1985). 'University Admission and the National Question'. In Social Scientists' Association (ed.), *Ethnicity and Social Change*, 166–78. Colombo: Social Scientists' Association.

——— (1993a). 'Fractional Politics: Dismantling Institutions of Democracy'. *Pravada*, 2(5).

——— (1993b). 'Growth vs. Welfare Populism: Capitalist Development in the Social Order-1992'. *Pravada* 2(1).

——— (2003a). 'Foreign Aid, Globalization and Conflict in Sri Lanka'. In Markus Mayer, Dharini Rajasingham-Senanayake and Yuvi Thangarajah (eds.), *Building Local Capacities for Peace; Rethinking Conflict and Development in Sri Lanka*, 132–52. New Delhi: Macmillan.

——— (2003b), 'The Political Economy of Electoral Reforms; Proportional Representation Sri Lanka'. In S. Bastian and R. Luckam (eds.), *Can Democracy Be Designed? The Politics of Institutional Choice in Conflict-torn Societies*, 201–07. London: Zed Books.

——— (2007) *The Politics of Foreign Aid in Sri Lanka: Promoting Markets and Supporting Peace*. Colombo: ICES.

Bastian, S. and R. Luckam (eds.) (2003). *Can Democracy Be Designed? The Politics of Institutional Choice in Conflict-torn Societies*. London: Zed Books.

Bastianpillai, B. and S. Wanasinghe. (1995). *Devolution in a Multi-Ethnic Society*. Colombo: Marga Publications.

Bates, T. (1975). 'Gramsci and the Theory of Hegemony'. *Journal of the History of Ideas* 36(2): 351–66.

Bayart, Jean-Francois (2009). *The State in Africa: The Politics of the Belly*, 2nd edn. New York: Wiley.

Bearfield, D. A. (2009). 'What Is Patronage? A Critical Reexamination'. *Public Administration Review* 69(1): 64–76.

BBC Sinhala (2005). '"Helping Hambantota" Probe Halted'. 28 September. https://www.bbc.com/sinhala/news/story/2005/09/050928_helping_hambantota (accessed 14 July 2010).

Bell, C. (1999). 'Foreword: A Comparative Perspective on Peace Agreements'. *Accord: An International Review of Peace Initiatives* 7: 6–9.

——— (2006). 'Peace Agreements: Their Nature and Legal Status'. *American Journal of International Law* 100(2): 373–412.

Berberoglu, B. (2000). 'Nationalism, Ethnic Conflict and Class Struggle; A Critical Analysis of Main Stream and Marxist Theories of Nationalism and National Movement'. *Critical Sociology* 26(3): 205–31.

Betz, H-G. (1994). *Radical Right-wing Populism in Western Europe*. New York: St.Martin's Press.

Bobbio, N. (1996). *Left and Right: The Significance of a Political Distinction*. Cambridge: Polity Press.

Boone, C. (1994). 'States and Ruling Classes in Postcolonial Africa: The Enduring Contradictions of Power'. In J. S. Migdal, Atul Kohli and Vivienne Shue (eds.), *State Power and Social Forces: Domination and Transformation in the 3rd World*, 108–48. Cambridge, New York and Melbourne: Cambridge University Press.

Boothman, D. (2008). 'The Sources for Gramsci's Concept of Hegemony'. *Rethinking Marxism* 20(2): 201–15.

Borland, K.W., Jr. (2001). 'Qualitative and Quantitative Research: A Complementary Balance'. *New Directions for Institutional Research* 112: 5–13. https://doi.org/10.1002/ir.25.

Bose, Sumantra (2004). 'Decolonisation and State Building in South Asia'. *Journal of International Affairs* 58(1): 95–113.

Bose, S. and A. Jalal (2004). *South Asia, History, Culture, Political Economy*, 2nd edn. New York: Routledge.

Bourdieu, P. (1977). *Outline of a Theory of Practice*. Translated by R. Nice, Vol. 16. Cambridge: Cambridge University Press.

Boutros-Ghali, B. (1992). 'An Agenda for Peace: Preventive Diplomacy, Peacemaking and Peacekeeping'. Report of the UN Secretary General, A/47/277-S/24111.

Bowden, Gilbert and Tony Binns (2016). 'Youth Employment and Post-war Development in Jaffna, Northern Sri Lanka'. *Conflict, Security and Development* 16(3): 197–218.

Box, Richard C., Gary S. Marshall, B. J. Reed and Christine M. Reed (2001). 'New Public Management and Substantive Democracy'. *Public Administration Review* 61(5): 608–19.

Brass, Paul R. (1991). *Ethnicity and Nationalism: Theory and Comparison*. London: Sage.

Brow, J. (1981). 'Class Formation and Ideological Practice: A Case from Sri Lanka'. *Journal of Asian Studies* 11(4):703–18.

——— (1988). 'In Pursuit of Hegemony: Representations of Authority and Justice in a Sri Lankan Village'. *American Ethnologist* 15: 311–27. https://doi.org/10.1525/ae.1988.15.2.02a00070.

——— (1990a). 'Notes on Community, Hegemony and the Uses of the Past'. *Anthropological Quarterly* 63(1): 1–6.

——— (1990b). 'The Incorporation of a Marginal Community within the Sinhalese Nation'. *Anthropological Quarterly* 63(1): 7–17.

——— (1996). *Demons and Development: The Struggle for Community in a Sri Lankan Village*. Tucson: University of Arizona Press.

Brow, J. and J. Weeramunda (eds.) (1992). *Agrarian Change in Sri Lanka*. New Delhi: Sage Publications.

Call, C. T. (2003). 'Democratization, War and State Building: Constructing the Rule of Law in El Salvador'. *Journal of Latin America Studies* 35(4): 827–62.

Caroll, W. K. (2006). 'Hegemony, Counter-Hegemony, Anti-Hegemony'. Keynote address to the Annual Meeting of the Society for Social Studies, York University, Toronto.

Central Bank of Sri Lanka (2008). *Annual Report: For the Year 2008*. Colombo: Central Bank of Sri Lanka.

——— (2010). *Annual Report: For the Year 2010*. Colombo: Central Bank of Sri Lanka.

────── (2020). *Economic and Social Statistics of Sri Lanka*. Colombo: Central Bank of Sri Lanka. http://www.cbsl.gov.lk (accessed on 29 June 2021).

Centre for Just peace and Democracy (CJPD) (2006). *Envisioning New Trajectories for Peace in Sri Lanka*. Luzern: CJPD.

Chandraprema C. A. (1991). *Sri Lanka: The Years of Terror—The JVP Insurrection 1987–1989*. Colombo: Lakehouse Bookshop.

Chang, E. (2005). 'Electoral Incentives for Political Corruption under Open-List Proportional Representation'. *Journal of Politics* 67(3): 716–30.

Chatterjee, P. (1986). *Nationalist Thought and the Colonial World*. Avon, UK: The Bath Press.

────── (2001). *The Politics of the Governed: Reflections on Popular Politics in Most of the World*. New York: Columbia University Press.

Cheran, R. (2001). *The Sixth Genre: Memory, History and the Tamil Diaspora Imagination*. Colombo: Marga Institute.

Chomsky N. and M. Foucault (2006). *The Chomsky–Foucault Debate on Human Nature*. New York: The New Press.

Chowdhury, Abdur and Syed Mansoob Murshed (2013). 'War and the Fiscal Capacity of the State'. Working Papers and Research 2013-03, Marquette University, Center for Global and Economic Studies and Department of Economics.

Clausewitz, Carl Von (1976). *On War*. Edited by Michael Howard and Peter Paret. Princeton, NJ: Princeton University Press.

Collier, P. (2003). *Breaking the Conflict Trap: Civil War and Development Policy*. Washington, DC: World Bank and Oxford University Press.

Collier, Paul and Anke Hoeffler (2002). 'Greed and Grievance in Civil War'. The Centre for the Study of African Economies Working Paper Series, Working Paper 160, 1 July. http://www.bepress.com/csae/paper160 (accessed on 12 April 2010).

Collier, Paul, V. L. Elliott, Håvard Hegre, Anke Hoeffler, Marta Reynal-Querol and Nicholas Sambanis (2003). *Breaking the Conflict Trap: Civil War and Development Policy – A World Bank Policy Research Report*. Washington, DC: World Bank and Oxford University Press.

Collins, Charles (1951). 'Public Administration in Ceylon'. Royal Institute of International Affairs, Michigan State University.

Coomaraswamy, R. (1984). *Sri Lanka's Ethnic Conflict: Mythology, Power and Politics*. Colombo: International Centre for Ethnic Studies.

────── (2003). 'The Politics of Institutional Design: An Overview of the Case of Sri Lanka'. In S. Bastian and R. Luckam (eds.), *Can Democracy Be Designed?*

The Politics of Institutional Choice in Conflict-torn Societies, 145–67. London: Zed Books.

——— (1987). 'Myths without Conscience: Tamil and Sinhalese Nationalist Writings of the 1980s'. In C. Abeysekara and N. Gunasinghe (eds.), *Facets of Ethnicity in Sri Lanka*. Colombo: Social Scientists' Association.

Counterpoint (2019). 'The JVP at a Crossroads: Bopage's Critical View of His Former Party'. 6 September. https://counterpoint.lk/the-jvp-at-a-crossroad-bopages-critical-view-of-his-former-party/ (accessed on 23 October 2020).

Crisis Group (2010). 'The Sri Lankan Tamil Diaspora after the LTTE'. Asia Report No. 186. https://www.crisisgroup.org/asia/south-asia/sri-lanka/sri-lankan-tamil-diaspora-after-ltte (accessed on 7 June 2010).

De Silva, K. M. (2007). *Sri Lanka's Troubled Inheritance*. Kandy: International Centre for Ethnic Studies.

Darby, J. (2001). *Effects of Violence on Peace Processes*. Washington, DC: United States Institute of Peace.

Darby, J. and R. McGinty (2000). *The Management of Peace Processes*. London: McMillan Press.

De Alwis, M. (2000). *Cat's Eye: A Feminist Gaze on Current Issues*. Colombo: Social Scientists' Association.

De Alwis, M. and K. Jayawardena (2001). *Casting Pearls: The Women's Franchise Movement in Sri Lanka*. Colombo: Social Scientists' Association.

——— (eds.) (1996). *Embodied Violence: Communalising Women's Sexuality in South Asia*. Delhi: Kali for Women/London: Zed Press.

De Alwis, M., W. Giles, E. Klein and N. Silva (2003). *Feminists under Fire: Exchanges across War Zones*. Toronto: Between the Lines.

De Alwis, R. K. (2009). 'History of and Prospects for Public Sector Reforms in Sri Lanka'. Unpublished PhD thesis, Victoria University of Wellington.

De Mel, N. (2001). *Women and the Nation's Narrative: Gender and Nationalism in Twentieth Century Sri Lanka*. Lanham, Boulder and New York: Rowman and Littlefield Publishers Inc.

——— (2007). *Militarizing Sri Lanka: Popular Culture, Memory and Narrative in the Armed Conflict*. New Delhi: Sage Publications.

De Silva, C. R. (1987). *Sri Lanka: A History*. New Delhi: Vikas Publishing House.

De Silva, K. M. (1981). *A History of Sri Lanka*. Berkeley: University of California Press.

——— (1985). *Managing Ethnic Tensions in Multiethnic Societies: Sri Lanka 1880–1985*. Lanham, MD: University Press of America.

——— (1993). *Sri Lanka: Problems of Governance*. Delhi: Konark Publishers.

——— (ed.) (1995). *A History of Ceylon*, vol. II. Peradeniya: University of Peradeniya.

——— (1998). *Reaping the Whirlwind: Ethnic Conflict, Ethnic Politics in Sri Lanka*. New Delhi: Penguin Books.

——— (2005). *A History of Sri Lanka*. Colombo: Vijitha Yapa Publications.

——— (2008). 'Sri Lanka'. In D. Mendis, *Electoral Processes and Governance in South Asia*, 134–58. New Delhi: Sage Publications.

De Silva, K. M., G. H. Peiris, S. W. R. de A. Samarasinghe, N. Thiruchelvam and Law and Society Trust (1999). *History and Politics: Millennial Perspectives—Essays in Honor of Kingsley de Silva*. Colombo: Law and Society Trust.

De Silva, Lakruwan (2010). 'Fonseka Arrest and the Govigama–Karawe Caste Equation in Sinhala Society'. 11 February. http://ideabullets.blogspot.com/2010/02/fonseka-arrest-and-govigama-karawe.html (accessed on 14 April 2010).

De Silva, N. (2002). *The Hybrid Island: Culture Crossing and the Invention of Identity*. Colombo: Social Scientists' Association.

De Silva, N. (No date). 'Rouge Ship and the Nobel Peace Prize'. www.kalaya.org (accessed on 12 May 2011).

De Silva Wijeratne, Roshan (2006). 'States of Mind and States of History: The Future in Sri Lanka Can Be Decentred'. In Centre for Just peace and Democracy (CJPD), *Envisioning New Trajectories for Peace in Sri Lanka*, 331–44. Luzern: CJPD.

De Soysa, N. (2000). 'The Truth behind Sri Lanka's Gender Development Statistics'. Third World Network. http://www.twnside.org.sg/title/2093.htm (accessed on 10 March 2012).

Deegalle, M. (2006) 'JHU Politics for Peace and Righteous State'. In M. Deegalle, *Buddhism, Conflict and Violence in Modern Sri Lanka*, 233–54. London: Routledge.

——— (ed.) (2009). *Buddhism, Conflict and Violence in Modern Sri Lanka*. London: Routledge.

Deiwiks, C. (2009). 'Populism'. *Living Reviews in Democracy*, 1–9. https://journaldatabase.info/articles/populism.html (accessed on 19 September 2010).

Demmers, Jolle (2015). *Theories of Violent Conflict: An Introduction*, 2nd edn. London and New York: Routledge.

Department of Census and Statistics (2010). *Bulletin of Labor Force Statistics in Sri Lanka*, Labor Force Survey First Quarter of 2010, No.50. Colombo: Department of Census and Statistics, Ministry of Finance and Planning.

—— (2012). *Census of Population and Housing 2012: Provisional information Based on 5% Sample*. Colombo: Department of Census and Statistics, Ministry of Finance and Planning.

—— (2018). *Sri Lanka Labour Force Survey*. Colombo: Central Bank of Sri Lanka.

DeVotta, N. (2000). 'Control Democracy, Institutional Decay, and the Quest for Eelam: Explaining Ethnic Conflict in Sri Lanka'. *Pacific Affairs* 73(19): 55–76.

—— (2002). 'South Asia Faces the Future Illiberalism and Ethnic Conflict in Sri Lanka'. *Journal of Democracy* 13(1): 84–98.

—— (2003). 'Illiberalism and Ethnic Conflict in Sri Lanka'. *Journal of Democracy* 13(1): 84–98.

—— (2005). 'From Ethnic Outbidding to Ethnic Conflict: The Institutional Bases for Sri Lanka's Separatist War'. *Nations and Nationalism* 11(1): 141–59.

—— (2004). 'Sri Lanka Ethnic Domination, Violence and Illiberal Democracy'. In M. Alagappa (ed.), *Civil Society and Political Change in Asia: Expanding and Contracting Democratic Space*, 292–323. Stanford, CA: Stanford University Press.

—— (2017). 'Civil War and the Quest for Transitional Justice in Sri Lanka'. *Asian Security* 13, no. 1: 74–79.

—— (2018). 'Religious Intolerance in Post-civil War Sri Lanka'. *Asian Affairs* 49(2): 278–300. DOI: 10.1080/03068374.2018.1467660.

—— (2019a). 'Sri Lanka's Christians and Muslims Weren't Enemies'. *Foreign Policy*. 25 April. https://foreignpolicy.com/2019/04/25/sri-lankas-christians-and-muslims-werent-enemies/ (accessed on 20 September 2019).

—— (2019b). 'Secularism and the Islamophobia Zeitgeist in India and Sri Lanka'. Middle East Institute. https://www.mei.edu/publications/secularism-and-islamophobiazeitgeist-india-and-sri-lanka (accessed on 2 March 2020).

—— (2021). 'Sri Lanka: The Return to Ethnocracy'. *Journal of Democracy* 32(1): 96–110.

Dewasiri, N. (2008). *The Adaptable Peasant: Agrarian Society in Western Sri Lanka under Dutch Rule, 1740– 1800*. Leiden and Boston: Brill Academic Publishers.

Dharmadasa, K. N. O. (1992). *Language, Religion and Ethnic Assertiveness: The Growth of Sinhala Nationalism in Sri Lanka*. Ann Arbor: The Michigan University Press.

Dizard, Jake, Christopher Walker and Sarah Cook (eds.) (2010). *Countries at the Crossroads: An Analysis of Democratic Governance*. London: Rowman and Littlefield Publishers, Inc.

Doornbos, M. (2006). *Global Forces and State Restructuring: Dynamics of State Formation and Collapse*. Houndsmill: Palgrave McMillan.

——— (2010). 'Researching African Statehood Dynamics: Negotiability and Its Limits'. *Development and Change* 41(4): 747–69.

Dunham, D. (1982). 'Politics and Land Settlement Schemes: The Case of Sri Lanka'. *Development and Change* 13(1):43–61.

——— (1983). 'Interpreting the Politics of Settlement Policy: A Background to the Mahaweli Development Scheme'. ISS Working Paper Series, No. 11, Institute of Social Studies, The Hague.

——— (Unpublished). 'Politics, Economic Policy and Social Provisioning: Growth and Dismantling of the Welfare State in Sri Lanka'.

Dunham, D. and C. Edwards (1997). 'Rural Poverty and an Agrarian Crisis in Sri Lanka, 1985–95: Making Sense of the Picture'. Research Studies: Poverty and Income Distribution Series No.1, Institute of Policy Studies, Colombo.

Dunham, D. and S. Kelegama (1994). 'Economic Liberalization and Structural Reforms: The Experience of Sri Lanka, 1977–93'. ISS Working Paper Series, No.163, Institute of Social Studies, The Hague.

——— (1995). 'Economic Reforms and Governance: The Second Wave of Liberalization in Sri Lanka 1989–93'. ISS Working Paper Series, No. 203, Institute of Social Studies, The Hague.

Dunham, D. and S. Jayasuriya (2000). 'Equity, Growth and Insurrection: Liberalization and the Welfare Debate in Contemporary Sri Lanka'. *Oxford Development Studies* 28(1): 97–110.

——— (2001). 'Liberalization and Political Decay: Sri Lanka's Journey from Welfare State to a Brutalized Society'. ISS Working Paper Series, No. 352, Institute of Social Studies, The Hague.

Dusza, K. (1989). 'Max Weber's Conception of the State'. *International Journal of Politics, Culture and Society* 3: 71–105.

Eddleston, M., M. H. R. Sheriff and K. Hawton (1998). 'Deliberate Self-harm in Sri Lanka: An Overlooked Tragedy in the Developing World'. *BMJ Clinical Research* 317(7151): 133–35.

Edrisinha, R. (1999). 'Constitutionalism, Pluralism and Ethnic Conflict: The Need for a New Initiative'. In R. I. Rotberg (ed.), *Creating Peace in Sri Lanka: Civil War and Reconciliation*, 169–89. Washington, DC: Brookings Institution Press.

Edrisinha, R. and N. Selvakumaran (2000). 'The Constitutional Evolution of Ceylon/Sri Lanka 1948–98'. In W. D. Lakshman and C. A. Tisdell (eds.), *Sri Lanka's Development since Independence: Socio-Economic Perspectives and Analyses*, 95–112. New York: Nova Science Publishers, Inc.

Edwards, C. 'Cutting Off the King's Head: The "Social" in Hannah Arendt and Michel Foucault'. www.sussex.ac.uk/cspt/documents/issue1-1.pdf (accessed on 6 August 2012).

Elhawary, S. and M. M. M. Aheeyar (2008). 'Beneficiary Perceptions of Corruption in Humanitarian Assistance: A Sri Lanka Case Study'. HPG Working Paper, Overseas Development Institute, London.

Epstein, D. J. (2009). 'Clientelism versus Ideology: Problems of Party Development in Brazil'. *Party Politics* 15(3): 335–55.

Evans, P. B., D. Rueschemeyer and T. Scokpol (eds.) (1985). *Bringing the State Back In*. Cambridge: Cambridge University Press.

Evans, Peter and James E. Rauch (1999). 'Bureaucracy and Growth: A Cross-National Analysis of the Effects of "Weberian" State Structures on Economic Growth'. *American Sociological Review* 64(5): 748–65.

Fearson, J. D. and D. D. Laitin (2003). 'Ethnicity, Insurgency and Civil War'. *American Political Science Review* 97(1): 75–90.

Fernando, S. 'Sri Lanka's UNP Govt. Pledged Not to Get Involved in Karuna–LTTE Split—Norway'. www.asiantribune.com/news/2011.

Fernando, T. (1973). 'Elite Politics in New States: The Case of Post-Independent Sri Lanka'. *Pacific Affairs* 46(3): 361–83.

FES (Friedrich-Ebert-Stiftung) (2008). 'United National Party: Preliminary Research Report on Inner Party Democracy'. FES, Colombo, November.

Flynn, P. (1973) 'Class, Clientelism and Coercion: The Mechanics of Internal Colonialism and Control'. Workshop on Dependency in Latin America, Centre for Latin American Research and Documentation, Amsterdam Centrum, 19–21 November.

Fonseka, Bhavani and Mirak Raheem (2011). *Land in the Northern Province: Post-War Politics, Policy and Practices*. Colombo: Centre for Policy Analysis.

Forgacs, D. and G. Nowell-Smith (eds.) (1985). *Antonio Gramsci: Selections from Cultural Writings*. Translated by William Boelhower. Cambridge, MA: Harvard University Press.

Foster, Erik K. (2004). 'Research on Gossip: Taxonomy, Methods and Future Directions'. *Review of General Psychology* 8(2): 78–99.

Foucault, M. (1977). *Discipline and Punish: The Birth of the Prison*. London: Allen Lane.

—— (1991). 'Governmentality'. In G. Burchell, C. Gordon and P. Miller (eds.), *The Foucault Effect: Studies in Governmentality*. London: Harvester Wheatsheaf.

—— (2000). 'Interview with Michel Foucault'. In J. D. Faubion (ed.), *Power: Essential Works of Foucault, 1954–1984*. New York: The New Press.

Fox, J. (1994). 'The Difficult Transition from Clientelism to Citizenship: Lessons from Mexico'. *World Politics* 46(28): 151–84.

Fraser, N. (1995). 'From Redistribution to Recognition? Dilemmas of Justice in a Post-Socialist Age'. *New Left Review* 1 (212) (old series): 68–93.

—— (2005). 'Reframing Justice in a Globalizing World'. *New Left Review* 36: 69–88.

Fujii, L. A. (2010). 'Shades of Truth and Lies: Interpreting Testimonies of War and Violence'. *Journal of Peace Research* 47(2): 231–41.

Fukuyama, F. (2004). *State-Building, Governance and World Order in the Twenty-first Century*. Ithaca: Cornell University Press.

—— (2011). *Origins of Political Order: From Prehuman Times to the French Revolution*, 1st paperback edn. New York, NY: Farrar, Straus and Giroux.

Galtung, J. (1969) Violence, Peace, and Peace Research, *Journal of Peace Research* 6(3): 167–91.

—— (1996). *Peace by Peaceful Means: Peace and Conflict, Development and Civilization*. London: Sage Publications.

Gerring, J. and S. C. Thacker (2004). 'Political Institutions and Corruption: The Role of Unitarism and Parliamentarism'. *Journal of Political Science* 34(2): 295–330.

—— (2005). 'Do Neo-Liberal Policies Deter Political Corruption'. *International Organization* 59(1): 233–54.

Giddens, A. (1994). *Beyond Left and Right: The Future of Radical Politics*. Stanford, CA: Blackwell Publishers.

Gunatilleke, G., N. Thiruchelvam and R. Coomaraswamy (eds.) (1983). *Ethical Dilemmas of Development in Asia*. Lexington, MA: Lexington Books.

Gunawardena, Chandra (2003). 'Gender Equity in Higher Education in Sri Lanka: A Mismatch between Access and Outcomes'. *McGill Journal of Education* 38(3): 437–51.

Goodhand, J. (2005). 'Frontiers and Wars: The Opium Economy in Afghanistan'. *Journal of Agrarian Change* 5(2): 191–216.

——— (2006). 'Internationalization of the Peace Process'. In *Envisioning New Trajectories for Peace in Sri Lanka*, 215–25. Luzern: Centre for Just Peace and Democracy.

——— (2010). 'Stabilising a Victor's Peace? Humanitarian Action and Reconstruction in Eastern Sri Lanka'. *Disasters* 34(3): 342–67.

——— (2012). 'Sri Lanka in 2012: Securing the State, Enforcing the "Peace"'. *Asian Survey* 53(1): 64–72.

Goodhand, J. and Bart Klem (eds.) (2005). *Aid, Conflict and Peacebuilding in Sri Lanka 2000–2005*. Colombo: The ASIA Foundation.

Goodhand, J., B. Klem and B. Korf (2009). 'Religion, Conflict and Boundary Politics in Sri Lanka'. *European Journal of Development Research* 21(5): 679–98.

Goonetileke, Ian (1984). 'July 1983 and the National Question in Sri Lanka: A Bibliographical Guide'. *Race and Class* 26(1): 159–193. http://rac.sagepub.com/content26/1/159.citation (accessed 19 July 2011).

Government of Sri Lanka (1961). *Report of the Salaries and Cadre Commission 1961, Part 1–111: Salaries and Connected Matters*. Colombo: Ceylon Government Press.

——— (2002). 'Relief, Rehabilitation, Reconciliation and Socio-Economic Development in the Conflict-Affected Areas of Sri Lanka, Summary of Donor Commitments, as of Nov/14/2002'. http://peaceinsrilanka.org/insidepages/RRR/RRRmain.asp (accessed on 14 November 2008).

Gramsci, A. (1972). *The Modern Prince and Other Writings*. New York: International Publishers.

Gregor, J. A. (1968). 'Political Science and the Uses of Functional Analysis'. *American Political Science Review* 62(2): 425–39.

Grindle, M. S. (2001). 'In Quest of the Political: The Political Economy of Development Policymaking'. In G. M. Meier and J. E. Stiglitz (eds.), *Frontiers of Development Economics: The Future in Perspective*, 345–84. New York: Oxford University Press.

Groth, A. J. (1970). 'Structural Functionalism and Political Development: Three Problems'. *Western Political Quarterly* 23(3): 485–99.

Grzymaka-Busse, A. (2000). 'Beyond Clientelism, Incumbent State Capture and State Formation'. *Comparative Political Studies* 41(4/5): 638–73.

Gunasekara, P. (1998). *Sri Lanka in Crisis: A Lost Generation—The Untold Story*. Colombo: S Godage & Brothers.

Gunasekare, T. (2010). 'Next the 19th Amendment'. *Sri Lanka Guardian*, 19 September.www.sundayleader.lk/2010/09/19 (accessed on 29 September 2011).

Gunasinghe N. (1996a). 'A Sociological Comment of the Political Transformations in 1956 and the Resultant Socio-Political Processes'. In S. Perera (ed.), *Newton Gunasinghe: Selected Essays*, 217–35. Colombo: Social Scientists' Association.

—— (1996b). 'Agrarian Relations in the Kandyan Countryside in relation to the Concept of Extreme Social Disintegration'. In S. Perera (ed.), *Newton Gunasinghe: Selected Essays*. Colombo: Social Scientists' Association.

—— (1996c). 'Anti-Tamil Riots and the Political Crisis'. in S. Perera (ed.), *Newton Gunasinghe: Selected Essays*. Colombo: Social Scientists' Association.

—— (1996d). 'Land Reform, Class Structure and the State in Sri Lanka: 1970–1977'. In S. Perera (ed.), *Newton Gunasinghe: Selected Essays*, 53–76. Colombo: Social Scientists' Association.

—— (1996e). 'The Symbolic Role of the Sangha'. In S. Perera (ed.), *Newton Gunasinghe: Selected Essays*, 236–39. Colombo: Social Scientists' Association.

—— (1996f). 'Class, Caste and the Political Process'. In S. Perera (ed.), *Newton Gunasinghe: Selected Essays*, 157–60. Colombo: Social Scientists' Association.

—— (1996g). 'The Open Economy and Its Impact on Ethnic Relations in Sri Lanka'. In S. Perera (ed.), *Newton Gunasinghe: Selected Essays*, 183–203. Colombo: Social Scientists' Association.

—— (2004) 'The Open Economy and Its Impact on Ethnic Relations in Sri Lanka'. In D. Winslow and M. D. Woost (eds.), *Economy, Culture and Civil War in Sri Lanka*, 99–114. Bloomington and Indianapolis: Indiana University Press.

Gunatillake, G. (2000). 'Development Policy Regimes'. In W. D. Lakshman and C. A. Tisdell (eds.), *Sri Lanka's Development since Independence; Socio-Economic Perspectives and Analysis*, 127–52. New York: Nova Science Publishers, Inc.

Gundogan, E. (2008). 'Conceptions of Hegemony in Antonio Gramsci's Southern Question and the Prison Notebooks'. *Journal of Marxism and Interdisciplinary Inquiry* 2(1): 45–60.

Gupta, A. (1995). 'Blurred Boundaries: The Discourse of Corruption, the Culture of Politics and the Imagined State'. *American Ethnologist* 22(2): 375–402.

Gurr, T. R. (1993). *Minorities at Risk: A Global View of Ethno-political Conflicts*. Washington, DC: United States Institute of Peace.

Guruge, Ananda (ed.) (1965). *Return to Righteousness: A Collection of Speeches, Essays and Letters of the Anagarika Dharmapala*. Colombo: Ministry of Education and Cultural Affairs.

Hagman, T. and D. Peclard. (2010). 'Negotiating Statehood: Dynamics of Power and Domination in Africa'. *Development and Change* 41(4): 539–62.

Hall, S. (1996). 'Gramsci's Relevance for the Study of Race and Ethnicity'. In D. Morley and K.-H. Chen (eds.), *Stuart Hall: Critical Dialogues in Cultural Studies*, 411–41. London: Routledge.

Haraway, Donna (1997). *Modest_Witness@Second_Millenium.FemaleMan©_Meets_OncoMouse™: Feminism and Technoscience*. New York: Routledge.

Hardt, M. and A. Nergi (2000). *Empire*. Cambridge, MA/London: Harvard University Press.

Hartzell, C. (1999). 'Explaining the Stability of Negotiated Settlements to Intrastate Wars'. *Journal of Conflict Resolution* 43(1): 3–22.

Hasbullah S. H. and B. Morison (eds.) (2004). *Sri Lankan Society in an Era of Globalization; Struggling to Create a New Social Order*. New Delhi: Sage Publications

Hass, E. B. (2000). *Nationalism, Liberalism and Progress*. Ithaca: Cornell University Press.

Heidenheimer, A. J. (2001). 'Parties, Campaign Finance and Political Corruption: Tracing Long term Comparative Dynamics'. In A. J. Heidenheimer and M. Johnston (eds.), *Political Corruption: Concepts and Contexts*, 761–76. New Brunswick: Transaction Publishers.

Heidenheimer, A.J. and M. Johnston. (eds.) (2001). *Political Corruption: Concepts and Contexts*. New Brunswick: Transaction Publishers.

Helbardt, Sascha, Dagmar Hellmann-Rajanayagam and Rüdiger Korff. (2010). 'War's Dark Glamour: Ethics of Research in War and Conflict Zones'. *Cambridge Review of International Affairs* 23(2): 349–69.

Helling, D. (2010). 'Tillian Footprints beyond Europe: War-making and State-making in the Case of Somaliland'. *St. Anthony's International Review* 6(1): 103–23.

Hellmann-Rajanayagam, D. (2008). 'From RPGs to MoUs: The LTTE and the Media, Perceptions of a "Terrorist" Movement among the Sri Lankan Tamil Diaspora'. *Diaspora Studies* 1(2): 85–104.

――― (2009). 'Drawing in Treacle: Mediation Efforts in Sri Lanka, 1983 to 2007'. *International Quarterly for Asian Studies* 40(1–2): 59–6.

Hennayake, S. (1993). 'Ethnicism in the studies of Ethno-nationalist Politics in Sri Lanka'. Ceylon Studies Seminar, University of Peradeniya.

Hennayake S. K. and N. Hennayake (2000). 'Anthropologists Misreading Sinhala-Buddhist Nationalism'. 2 January. https://www.lankaweb.com/news/features.html (accessed on 15 April 2022).

Herbst, J. (1990). 'War and the State in Africa'. *International Security* 14(4): 119–39.

Herring, R. (1987). 'Economic Liberalization Policies in Sri Lanka: International Pressures, Constrains and Supports'. *Economic and Political Weekly* 22(8): 325–33.

Hettige, S. T. (ed.) (1992). *Unrest or Revolt: Some Aspects of Youth Unrest in Sri Lanka*. Colombo: Goethe Institute.

Hettige, S. (2000). 'Transformation of Society'. In W. D. Lakshman and C. A. Tisdell (eds.), *Sri Lanka's Development since Independence: -Socioeconomic Analysis*, 19–40. New York: Nova Science Publishers, Inc.

Hoare, Q. and G. Nowell Smith (eds. and trans.) (1971). *Selections from the Prison Notebooks of Antonio Gramsci*. New York: International Publishers.

Hobsbawm, E. J. (1992). *Nations and Nationalism since 1780: Programme, Myth, Reality*, 2nd edn. Cambridge: Cambridge University Press.

Höglund, Kristine and Camilla Orjuela (2013). 'Friction and the Pursuit of Justice in Post-war Sri Lanka'. *Peacebuilding* 1(3): 300–16.

Holt, J. C. (ed.) (2016). *Buddhist Extremists and Muslim Minorities: Religious Conflict in Contemporary Sri Lanka*. New York City: Oxford University Press.

Hoole, R. and R. Thiranagama (2001). *Sri Lanka: Arrogance of Power, Myths, Decadence and Murder*. Colombo: University Teachers for Human Rights.

Hopkin, J. (2006). Conceptualizing Political Clientelism: Political Exchange and Democratic Theory'. Paper presented for APSA Annual Meeting, Philadelphia (31 August–3 September).

Horowitz, D. (1989). 'Incentives and Behaviour in the Ethnic Politics of Sri Lanka and Malaysia'. *Third World Quarterly* 11(4): 18–35.

Houtart, F. (1976). 'Buddhism and Politics in South East Asia–Part One'. *Social Scientist* 5(3): 3–23.

Hulme, David and Nimal Sanderatne (1996). *Public Accountability, Public Expenditure Management and Government in Sri Lanka, 1948–1993*. Colombo: Institute of Policy Studies.

Hyndman, P. (1988). *Sri Lanka: Serendipity under Siege*. Nottingham: Spokesman.

IDEA (2007). *Political Parties in South Asia: The Challenge of Change—South Asia Regional Report*. Sweden: International IDEA.

IDSN (2008). 'Dalits of Sri Lanka: Caste-blind Does Not Mean Casteless'. IDSN.

ILO Laborsta (2008). 'Sectoral Activities Department, Sri Lanka'. Geneva: ILO.

IMF (2001). *Sri Lanka: Recent Economic Developments, IMF Country Report 1/70*. Washington, DC: IMF.

Imtiyaz, A. R. M. and Amjad Mohamed-Saleem (2015). 'Muslims in Post-war Sri Lanka: Understanding Sinhala-Buddhist Mobilization against Them'. *Asian Ethnicity* 16(2): 186–202.

Imtiyaz, A. R. M. and M. C. M. Iqbal (2011). 'The Displaced Northern Muslims of Sri Lanka: Special Problems and the Future'. *Journal of Asian and African Studies* 46(4): 375–89.

IPS (2011). *Sri Lanka, State of the Economy: Post-conflict Growth, Making It Inclusive*. Colombo: Institute of Policy Studies.

Irwin, C. (2008). 'Peace in Sri Lanka: From Symbols to Substance'. Institute of Irish Studies, University of Liverpool. https://www.cpalanka.org/wp-content/uploads/2008/12/Peace_in_Sri_Lanka.pdf (accessed on 18 May 2010).

Ismail, Q. (2005) *Abiding by Sri Lanka: On Peace, Place and Postcoloniality*. Minneapolis: University of Minnesota Press.

Ismail, Q. and P. Jeganathan (eds.) (1995). *Unmaking the Nation: The Politics of Identity and History in Modern Sri Lanka*. Colombo: Social Scientists' Association.

Ivan, V. (1989). *Sri Lanka in Crisis: Road to Conflict*. Ratmalana: Sarvodaya Book Publishing Services.

——— (2007). *The Queen of Deceit*. Maharagama: Ravaya Publishers.

Jalal, A. (1995). *Democracy and Authoritarianism in South Asia: A Comparative and Historical Perspective*. Cambridge: Cambridge University Press.

Jayantha, D. (1992). *Electoral Allegiance in Sri Lanka*. New York: Cambridge University Press.

Jayasundara, Shyamika (2004). 'Worldview Analysis of the Norwegian Peace Makers in Sri Lanka'. Master'sthesis (unpublished), Eastern Mennonite University, Harrisonburg, Virginia.

——— (2010). 'Patronage in Sri Lanka'. Conference paper presented at Bath University, UK, 14–16 September. www.bath.ac.uk/cds/events/sym-papers/Jayasundara2.pdf (accessed on 20 December 2011).

Jayasundara-Smits, Shyamika (2015). 'Sri Lanka's Civil War: What Kind of Methodologies for Identity Conflict?' In Helen Hintjens and Dubravka Zarkov (eds.), *Conflict, Peace, Security and Development, Theories and Methodologies*, 187–201. Oxon and New York: Routledge.

——— (2018). 'Lost in Transition: Linking War, War Economy and Post-war Crime in Sri Lanka'. *Third World Thematics: A TWQ Journal* 3(1): 63–79.

Jayatilleka, D. (1999). 'Marxism and the Millennium'. In K. M. De Silva, G. H. Peiris, S. W. R. de A. Samarasinghe and Law and Society Trust,

History and Politics, Millennium Perspectives, Essays in Honor of Kingsley De Silva. Colombo: Law and Society Trust.

Jayawardane, L. (1992). 'Foreword'. In S. J. Tambiah (ed.), *Buddhism Betrayed? Religion, Politics and Violence in Sri Lanka*, ix–xvi. Chicago: Chicago University Press.

Jayawardena, K. (1984). 'Class Formation and Communalism'. *Race and Class* 26(51): 51–62.

——— (1985a). *Ethnic and Class Conflicts in Sri Lanka: Some Aspects of Sinhala Buddhist Consciousness over the Past 100 Years*. Colombo: Centre for Social Analysis.

——— (1985b). 'Some Aspects of Class and Ethnic Consciousness in Sri Lanka in the Late 19th and Early 20th Centuries'. In Social Scientists' Association (ed.), *Ethnicity and Social Change in Sri Lanka*, 74–92. Colombo: Social Scientists' Association.

——— (1987a). 'Ethnic Conflict in Sri Lanka and Regional Security'. Social Scientists' Association. www.infolanka.com/org/srilanka/issues/kumari.html (accessed on 14 April 2022).

——— (1987b). 'The National Question and the Left Movement in Sri Lanka'. In C. Abeysekera and N. Gunasinghe (eds.), *Facets of Ethnicity*, 226–71. Colombo: Social Scientists' Association.

——— (2000). *Nobodies to Somebodies: The Rise of the Colonial Bourgeoisie in Sri Lanka*. London and New York: Zed Books.

——— (2003). *Ethnic and Class Conflicts in Sri Lanka: The Emergence of Sinhala-Buddhist Consciousness 1883–1983*. Colombo: Sanjiva Books.

——— (2007). *Nobodies to Somebodies: The Rise of Colonial Bourgeoisie in Sri Lanka*. Colombo: SSA and Sanjiva Books.

——— (2010). *Perpetual Ferment, Popular Revolts in Sri Lanka in the 18th and 19th Centuries*. Colombo: Social Scientists' Association.

——— (1974). 'Origins of the Left Movement in Sri Lanka'. *Social Scientist* 2(6/7): 3–28.

Jayawardena, V. K. (1972). *The Rise of the Labor Movement in Ceylon*. Durham: Duke University Press.

Jayaweera, S. (2001). *The Ethnic Conflict and Sinhala Consciousness*. Colombo: Marga Institute.

Jennings, I. (1954). 'Politics in Ceylon since 1952'. *Pacific Affairs* 27(4): 338–52.

Jennings, W. I. (1952). 'Politics in Ceylon'. *Far Eastern Survey* 21(17): 177–80.

Jessop, B. (1990). *State Theory: Putting the Capitalist State back in Its Place*. Cambridge: Penn State Press.

Jiggins, J. (1979). *Caste and Family in the Politics of the Sinhalese 1947–1976*. Cambridge: Cambridge University Press.

Jogernsen, W. M. and L. J. Phillips (2002). *Discourse Analysis as Theory and Method*. London: Sage.

Joseph, F. V. (1981). *Gramsci's Political Thought: Hegemony, Consciousness and the Revolutionary Process*. Oxford: Clarendon Press.

Joseph, J. (2002). *Hegemony: A Realist Analysis*. London: Routledge.

Jou, W. (2010). 'The Heuristic Value of the Left and Right Schema in East Asia'. *International Political Science Review* 31(3): 366–94.

Jupp, J. (1968). 'Constitutional Developments in Ceylon since Independence'. *Pacific Affairs* 41(2): 169–83.

——— (1978). *Sri Lanka: Third World Democracy*. London: Frank Cass and Company.

Kadirgamar, A. (2010). 'State Power, State Patronage and Elections in Sri Lanka'. *Economic and Political Weekly* 45(2): 21–24.

——— (2012). 'Legitimacy and Crisis in Sri Lanka'. *Economic and Political Weekly* 47(9): 25–29.

———. (2016). 'Time to Look Within, Not Westwards'. *The Hindu*, 23 September.

——— (2017). 'The Failure of Post-War Reconstruction in Jaffna, Sri Lanka: Indebtedness, Caste Exclusion and the Search for Alternatives'. PhD dissertation, CUNY Academic Works. https://academicworks.cuny.edu/gc_etds/1901 (accessed on 10 May 2020).

——— (2020). 'Polarization, Civil War, and Persistent Majoritarianism in Sri Lanka'. In Thomas Carothers and Andrew O'Donohue (eds.), *Political Polarization in South and Southeast Asia: Old Divisions, New Dangers*, 53–66. Carnegie Endowment for International Peace. https://carnegieendowment.org/2020/08/18/polarization-civil-war-and-persistent-majoritarianism-in-sri-lanka-pub-82437 (accessed on 14 December 2020).

Kapferer, B. (1988). *Legends of People, Myths of State: Violence, Intolerance and Political Culture in Sri Lanka and Australia*, 2nd edn. Washington, DC and London: Smithsonian Institution Press.

——— (2001). 'Ethnic Nationalism and the Discourse of Violence in Sri Lanka'. *Communal/Plural* 9(1): 33–67.

Kaplan, B. and J. A. Maxwell (1994). 'Qualitative Research Methods for Evaluating Computer Information Systems'. in J. G. Anderson, C. E. Aydin and S. J. Jay (eds.), *Evaluating Health Care Information Systems: Methods and Applications*, 45–68. Thousand Oaks, CA: Sage.

Karunaratne D. H. (2007). 'Structural Change and the State of the Labour Market in Sri Lanka'. Hosei University repository. http://doi.org/10.15002/00003106 (accessed on 20 January 2011).

Kearney, R. (1971). *Trade Unions and Politics in Ceylon*. Berkeley: University of California Press.

——— (1973). 'The Marxist Parties of Ceylon'. In P. Brass and M. P. Franda (eds.), *Radical Politics in South Asia*, 400–39. Cambridge, Cambridge University Press.

——— (1981). 'Women in Politics in Sri Lanka'. *Asian Survey* 21(7): 729–46

Kearney, R. N. (1985). 'Ethnic Conflict and the Tamil Separatist Movement in Sri Lanka'. *Asian Survey* 25(9): 898–917.

——— (1987/88). 'Territorial Elements of Tamil Separatism in Sri Lanka'. *Pacific Affairs* 60(4): 561–77.

Kedourie, E. (1960). *Nationalism*. London: Hutchinson & Co. Ltd.

Keefer, P. and R. Vlaicu (2008). 'Democracy, Credibility and Clientelism'. *Journal of Law, Economics and Organization* 24(2): 371–406.

Keefer, P. (2005). 'Clientelism, Credibility and the Policy Choices of Young Democracies'. Development Research Group, The World Bank, Washington, DC.

——— (2009) 'The Ethnicity Distraction? Political Credibility, Clientelism and Partisan Preference in Africa'. The World Bank, Washington, DC. http://www.saylor.org/site/wp-content/uploads/2012/05/polsc325-2.5-Keefer.pdf (accessed on 12 May 2010).

Keerawella, G. and R. Samarajiva. (1994). 'Sri Lanka in 1993: Eruption and Flow'. *Asian Survey* 34(2): 168–74.

——— (1995). 'Sri Lanka in 1994: A Mandate for Peace'. *Asian Survey* 35(2): 153–59. DOI:10.2307/2645024.

Keethaponcalan, S. I. (2008). *Sri Lanka: Politics of Power, Crisis and Peace 2000–2005*. New Delhi: Kumaran Book House.

Kelegama, S. (2000). 'Development in Independent Sri Lanka: What Went Wrong?' *Economic and Political Weekly* 35(17): 1477–90.

Khan, M. (1998). 'Patron–Client Networks and the Economic Effects of Corruption'. *European Journal of Development Research* 10(1): 15–39.

——— (2000). 'Class, Clientelism and Communal Politics in Bangladesh. University of London. http://eprints.soas.ac.uk/2418/1/Class_Clientelism_and_Communalism_in_Bangladesh.pdf (accessed on 9 July 2009).

Kiribamune, S. (1999a). 'The State and Sangha in Pre-modern Sri Lanka'. In K. M. De Silva, G. H. Peiris, S. W. R. de A. Samarasinghe and Law and

Society Trust. *History and Politics: Millennial Perspectives—Essays in Honor of Kingsley De Silva*, 201–16. Colombo: Law and Society Trust.

——— (ed.) (1999b). *Women and Politics in Sri Lanka: A Comparative Perspective*. Colombo: International Centre for Ethnic Studies.

Knight-John, M. and P. P. A. W. Athukorala (2005) 'Assessing Privatization in Sri Lanka: Distribution and Governance'. In N. Birdsall and John R. Nellis (eds.), *Reality Check: The Distributional Impact of Privatization in Developing Countries*, 389–426. Washington, DC: Center for Global Development.

Kodikara, C. (2009). *The Struggle for Equal Political Representation of Women in Sri Lanka: A Stocktaking Report for the Ministry of Child Development and Women's Empowerment and the United Nations Development Programme*. Kiribathgoda: Sarasavi.

Kohli, A. (1994). 'Centralization and Powerlessness in India'. In J. S. Migdal, Atul Kohli and Vivienne Shue (eds.), *State Power and Social Forces: Domination and Transformation in the 3rd World*, 89–107. Cambridge: Cambridge University Press.

Kohli, A. and V. Shue (1994). 'State Power and Social Forces: On Political Contention and Accommodation in the Third World'. In J. S. Migdal, Atul Kohli and Vivienne Shue (eds.), *State Power and Social Forces: Domination and Transformation in the 3rd World*, 293–326. Cambridge: Cambridge University Press.

Korf, B. (2010). 'Sri Lanka: The Third Wave'. *International Development Planning Review* 32(1): i–vii.

Krishna, S. (1999). *Post-colonial Insecurities: India, Sri Lanka, and the Question of Nationhood*. Minneapolis: University of Minnesota.

Kumar, Ravi. (2016). *Neoliberalism: Critical Pedagogy and Education*. Oxon and New York: Routledge.

Kunicova, J. and S. Rose-Akerman (2005). 'Electoral Rules and Constitutional Structures as Constrains on Corruption'. *Journal of Political Science* 35(4): 573–606.

Kurien C. T. (2005). 'The Politics of Economics: Book Review, Saman Kelegama, *Economic Policy in Sri Lanka – Issues and Debates*, New Delhi: Sage Publications'. *Frontline*, 22 April. https://frontline.thehindu.com/other/article30204252.ece (accessed on 14 May 2009).

Kutsen, O. (1998). 'The Strength of the Partisan Component of Left–Right Identity: A Comparative Longitudinal Study of Left–Right Party Polarization in Eight Western European Countries'. *Party Politics* 4(1): 5–31.

Laclau, E. and Chantal Mouffe (1985). *Hegemony and Socialist Strategy: Towards a Radical Democratic Politics*. London and New York: Verso.

Lakshamn, W. D. (1985). 'The IMF–World Bank Intervention in Sri Lankan Economic Policy: Historical Trends and Patterns'. *Social Scientist* 13(2): 3–29.

——— (1987). 'Active State Control vs. Market Guidance in Dependent Capitalist Economy: The Case of Sri Lanka 1970–84'. *Social Scientist* 15(4/5): 10–44.

——— (1989). 'Lineages of Dependent Development'. In P. Viganarajah and A. Hussain (eds.), *The Challenge in South Asia: Development, Democracy and Regional Cooperation*, 105–38. New Delhi: Sage Publications.

Lakshman, W. D and C. A. Tisdell (2000). *Sri Lanka's Development since Independence: Socio-Economic Perpectives and Analyses*. New York: Nova Science Publishers, Inc.

LaPorte, R., Jr (1970). 'Administrative, Political and Social Constraints on Economic Development in Ceylon'. *International Review of Administrative Science* 35: 158–79.

——— (1981). 'Public Administration in South Asia since the British Raj'. *Public Administration Review* 41(5): 581–588.

Lears, J. T. J. (1985). 'The Concept of Cultural Hegemony: Problems and Possibilities'. *American Historical Review* 90(3): 567–95.

Lederach, J. P. (1997). *Building Peace: Sustainable Reconciliation in Divided Societies*. Washington, DC: United States Institute of Peace.

——— (1999) 'Justpeace: Challenge in 21st Century'. In *People Building Peace: 35 Inspiring Stories around the World*, 27–36. Utrecht: European Centre for Conflict Prevention.

——— (2003). *The Little Book of Conflict Transformation*. New York: Good Books.

——— (2005). *Moral Imagination: The Art and Soul of Peacebuilding*. Oxford and New York: Oxford University Press.

Leftwitch, A. (ed.) (2004). *What Is Politics? The Activity and Its Study*. Cambridge and Malden, MA: Polity Press.

Lee, Jones and Shahar Hameiri (2020). 'Debunking the Myth of 'Debt-Trap Diplomacy': How Recipient Countries Shape China's Belt and Road Initiative'. Research Paper, Chatham House. https://www.chathamhouse.org/2020/08/debunking-myth-debt-trap-diplomacy/4-sri-lanka-and-bri (accessed on 18 January 2021).

Lemarchand, R. (1972). 'Political Clientelism and Ethnicity in Tropical Africa: Competing Solidarities in Nation-Building'. *American Political Science Review* 66(1): 68–90.

Lester, J. C. (1994). 'The Political Compass and Why libertarianism Is Not Right-Wing'. https://philarchive.org/archive/JCLTPC (accessed on 12 August 2010).

Lipchutz, R. D. (1998). 'Beyond the Neoliberal Peace: From Conflict Resolution to Social Reconciliation'. *Social Justice* 25 (4): 5–19.

Lipset, S. M. (1963). *Political Man: The Social Bases of Politics.* New York: Anchor Books.

Lucardie, P. (2009). 'Populism: Some Conceptual Problems'. *Political Studies Review* 7 (3): 319–21.

Ludden D. (ed.) (2002). *Reading Subaltern Studies: Critical Histories, Contested Meanings, and the Globalisation of South Asia.* New Delhi: Permanent Black Publishers/London: Anthem Press.

Mahinda Chinthana: Towards a New Sri Lanka (2005). Election Manifesto of Mahinda Rajapaksa.

Mahinda Chinthana: Vision for a Brighter Future (2010). Election Manifesto of Mahinda Rajapakse.

Malalgoda, Kitsiri (1976). *Buddhism in Sinhalese Society 1750–1900: A Study of Religious Revival and Change.* Berkeley: University of California Press.

Mann, M. (2005). *The Dark side of Democracy: Explaining Ethnic Cleansing.* New York: Cambridge University Press.

Manor, J. (ed.) (1984) *Sri Lanka in Change and Crisis.* London and Sydney: Croom Helm.

——— (1989). *The Expedient Utopian: Bandaranaike and Ceylon.* Cambridge: Cambridge University Press.

Matthews, B. (1978). 'Recent Developments in Sri Lanka Politics'. *Pacific Affairs* 51(1): 84–100

——— (1979). 'The Problem of Communalism in Contemporary Burma and Sri Lanka'. *International Journal* 34(3): 430–56.

——— (1982). 'District Development Councils in Sri Lanka'. *Asian Survey* 22(11): 1117–34.

——— (1986). 'Radical Conflict and the Rationalization of Violence in Sri Lanka'. *Pacific Affairs* 59(1): 28–44.

——— (1988). 'Sinhala Cultural and Buddhist Patriotic Organizations in Contemporary Sri Lanka'. *Pacific Affairs* 61(4): 620–63.

——— (1990). 'Sri Lanka in 1989: Peril and Good Luck'. *Asian Survey* 30(2): 144–49.

——— (2004). 'Tightening Social Cohesion and Excluding "Others" among the Sinhalese'. In S. H. Hasbullah and B. M. Morrison (eds.), *Sri Lankan Society in an Era of Globalization Struggling to Create a New Social Order*, 85–101. New Delhi: Sage Publications.

Marx, Karl. (1981). *A Contribution to the Critique of Political Economy*. Cambridge, London, New York, New Rochelle, Melbourne, Sydney: Cambridge University Press.

Max-Neef, Manfred A. (2005). 'Foundations of Transdisciplinary'. *Ecological Economics* 53(1): 5–16.

Medina, L. F. and S. Stokes (2002). 'Clientelism as Political Monopoly'. www.ccd.uchicago.edu/MedinaStokesAPSA.pdf (accessed on 14 April 2008).

McGilvray, Dennis, B. (2010). 'Sri Lankan Muslims: Between Ethno-nationalism and the Global Umma'. *Nations and Nationalisms* 17(1): 45–64.

McGinty, R. (2008). 'Indigenous Peace-Making versus the Liberal Peace'. *Cooperation and Conflict* 43(2): 139–63.

McCourt, Willy (2007a). *Human Factor in Governance, Managing Public Employees in Africa and Asia*. New York: Palgrave McMillan.

——— (ed.) (2007b). 'Impartiality through Bureaucracy? A Sri Lankan Approach to Managing Values'. *Journal of International Development* 19(3): 429–42.

——— (No date). 'Finding a Way Forward on Public Employment Reform: A Sri Lankan case Study'. Institute for Development Policy and Management, University of Manchester, Manchester.

McGrail, Richard. 'Subaltern Studies: A Conversation with Partha Chatterjee'. *Cultural Anthropology*. https://journal.culanth.org/index.php/ca/subaltern-studies-partha-chatterjee (accessed on 18 June 2020).

Migdal, J. S. (2001). *State in Society: Studying How State and Societies Transform and Constitute Each Other*. Cambridge: Cambridge University Press.

——— (2002). *State in Society: Studying How States and Societies Transform and Constitute One Another*. New York: Cambridge University Press.

Migdal, J. S., Atul Kohli and Vivienne Shue (eds.) (1994). *State Power and Social Forces: Domination and Transformation in the 3rd World*. Cambridge: Cambridge University Press.

Ministry of National Policies and Economic Affairs (2016). *National Human Resources Development Council of Sri Lanka: Annual Report*. Colombo: Ministry of National Policies and Economic Affairs.

Mohammed, Nadir A. L. (1999). *Civil Wars and Military Expenditures: A Note*. Washington, DC: The World Bank.

Moore, M. (1985). *The State and Peasant Politics in Sri Lanka*. Cambridge: Cambridge University Press.

―― (1989). 'The Ideological History of the Sri Lankan Peasantry'. *Modern Asian Studies* 23(1): 179–207.

――(1990). 'Economic Liberalization versus Political Pluralism in Sri Lanka?' *Modern Asian Studies* 24(2): 341–83.

―― (1993). 'Thoroughly Modern Revolutionaries: The JVP in Sri Lanka'. *Modern Asian Studies* 27(3): 593–642.

―― (1997a). 'Leading the Left to the Right: Populist Coalitions and Economic Reform'. *World Development* 25(7): 1009–28.

―― (1997b). 'The Identity of Capitalists and the Legitimacy of Capitalism: Sri Lanka since Independence'. *Development and Change* 28 (2): 331–66.

Morton, A. D. 'New Follies on the State of Globalization Debate?' *Review of the International Studies* 30(1): 133–47.

Mouffe, C. (ed.) (1979). *Gramsci and Marxist Theory*. London: Routledge and Kegan Paul.

――(2005). *On the Political: Thinking in Action*. London: Routledge.

―― (2013). 'Hegemony and Ideology in Gramsci (1979)'. In James Martin (ed.). *Hegemony, Radical Democracy and the Political*, 15–44. New York and London: Routledge.

Murshed, S. M. (2010). *Explaining Civil Wars: A Rational Choice Approach*. Cheltenham, UK, and Northampton, MA: Edward Elgar Publishing Ltd.

Nanayakkara, V. K. (2006). 'From Dominion to Republican Status: Dilemmas of Constitution Making in Sri Lanka'. *Public Administration and Development* 26(5): 425–37.

Nandi, P. (2000). 'Visions of Nationhood and Religiosity among Early Freedom Fighters in India'. In S. L. Sharma and T. K. Oommen (eds.), *Nation and National Identity in South Asia*, 135–50. New Delhi: Orient Longman Limited.

Naurath, N. (2007). 'Sri Lanka's Hope for Peace Dwindles'. https://news.gallup.com/poll/28573/Sri-Lankans-Hope-Peace-Dwindles.aspx (accessed on 11 June 2010).

Nesiah, D. (2001). *Tamil Nationalism*. Colombo: Marga Institute.

Nicholas, R. W. (1977). 'Factions: A Comparative Analysis'. In S. W. Schmidt (ed.), *Friends, Followers and Factions*. Berkeley: University of California Press.

Niemann, M. (2007). 'War Making and State Making in Central Africa'. *Africa Today* 53(3): 21–39.

Nigam, A. (1999). 'Marxism and the Postcolonial World: Footnote to a long March, Economic and political Weekly, 34(1/2).

Nimni, E. (1991) *Marxism and Nationalism: Theoretical Origins of a Political Crisis*. London: Pluto Press.
Nissan, E. (1997) 'History in the Making: Anuradhapura and the Sinhala Buddhist Nation'. in H. L. Seneviratne (ed.), *Identity, Consciousness and the Past: Forging of Caste and Community in India and Sri Lanka*, 23–41. Delhi: Oxford University Press.
Nye, J. S. (1967). 'Corruption and Political Development: A Cost–Benefit Analysis'. *American Poltical Science Review* 61(2): 417–27.
OECD-DAC (2008). 'State Building in Situations of Fragility: Initial Findings'. OECD, Paris.
―――― (2011). *Supporting Statebuilding in Situations of Fragility and Conflict: Policy Guidance*. DAC Guidelines and Reference Series. Paris: OECD.
O'Gorman, F. (2001). 'Patronage and the Reform of the State in England, 1700–1860'. In S. Piattoni (ed.), *Clientelism, Interests and Democratic Representation: The European Experience in Historical and Comparative Perspective*, 54–76. Cambridge: Cambridge University Press.
Oberst, R. (1986). 'Administrative Conflict and Decentralization: The Case of Sri Lanka'. *Public Administration and Development* 6: 163–74.
Obeysekara, G. (1967). *Land Tenure in Village Ceylon*. London: Cambridge University Press.
―――― (1979). 'The Vicissitudes of the Sinhala-Buddhist Identity through Time and Change'. In M. Roberts (eds.), *Collective Identities, Nationalisms and Protest in Modern Sri Lanka*, 279–314. Colombo: Marga Institute.
Obeysekara, G. (2002). 'Buddhism, Nationhood and Cultural Identity: The Premodern and Pre-Colonial Formations'. Lecture delivered at the Course on Ethnicity, Identity and Conflict, ICES Auditorium, Colombo, 9 August (printed version by ICES, January 2004).
Orlikowski, W. J. and J. J. Baroudi (1991). 'Studying Information Technology in Organizations: Research Approaches and Assumptions'. *Information Systems Research* 2(1): 1–28.
Paris, R. (2004). *At War's End: Building Peace after Civil Conflict*. Cambridge: Cambridge University Press.
Pasha, M. K. (1996). 'Security as Hegemony'. *Alternatives: Global, Local and Political*. 21(3): 283–302.
Patnaik, A.K. (1988). 'Gramsci's Concept of Common Sense: Towards a Theory of Subaltern Conciousness in Hegemony Processes'. *Economic and Political Weekly* 23(5): 2–10.

Patton, M. Q. (2002). *Qualitative Research and Evaluation Methods*, 3rd edn. Thousand Oaks, CA: Sage Publications.

Paulantzas, N. (1973). 'On Social Classes'. *New Left Review* 1(78). https://newleftreview.org/issues/i78/articles/nicos-poulantzas-on-social-classes (accessed on 20 June 2008).

Peebles, P. (1973). 'The Transformation of Colonial Elite: The Mudliyars of Nineteenth Century Ceylon'. MPhil dissertation, University of Chicago.

——— (1991). 'Colonization and Ethnic Conflict in the Dry Zone of Sri Lanka'. *Journal of Asian Studies* 49(1): 30–55.

——— (1993). 'Review: *Electoral Allegiances in Sri Lanka* (1992) by Dilesh Jayantha'. *Pacific Affairs* 66(3): 444–45.

Perera, S. (1995). *Living with Tortures and Other Essays of Intervention: Sri Lankan Society, Culture and Politics in Perspective*. Colombo: ICES.

——— (ed.) (1996). *Newton Gunasinghe: Selected Essays*. Colombo: Social Scientists' Association.

——— (1997). 'Political Violence, Structural Amnesia and Lack of Remorse'. *Pravada* 5(1): 11–13.

——— (2021). 'Social Sciences and Humanities in Sri Lanka'. *Sunday Observer*, 28 March.

Persson, T., G. Tabellini and Franco Trebbi (2003). 'Electoral Rules and Corruption'. *European Economic Association* 1(4): 958–89.

Pfaff-Czarnecka J., D. Rajasingham-Senanayake, A. Nandy and E.T. Gomez (1999). *Ethnic Futures: The State and Identity Politics in Asia*. New Delhi: Sage Publications.

Phandis, U. (1976). *Religion and Politics in Sri Lanka*. New Delhi: Dhawan Printing Works.

Piattoni, S. (2001). *Clientelism, Interests and Democratic Representation: The European Experience in Historical and Comparative Perspective*. New York: Cambridge University Press.

Pieris, Anoma (2019). *Sovereignty, Space and Civil War in Sri Lanka: Porous Nation*. Oxon and New York: Routledge.

Pieris, G. H. (1978). 'Land Reform and Agrarian Change in Sri Lanka'. *Modern Asian Studies* 12(4): 611–28.

——— (2006). *Sri Lanka: Challenges of the New Millennium*. Colombo: Kandy Books.

Pieris, G. (1999). 'Insurrection and Youth Unrest in Sri Lanka'. In K. M. De Silva, S. W. R. De A. Samarasinghe and Law and Society Trust, *History and Poltics: Millenium Perspectives—Essays in Honor of Kingsley De Silva*, 165–200. Colombo: Law and Society Trust.

Plattner, M. F. (2010). 'Populism, Pluralism and Liberal Democracy'. *Journal of Democracy* 21(1): 81–92.

Polychroniou, C. (2001). 'An Interview with Erik Olin Wright'. www.ssc.wisc.edu/~wright/Polyc-int.PDF (accessed on 19 September 2010).

Prazauskas, A. (1998). 'Ethnicity, Nationalism and Politics'. ISS Working Paper Series, No. 280, Institute of Social Sciences, The Hague.

Raheem, M. (2010). 'Post War Muslim Minority Party Politics: Surviving Political Quietus'. www.groundviews.org/2010/04/09/post-war-muslim-minority-party-politics-surviving-the- political-quietus (accessed on 12 December 2011).

Rajasingham-Senanayake, D. (2003). 'Beyond Institution and Constitution Building: Linking Post/Conflict Reconstruction and Deep Democracy'. In M. Mayer, Darini Rajasingham- Senanayake and Yuvi Thangarajah (eds.), *Building Local Capacities for Peace: Rethinking Conflict and Development in Sri Lanka*, 107–31. New Delhi: McMillan.

——— (2011a). 'Is Post-War Sri Lanka Following the "Military Business Model"?' *Economic and Political Weekly* 46(14): 27–30.

——— (2011b). 'Lanka @ 63: The Military Business Model of Post-war Economic Development'. 26 February. https://groundviews.org/2011/02/27/lanka-63-the-%E2%80%98military-business-model%E2%80%99-of-post-war-economic-development/ (accessed on 18 February 2012).

Rambukwella, H. (2018). 'Anagarika Dharmapala: The Nation and Its Place in the World'. In *Politics and Poetics of Authenticity: A Cultural Genealogy of Sinhala Nationalism*, 48–72. London: UCL Press.

Rampton, David (2011). '"Deeper Hegemony": The Politics of Sinhala Nationalist Authenticity and the Failures of Power-sharing in Sri Lanka'. *Commonwealth and Comparative Politics* 49(2): 245–273.

Ramsbotham, O., T. Woodhouse and H, Miall (eds.) (2009). *Contemporary Conflict Resolution*, 2nd edn. Cambridge, MA: Polity Press.

Ranugge, S. (2000). 'State, Bureaucracy and Development'. In S. Hettige, and M. Mayer (eds.), *Sri Lanka at Crossroads: Dilemmas and Prospects after 50 Years of Independence*, 50–62. Delhi: Macmillan.

Rayner, M., P. Scarborough and S. Allender (2006). 'Values underlying the National Service Framework for Coronary Heart Disease in England: A Discourse Analysis'. *Journal of Health Services Research and Policy* 11(2): 67–73.

Redcliffe-Brown, A. R. (1940). *Structure and Function in Primitive Society: Essays and Addresses*. London: Cohen and West.

Riaz, Ali. (2021). *Religion and Politics in South Asia*, 2nd edn. London: Routledge.

Rischardson, J. M. (2005). *Paradise Poisoned: Learning about Conflict, Terrorism and Development from Sri Lanka's Civil Wars*. Kandy: International Centre for Ethnic Studies.

Richmond, O. P. (2006). 'The Problem of Peace: Understanding the Problem of "Liberal Peace"'. *Conflict, Security and Development* 6(3): 291–314.

——— (2014). *Failed Statebuilding: Intervention, the State, and the Dynamics of Peace Formation*. New Haven and London: Yale University Press.

——— (2020). 'Interventionary Order and Its Methodologies: The Relationship between Peace and Intervention'. *Third World Quarterly* 41(2): 207–27.

Riesman, Catherine K. (1993). *Narrative Analysis*. Newbury Park, London and New Delhi: Sage Publications.

Roberts, M. (1974). 'Problems of Social Stratification and the Demarcation of National and Local Elites in the British Ceylon'. *Journal of Asian Studies* 33(4): 549–77.

——— (ed.) (1979). *Collective Identities, Nationalisms and Protest in Modern Sri Lanka*. Colombo: Marga Institute.

——— (1982). *Caste Conflict and Elite Formation: The Rise of Karava Elite in Sri Lanka 1500–1931*. Cambridge: Cambridge University Press.

——— (1994). *Exploring Confrontation: Sri Lanka: Politics, Culture and History*. Chur: Harwood Academic Publishers.

——— (2000). 'Himself and Project: A Serial Autobiography—Our Journey with A Zealot, Anagarika Dharmapala'. *Social Analysis: The International Journal of Anthropology* 44(1): 113–14.

——— (2001). *Burden of History: Obstacles to Power Sharing in Sri Lanka*. Colombo: Marga Institute.

——— (2005). *Narrating Tamil Nationalism: Subjectivities and Issues*. Colombo: Vijitha Yapa Publications.

——— (2010). 'Caste in Modern Sri Lankan Politics'. Thuppahi's Blog, 24 February. https://thuppahis.com/2010/02/23/caste-in-modern-sri-lankan-politics/ (accessed on 14 April 2010).

Roberts, Peter and Michael A. Peters. (2003). *Neoliberalism, Higher Education and Research*. Rotterdam: Sense Publishers.

Robinson, J. A. and T. Verdier (2003). 'The Political Economy of Clientelism'. Unpublished paper. www.scholar.harvard.edu/jrobinson/publications/political-economy-clientelism (accessed on 12 June 2011).

Rogers J. D. (2004). 'Caste as a Social Category and Identity in Colonial Lanka'. *Indian Economic Social History Review* 41(1): 51–77.

—— (2005). 'Prospects and Problems in Sri Lankan Studies'. www.aisls.org/pdfs/2005prob-prospects.pdf (accessed on 10 January 2009.

Rogers J. D., J. Spencer and J. Uyangoda (eds.) (1998). 'Sri Lanka: Political Violence and Ethnic Conflict'. *Journal of American Psychologist* 53(7): 771–77.

Roniger, L. (2004). 'Political Clientelism, Democracy, and Market Economy'. *Comparative Politics* 36(3): 353–75.

Ross, Rupert (1996). *Returning to the Teachings: Exploring Aboriginal Justice*. Toronto: Penguin Books.

Rotberg, R. I. (ed.) (1999). *Creating Peace in Sri Lanka: Civil War and Reconciliation*. Washington, DC: Brooking Institute Press.

Rothman, S. (1971). 'Functionalism and Its Critics: An Analysis of the Writings of Gabriel Almond'. *Political Science Reviewer* 1(1): 236–76.

Rupasinghe, K. 'The Rajapakse Presidency: Consequences for the Peace Process'. *Polity* 3(1/2): Colombo: Social Scientists' Association.

—— (2006). 'Analysis of the Implementation of the Ceasefire Agreement'. In *Envisioning New trajectories for Peace in Sri Lanka*.Maharagama: CJPD and Ravaya Publication.

Ryan, B. (1953). *Caste in Modern Ceylon: The Sinhalese System in Transition*. New Brunswick: Rutgers University Press.

Sabaratnam, L. (2001). *Ethnic Attachments in Sri Lanka: Social Change and Cultural Continuity*. New York: Palgrave.

Sabaratnam, T. (No date). 'Out of Bondage: The Thondaman Story'. http://www.lankalibrary.com/pol/thondaman.htm (accessed on 14 February 2010).

Sadowski, Y. (1998). 'Ethnic Conflict'. *Foreign Policy* 111(Summer): 12–23. DOI:10.2307/1149375.

Salam, R. (2000). 'The Confounding State: Public Ignorance and the Politics of Identity'. *Critical Review* 14(2/3): 299–325.

Samaranayake, G. (1987). 'The Changing Attitude towards the Tamil Problem within the Janatha Vimukthi Peramuna (J.V.P.)'. In C. Abeysekara and N. Gunasinghe (eds.), *Facets of Ethnicity in Sri Lanka*, 272–97. Colombo: Social Scientists' Association.

Samarasinghe, S. W. R. De A. (1994). 'The Parliamentary Elections in Sri Lanka: A Vote for Good Governance'. *Asian Survey* 34(12): 1019–22.

Samaratunge, Ramanie and Lynne Bennington. (2002). 'New Public Management: Challenge for Sri Lanka'. *Asian Journal of Public Administration* 24(1): 87–109.

Samaraweera, V. (1981). 'Land, Labor, Capital and Sectional Interests in the National Politics of Sri Lanka'. *Modern Asian Studies* 15(1): 127–62.

Sambandan V.S. (2000). 'The Fall of Elephant Pass'. *Frontline*, 29 April, 17(9). https://frontline.thehindu.com/world-affairs/article30253885.ece (accessed 20 April 2010).

Sambanis, N. (2004). 'What Is Civil War? Conceptual and Empirical Complexities on an Operational Definition'. *Journal of Conflict Resolution* 48(6): 814–58.

Sarvananthan, M. (2016). 'Elusive Economic Peace Dividend in Sri Lanka: All That Glitters Is Not Gold'. *GeoJournal* 81: 571–96.

Schaffer, H. (1995). 'The Sri Lankan Elections of 1994: The Chandrika Factor'. *Asian Survey* 35(5): 409–25.

Schaffer, T. (1999). 'Peacemaking in Sri Lanka: The Kumaratunga Initiative'. In R. I. Rotberg (ed.), *Creating Peace in Sri Lanka: Civil War and Reconciliation*, 132–41. Washington, DC: Brooking Institute Press.

Schwarzmantel, J. (2005). 'Challenging Neo-Liberal Hegemony'. *Contemporary Politics* 11(2–3): 85–98.

Scott, J. (1969). 'Corruption, Machine Politics and Political Change'. *American Political Science Review* 63(4): 42–59.

——— (1990). *Domination and the Arts of Resistance: Hidden Transcripts*. Ann Arbor: Yale University Press.

——— (1996). 'Religion in Colonial Society: Buddhism and Modernity in 19th Century Sri Lanka'. *Cultural Dynamics* 8(1): 7–23.

——— (1999). *Refashioning Futures: Criticism after Postcoloniality*. Princeton, NJ: Princeton University Press.

Selvanathan, Saroja and Eliyathamby A. Selvanathan (2014). 'Defence Expenditure and Economic Growth: A Case Study of Sri Lanka using Causality Analysis'. *International Journal of Development and Conflict* 4(2): 69–76.

Sen, A. (1988). 'The Frontiers of the Prison Notebooks'. *Economic and Political Weekly* 23(5): 31–36.

Seneviratne, B. (2001). *The Broken Palmyra: A Collection of Essays*. Jaffna: UTHR, University of Jaffna.

Seneviratne, H. L. (1997). 'Identity and the Conflation of Past and Present'. In H. L. Seneviratne (ed.), *Identity, Consciousness and the Past: Forging of Caste and Community in India and Sri Lanka*, 3–41. Delhi: Oxford University Press.

——— (1999). *The Work of Kings: The New Buddhism in Sri Lanka*. Chicago: The University of Chicago Press.

Shanmugaratnam, N. (1993). 'The National Question and Obstacles to Peace in Sri Lanka: Some Reflections'. *Pravada* 2(5): 15–18.

——— (2007). 'Interrogating an Obscured Legacy'. In R. Vaitheespara (ed.), *Theorizing the National Crisis: Sanmugathasan, the Left and the Ethnic Conflict in Sri Lanka*, 1–10. Colombo: Social Scientists' Association.

Sharma, S. L. and T. K. Oommen (eds.) (2000). *Nation and National Identity in South Asia*. New Delhi: Orient Longman Limited.

Shastri, A. (1990). 'The Material Basis for Separatism: The Tamil Eelam Movement in Sri Lanka'. *Journal of Asian Studies* 49(1): 56–77.

——— (1992). 'Sri Lanka's Provincial Council System: A Solution to the Ethnic Problem?' *Asian Survey* 32(8): 723–43.

Shastri, A. and A. J. Wilson (eds.) (2001). *Post-Colonial States of South Asia: Democracy, Development and Identity*. New York: Palgrave.

Shefner, J. (2001). 'Coalitions and Clientelism in Mexico'. *Theory and Society* 30(5): 593–628.

Shefter, M. (1994). *Political Parties and the State: The American Historical Experiences*. Princeton, NJ: Princeton University Press.

Shils, Edward A. and Henry A. Finch (eds.) (2011). *Methodology of Social Sciences*. New Brunswick, NJ: Transaction Publishers.

Sim, S. F. (2006). 'Hegemonic Authoritarianism and Singapore: Economics, Ideology and the Asian Economic Crisis'. *Journal of Contemporary Asia* 36(2): 143–59.

Sivatamby, K. (2004). 'The Sri Lankan Ethnic Conflict: A Tamil Perspective'. Sri Lanka: Marga Institute.

Somasundaram.M. (ed.) (2000). *Constitution 2000: Parliamentary Debates*. Colombo: Ethnic Affairs and National Integration Division, Sri Lanka.

Sorensen, G. (2001). 'War and State Making: Why Doesn't It Work in the Third World?' Failed Conference, Florence, 10–14 April.

Sotiris, Panagiotis. (2018). 'Gramsci and the Challenges for the Left: The Historical Bloc as a Strategic Concept'. *Science and Society* 82(1): 94–119.

Spiro, H. J. (1967). 'Review of *Comparative Politics: A Developmental Approach* by Gabriel Almond and G. Bingham Powell Jr.' *Journal of Politics* 29(4): 903–05.

Spencer, J. (2000). 'On Not Becoming a Terrorist: Problems of Memory, Agency and Community in Sri Lankan Conflict'. In V. Das, Arthus Kleinman, Mamphela Ramphele and Pamela Reynolds (eds.), *Violence and Subjectivity*, 120–40. Berkeley and London: The Regents of the University of California Press.

——— (2002). 'The Vanishing Elite: The Political and Cultural Work of Nationalist Revolution in Sri Lanka'. In C. Shore and S. Nugent (eds.), *Elite Cultures: Anthropological Perspectives*, 91–109. London: Routledge.

——— (2007). *Anthropology, Politics and the State: Democracy and Violence in South Asia*, Cambridge: Cambridge University Press.

——— (2008). 'A Nationalism without Politics? The Illiberal Consequences of Liberal Institutions in Sri Lanka'. *Third World Quarterly* 29(3): 611–29.

——— (2016). 'Securitization and Its Discontents: The End of Sri Lanka's Long Post-war?' *Contemporary South Asia* 24(1): 94–108.

——— (ed.) (1990). *Sri Lanka: History and Roots of Conflict*. London: Routledge.

Spencer, J., R. Handler, B. Kapferer, R. Khare, D. McGilvray, G. Obeyesekere and M. Southwold (1990). 'Writing Within: Anthropology, Nationalism, and Culture in Sri Lanka'. *Current Anthropology* 31(3): 283–300.

Srinivas, R. and S. Crabtree (2005). 'Sri Lankan Maintains Hope in the Midst of Chaos'. https://news.gallup.com/poll/22678/sri-lankans-maintain-hope-midst-chaos.aspx (accessed on 2 February 2009).

Standing G. (2011). *The Precariat: The New Dangerous Class*. London, New York, New Delhi and Sydney: Bloomsbury Academic.

Stedman, S. J. (1997). 'Spoiler Problems in Peace Processes'. *International Security* 22(2): 4–53.

Stedman, S. J., Donald Rothchild and Elizabeth M. Cousens (eds.) (2002). *Ending Civil Wars: Implementation of Peace Agreements*. Boulder, CO: Lynne Reinier Publishers Inc.

Stokke, K. (2010). 'Liberal Peace in Question: The Sri Lankan Case'. In K. Stokke and J. Uyangoda (eds.), *Liberal Peace in Question: Politics of State and Market Reform in Sri Lanka*, 1–34. London, New York and Delhi: Anthem Press.

Strinati, D. (1995). *An Introduction to Theories of Popular Culture*. London: Routledge.

Swaris, N. (1973). 'Traditionalism and Patronage in Sinhalese Society'. Unpublished MA thesis, Institute of Social Studies, The Hague.

Szeftel, M. (2000). 'Clientelism, Corruption and Catastrophe'. *Review of African Political Economy* 27(85): 427–41.

Tambiah, S. J. (1986). *Sri Lanka: Ethnic Fratricide and the Dismantling of Democracy*. London: Tauris.

——— (1989). 'Ethnic Conflict in the World Today'. *American Ethnologist* 16(2): 335–49.

——— (1992). *Buddhism Betrayed: Religion, Politics and Violence in Sri Lanka*. Chicago and London: The University of Chicago Press.
Taylor, B. D and R. B. Tilly (2008). 'Tilly Tally: War-Making and State-Making in Contemporary Third World'. *International Studies Review* 10: 27–56.
Taylor, Michael (ed.) (2008). *Rationality and Revolution*, Cambridge, New York, Paris: Cambridge University Press.
Tennakoon, N. S. (1988). 'Rituals of Development: The Accelerated Mahaweli Development Program of Sri Lanka'. *American Ethnologist* 5(2): 294–310.
Thangarajah, C. Y. 2000. 'The Genealogy of Tamil Nationalism in Post-Independent Sri Lanka'. In S. T. Hettige and M. Mayer (eds.), *Sri Lanka at Crossroads: Dilemmas and Prospects after 50 Years of Independence*, 119–36. New Delhi: Macmillan.
Thangarajah, Yuvi (2003). 'Ethnicization of the Devolution Debate and the Militarization of Civil Society in North-Eastern Sri Lanka'. In M. Mayer, D. Rajasingham-Senanayake and Y. Thangarajah (eds.), *Building Local Capacities for Peace: Rethinking Conflict and Development in Sri Lanka*, 13–36. New Delhi: Macmillan.
Theis, C. G. (2005). 'War, Rivalry and the State Building in Latin America'. *American Journal of Political Science* 49(3): 451–65.
Thiranagama S. (2011). *In My Mother's House: Civil War in Sri Lanka*. Philadelphia, PA: University of Pennsylvania Press.
——— (2018). 'The Civility of Strangers? Caste, Ethnicity, and Living Together in Postwar Jaffna, Sri Lanka'. *Anthropological Theory* 18(2–3): 357–81. https://doi.org/10.1177/1463499617744476.
Thiruchelvam, N. (1984a). 'Ethnicity and Resource Allocation'. In R. B. Goldmann and A. J. Wilson (eds.), *From Independence to Statehood: Managing Ethnic Conflict in Five African and Asian States*, 185–95. London: Palgrave Macmillan.
Thiruchelvam, N. (1984b). *The Ideology of Popular Justice in Sri Lanka: A Social–Legal Inquiry*. New Delhi: Vikas.
——— (1984c). 'The Politics of Decentralization and Devolution: Competing Concepts of District Development Councils'. In R. B. Goldmann and A. J. Wilson (eds.), *From Independence to Statehood: Managing Ethnic Conflict in Five African and Asian States*. Palgrave Macmillan.
——— (1999a). *Neelan Thiruchelvam: Selected Writings*. Colombo: International Centre for Ethnic Studies.
——— (1999b). 'Devolution and the Elusive Quest for Peace in Sri Lanka'. In R. I. Rotberg (ed.), *Creating Peace in Sri Lanka: Civil War and Reconciliation*. Washington, DC: Brookings Institution Press.

Tilly, C. (1985). 'War Making and State Making as Organized Crime'. In P. Evans, D. Rueschemeyer and T. Skocpol (eds.), *Bringing the State Back*, 169–91. Cambridge: Cambridge University Press.
—— (1990). *Coercion, Capital, and European States, AD 990–1990*. Cambridge, MA: B. Blackwell.
Tilly, C. and Gabriel Ardant (eds.) (1975). *The Formation of National States in Western Europe*. Princeton, NJ: Princeton University Press.
Tompson, W. (2007). 'From "Clientelism" to a "Client Centered Orientation"? The Challenges of Public Administration Reform in Russia'. Economic Department Working Papers No.536, OECD.
Transparency International (2008). *Corruption Perception Index 2008*. http://archive.transparency.org/policy_research/surveys_indices/cpi/2008 (accessed on 9 June 2010).
—— (2005). 'Mega Cabinets in Sri Lanka: Perceptions and Implications', Report 1. Colombo, Sri Lanka. http://www.tisrilanka.org/pub/pp/pdf/megacabengpospaper.pdf (accessed on 9 June 2010).
Transparency International, Cambridge University Press and Ernst and Young (2009). *Global Corruption Report 2009: Corruption and the Private Sector*. Cambridge: Cambridge University Press.
Urbinati, N. (1998). 'From the Periphery of Modernity: Antonio Gramsci's Theory of Subordination and Hegemony'. *Political Theory* 6(3): 370–91.
Uyangoda, J. (1991). 'Impeachment and the Constitutional Crisis'. *Pravada* 1(1): 6–9.
—— (1993). 'Premadasa as President: A Posthumous Assessment'. *Pravada* 2(4): 5–8.
—— (1997a). 'Academic Texts on the Sri Lankan Ethnic Question as Biographies of a Decaying Nation-state'. *Nethra* 1(3): 7–23.
—— (1997b). 'Local Bodies as Domains of Localized Power'. *Pravada* 5(1): 5–10.
—— (2000). 'Post-Independence Social Movements in Post-Independent Sri Lanka'. In W. D. Lakshman and C.A. Tisdell (eds.), *Sri Lanka's Development since Independence: Socio-Economic Perspectives and Analysis*, 61–76. New York: Nova Science Publishers, Inc.
—— (2003). 'Social Conflict, Radical Resistance and Projects of State Power in Southern Sri Lanka: The case of the JVP'. In Markus Mayer, Darini Rajasingham-Senanayake and Yuvi Thangarajah (eds.), *Building Local Capacities for Peace: Rethinking Conflict and Development in Sri Lanka*, 37–76. London: Macmillan.

―――― (2005). *Ethnic Conflict, Ethnic Imagination and Democratic Alternatives for Sri Lanka*. Colombo: Social Scientists' Association.

―――― (2006a). *Dakune Kerella and Sri Lankave Keralikara Deshapalaneye Anagathaya*. Colombo: Social Scientists' Association.

―――― (2006b). *Jathika Chinthanaye Ghanadura*. Colombo: Social Scientists' Association.

―――― (ed.) (2008). *The Way We Are: Politics of Sri Lanka 2007–2008*. Colombo: Social Scientists' Association.

―――― (2006c). 'Sri Lanka's Ethnic Conflict: Root Causes'. In Centre for Just Peace and Democracy, *Envisioning New trajectories for Peace in Sri Lanka*. Luzern: CJPD and Ravaya Publication.

―――― (2007a). 'Ethnic Conflict in Sri Lanka: Changing Dynamics'. *Policy Studies* 32. Washington D.C.: East-West Centre.

―――― (ed.) (2007b). *Religion in Context: Buddhism and Socio-Political Change in Sri Lanka*. Colombo: Social Scientists' Association.

―――― (2007c). 'Sri Lanka: Back to Square One?' *Economic and Political Weekly* 42(24): 1800–01

―――― (2008a). 'Gangsterism: It's Political Sociology'. In Uyangoda, J. (ed.), *Matters of Violence: Reflections on Social and Political Violence in Sri Lanka*, 113–15. Colombo: Social Scientists' Association.

―――― (2008b). 'Local Bodies as Domains of Localized Power'. In J. Uyangoda (ed.), *Matters of Violence: Reflection on Social and Political Violence in Sri Lanka*, 71–85. Colombo: Social Scientists' Association.

―――― (2010). *Writing Research Proposals in the Social Sciences and Humanities: A Theoretical and Practical Guide*. Colombo: Social Scientists' Association.

Uyangoda, J. and M. Perera (eds.) (2003*). Sri Lanka's Peace Process 2002: Critical Perspectives*. Colombo: Social Scientists Association.

Van de Walle, N. (2009). 'The Democratization of Political Clientelism in Sub-Sahara Africa'. A paper prepared for delivery at the conference, Democracy and Development in the Middle East, in honour of John Waterbury, at Princeton University, 23 April.

Van Dijk, T. A. (1993). 'Principles of Critical Discourse Analysis'. *Discourse and Society* 4(2): 249–98.

―――― (2002). 'Political Discourse and Political Cognition'. In A. P. Chilton and C. Schafner (eds.), *Politics as Texts and Talk: Analytical Approaches to Political Discourse*, 203–37. Amsterdam: Benjamin.

Venugopal, R. (2008). 'The Politics of Sri Lanka's Janatha Vimukthi Peramuna (JVP)'. Department of International Development, University of Oxford.

——— (2009). 'The Making of Sri Lanka's Post-Conflict Economic Package and the Failure of the 2001–2004 Peace Process'. CRISE Working Paper No.64, Centre for Research on Inequality, Human Security and Ethnicity, Oxford.

——— (2010). 'Business for Peace, or Peace for Business? The Role of Corporate Peace Activism in the Rise and Fall of Sri Lanka's Peace Process'. In K. Ravi Raman and Ronnie D. Lipschutz (eds.), *Corporate Social Responsibility: Comparative Critiques*, 148–64. New York: Macmillan.

——— (2011). 'The Politics of Market Reform at a Time of Civil War: Military Fiscalism in Sri Lanka'. *Economic and Political Weekly* 46(49): 67–75.

——— (2018). *Nationalism, Development and Ethnic Conflict in Sri Lanka*. Cambridge: Cambridge University Press.

Vincente, P. C. and L. Wantchekon (2009). 'Clientelism and Vote Buying: Lessons from Field Experiments in African Elections'. Paper prepared for a special issue of the Oxford Review of Economic Policy in collaboration with iiG. www.iig.ox.ac.uk/output/articles/OxREP/iiG- OxREP-Vicente-Wantchekon.pdf (accessed on 11 October 2010).

Verite Research (2019). 'Sri Lanka: Resolution 30/1 Implementation Monitor: Statistical & Analytical Review No. 4'. https://www.veriteresearch.org/publication/unhrc-resolution-30-1-implementation-monitor-statistical-analytical-review-no-3-2/ (accessed on 9 September 2020).

Volkan, V. D. (2004). *Blind Trust: Large Groups and Their Leaders in Times of Crises and Terror*. Charlottesville, VA: Pitchstone Publishing.

Voss, Karen-Claire (2002). 'Review Essay of Basarab Nicolescu's *Manifesto of Transdisciplinarity*, Albany: State University of New York Press'. http://www.esoteric.msu.edu/Reviews/NicolescuReview.htm (accessed 27 April 2013).

Waldner, D. (1999). *State Building and Late Development*. Ithaca: Cornell University.

Wallensteen, P. (1997). 'Armed Conflicts, Conflict Termination and Peace Agreements, 1989–96'. *Journal of Peace Research* 34(3): 339–58.

Walton, Oliver (2015). 'Framing Disputes and Organizational Legitimation: UK-based Sri Lankan Tamil Diaspora Groups' Use of the "Genocide" Frame since 2009'. *Ethnic and Racial Studies* 38(6): 959–75.

Warnapala, W. A. W. (1972). 'District Agencies of Government Departments in Ceylon'. *International Review of Administrative Sciences* 38(2): 133–40.

——— (1974). 'Sri Lanka in 1973: A Test for Both the Rulers and the Ruled'. *Asian Survey* 14(2): 148–56.

——— (1975). 'The Marxist Parties of Sri Lanka and the 1971 Insurrection'. *Asian Survey* 15(9): 745–57.

——— (1978). 'Sri Lanka 1978: Reversal of Policies and Strategies'. *Asian Survey*. 19(2): 178–90.

——— (1993). *The Sri Lankan Political Scene*. New Delhi: Navarang.

Weber, M. (1964). *The Theory of Social and Economic Organization*. New York: The Free Press.

Weerakoon, B. (2004). *Rendering unto Caesar: A Fascinating Story of One Man's Tenure under Nine Prime Ministers and Presidents of Sri Lanka*. Colombo: Vijitha Yapa Books.

Weerakoon, B. and S. Wanasinghe (1994). *Reflections on Governance*. Colombo: Marga Institute.

Weingrod, A. (1968). 'Patrons, Patronage and Political Parties'. *Comparative Studies in Society and History* 10(4): 377–400.

Weiner, M. (1965). 'The Politics of South Asia'. In G. A. Almond and J. Coleman, *The Politics of the Developing Areas*, 153–246. Princeton, NJ: Princeton University Press.

Wickramaratne, A. (1995). *The Roots of Nationalism in Sri Lanka*. Colombo: Karunaratne and Sons Ltd.

——— (1999). 'Buddhist Nationalism in Sri Lanka: Perceptions, Change and Reality'. In K. M. De Silva, S. W. R. De A. Samarasinghe and Law and Society Trust, *History and Politics: Millenial Perspectives*, 193–224. Colombo: Law and Society Trust.

Wickramasinghe, N. (1995a). *Ethnic Politics in Colonial Sri Lanka, 1927–1947*. New Delhi: Vikas Publication House.

——— (1995b). 'History outside the Nation'. *Economic and Political Weekly* 30(26): 1570–72.

——— (2006). *Sri Lanka in the Modern Age: A History of Contested Identities*. London: C. Hurst & Co. Ltd.

——— 2008). 'Sri Lanka in 2007: Military Successes, but at Humanitarian and Economic Costs'. *Asian Survey* 48 (1): 191–97.

——— (2009). 'After the War: A New Patriotism in Sri Lanka'. *Journal of Asian Studies* 68(4): 1–10.

——— (2010). 'In Sri Lanka: The Triumph of Vulgar Patriotism'. *Current History* 109(729): 158–61. http://www.currenthistory.com/pdf_org_files/109_726_158.pdf (accessed on 14 April 2011).

——— (2014). 'Sri Lanka in 2013: Post-war Oppressive Stability'. *Asian Survey* 54(1): 199–205.

Wickramasinghe, R. (2006). 'Peace Process in Sri Lanka'. *South Asian Survey* 13(5): 5–15.

Wijesinghe, R. (2007). *Declining Sri Lanka: Terrorism and Ethnic Conflict—The Legacy of J. R. Jayawardena (1906–1996)*. New Delhi: Cambridge University Press.

Wijeweera, Albert and Matthew J. Webb (2009). 'Military Spending and Economic Growth in Sri Lanka: A Time Series Analysis'. *Defence and Peace Economics* 20(6): 499–508.

Wijeweera, B. S. (1989). 'Policy Developments and Administrative Changes in Sri Lanka: 1948–1987: Introduction'. *Public Administration and Development* 9(3): 287–300.

Wijeweera, R. (1986). *Demala eelam aragalayata visaduma kumakda?* Pitakotte: Niyamuwa Prakashaka.

Wilson A. J. (1975). *Electoral Politics in an Emergent State: The Ceylon General Election of May 1970*. London: Cambridge University Press.

——— (1980). *Gaullist System in Asia: The Constitution of Sri Lanka*. London: Palgrave Macmillan.

——— (1988). *The Break-up of Sri Lanka: the Sinhalese–Tamil Conflict*. Honolulu: University of Hawaii Press.

——— (2000). *Sri Lankan Tamil Nationalism: Its Origins and Development in the 19th and 20th Centuries*. London: C. Hurst & Co. Ltd.

Wilson, J. (1975). *Electoral Politics in an Emergent State: The Ceylon General Election of May 1970*. London: Cambridge University Press.

——— (1979). 'Review of Michael Roberts, editor, *Documents of the Ceylon National Congress and Nationalist Politics in Ceylon, 1929–1950*, Four Volumes, Department of National Archives, Colombo, Sri Lanka'. *American Historical Journal Review* 84(4): 1131–32.

World Bank (2011). 'From Violence to Resilience: Restoring Confidence and Transforming Institutions'. In *World Development Report 2011: Conflict, Security and Development*, ch. 3. New York, NY: World Bank.

Wriggins, H. W. (1982). 'Sri Lanka in 1981: Year of Austerity, Development Councils and Communal Disorders'. *Asian Survey* 22(2): 171–79.

Xavier, Sujith (2015). 'Looking for "Justice" in All the Wrong Places: An International Mechanism or Multidimensional Domestic Strategy for Mass Human Rights Violations in Sri Lanka?' Osgoode Legal Studies Research Paper Series, 86.

Zaartman, W. I. (ed.) (1995a). *Elusive Peace*. Washington, DC: Brooking Institutions.

——— (ed.) (1995b). *Ripe for Resolution*. New York: New York University Press.

——— (2001). 'The Timing of Peace Initiatives: Hurting Stalemates and Ripe Moments'. *Global Review of Ethnopolitics* 1(1): 8–18.
——— (ed.) (2007). *Peacemaking in International Conflict: Methods and Techniques*. Washington, DC: United States Institute of Peace.
Zarkov, Dubravka (2015). 'Identity Politics of War: Theorising, Policy and Intervention'. In Helen Hintjens and Dubravka Zarkov (eds.), *Conflict, Peace, Security and Development: Theories and Methodologies*. Abingdon, Oxon and New York: Routledge.

NEWSPAPER ARTICLES

Aneez, Shihar and Ranga Sirilal (2010). 'Arrested General "Hell-bent" on Betrayal: Sri Lanka'. Reuters, 9 February. https://www.reuters.com/article/us-srilanka-politics-idUSTRE6180ZM20100209 (accessed on 21 May 2011).
Athas, Iqbal (2007). 'MiGs Loaded with Millions in Mega Frauds'. 12 August. https://www.sundaytimes.lk/070812/Columns/sitreport.html (accessed on 9 June 2009).
Bell. Stewart (2009). 'Sri Lanka Waging a War without Witnesses'. *National Post*, 7 May. https://sunandadeshapriya.wordpress.com/2009/05/08/sri-lanka-waging-a-war-without-witnesses/ (accessed on 21 May 2009).
Business Times Team (2009). 'Political Parties, Companies Must Declare Funding, BT Poll of Accountability of Political Finances'. *Sunday Times*, 13 December. www.sundaytimes.lk/091213/BusinessTimes/bt01.html (accessed on 15 January 2010).
Colombo Telegraph (2021). 'Nandasena Issues Chilling Warning to Opposition: "I Killed Prabhakaran Like a Dog—I Can Become That Person"'. 10 January. https://www.colombotelegraph.com/index.php/nandasena-issues-chilling-warning-to-opposition-i-killed-prabhakaran-like-a-dog-i-can-become-that-person/ (accessed on 19 March 2021).
Daily Mirror (2007). 'Is Sri Lanka Really Ready for the COPE Findings?' 24 May. http://www.colombopage.com/archive.
Daily News (2012). 'Sri Lanka: Women in Politics'. 18 August. http://www.peacewomen.org/news_article.php?id=5218&type=news (accessed on 1 November 2012).
Fernando, R. K. H. M. (2007). 'COPE Report: What Next'. *The Island*, 9 March. http://servesrilanka.blogspot.nl/2007/03/cope-report-what-next.html (accessed on 27 June 2007).

Fuard, Asif (2006). 'The Fraud of Frauds in VAT'. *Sunday Times*, 26 January. http://sundaytimes.lk/060402/news/3.html (accessed on 27 June 2009).

Gunaratne, Natasha (2007). 'Latest COPE Report Identifies Miscreants and Mismanagement: Unlike Past Parliamentary Reports on State Institutions'. *Financial Times*, 3 June. http://www.sundaytimes.lk/070603/FinancialTimes/ft317.html (accessed on 27 June 2009).

Handunnetti, Dilrukshi (2009). 'Anything but "Safe" Zones'. *Sunday Leader*, 10 May. www.thesundayleader.lk, website is now banned, last accessed in 2010.

Lanka News Papers.com (2006). 'Govt. Hunts for CBK Friend Who Made Millions. 28 January. http://www.lankanewspapers.com/news/2006/1/5423.html (accessed on 30 January 2009).

——— (2009). 'Alleged Arms Deals Frauds: All Arms Deals Done by Lanka Logistics Co. Gotabaya Is Its Chairman. 29 November. http://www.lankanewspapers.com/news/2009/11/50676.html (accessed on 1 December 2009).

Reuters (2010). 'WikiLeaks Renews Accusations over Sri Lanka War Crimes'. 2 December. https://www.reuters.com/article/uk-wikileaks-srilanka/wikileaks-renews-accusations-over-sri-lanka-war-crimes-idUKTRE6B16CO20101202 (accessed on 12 December 2010).

Sirilal, Ranga (2010). 'Sri Lanka Tamils Back War-Winning General for President'. Reuters, 2 January. https://www.reuters.com/article/us-srilanka-politics-idUSTRE6051DX20100106 (accessed on 15 January 2010).

Sri Lanka Guardian (2009). 'Sarath Fonseka Hints about His Future Political Plans in Washington—Updated'. 27 October. http://www.srilankaguardian.org/2009/10/sarath-fonseka-hints-about-his-future.html (accessed on 27 October 2009).

Srinivasan, Meera (2020). 'Sri Lanka: Controversial 20th Amendment Passed'. *The Hindu*, 22 October. https://www.thehindu.com/news/international/sri-lanka-controversial-20th-amendment-passed/article32921800.ece (accessed on 20 March 2021).

Sunday Times (2000). 'Military Procurement and Corruption'. 25 June. http://www.sundaytimes.lk/000625/sitrep.html (accessed on 30 June 2000).

——— (2006a). 'Big Fraud and Billion-Rupee Scandal in Latest MiG Deal'. 3 December. http://www.sundaytimes.lk/061203/News/n126.html (accessed on 12 December 2006).

——— (2006b). 'Presidential Commission to Probe Sandagiri's Huge Deals'. 8 January. http://www.sundaytimes.lk/060108/index.html (accessed on 3 March 2006).

——— (2006c). 'Who Was behind the Rs. 892 Million Urea Deal'. 21 May. http://sundaytimes.lk/060521/news/urea.html (accessed on 1 June 2006).

——— (2007a). 'Business: Be Truthful on Corruption'. 3 June. http://www.sundaytimes.lk/070603/FinancialTimes/ft325.html (accessed on 11 November 2009).

——— (2007b). 'Case against CBK: More Respondents Added'. 42(25), 18 November. https://www.sundaytimes.lk/071118/News/news00012.html (accessed on 15 January 2011).

———(2008). 'Chandrika Kumaratunga Should Be Dealt with under the Law'. 3 August. https://www.sundaytimes.lk/080803/News/sundaytimesnews_29.html (accessed 20 June 2009).

———(2009). 'Politicians Selling Beach Land in East". 23 August. http://www.sundaytimes.lk/090823/News/nws_01.html .

The Economist (2007). 'The Worsening War in Sri Lanka'. 7 June.

The Hindu (2019). 'Gotabaya Rajapaksa: Controversial 'War Hero' Who Ended Sri Lanka's 3-Decade-Long Bloody Civil Conflict'. 17 November. https://www.thehindu.com/news/international/gotabaya-rajapaksa-controversial-war-hero-who-ended-sri-lankas-3-decade-long-bloody-civil-conflict/article29998358.ece (accessed on 25 August 2009).

Uyangoda, Jayadeva. 2002. 'Still Waters: Narcissism of Minor Differences'. *Daily News*, 17 August. http://archives.dailynews.lk/2002/08/17/fea02.html (accessed on 21 August 2008).

Venkataraman, K. (2009). 'Rajapaksa Needs to Devolve Powers to Inspire Hope for Moderate Tamils'. *Times of India*, 20 May. https://timesofindia.indiatimes.com/city/chennai/rajapaksa-needs-to-devolve-powers-to-inspire-hope-in-moderate-tamils/articleshow/4552785.cms (accessed on 14 September 2009).

WEBSITES

Batha, Emma. (2005). 'Q & A: Corruption and Aid'. http://www.alertnet.org/thefacts/reliefresources/11315551833.htm (accessed on 18 April 2009).

Commissioner of Elections (1982). 'Presidential Election – 20.10.1982'. https://elections.gov.lk/web/wp-content/uploads/election-results/presidential-elections/PresidentialElections1982.pdf (accessed on 14 April 2022).

COPE (Committee of Public Enterprises) (2011a). 'First Report of the Committee on Public Enterprises of the Parliament of the Democratic

Socialist Republic of Sri Lanka'. 1 December. https://www.parliament.lk/uploads/comreports/COMDOC1032_document.pdf#page=1 (accessed 6 January 2012).

——— (2011b). 'Third Report of the Committee on Public Enterprises of the Parliament of the Democratic Socialist Republic of Sri Lanka'. https://www.parliament.lk/uploads/comreports/COMDOC1032_document.pdf#page=1 (accessed 6 January 2012).

——— (2017). 'First Report of the Committee on Public Enterprises of the Parliament of the Democratic Socialist Republic of Sri Lanka'. 8 February. https://www.parliament.lk/uploads/comreports/COMDOC1032_document.pdf#page=1 (accessed on 6 January 2022).

DCAF (Geneva Centre for the Democratic Control of the Armed Forces) (2010). *Building Integrity and Reducing Corruption in Defence: A Compendium of Best Practices*. Geneva: DCAF.

Department of Census and Statistics (2010–2018). *Population and Housing Survey*. http://www.statistics.gov.lk (accessed on 14 July 2019).

DeVotta, N. (2019). 'Secularism and the Islamophobia Zeitgeist in India and Sri Lanka'. Middle East Institute. https://www.mei.edu/publications/secularism-and-islamophobiazeitgeist-india-and-sri-lanka (accessed on 2 March 2020).

Department of Labour, Government of Sri Lanka (2012–2020). *Annual Reports*. http://www.labourdept.gov.lk/ (accessed on 14 April 2022).

Dias, Wije (2003). 'Bitter Sri Lankan Power Struggle Flares Up over Lotteries Board'. 23 May. http://www.wsws.org/articles/2003/may2003/sril-m23.shtml (accessed on 5 February 2008).

Government of Sri Lanka (2005). *Mahinda Chinthana: Towards a New Sri Lanka*. Colombo: Department of National Planning, Padukka; Ministry of Finance and Planning. https://www.thegef.org/sites/default/files/ncsa-documents/MahindaChintanaTenYearDevelopmentPlan.pdf (accessed 20 May 2008).

——— (2009). 'Sri Lanka: No Time for Ceasefire, Time yet for Surrender – President'. 30 April. https://m.reliefweb.int/report/306685?lang=ru (accessed on 15 July 2009).

Groundviews (2008). 'Rohan Edrisinha on the APRC Proposals and the 13th Amendment to the Constitution'. 30 January. https://groundviews.org/2008/01/30/rohan-edrisinha-on-the-aprc-proposals-and-the-13th-amendment-to-the-constitution/ (accessed on 18 June 2008).

Gunadasa, Saman (2011). 'Sri Lankan Government Boosts Military Spending'. https://www.wsws.org/en/articles/2011/11/slec-n02.html (accessed on 4 May 2012).

Haviland, Charles (2010). 'Where Now for Post-election Sri Lanka?' BBC News, Colombo, 29 January. http://news.bbc.co.uk/2/hi/south_asia/8487405.stm (accessed on 4 March 2010).

HRW (Human Rights Watch) (2019). *World Report 2019: Sri Lanka Events of 2018*. https://www.hrw.org/world-report/2019/country-chapters/sri-lanka (accessed on 19 January 2020).

HRW (Human Rights Watch) (2020). 'Sri Lanka: Repeal Abusive Counterterrorism Law – Uphold Pledges to United Nations, European Union'. 10 January. https://www.hrw.org/news/2020/01/10/sri-lanka-repeal-abusive-counterterrorism-law (accessed 20 January 2020).

ICJ (International Commission of Jurists) (2020). 'Sri Lanka: Newly Adopted 20th Amendment to the Constitution Is Blow to the Rule of Law'. 20 October. https://www.icj.org/sri-lanka-newly-adopted-20th-amendment-to-the-constitution-is-blow-to-the-rule-of-law/ (accessed on 20 November 2020).

LBO (Lanka Business Online) (2010a). 'Sri Lanka Creates More State Jobs, but Costs Mount'. https://www.lankabusinessonline.com/sri-lanka-creates-more-state-jobs-but-costs-mount/ (accessed on 12 May 2011).

——— (2010b). 'Sri Lanka Opposition Says Politicians Could Be Taxed'. 12 January. https://www.lankabusinessonline.com/sri-lanka-opposition-says-politicians-could-be-taxed/ (accessed on 15 March 2010).

Nanayakkara, Wimal (2016). 'Can Sri Lanka Eradicate Poverty and Reduce Income Inequality by 2030?' 3 June. https://www.ips.lk/talkingeconomics/2016/06/03/can-sri-lanka-eradicate-poverty-and-reduce-income-inequality-by-2030/ (accessed on 20 April 2022).

Nesan, K. (2006). 'European Union Ban on LTTE Heightens Danger of War in Sri Lanka'. 2 June. https://www.wsws.org/en/articles/2006/06/sril-j02.html (accessed 20 June 2011).

Nesiah, Devanesan (2010). 'Citizen's Commission: Expulsion of the Northern Muslims by the LTTE in October 1990'. 2 March. https://groundviews.org/2010/03/02/citizens-commission-expulsion-of-the-northern-muslims-by-the-ltte-in-october-1990/ (accessed on 12 April 2010).

Parliament Secretariat (2021). *The Constitution of the Democratic Socialist Republic of Sri Lanka*, revised edn. https://www.parliament.lk/files/pdf/constitution.pdf (accessed on 14 April 2022).

PeaceinSriLanka. 2009. 'Ceasefire Violations, as Ruled by the Monitoring Mission'. www. http://www.peaceinsrilanka.lk/negotiations/slmm-statistics (accessed on 18 September 2009).

Peiris, Pradeep, Sakina Moinudeen and M. Krishmamoorthy (2020). 'Authoritarianism Is No Remedy to the Country's Wounded Democracy'. Groundviews, 14 June. https://groundviews.org/2020/06/14/authoritarianism-is-no-remedy-to-the-countrys-wounded-democracy/ (accessed on 18 March 2021).

Reliefweb 2007. 'Sri Lanka: Tsunami Aid "Missing", Says Anti-corruption Group'. 28 December. https://reliefweb.int/report/sri-lanka/sri-lanka-tsunami-aid-missing-says-anti-corruption-group (accessed 10 January 2010).

Satyendra, Nadesan (2008). 'Yet Again Military Expenditure Took a Lion's Share of Sri Lanka's 2006 Budget'. https://tamilnation.org/tamileelam/aid/#2005 (accessed on 14 December 2008).

Trading Economics. 'Summary: Sri Lanka Inflation Rate'. https://tradingeconomics.com/sri-lanka/inflation-cpi (accessed on 14 April 2022).

Transparency International Sri Lanka (2012). 'MPs Trapped in Bribery Net'. 30 May. https://www.tisrilanka.org/mps-trapped-in-bribery-net/ (accessed on 30 May 2012).

United National Party. *The 2000 Manifesto: This Is Your Future.* https://unitednationalparty.tripod.com/manifesto.htm (accessed on 9 June 2011).

Wickramatunge, Raisa (2018). 'UPDATE: Flip-flopping on Accountability – A Timeline'. 23 March. https://groundviews.org/2018/03/23/update-flip-flopping-on-accountability-a-timeline/ (accessed on 20 March 2019).

Wright, E. O. (2001). 'Interview with Chronis Polychroniou, Reflections on Marxism, Class and Politics'. https://www.ssc.wisc.edu/~wright/Polyc-int.PDF (accessed on 6 December 2008).

INDEX

Accelerated Mahaweli Development Project (AMDP), 149
administrative reforms, 4
agrarian reform in 1972, 18, 128
agrarian services, 178
All Party Representatives Committee (APRC), 19, 262–63
Almond, Gabriel, 6
Ambedkar, 69
anti-colonial nationalism, 62
anti-Western sentiments, 58
ape (our)
   ape (ness), 217
   ape rajaya, 217
   ape syndrome, 217–20
Arunachalam, Ponnambalam, 64
Ashraff, M. H. M, 134, 230, 231, 238
Asian Development Bank (ADB), 19
authoritarianism
   authoritarian politics, 287
   authoritarian populism, 289–94
   Bonaparte style, 226, 228, 230
   global new right, 246
   left-wing, 119
   new right, 244, 246
   populism, 16, 289–94
   right-wing politics, 31, 90–101

Bandaranaike-Chelvanayakam pact, 102
Bandaranaike, Sirimavo, 128, 220n10, 229
Bandaranaike, S. W. R. D., 86, 110n30, 121–22
Barad, Karen, 50
Barth, Federick, 223
Black July, 37, 41, 43–44, 48, 54n6
Bolawattha village, 53n1
Bolshevik Leninist Party, 93
Bourdieu, Pierre, 118
British civil service, 176
British colonial period, 59–60, 62, 125, 174–77
Brow, J., 117
bureaucracy, 4, 31, 71, 82, 173–85, 191–94, 197, 199, 210, 214–15, 217, 219

capitalism
   socialism, 145
   socialist democracy, 189
capitalist transformation, 4
caste
   caste hierarchy, 8, 70, 184
   Durawa, 8
   Goyigama, 8, 82, 115, 154, 188, 259
   Karava, 8, 82, 115

Salagama, 8, 82, 115
Vellala, 8, 64
caste-based patronage, 116–17
celebrities, 213, 240
central state institutions, 177
Ceylon Civil service (Colonial civil service), 175–77, 181–82, 184
Ceylon Labour Party (CLP), 119
Ceylon National Congress (CNC), 118
Ceylon Workers' Congress (CWC), 126, 221n13, 230, 238, 245
Chelvanayagam, S. V. J., 64, 87–88
Cheran, R., 64, 102
China, 16, 22–23, 284, 300n9
chit system, 149
the civil war, 4
class
   bourgeois class, 59–62, 66, 70–71, 77–78, 81–83, 85, 108n5, 110n25, 127, 153
   class analysis, 59
   class awakening, 62
   class-consciousness, 62, 77, 92, 156
   class dynamics, 78, 296
   class-for-itself, 62, 106
   class formation, 297
   class-in-itself, 140
   class interests, 60, 66–68, 73–74, 80, 108
   class relations, 3–4, 29–30, 34, 57, 59, 73, 79–80, 93, 106, 117, 143, 295, 297
   cross class alliance, 72–73, 106, 196
   cross-class coalitions, 106
   dominant class, 24–27, 59, 75, 77–78, 80, 184, 293–94, 296–97
   land-holding class, 84
   local capitalist class, 88, 186
   lower classes, 17, 30–31, 60–62, 64–65, 67–71, 74, 80–81, 84–85, 88, 91–92, 106–07, 113–16, 118–20, 124–26, 130, 136, 141, 154–55, 167–68, 173, 176, 179, 181, 185, 199, 216, 219, 260, 276, 297
   nouveau riche, 82, 115
   oppressed classes, 94
   rural petty bourgeoisie, 54–55n11, 68, 83, 85, 86, 124, 129, 192
   subaltern classes, 25, 295
   torturable class, 130
   upper classes, 60–63, 68, 71, 73–74, 79, 84–85, 105–06, 127, 156, 176, 179, 182
class, ethno-religious nationalism, 75–80
Clawzewitz, Carl Von, 31, 225
coconut cultivation, 178
Colebrook-Cameron Commission (CCC), 175
Collins, C., 175
Colombo consumer price index, 242
'colonial bourgeoisie', 116
colonialism
   anti-colonial, 79, 89
   anti-imperial struggles, 119
   British colonialism, 22, 124
   Dutch colonial rule, 16
   Portuguese, 16, 82, 110n26, 113
   post-colonial, 3, 11–14, 25, 34n15, 39–40, 53, 73, 81, 83, 85–86, 91, 94, 100–01
   pre-colonial, 8, 60, 62–63, 68–70, 113–15, 167
colonial practices, 176
Communist Party, 92–93
conflict
   ethnic conflict, 1–3, 15–16, 33n1, 39–44, 46, 48, 51–52, 96, 134–35, 146, 174, 209, 223, 235, 250, 271n10, 296
   ethno-religious conflict, 107
constitution, 15, 81, 93, 127–28, 145–47, 199, 215–16, 233, 236, 239–40
13th amendment to the constitution, 210, 262, 273n31
17th amendment to the constitution, 214–16, 300n5
18th amendment to the constitution, 198, 216, 290–91, 300n5

INDEX

19th amendment to the constitution, 290–91, 300*n*5
20th amendment to the constitution, 101, 290–91
Donoughmore Constitution (1931–1941), 118–19
first republican, 91, 127, 190, 198
second republican, 146, 171*n*22, 197–98, 210
Soulbury Constitution, 179, 190
Constitutional Bill of 2000, 238, 240
contemporary civil wars, 224
corruption, 2, 131–32, 147–48, 154, 158–59, 161, 163, 165, 171*n*25, 172*n*35, 187, 189, 205, 210–12, 215, 226, 270*n*2, 276, 279–81, 299*n*1
cultural and political rituals, 5
cultural services, 178

decentralisation, 151–52, 209–11
De Mel, Neloufer, 15, 49, 110*n*21, 172*n*34
demography, 7–12
De Silva K.M., 7, 16–17, 46, 62, 70, 101, 103, 112*n*46, 115–16, 118, 120–23, 126, 169*n*2, 170*n*10, 175, 179, 183, 187, 192, 232, 279
development
  dry-zone, 114
  dry zone land settlements, 114
  economic development, 11, 17–19, 39, 65–67, 90, 109*n*14, 138, 157, 166, 169*n*7, 175, 178, 186, 188, 191, 196, 209, 241–44, 246, 253, 282, 298
  Kandyan peasantry, 114, 178
  rural poverty, 17–18, 143
Dharmapala, Anagarika, 65–72, 78–79, 86, 89, 99, 105, 109*n*12
District Development Councils (DDC), 18, 151–52, 199, 209–10, 221*n*14
Donoughmore Commission (1931), 177
Donoughmore Constitution, 118–19, 135, 176–77

Dudley-Chelvanayakam pact, 102
Dunham, D., 117
dynastic politics, 4

early anti-colonial leadership, 65–75
early presidential election, 278
early Tamil nationalism, 63–65
Eastphalian led global order, 298
economic liberalisation, 4
economic reforms, 15–16, 143, 158, 195
Eksath Bhikku Peramuna (United Buddhist Front), 123
election campaigns, 5
elite civil servants, 182–85
elites
  dominant elites, 76, 78, 84, 205–06
  factionalised elites, 32, 125, 219, 225, 232, 260
ethnic civil war, 39
ethnic conflict, 39, 43, 46, 52, 271*n*10
ethnic identity, 39
ethnic-identity-based consciousness, 58
European Union, 263, 273*n*32, 303
external international actors, 251–54

Facilitating Local Initiatives for Conflict Transformation (FLICT), 55*n*13
factional polity, 80–90
finance party patronage system (1948–1977), 178–81
first and second Republican constitutions, 198
'first generation nationalism', 58
Fonseka, Sarath, 255, 277–83, 286, 300*n*3
Foucauldian discourse analysis, 38
Fujii, LeAnne, 33*n*4, 49

Gam Udawa, 154
the general election in 2001, 241–43, 245–46

Generalized System of Preferences (GSP+), 284, 303
German Technical Cooperation (GTZ), 55n13
Golden Age, 62, 160
Goonatileke, Ian, 43
governors, 283
Gramsci, Antonio, 15, 22, 24–26, 31, 34n12, 59, 71, 75, 78, 104, 108n4, 118, 138
greater Colombo consumer price index, 242
Grindle, Merilee, 144, 219
Gunasinghe, A. E., 70, 119
Gunasinghe, Newton, 13, 15, 18, 70, 90, 117, 121–23, 129, 137, 141, 150–53

Hakeem, Rauf, 134, 238, 262–63
Harischandra, Walisinha, 98
hegemony
  coercion, 78, 104, 107
  common sense, 118
  consent, 107, 276
  domination, 125, 143, 166, 168
  hegemony building, 3, 6–7, 9, 14, 16–32, 57, 59, 63, 65, 73, 75–78, 84, 100–01, 103–05, 107–08, 113, 118, 125, 127, 129, 131, 144, 146, 154, 162, 166, 168, 172n34, 173–74, 183, 191, 195, 206, 218, 223–25, 239, 264, 269–70, 275–76, 280, 283, 293–99, 301
  historical bloc, 26, 27, 79, 125, 138, 292–93, 295, 297, 303
  morbid symptoms, 298, 303
  national popular, 26, 61, 63, 86, 108n6
  subordination, 15
Helbardt, Hellmann-Rajanayagam and Korff, 52
Herbst, Jeffrey, 22
'hidden transcripts', 4

identity
  ape (rajaya, aanduwa, kena), 217
  authenticity, 6, 159, 161
  Buddhist, 81, 86, 106, 164–65
  Catholic, 10, 36–37
  class, 37, 59, 63, 87
  ethnic, 7, 11, 37–47, 52–53, 54n7, 55n20, 58, 84, 91, 134, 206, 271n10, 296
  gender, 52
  Hindu, 291
  Kandyan, 114
  Muslim, 8–10, 72
  primordialist, 47, 75
  regional, 53, 260, 278
  religious, 36, 43, 57–58, 84, 90, 106, 219
  Roman catholic, 9–10
  Shia, 8–9, 212
  Sinhala, 72
  Sunni, 8–9
  Tamil, 8–9, 90
India, 7, 14–16, 22–23, 34n14, 63, 69–70, 109n17, 115, 210, 266, 272n18, 284, 286
Indian peacekeeping forces (IPKF), 234
Indo-Lanka Accord, 18
Industrialisation, 141–42
interdepartmental committee system, 177
Interim Self Governing Administration (ISGA), 255, 272n24
intra-elite competition, 4
Introduction of State Industrial Act of 1957, 186
Ismail, Quadri, 15, 49

Jaathika Sevaka Sangamaya (JSS), 150
Jaffna Youth Congress, 64
Janasaviya, 154
Janatha Vimukthi Peramuna (JVP), 37–38, 54n11, 78, 94–97, 99, 100, 111n39, 129–32, 134, 155–56, 160, 191, 207–08, 226, 228–29, 234, 243–45,

INDEX

247, 249–50, 252, 256–57, 259, 260, 262–64, 268, 271n10, 272n26
Jathika Hela Urumaya (JHU), 78, 94, 98–100, 131–32, 134, 160, 259–60, 263–64, 268, 273n30293
Jayawardene, J. R., 18, 49, 100
Jayawardena, Kumari, 13, 49, 57–59, 61–62, 65, 67–68, 76–77, 82, 84, 87, 89, 92–94, 97, 100, 104
Jayawardene regime (1977–1988), 144–54

Kandyan peasantry, 178
Kapferer, Bruce, 13, 18, 46–47, 55n19, 75, 109n8
Karuna faction, 134, 258, 262
Kedourie, Elie, 89
King Devanampiyatissa, 98
King Dutugemunu, 260, 274n35
Korean war, 139, 170n17
Kumaratunga, Chandrika Bandaranaike, 32, 157–60, 221n13, 225–41
Kumaratunga regime (1993–2004), 157–60
Kumaratunga, Vijaya, 228

labour movement, 77, 92, 118
Lakshman, W. D., 139, 180, 186–87, 192, 194, 220n5
Land Reform Commission (LRC), 192
The Language Act of 1956, 125
Lanka Sama Samaja Party (LSSP), 92–93, 111n34, 119–20
Lederach, John Paul, 38, 45, 48, 55n18
'Leftist', 42
Lessons Learnt and Reconciliation Commission (LLRC), 19, 287–88
liberal democratic political principles and institutions, 45
liberal-ideology-inspired scholarship, 13
Liberation Tigers of Tamil Eelam (LTTE), 1–2, 5, 8–9, 18–19, 32, 37, 41, 44, 48, 54n8, 55n21, 97, 100–05,

112n48, 150, 154, 156, 165–67, 224, 226–29, 231–37, 241, 244–53, 256–70, 271n10, 275

Mahajana Eksath Peramuna (MEP), 94, 111n33, 111n34, 180
  10-year Economic Plan of 1959, 180
Mahinda Chinthana, 19, 35n19, 160, 201–02, 259, 261
Malalgoda, Kitsiri, 73
Mann, Michael, 74, 81
Marxism
  Marxist class schema, 11
  Marxist epistemology, 13, 45
  Marxist theory of state, 13
  Marxist political parties, 42, 88, 94–95, 122, 130
mass mobilisation, 63
Max-Neef's classification, 50
Memorandum of Understanding (MOU), 243–44, 247–48
Migdal, Joel S., 20–23, 27–29, 63, 194
Migdal's approach, 21, 27–28
militarisation, 4
Moor, Mick, 7, 18, 35n18, 61, 66, 93, 96, 98, 115, 120, 124, 130, 140, 149, 153, 155, 188, 193–94, 234
Mouffe, Chantal, 24–26, 291, 293–94, 297
Mudliyar families, 115–16
Mudliyar system, 115–16, 119
multilateral financial institutions, 227, 252

narcissism of minor differences, 245
National Freedom Front (NFF), 131–134
National Integration Programme Unit (NIPU), 233, 268
nationalisation, 119–20, 126, 128, 141–42, 187–88, 192
nationalism, 6
  cultural revivalism, 64, 71–72
  ethnic nationalism, 15, 57, 59, 74–78, 81

militarization (of the state), 247
nationalist interest, 62
nationalist movement, 65, 72, 74, 78–79, 83, 104
Navalar centrism, 102
Navalar-Ramanathan tradition, 64
pan-Sinhala-Buddhist nationalism, 87
religious nationalism, 58, 75–80
right-wing nationalism, 81
ruling ideology, 25, 95, 193
Saivite, 63
Sinhala-Buddhist exclusivism, 120
Sinhala-Buddhist hegemonic state, 14, 28, 98–99, 105, 107, 287
Sinhala-Buddhist ideology, 31, 49, 86, 95, 124–25, 130, 206, 218, 269–70, 277–78, 282
Sinhala-Buddhist nationalism, 2, 20, 24–25, 29, 30, 57–65, 72–74, 78, 80–81, 83, 85–86, 88–91, 97, 99–100, 103–08, 110n21, 123, 125, 134, 168
state ideology, 95
Tamil militarism, 103
Tamil nationalism, 30, 58, 63–65, 75, 101–08, 110n29
National Unity Alliance (NUA), 134, 238
neo-liberalism
  corruption, 32
  economic policies, 95
  free-market dictatorship, 196
  liberal economic plan, 242–43
  liberal international order, 276, 284, 294, 299
Nesiah, Devanesan, 58, 65, 74, 103
New Democratic Front (NDF), 279, 281, 300n3
New Public Management (NPM), 214
non-governmental organisations (NGOs), 1, 33n1, 44
non-Western contexts, 44
'North-East war', 246

North Western Province, 10, 36
Norway, 33n8, 246, 251, 271n16, 272n18

open economy, 11, 94–95, 145–46, 168, 196, 208–09
organic intellectuals, 26
Overseas Development Institute (ODI), 23

Parliamentary Committee on Public Enterprises (COPE), 159, 165
party-sponsored patronage, 117–29
patronage
  clientelism, 52
  horizontal patronage, 132, 206–09
  party based patronage system, 30–31, 125, 174
  patronage networks, 115–19, 121–22, 124, 128, 136–37, 140–41, 143, 159, 162, 166–67, 193, 197, 202, 210–11, 218
  patronage politics, 4, 6, 30–31, 113–18, 133, 143–44, 146, 167, 172n34, 174, 179, 181, 184–85, 189–90, 197
  patronage relationships, 85, 193
  patronage system, 30–31, 113–14, 117–18, 125, 132, 144, 147, 157, 161–62, 166–68, 173, 187, 189, 194, 196, 200, 206, 209, 212, 214
  political patronage, 6–7, 30, 113, 133, 168, 173, 179, 181, 192, 200, 206–08, 219
  politics, 4, 6
  quasi-patronage, 174–77
peace
  agenda for peace, 227
  liberal peace, 1, 32, 33n3, 225, 246–49, 252, 253–56
  (neo) liberal peace, 246–49, 252
  peace by peaceful means, 32, 225–30, 235–37

INDEX

peace deal, 250
peace-making, 31–32, 269, 295
    Saama Balakaaya (peace solidarity force), 233
    Saama Thawalama (peace caravan), 233
    Sudu Nelum Vyapaaraya (White lotus movement), 233
    victor's peace, 258–61
peace-building, 277
peace processes, 4
Peebles, 114
People's Alliance (PA), 32, 157–61, 207–08, 225–26, 228–32, 234–39, 241–49, 254, 256, 270n7
Pillaian faction, 134
political elites, 182–85
political incorporation, 125, 167, 185, 191
political parties, 118
political party development, 4
politics, 51
    badagoastharavaadaya, 145
    belly politics, 142, 170n18
    dynastic politics, 3, 4, 86, 258–61
    nationalist politics, 2–3, 61
    political development, 3, 17, 22, 88, 92, 118, 143–44, 166, 254, 279, 289, 294
    political favouritism, 157–59, 165, 187, 189, 211
    politicisation, 136, 153, 174, 177, 179–81, 183, 185, 192, 194, 199, 211, 215–16, 218, 279, 283
    politics of development, 118
    rice politics, 142
    temple politics, 289
    Tsunami politics, 117, 256–57
population, 7–12
post-1977 period, 195–97
post-positivism, 46
Post-Tsunami Joint Operation Mechanism (P-TOMS), 19, 232, 257, 259
post-war reconstruction, 4

post-war transitional justice, 285–89
power devolution, 209–13
Prabakaran, Velupillai, 48
pre-colonial patronage relations, 113
Premadasa, R., 126, 154–57, 169n5, 226, 228–31, 234, 261
Premadasa regime (1989-1993), 154–57
Prevention of Terrorism Act of 1972 (PTA), 248
privatisation
    peoplelisation, 227
    privatisation with a human face, 227
proportional representation (PR), 132, 146, 152–53, 202, 207–08
provincial councils (PC), 5, 18–19, 33n6, 169n2, 201, 209–11, 213, 220n10, 221n17, 229, 273n31
public and private sector employment, 201
public bureaucracies, 173
public sector employment, 204
public sector investment programmes (PSIP), 148
public sector reforms, 214, 216
Public Service Commission (PSC), 179, 195, 199, 215

Rajapaksa regimes, 9, 32, 41, 97, 101, 160–69, 268, 287–89, 302
Rajapaksa, Gotabaya, 9, 20, 162–63, 286–93, 298, 300n6, 301–03
Rajapaksa, Mahinda, 9, 19–20, 32, 35n19, 144, 160–69, 172n35, 257–69, 272n28, 273n29–30, 274n35, 276–88, 290–93, 299n2, 300n3, 301–02
Ramanathan, Ponnambalam, 64
Ranawaka, Champika, 100
'reflective practitioner', 38
regaining Sri Lanka, 19, 253
registered unemployed female graduates, 205

relations of production, 10–11, 29, 85, 115, 117, 295
'religious nationalism', 58
Roberts, Michael, 8, 15, 34*n*11, 64, 82, 87–88, 98, 102, 104, 109*n*9, 110*n*23, 116, 169*n*2
Rwanda, 49

Sangha
  Buddhist clergy, 19, 278, 290
  monks, 70
  Vinayankalara, 71
Scott, David, 11, 73
Scott, James, 4
Second Five-year Plan (1972–1976), 189
secretaries, 283
semi-government sector employees, 201, 203–04
Senanayake, D. S., 121–22
Seneviratne, H. L., 66–71, 86, 98, 109*n*14, 112*n*44
shared ethno-religious victimhood, 58–59
Sinhala-Buddhist nationalism, 2, 58–60, 64
Sinhala-Buddhist politics, 101–08
'Sinhala consciousness', 58
Sinhala Jathika Sangamaya, 123
Sinhala Maha Sabhas, 121
Sinhala Only Act of 1956, 91, 111*n*36, 124–25
Sirisena, Maithripala, 286, 288–91, 299*n*2
Six Year Economic Development Plan, 138
socialism, 190–94
  negative development model, 142
  premature welfarism, 142
  socialist era, 194
  socialist state policies, 186, 193
  social welfare, 1, 135, 138, 141, 269
  social welfarism, 186

state institutions, 15–17, 21–22, 31, 90, 136, 138, 143, 147, 150, 171*n*22, 173–220
  welfare, 1, 135, 138, 141
  welfare policies, 1, 134–39, 142–43, 190, 217, 219
society
  righteous society, 170*n*21, 196, 199
  Sinhalese polity, 3–4, 9–10, 16–18, 30, 41, 81, 84, 86–87, 91, 96–97, 101, 106–107, 112*n*47, 114, 126, 128–31, 134, 137, 156, 166, 202–03, 210, 232–33, 236, 245–46, 251–52, 258–59, 261, 268
  state-in-society model, 5, 12, 20, 27–29, 40, 63, 72, 76, 104, 106–07, 167, 177, 185, 194, 225, 276, 294
  state-in-society relations, 5, 12, 20, 27–29, 40, 63, 72, 76, 104, 106–08, 167, 177, 185, 194, 225, 276, 294, 295
Soulbury Constitution, 179, 189–90
South Asian scholarship, 1–2
Soviet Union, 13, 45, 270*n*1
Spencer, Jonathan, 11, 16, 46, 55*n*19, 117, 149, 151, 153, 196–97, 205, 220*n*7, 234, 277, 280
Sri Lanka Freedom Party (SLFP), 8, 86–87, 89–90, 93–95, 97, 110*n*30, 111*n*34, 120, 123–24, 125, 129–31, 147, 156, 159–60, 170, 180, 185–88, 225, 279
Sri Lanka Mahajana Peramuna (SLMP), 228–29
Sri Lanka Muslim Congress (SLMC), 134, 230–31, 238, 243, 245, 258, 272*n*20
standardisation of university education, 127
state-building
  European state-making, 21, 224
  nation-building, 23, 76, 276, 277

INDEX

state-making, 21, 31, 224, 267, 269
state re-building, 19, 20, 32, 35*n*20
state bureaucracy, 4, 183
state institutions, 15–17, 21–22, 31, 90, 136, 138, 143, 147, 150, 161, 171*n*22, 173–222, 290, 302
state-managed industrial corporations, 186
state patronage, 114, 279
state reforms, 4, 6, 185–90
state welfare policy, 134–44
structural adjustment programmes, 15
subaltern
    subaltern groups, 26–27, 296–97, 299
    subaltern politics, 4, 20, 24, 295, 298–99
    subaltern study project, 14

Tambiah, Stanley, 46, 68, 223
Tamil National Alliance (TNA), 246–47, 286
Tamil nationalism, 101–08
Tamil People's Liberation Tigers (TMVP), 134
Tamil United Liberation Front (TYLF), 112*n*49
Thimpu Principles, 249, 272*n*17
Thondaman, Saumiyamurthi, 126–27, 221*n*13, 230
Tilly, Charles, 20–21, 31, 223–25, 267, 269
Toddy, alcoholic beverage, 53*n*2
transdisciplinarity, 50
'Triple R framework', 19
tsunami politics, 117, 256–57

unemployment (2003–2008), 204
United National Party (UNP), 54*n*5, 83, 120, 124, 180, 225, 275
Uyangoda, Jayadeva, 12, 18–19, 65, 70–72, 94, 98–99, 101, 121, 151, 154–56, 174, 228, 241, 245–50, 267, 271*n*14, 274*n*36, 280, 285

village councils (*gam sabha*s), 175
village headman (*grama sevaka*), 184, 188
violence
    armed insurrection, 18, 129, 228
    armed youth movement, 18
    Bodu Bala Sena (BBS), 101, 289, 302
    communal violent incidents, 1, 13
    defence, 254–56
    Easter attacks, 289
    military movement, 18
    political violence, 144, 168–69, 194, 220, 226, 298
    security sector, 275
    structural violence, 226

Waldner, David, 138, 141, 143, 169*n*1, 173, 185, 297
war
    civil war, 1–4, 8–9, 13–15, 19, 23, 32, 36, 38–44, 46–50, 52–53, 54*n*6, 59, 73–74, 76–78, 96, 125, 133, 154, 158, 162–63, 166, 174, 198, 202, 205–06, 220, 223–24, 227, 232, 285, 289, 295–96
    just war post-war, 167
    North-East War, 246
    war against terrorism, 32, 225, 261, 263, 285
    war for peace, 32, 225, 269, 278
    war in the North and the East, 224, 250
    war making, 21, 31, 223–24, 267, 269, 295
war and peace, 6
Warnapala, Wiswa, 70, 152, 175, 178–79, 187, 189, 197, 199
Wennappuwa town, 54*n*5
Western-dominated international financial markets, 284
Western donor countries, 33*n*1, 39, 166, 227

white elephant, 211, 221*n*19
Wickramasinghe, Nira, 15–17, 19, 32, 34*n*11, 49, 58, 64, 114, 117–18, 120–21, 125, 129, 139, 161, 221*n*16, 235, 254, 256, 284, 286, 289
Wickremasinghe, Ranil, 225, 235–36, 240, 246

The Wilmot Perera Commission Report of 1961, 183–84, 220*n*3
World Bank (WB), 19, 23, 35*n*17, 140–41, 157, 164, 205, 213, 251
World Development Report, 174

Zarkov, Dubravka, 12–13, 15